Social-Imperialism in Britain

Historical Materialism Book Series

The Historical Materialism Book Series is a major publishing initiative of the radical left. The capitalist crisis of the twenty-first century has been met by a resurgence of interest in critical Marxist theory. At the same time, the publishing institutions committed to Marxism have contracted markedly since the high point of the 1970s. The Historical Materialism Book Series is dedicated to addressing this situation by making available important works of Marxist theory. The aim of the series is to publish important theoretical contributions as the basis for vigorous intellectual debate and exchange on the left.

The peer-reviewed series publishes original monographs, translated texts, and reprints of classics across the bounds of academic disciplinary agendas and across the divisions of the left. The series is particularly concerned to encourage the internationalization of Marxist debate and aims to translate significant studies from beyond the English-speaking world.

For a full list of titles in the Historical Materialism Book Series available in paperback from Haymarket Books, visit:
https://www.haymarketbooks.org/series_collections/1-historical-materialism

Social-Imperialism in Britain

*The Lancashire Working Class
and Two World Wars*

Neil Redfern

Haymarket Books
Chicago, IL

First published in 2018 by Brill Academic Publishers, The Netherlands
© 2018 Koninklijke Brill NV, Leiden, The Netherlands

Published in paperback in 2020 by
Haymarket Books
P.O. Box 180165
Chicago, IL 60618
773-583-7884
www.haymarketbooks.org

ISBN: 978-1-64259-049-4

Distributed to the trade in the US through Consortium Book Sales and Distribution (www.cbsd.com) and internationally through Ingram Publisher Services International (www.ingramcontent.com).

This book was published with the generous support of Lannan Foundation and Wallace Action Fund.

Special discounts are available for bulk purchases by organizations and institutions. Please call 773-583-7884 or email info@haymarketbooks.org for more information.

Cover design by Jamie Kerry and Ragina Johnson.

Printed in the United States.

10 9 8 7 6 5 4 3 2 1

Library of Congress Cataloging-in-Publication data is available.

Crowds outside Buckingham Palace on the day that war was declared in 1914
SOURCE: FROM THE COLLECTIONS OF THE IMPERIAL WAR MUSEUMS, CALL NUMBER: Q 81832. PUBLIC DOMAIN

Dedicated to the memory of John McLean, Arthur MacManus, Sylvia Pankhurst and all the others, known and unknown, who resisted the social-chauvinist tides of the two world wars.

Contents

Acknowledgements XI

Introduction 1

1 Rallying Round the Flag 11
   1 The Labour Movement and the War 12
   2 Mustering the Masses for War 20
   3 The End of the Road for Liberalism? 27
   4 The Discontents and Demands of the Labour Movement 33
   5 'Dilution' and the Mobilisation of Women 40

2 Labour's Unrest and Capital's Promises 49
   1 Conscriptions and 'Conchies' 49
   2 Social Patriots and (a Few) Internationalists 52
   3 Labour Unrest and (Eventual) Government Response 59
   4 Strikes, Shop Stewards and Revolutionaries 66
   5 A Better World Coming? 71
   6 More Strikes, More Shop Stewards and Some Revolutionaries 81

3 1919: a 'Red Year'? 95
   1 A Revolutionary Situation in Britain? 96
   2 Expanding the Franchise: Suffragettes, Suffragists and the Labour Party 98
   3 Labourists, Feminists and Socialists: Labour's New Platform 102
   4 The Labour Movement in the General Election of 1918 108
   5 1919: a Tumultuous but Not 'Red Year' in Lancashire 117
   6 Housing Reform and the Municipal Elections of 1919 124
   7 The Post-war Crisis, the Working Class, and the Empire 128

4 Rallying Round the Flag Again 141
   1 An Imperialist War in Anti-fascist Clothing 141
   2 The Crisis of 1940 149
   3 Building a Labour-Capital Pact 152
   4 Never Again! The Early Growth of Popular Reform Sentiment 158
   5 Dissent and Discontent in the Working Class and in the Labour Movement 163
   6 Joint Production Committees: a 'Nazi System of Labour Organisation'? 168

    7   Out of the Kitchen Again: Mobilising Women to 'Do Their Bit'   173
    8   Not Counting the Colonies: the Labour Movement and the
        Empire   178
    9   A Social-Imperialist Surge for Reform   183

5 **Building the Social-Imperialist Settlement**   189
    1   Beveridge Promises a New World   189
    2   The 'Old Gang' Takes an Ideological and Political Beating   195
    3   A Resurgence of Industrial Unrest   199
    4   A Touch on the Reform Accelerator   201
    5   More Promises, More Unrest, More Discontent   207
    6   Social Imperialism Triumphant: the Last Phase of the War   214
    7   Labour to Power: the End of the War and the General Election   223

Conclusion and Postscript   236

Bibliography   243
  Index   258

Acknowledgements

Although the opinions expressed here are my own, there are many people who in one way or another have contributed to this work. I do not know the names of many of them, although I should mention first my parents, Joseph and Mary Redfern (née McDonald), who instilled in me a strong class consciousness and a strong sense of identification with struggles (though they would not have expressed such things this way) against exploitation and oppression wherever they may be. I should acknowledge also the political experiences, both positive and negative, of many years of political activity, which helped to form the ideological and political outlook expressed in this work.

The criticism and advice of many people, in particular two anonymous peer reviewers, as well as Alan Fowler, Tony Adams, Neville Kirk, Andrew Thompson, Deidre Beddoe, Nick Mansfield, David Swift and David Monger, greatly improved the work. Pertinent criticisms and comments came from staff and students who attended seminars at Manchester and Manchester Metropolitan universities and members of the public at a talk at Tameside History Club. The librarians and archivists at the John Rylands University Library, Deansgate, Manchester, the Lancashire County Record Office at Preston, Manchester Central Library, the National Archives at Kew, Oldham Local Studies and Archives, the Archives and Study Centre at the People's History Museum, Manchester and Tameside Local Studies and Archives Centre were unfailingly helpful. Finally, Jenny Taylor painstakingly worked on copy-editing and proofreading and made more than a few suggestions regarding the arguments herein. Simon Mussell also did an excellent job of copy-editing. Without the help and encouragement of all these people, this work could not have been written.

Introduction

Serving with the Manchester Regiment in India in 1944, during the bitter fighting between Britain and Japan in Assam, Private Wolstenholme was moved to write home that the regiment had 'played a big part in clearing the Japs out of Kohima and chasing them down the Imphal Road ... our machine guns were working beautifully ... and the rattle of tommy-guns and stens could be heard faintly in the distance as they finished off the Japs in their bunkers'.[1] In civilian life, Wolstenholme lived and worked in Mossley, a Lancashire cotton town. Like the great majority of British working class people in the twentieth century, he was probably not a Jingoist, but a patriot, who simply assumed that Britain's cause was just. Objectively, like the great majority of British working class people, more particularly those of them in the trade unions and the Labour Party, he was collaborating with British capital in its attempts to maintain its dominant position in the international imperialist order. This work of political history seeks to examine this collaboration. It will be argued that it was rooted in the political economy of imperialism.

Stimulated by the resurgence of popular patriotism during the Falklands War, there were several studies of popular patriotism in its wake. Geoffrey Field considered 'social patriotism' – defined by him as 'an inwardly focused patriotism, one that is oriented toward domestic social reform'[2] – in the Second World War. Miles Taylor examined the British left's rather sniffy attitude to popular patriotism in the twentieth century.[3] Paul Ward, aptly defining social-patriotism as 'a reciprocal arrangement between social classes when the ruling class offers social reform in return for patriotism', studied the emergence and persistence of social-patriotism in the late nineteenth and early twentieth centuries.[4] Why then a new study? These earlier works were concerned with the language, psychology and politics of patriotism, having little, if anything, to say on the political economy of the matter, in particular its connection with imperialism (in the Leninist sense of monopoly capitalism rather than as a synonym for colonialism).[5] Nor did they have much to say on the interaction between rulers and ruled, concentrating overwhelmingly on the latter. For

---

1 *Mossley and Saddleworth Reporter*, 21 July 1944.
2 Field 1992, p. 36.
3 Taylor 1992.
4 Ward 1998, p. 4.
5 Equating imperialism with colonialism is common in British historiography. We find this tendency in, for instance, all the contributions to Frank (ed.) 2010.

these reasons, I use the term 'social-imperialism'[6] rather than 'social patriotism'. Finally, offered here is an analysis of the hardly examined local roots of social-imperialism.

While the national picture is prominent, the main focus is on Lancashire (an excellent focus for a study of social-imperialism in action, given its main industry, cotton, was a prime beneficiary of imperialism) and its industry, working class and labour movement.[7] In particular, we will consider three towns: Ashton-under-Lyne (hereinafter Ashton), Mossley[8] and Oldham. These towns – all three within the great cotton conurbation of South-East Lancashire/North East Cheshire – were products of the first phase of the Industrial Revolution, based on land enclosures, sugar, iron, coal, cotton and sweated labour, including slavery.[9] Ashton's population increased by 437 percent between 1801 and 1861.[10] Oldham experienced a similarly rapid expansion, from 12,024 in 1801 to 52,280 in 1851.[11] Data are not available for Mossley, but the town probably grew at roughly the same rate as the other towns in the area. By the start of the twentieth century, modern factory production had been fully established. Populations had more than doubled: Oldham's, for instance, had swollen to 137,246[12] and Mossley's to 13,542.[13] (Mossley's small size and geographical isolation had a considerable impact on its society and politics in our period).[14] Old-

---

6   Here the terms 'social-imperialism' and 'social-imperialist' are used to describe the advocates of financing social reform through imperialism and practitioners of pro-imperialist collaboration between labour and capital. The concept has been used in other ways, for instance, as a means of diverting working class unrest through imperial expansion. See, e.g., Mason 1996.
7   There are several academic studies of the Lancashire working class in our period, of the growth of the labour movement in particular. See, e.g., Griffiths 2001, Savage 1987, and Adams 2000.
8   Mossley was spread over three counties (Lancashire, Cheshire and Yorkshire), but came under the jurisdiction of Lancashire County Council and was essentially a Lancashire town.
9   There were of course significant differences within the Lancashire cotton trade. Probably the most important was the division between spinning – predominant in our three towns – and weaving, found mostly outside the Manchester conurbation, in such places as Preston and Blackburn. Within these divisions there was a marked sexual division of labour: spinners were almost entirely male, weavers mostly female; Jowitt and McIvor (eds.) 1988, Introduction and Chs. 4, 6 and 11. But as far as our subject – social-imperialism – is concerned, these differences are relatively unimportant.
10 Newell 1993, p. 11.
11 Bateson 1949, p. 232.
12 Ibid.
13 Newell and Walker 2001, p. 36.
14 See Redfern 2013, for a discussion of the peculiarities of Mossley.

ham and the small towns around it, such as Chadderton, Failsworth and Royton accounted for 12 percent of world cotton spinning[15] and was 'the metropolis of the textile machine industry as well as the metropolis of cotton spinning'.[16] Of course, not everyone worked in cotton – engineering, brewing, domestic service, mining, transport and many other trades offered employment. A distinctive feature of Lancashire's industry, one that had a significant effect on the politics of our period, was the high proportion of women, including, untypically, married women, in its workforce.

Possession of such colonies as India and the West Indies and domination over such countries as China and Egypt had helped British capitalism to emerge successfully from the storms of the first half of the nineteenth century. The early Lancashire cotton industry had been protected against Indian cotton goods: later, during the formal colonisation of India, the Indian cotton industry had been destroyed when India was opened up to cheap Lancashire cotton goods and became a supplier of raw cotton to Lancashire rather than a supplier of finished luxury goods for Britain as a whole.[17] By the end of the century Lancashire's prosperity and the living standards of its workers was founded not on the superiority of its goods but on a monopoly of an imperial market enforced by parliament (Andrew Thompson has shown how the Lancashire working class benefited for decades from the protection against Indian textiles afforded to its textile industry),[18] the army and the Royal Navy.

The working class of the Manchester conurbation had a direct military connection with the Empire – since 1881 the Manchester Regiment's headquarters had been at what after the Boer War was called the Ladysmith Barracks, on Mossley Road, Ashton. Prior to the outbreak of war in 1914 the army had provided employment for many men from our three towns and helped to sustain many of their businesses. More importantly, the Army was the ultimate protector of the imperial order dominated by Britain. The battalions of the Manchesters (celebrated today in the Museum of the Manchesters, next to Tameside Town Hall, Ashton) were deployed in various colonial campaigns: in India in 1902–14 and again in 1922–32; in the Anglo-Irish War in 1920–22; and in Egypt during the 'Arab Revolt' of 1936–39. But in our period the army's primary task was not to subdue unruly colonial subjects but to defend Britain's pre-eminence in the imperial order against the challenge of other powers, prin-

---

15 Farnie 1982, p. 42.
16 Farnie 1998, pp. 1–4.
17 Between 1806 and 1842 exports of raw cotton from India to Britain rose from 2.725 million lbs. to 96.555 million lbs. (Silver 1966, p. 85).
18 Thompson 2005, pp. 75–6.

cipally Germany. The Manchesters participated in this task in France, Turkey, Mesopotamia and Palestine during the First World War, and in France, Italy, Singapore, India and Burma during the Second World War.[19]

In folk memory, the warm welcome given to Gandhi during his famous visit to Lancashire in 1931 was a manifestation of solidarity with India's cause. It is possible, however, and perhaps more likely, that it was mainly an expression of hopes that Gandhi would call off the Indian boycott of Lancashire's finished cotton goods.[20] Gandhi of course regarded the glaring economic inequality between India and Britain as a moral question. In a sense it was, but from a materialist point of view it would not be surprising if unemployed cotton workers surviving on a pittance should perceive Gandhi as someone who might help to alleviate their distress rather than as a possible co-fighter against imperialism. While it is futile and moralistic to expect that Lancashire's workers should have reflected on the political economy of imperialism during Gandhi's visit, it is necessary to understand why this political economy led not just Lancashire's workers but the British working class as a whole to consistently support their own ruling class in various imperialist ventures.

Contemporaries were well aware of the crucial role played by imperialism in containing class antagonisms. John MacKenzie has vividly described attempts to persuade a mass electorate of imperialism's benefit to them.[21] A project dedicated to this end was the Primrose League, founded in 1883 to win working class support for the ardently pro-imperialist Conservative Party through dances, teas, fêtes and so on. Conservatism in general and the Primrose League in particular became notably strong in such cotton towns as Ashton.[22] Indicative of support for imperialism and Conservatism among working class people, particularly in Lancashire, was the joint Conservative candidature of James Mawdsley, the leader of the spinner's union, and the arch-imperialist Winston Churchill in the Oldham double by-election of 1899. Churchill frequently stressed imperial matters during this election campaign (held during the Boer War), as would another keen imperialist Max Aitken (the future Lord Beaverbrook), when standing for Ashton in the general election of 1910.[23]

Social-imperialist sentiment accelerated after the national panic caused by the poor physical condition of many would-be army recruits for the Boer War.[24]

---

19   Bonner 2011.
20   Barrow 2010, p. 89.
21   MacKenzie 1985.
22   Pugh 1985, p. 123.
23   Chisholm and Davis 1992, p. 89.
24   38 percent of potential recruits had been rejected as unfit. Jones 1994, p. 22.

Of particular relevance here are the views of Sydney Webb, who we shall encounter several times in this work. Webb was a prominent member of the Fabian Society, which was to become the principal intellectual influence on the Labour Party and trade unions, eventually the primary agents of social-imperialism within the working class. A keen social-imperialist, Webb argued in 1901 that imperialism and social reform were both essential to 'ensure the rearing of an imperial race' in the interest of 'national efficiency'.[25] Such views were then entering the mainstream of bourgeois ideology and politics. Bernard Semmel showed that in the early twentieth century both main parties, the Liberals and the Conservatives, were quick to see the possibilities offered by social reform in appealing to new mass electorates. In the general election of 1906, the Conservative and Liberal Parties both argued that their programme would strengthen the Empire and would best provide for urgently needed social reforms.[26]

British capital had begun to regard imperialism as an important means of ensuring that resources were available to foster the loyal, strong, healthy men and women necessary to ensure that Britain could compete in the Darwinian struggle for national supremacy. Moreover, it was increasingly realised that the problem was not moral turpitude or fecklessness on the part of the poor, but poverty itself and environmental factors. Government increasingly took on some responsibility for the state of working class being. Early steps were the introduction of old age pensions, free school meals for poor children and a state-backed health insurance scheme for poor and middling income workers.

By 1914 as a result of these and earlier reforms on employment, public health, housing and so on, the harsh and heartless early industrial capitalism of the cotton towns depicted in such novels as *Hard Times* and *Mary Barton* had been ameliorated to such an extent that, as Patrick Joyce argued some years ago, 'the rule of the tall chimney' had 'entered into the workpeople's lives to a degree that made their acceptance of the social regime of capitalist industry a matter of inward emotion as much as of outward calculation'.[27] A practical confirmation of Joyce's contention is provided by Sam Fitton's cartoons in the *Cotton Factory Times*, widely read and enjoyed by cotton workers. Fitton's cartoons, while exhibiting a keen class consciousness, exhibited also a fundamental acceptance of capitalism and the rule of the bourgeoisie.[28]

---

25   Cited in Himmelfarb 1991, p. 78.
26   Semmel 1960, p. 28.
27   Joyce 1980, p. xiii.
28   The paper was published between 1885 and 1937. (See Cass et al. 1998). Reproductions of many of Fitton's cartoons can be seen in Fowler and Wyke 1995.

British domestic history is then inextricably bound up with the history of the British Empire. But as David Cannadine observed, 'the history of the British Empire is still far too often written as if it were completely separate and distinct from the history of the British nation'.[29] (There were and are of course such exceptions as Linda Colley).[30] Taking our cue from Cannadine, we might observe that the history of the home front in Britain in the two world wars and also the history of the British labour movement are far too often written as if they were completely separate and distinct from the history of the British Empire. In such accounts of the home front in war as Arthur Marwick's *The Deluge*, Adrian Gregory's *The Last Great War*, Angus Calder's *The People's War*, Paul Addison's *The Road to 1945* and Geoffrey's Field's recent *Blood Sweat and Toil: Remaking the British Working Class 1939–45*,[31] we find excellent discussions of the interaction between working class demands for reform and, in the first of the two world wars, rising industrial militancy, and elite anxieties regarding maintaining working class commitment to war.

But in these and most other works working class support for the defence, expansion and reconquest of Empire is a given. Probably, in most cases, it is seen as unproblematic. Since the Second World War (the 'good' war, as the title of Stud Turkel's oral history of the war suggests),[32] there has been a marked tendency, Semmel apart, to either deny the link between imperialism and social reform or to ignore the question. For liberals and conservatives, to accept that working class national loyalty is based at least in part on imperialist booty is to accept that this loyalty cannot be taken for granted. For those on the left, to accept that social reform was obtained at the expense of the peoples of the Empire would be to question the legitimacy of those reforms.

In the early post-World War II period Schumpeter insisted, in his *Imperialism and the Social Classes*, that the working class had no interest in imperialism: 'even less than peasant imperialism is there any such thing as socialist or working class imperialism'.[33] This trend has continued in, for instance, the work of the celebrated conservative economic historian D.K. Fieldhouse.[34] Mike Savage[35] and Trevor Griffiths[36] are typical of the mainstream of labour

---

29 Cannadine 2001, p. xvii.
30 Colley 1996.
31 Marwick 1991; Gregory 2008; Calder 1969; Addison 1977; Field 2011.
32 Terkel 1985.
33 Schumpeter 1951, p. 94.
34 Fieldhouse 1984. See O'Brien 1988, for a summary of the arguments on the matter and also Davis and Huttenback 1986.
35 Savage 1987.
36 Griffiths 2001.

historiography in having little to say at all of the connections between the British labour movement and imperialism. Granted, there are exceptions. Stephen Howe has provided an illuminating account of the labour movement and colonialism.[37] More recently, Neville Kirk has shown how what he has called the 'politics of loyalism' – loyalty to flag, crown, country and Empire – was far stronger than internationalism in both the British and Australian working class.[38]

Yet even in such literature, the social-imperialist content of the two world wars is a blind spot. In a staggeringly complacent introduction to a recent collection of essays on the labour movement and imperialism, Tony Benn made the highly dubious claim that post World War Two colonial independence 'was made possible because of the links that the British labour movement and socialists had established with colonial liberation movements'. Of the determined participation of British labour in the defence and expansion of British imperialism during and after the two world wars – in, for example, Ireland, Iraq, Burma, Indonesia, Malaya, and Korea, Benn has nothing to say.[39] The other contributors in this volume all have valuable points to make, yet all have virtually nothing to say on social-imperialism.

To many on the left, the influence of a 'labour aristocracy' benefiting from imperialism on the mass of workers could be the only explanation for the support for war offered in 1914 by the vast majority of Europe's workers. Partha Sarathi Gupta, in his *Imperialism and the British Labour Movement 1918–1964*,[40] sought to demolish the notion of a labour aristocracy, concentrating on Lenin, who, desperately seeking an explanation for the support of the working class for imperialist war, had blamed the 'treachery' of labour leaders, the 'influence' of a 'privileged stratum', the 'craft mentality' of skilled workers and so on.[41]

It was not difficult to refute Lenin's rather crude analysis by examining the ideas and policies of labour leaders and intellectuals. Gupta based his analysis almost entirely on such people. He provided many quotes from labour movement leaders who were sympathetic to the aspirations of the colonial peoples. He had virtually nothing to say on social-imperialism as it was experienced among the rank-and-file of the labour movement and the working class in general. He made virtually no attempt to grapple with the key question of why the vast majority of the labour movement, including its leaders, no matter how

---

37 Howe 1994.
38 Kirk 2011.
39 Frank et al. (eds) 2010, pp. 1–7.
40 Gupta 1975.
41 See, for instance, Lenin 1974, pp. 105–20 and 205–9.

many lofty internationalist sentiments they might have expressed (or still held, for that matter) supported the war effort in 1914.

Marxist scholars such as Samir Amin, Raymond Lotta and Dan Nabudere have offered a much more nuanced explanation than Lenin's for working class support for imperialism. The problem is not simply the influence of a 'labour aristocracy' but that in the imperialist countries all working class people – even the poorest – benefit to some degree from imperialism. Their argument, their convincing argument, is that superprofits from what came to be called the Third World have helped capitalism to continually develop the means of production in the advanced capitalist countries. Finance for social reform thus comes from domestic production as well as from the developing world. In consequence, rising living standards and social reform help to create a strong mood of social patriotism resulting in the co-operation with capital of the working class, particularly the organised labour movement, in asserting the national interest.[42]

By the start of our period, the British working class had become the mature, 'respectable' working class of 'cup finals, fish-and-chip shops, palais de dance and Labour with a capital L'.[43] They might be increasingly alienated from the product of their labour, yet capitalism had produced diversions – public parks, association football, the music hall, days at the seaside and so on – to provide balm for that alienation.[44] For those so inclined, numerous churches and non-conformist chapels also provided balm, for religion was not only 'the opium of the people', it was 'the sigh of the oppressed ... the heart of a heartless world'.[45] Materially, modern manufacturing methods were starting to allow the production of relatively cheap consumer goods – clocks, ornaments, bicycles, clothes and suchlike – which workers could increasingly afford. While the workers of the Lancashire cotton towns worked long hours (until 1919, work in the cotton trade started at 6 a.m. each day in the punishing standard working week of 55½ hours) and suffered poor housing, they were not the unstable, unorganised proletariat typical of, say, inner Manchester or Liverpool. Cotton and engineering provided the working class, men especially, of our towns with relatively stable employment, better than average pay and facilitated high levels of unionisation.[46]

---

42 Amin 1977; Lotta 1984; Nabudere 1977.
43 Hobsbawm 1984, p. 194.
44 See Wild 1979 for a discussion of recreation in Rochdale, a typical cotton town. See also Bowker 1990 for a discussion of recreation in Ashton later in the century.
45 Marx 1974, p. 38.
46 Around 90–95 percent of spinners belonged to the Amalgamated Association of Operative Cotton Spinners and Twiners (Spinners' Amalgamation). (Howell 1983, p. 53).

It is unsurprising then that on the outbreak of war the great majority of working class people favoured the cloying embrace of patriotism rather than the icy waters of internationalism. During the two world wars neither class nor political antagonism – in, say, Great War belief that 'profiteers' were making fortunes at the expense of the workers or in Second World War anger regarding the allegedly 'broken promises' of the first war – significantly undermined working class patriotism: as Bernard Waites argued, 'National consciousness was not necessarily antithetical to class consciousness'.[47] For the great majority, the national interest was perceived to transcend class, political and sectional interests. This was manifest early in both wars. The outbreak of war in 1914 brought to an abrupt end the unprecedented industrial conflict of the previous four years. In 1939 the labour movement swiftly announced industrial and electoral truces.

But the experience of war raised the possibility, however slight, of a fracturing of class collaboration. In both wars there were serious outbursts of industrial conflict in crucial parts of the war economy. And 1917 raised the spectre of revolution. Ruling class anxiety regarding the loyalty of the working class and concern regarding its physical state – 1914 had seen a new recruitment crisis when the majority of would-be volunteers failed to meet the army's not very exacting standards[48] – served to accelerate the pace of reform. During and in the wake of the two world wars, British society and the place of the working class within it were transformed by fundamental and far-reaching social, economic and political reforms. Of particular importance were the introduction of universal adult suffrage in the decade from 1918 and the post-World War Two 'welfare state', promised after the defeat of British arms in 1940, which sealed and consolidated the social-imperialist bargain struck in 1914. In both wars, reforms were primarily the result of bourgeois anxieties regarding working class loyalty and fitness, rather than revolutionary upheavals and were thus fundamentally conservative, delivered *de haut en bas*.

Let us now consider how the social-imperialist bargain was struck, sealed and consolidated. The five chapters which follow correspond to clearly delineated stages of the two world wars. Chapter 1 covers the period from the outbreak of war in 1914 to the end of 1915. Chapter 2 discusses the period from the introduction of conscription in January 1916 to the end of the war in November 1918. Chapter 3 deals with the postwar crisis which erupted in 1919. Chapter 4

---

47   Waites 1987, p. 181.
48   Beckett and Simpson 1985, p. 44. At the start of Ashton's recruiting drive in 1914 it was reported that a 'lot of able-bodied men ... have had to be rejected ... owing to lack of good teeth'. *Ashton Herald*, 22 August 1914.

examines the period from the outbreak of the Second World War to the British victory over Germany at El Alamein. Chapter 5 deals with the period from El Alamein to Labour's victory in the General Election of 1945. This was the period, defined by the Beveridge Report of 1942, which sealed the social-imperialist bargain between British labour and British capital.

CHAPTER 1

Rallying Round the Flag

In Britain, the centenary of the outbreak of the First World War in 1914 was met by right-wing historians asserting the justness of Britain's cause and by media coverage which was sentimental, nostalgic even, and vaguely patriotic. Concepts such as 'the fallen', 'valour', 'heroism' and 'sacrifice' served to sanitise the suffering and death of those, the great majority of them working class, ground under the military juggernauts of capital in the various fronts of the war. The opposing voice of internationalism has virtually been lost during the rightward ideological drift of the past forty years or so, to which most of the left have succumbed. Gordon Brown, when Chancellor of the Exchequer in the Labour governments of 1997–2010, asserted that Britain should 'stop apologising for its colonial past' and laid a wreath on the graves of British soldiers killed in German East Africa during the First World War.[1]

Only from the most complacently or ignorantly patriotic or nationalistic stance can it be considered that the First World War was anything other than an imperialist war. German East Africa (now Burundi, Rwanda and Tanzania), for instance, was divided between Belgium and Britain after Germany's defeat. The war was the result of twenty or so years of contention between the European great powers over the balance of power in Europe, over spheres of influence and over colonies. France and Russia cemented an anti-German alliance in 1894. The Franco-British *Entente Cordiale* of 1904 marked an end to their rivalry in North Africa (France recognised British control of Egypt, while Britain accepted French interests in Morocco). Their naval agreement of 1912 brokered a division of labour: Britain would defend France's channel ports, France would protect British interests in the Mediterranean. The Russo-British Convention of 1907 settled the two parties' historic disputes over Afghanistan, Persia and Tibet. The war that erupted in 1914 between Germany and Austria-Hungary on the one hand, and the *Triple Entente*, the coalition of Britain, France and Russia, on the other, was the culmination of these imperialist settlements and rivalries.

In November 1914 Turkey entered the war as an ally of Germany. Within months it had to mount a defensive war against Britain and France in the Dardanelles. The Gallipoli campaign (as it became known in Britain) was in part intended to forestall a putative Turkish attack on the Suez Canal, a vital pas-

---

1 *Daily Mail*, 15 January 2005.

sage to British imperial possessions in the Far East. The campaign ended in victory for Turkey, but ultimately led to its defeat and, under the provisions of the Anglo-French Sykes-Picot agreement of 1916, to the postwar sharing of the spoils of Turkey's Ottoman Empire between Britain and France. What the Labour members of the British Government (Labour had joined the coalition government formed in 1915) knew of Sykes-Picot is unclear, but they saw no reason to resign when its provisions were revealed by the Bolsheviks after the second Russian Revolution of 1917. This was but one example of the ingrained social-chauvinism of the British labour movement, manifest since the start of the war.

1   The Labour Movement and the War

In 1914 the parties of the Second International, to which the main party of the left in Britain, the Labour Party, was affiliated, were committed to opposing the general European war which they had long expected. They would call a general strike and thus thwart the plans of the militarists and warmongers.[2] For the Marxist parties (among which the Labour Party should not be numbered), it had been axiomatic that such a war would be an unjust predatory war, the result of the innate contradictions of imperialism, an outmoded and moribund capitalism, ripe for overthrow by revolution, which the working class had no objective interest in supporting.

The Labour Party's attitude to war owed more to pacifism and classical liberal internationalism than to Marxism. Unlike its affiliate, the Independent Labour Party (ILP), Labour had not committed itself to call a general strike to oppose war. Even so, it was in principle opposed to war as a means of settling international disputes. It seemed for a short while after the crisis which erupted in the summer of 1914 that British Labour would refuse to support war. An editorial in the *Daily Herald*, edited by the veteran socialist George Lansbury, highly regarded in labour circles, which must have been written immediately after Austria-Hungary's declaration of war on Serbia, insisted that:

> The present European crisis throws a grave responsibility on the trade unions. At any moment the working classes of Europe may be called upon to defend interests in which they are not concerned, for a cause that it no

---

2   See Newton 1985, pp. 251–93, for a discussion of the debates within the Second International on the general strike weapon.

way promises to uplift ... The capitalists for whose benefit the war will be waged will lose nothing ... The railways and the telegraphs throughout Europe are in the hands of powerful trade unions. War cannot be carried on without their use [these workers] must strike against war. Let the International Bureau [of the Second International] call upon [the workers] to wage a real war for the interest of the working class.[3]

The left-wing *Herald* was not the most representative of labour movement[4] opinion, but on the 1st August, shortly after German troops crossed the French border and Britain warned Germany that it could not remain neutral, a manifesto of the 'British Section of the International' (i.e. the Labour Party), signed by Arthur Henderson, erstwhile leader of the Party and shortly to be leader again, and Keir Hardie, first leader of the Party, called upon the working class to oppose the war. Workers should 'hold vast demonstrations in all industrial centres'. The manifesto concluded with such stirring slogans as 'Down with Class Rule!', 'Down with the Rule of Brute Force!' and 'Down with War!'[5]

The next day, the Labour Party did mount an anti-war demonstration. Under page one banner headlines – 'The Workers War on the War', '20,000 in Trafalgar Square', 'Cheers for Proposed General Strike' – the *Herald* reported that 'During the progress of the meeting, a Russian, a German, a Frenchman and a Swiss embraced each other ... Thus was true international amity demonstrated'.[6] But it soon became clear that very few leaders of European socialism were able to withstand or were prepared to oppose intense ideological pressure to support the war.

The vast majority of European socialist parties, the Russian a notable exception, found specious reasons to support the war. The Germans, for instance, argued that German democracy was threatened by Russian autocracy. Of course, most labour movement people were probably unaware of the underlying contradictions of imperialism which had given rise to the war. And we should make a distinction between the ideological capitulation, the social-chauvinism, the breaking of solemn pledges of labour leaders, and the simple patriotism of the rank-and-file and of the working class in general. But subjective motivation is not the point: the point is that the reforms and rising

---

3   *Daily Herald*, 29 July 1914.
4   In this work, 'labour movement' is not used as a synonym for 'working class'. It is taken to mean not just the trade unions, trades councils and Labour Party, but also other left-wing political parties such as the ILP, the British Socialist Party (BSP) and the Communist Party (CP).
5   *Daily Herald*, 1 August 1914.
6   *Daily Herald*, 3 August 1914.

prosperity of the previous half-century had nurtured an ideological and political climate in which patriotism proved far more congenial to the great majority than internationalism.

On the 4th of August, Germany's invasion of neutral Belgium the previous day provided a pretext for British entry into the war. In parliament, nearly all Labour's MPs supported a declaration of war on Germany.[7] The next day, Labour's National Executive Committee (NEC) resolved to support the war.[8] Labour argued that the national enemy must be defeated; a German victory would mean that 'working class aspirations for greater economic and political power would be checked, thwarted and crushed, as they have been in the German Empire'.[9] The anti-war *Herald*, perhaps recognising that such calls would not be answered, made no more calls for a general strike. The support of foreign socialists for war was used in justification: 'there are four and a half million social-democrats in Germany – they have done nothing', while the French unions were 'cravenly supporting a general mobilisation'.[10]

When war seemed imminent Henderson had convened a conference to organise a general strike, but by the time the delegates assembled (two from the Amalgamated Weavers Association (Weavers' Amalgamation) among them),[11] Britain had declared war. Rather than organise a general strike, the delegates established on the 5th of August the War Emergency Workers National Committee (WEWNC). It was intended that the committee would defend during the war the particular interests of the working class. As well as Henderson, who had strong links with the unions (he had once been an organiser for the iron foundry workers), such labour stalwarts as the leader of the ILP, Ramsay MacDonald, Sydney Webb, Mary MacArthur of the National Federation of Women Workers and the leader of the miners' union, Robert Smillie, were crucial in building the authority of the committee (though MacDonald lost credibility with most labour movement activists when he became a prominent opponent of the war). Its secretary was James Middleton, Assistant Secretary of the Labour Party.[12] Once established, the Committee moved to make itself more

---

7   Thorpe 1997, p. 33.
8   Winter 1974, p. 142.
9   Horne 1991, p. 54.
10 *Daily Herald*, 4 August 1914.
11 Minutes of the Central Committee of the Weavers' Amalgamation, August 1914. TU/Weavers/006 @ Working Class Movement Library, Salford. (WCML).
12 Harrison 1971, pp. 213–14. See also Swift 2016. Swift's is a much more empirical account of the committee's work than Harrison's. It provides invaluable information on such matters as the committee's monitoring of 'profiteering' and campaigning against surveillance of the sexual activities of the wives of men on active service.

representative by co-opting such people as Margaret Bondfield[13] from the Co-operative movement. The Women's Labour League (WLL)[14] was represented by Marion Phillips, its Secretary.[15]

The openly pro-imperialist views of some labour movement notables suggest that for these at least the defence of Belgium was merely a rationalisation of social-chauvinism. James Seddon, Labour MP for Newton in Lancashire, once President of the Trades Union Congress (TUC) and once President of the National Amalgamated Union of Shop Assistants, argued, in a widely-read pamphlet, that while he had once been anti-war, it was clear that 'Germany's purpose [in the war] was to secure world domination'. Labour had 'learned that Prussian militarism must be destroyed, root and branch ... this war is a death grapple between systems which cannot co-exist if freedom is to be something more than a name'.[16] Admittedly, Seddon was on the far right of the Labour Party (in 1916 he joined the jingoist British Workers National League and in 1917 he resigned from the Labour Party[17]), but his forthright support for Britain's imperial war aims was far from exceptional.

The great majority of the labour movement in Lancashire followed the national leadership. J.R. Clynes, the MP for Manchester North East and a major figure in national and Lancashire labour politics (Clynes had excellent labour movement credentials – he had started his working life as a piecer[18] in an Oldham cotton mill when ten years old), probably set the tone for mainstream union opinion at the outbreak of war. Writing in the Liberal *Oldham Weekly Chronicle*, he argued:

> The little the Labour Party could do to maintain peace was done up to the moment when the voice of peace was drowned in the blast of war. Now that peace appeals are of no value and that parties are sunk in the greater interest and concerns of the nation, Labour joins with every other force in facing the tests which war imposes.[19]

---

13   Bondfield, who had started her working life as a shop assistant, had for some time been a union organiser.
14   The WLL was, as its name implies, an organisation of women members of the Labour Party. It fought for suffrage reform and for social-reform, especially on housing (Ada Salter, a prominent member of the league, had cut her political teeth working for improvement of the terrible slums of the East End of London).
15   Women's Labour League 1915, p. 21. Phillips became Labour MP for Sunderland in 1929.
16   Seddon 1917, p. 6.
17   Martin 1974, pp. 333–4.
18   Piecers pieced together thread broken in the spinning process.
19   *Oldham Weekly Chronicle*, 8 August 1914.

Addressing a public meeting in Oldham a few months later, James Sexton, the General Secretary of the National Union of Dock Labourers, which, as he was careful to inform his audience, 'had to get war materials to "the men at the front"', demonstrated how many labour leaders had rationalised their support for the war. Sexton said that he had been 'anti-military' and had 'questioned the wisdom of a big navy', but he could now see that Britain must 'have command of the seas'. Without the navy Britain would have been 'at the mercy of one of the most brutal systems of military despotism the world had ever seen'. Germans could not 'hold meetings on street corners'. His stock of examples of German despotism exhausted, Sexton informed the meeting that German workers 'had no Saturday afternoons off'.[20]

But for most trade union movement leaders such intellectual somersaults had probably not been necessary. They virtually all regarded support for the war effort as axiomatic. On the 24th of August, the TUC resolved to work to quickly resolve existing and future industrial disputes. On the 2nd of September, its Parliamentary Committee resolved to follow the Labour Party in supporting recruitment campaigns. A year later, at its annual congress, only seven out of 607 delegates opposed a pro-war resolution.[21]

William Mullins, the Secretary of the Amalgamated Association of Card and Blowing Room Operatives (Cardroom Amalgamation) (Card and Blowing Rooms were where raw cotton was prepared for spinning) vied with the far right in invective against that 'brutal, vain poltroon Kaiser of Germany, who is very largely responsible for this murderous war'. There could be 'no withdrawing from the war until the power that caused it is irreparably broken and scattered'. Like many others in the labour movement, Mullins could not see the mote in his own eye: German socialists 'in spite of their protestations to the contrary ... are fighting for German imperialism'.[22]

At a lower level, the great majority of labour movement activists seem to have taken for granted that they should support the war. The Manchester branch of the Municipal Employees Association was quick to assure local authorities that it desired to 'cause as little trouble as possible during the crisis through which the country is passing' and was accordingly 'withdrawing their

---

20 *Oldham Weekly Chronicle*, 23 January 1915. For his services to capital, the King bestowed upon Sexton in 1917 one of the highest British honours, a CBE (Commander of the British Empire). He was knighted in 1931. (Taplin 1993, pp. 248–55).
21 Pelling 1987, p. 140.
22 Cardroom Amalgamation, Reports and Minutes March 1913–December 1916. Quarterly Report and Balance Sheet for the Quarter ending 26 September 1914. Report to District Officials from William Mullins, Secretary. TU/TEX/CARD/12 @ WCML.

claim for a pay increase'.²³ A letter to a local newspaper from a branch of the railwaymen's union stated that it would not be holding the usual annual benefit concert for orphans; instead, it was hoped that those who usually contributed would instead give to the 'support of those whose husbands and fathers have been called up to do their duty for their native land'.²⁴

The Executive Committee (EC) of Oldham Trades and Labour Council (T&LC)²⁵ met on the 4th of August to decide their attitude to the war. The meeting seems to have been inconclusive, but their decision not to hold a 'public meeting against this country taking any part in the war arising out of Austria's declaration of war against Servia [the Cyrillic alphabet was then often transliterated this way] ... on account of the developments which had taken place, and the presentation of an ultimatum against Germany by this country' suggests that anti-war sentiments were in a minority. The members of the EC did, however, regret 'that the civilised nations of Europe have not been able to settle their disputes without recourse to the cruel method of war'. On the 25th of August, though a formal decision on the stance to be taken towards the war had still not been taken, the EC decided that the council would respect the decision by the leaders of the main political parties that there would be an electoral truce for the duration of the war. On the 16th of October, a full delegate meeting endorsed the Labour Party's national leadership's policy and decided 'to take part ... in the organisation of Public Meetings for the purpose of recruiting'.²⁶

In both Ashton and Mossley the labour movement gave full support to the war. The Ashton, Dukinfield and District Trades Council (hereafter referred to as Ashton Trades Council) agreed early in September to support collections for the war effort organised by the town council. Weavers 'at the Stamford Mill had already arranged to pay 2d. per loom ... and that overlookers and other officials would pay in proportion'.²⁷ The leaders of a local cotton union resolved that 'any member of this society called up for service with the colours shall be exempt

---

23 Ashton Municipal Borough Council (Ashton Council), Minutes of the General Purposes Committee, 14 August 1914. CA/ASH/111/26 @ Tameside Local Studies and Archives Centre (TLSAC), Ashton-under-Lyne.
24 *Ashton Reporter*, 22 August 1914.
25 Trades councils fought for the common interests of trade unions in a given town or city. Trades and Labour Councils were such councils as had affiliated to the Labour Party. In 1914 these were in a minority; the councils in Ashton and Mossley were not so affiliated.
26 Minutes of Oldham T&LC 1914–20. M17/1/2 @ Oldham Local Studies and Archives (OLSA), Oldham.
27 *Ashton Reporter*, 5 September 1914.

from paying contributions until he returns to civil life'.[28] The trades council also agreed to support the electoral truce (there was as yet no branch of the Labour Party in Ashton, but the trades council had for years fielded 'labour' candidates in municipal elections). In October it accepted that in Portland Ward only a Conservative candidate would stand.[29]

Despite its anti-war stance, the *Herald* retained much influence in labour circles. Its insistence that 'we must ceaselessly bear in mind that side by side with this warfare of the nations there is waged the relentless warfare of labour and capital. In their enthusiasm for their country [workers] must not lose sight of the industrial struggle'[30] doubtless resonated with many. While few working class people or even labour movement activists shared the *Herald's* overtly class-war stance, probably most British working class people did have a sense of a distinctive class interest. While their support for the war was solid, we shall see that for many this support was to be sorely tested. By the autumn of 1917 many had abandoned their initially unqualified support for war and some had come to share the *Herald's* class-war perspectives.

What of initial labour movement opposition to the war? In an appeal to the working class, the ILP insisted that the workers of Britain had 'no quarrel with the workers of Europe. They have no quarrel with you. The quarrel is with the RULING classes of Europe'.[31] A few of its leaders, including Clynes, resigned in protest at the party's anti-war stance. Within days of the outbreak of war, the eccentric and jingoist leader of the ostensibly Marxist British Socialist Party (BSP), Henry Mayers Hyndman declared that the German invasion of Belgium was the *casus belli* and that therefore 'everybody must eagerly desire the defeat of Germany'.[32] Initially, the only consistent revolutionary opposition to the war came from a mainly Scottish minority of the BSP, centred around John MacLean, and the also mainly Scottish Socialist Labour Party (SLP). A few days after the outbreak of war members of these two organisations organised a large anti-war demonstration in Glasgow. In 1916 the internationalists in the BSP gained a majority.[33]

As in London, the Labour Party in Manchester organised an anti-war demonstration on the 2nd of August,[34] but thereafter followed the national leader-

---

28   Minutes of Ashton District of SE Lancs and Cheshire Weavers and Winders Association, September 7 1914. TU/6/7 @ TLSAC.
29   *Ashton Reporter*, 10 October 1914.
30   *Daily Herald*, 6 August 1914.
31   *Labour Leader*, 6 August 1914. Emphasis in the original.
32   *Justice*, 13 August 1914.
33   Redfern 2005, pp. 35–7.
34   *Manchester Guardian*, 3 August 1914.

ship. The ILP mounted small anti-war demonstrations in Oldham, Hyde and Rochdale.[35] Harry Pollitt, the future General Secretary of the Communist Party of Great Britain (CP), then the minute secretary of the Openshaw branch of the BSP, attempted anti-war agitation in Ashton's market place.[36] But hecklers shouted 'rule Britannia' and 'three cheers for the navy' and attempted to rush the lorry from which Pollitt was speaking.[37] Pollitt himself remembered that it was a 'rough house ... and finally two policemen arrived ... and took me to the Openshaw tram'. Pollitt made another attempt at anti-war agitation the next day, but the 'crowd was there, ready to lynch me if I dared to say a word ... The same policeman was there and once again, gently but firmly, led me to the tram'.[38]

In Oldham, agitators from an unspecified organisation made anti-war speeches at the park gates. We know of the agitators only because their fiery speeches caused concern on the town council. One councillor thought their speeches 'should not be allowed seeing that political controversy has been dropped ... if people were to be allowed to speak such opinions as he understood were spoken last Sunday night then there was every possibility of a riot'. But Alderman Ashworth, the chairman of the Parks Committee, had himself gone to the park to listen to the speeches. He told the Parks Committee that while he had heard much that was 'foolish' and 'unwise', he was not 'aggravated'. Another Committee member thought that the council 'ought to be very careful before they [prohibited] free speech'. The Committee decided to take no action.[39]

In Mossley, the ILP was conflicted. At the 1915 annual meeting of Mossley's spinners, their secretary, ILP member Wright Mosley, supported the war while piously hoping that 'God would give to us and the whole world a speedy, righteous peace' and that the outcome of the war would be 'a true brotherhood of man, and a lasting fellowship of nations'.[40] The ILP's Mathew Farr, Executive Council member of the Cardroom Amalgamation and town Alderman, served on the town's military tribunal after the introduction of conscription in 1916.

---

35   *Labour Leader*, 6 August 1914.
36   Quite possibly, Pollitt acted unilaterally. The minutes show no evidence of anti-war sentiment; indeed the meeting of the 1st of October resolved not to contest the November municipal election, presumably because of the electoral truce. Communist Party Archive (CPA), Minutes of Openshaw BSP branch CP/ORG/MISC/3/5 @ Labour History Archive and Study Centre @ People's History Museum, Manchester (PHM).
37   *Ashton Reporter*, 8 August 1914.
38   Pollitt 1940, pp. 64–6.
39   *Oldham Weekly Chronicle*, 12 September 1914.
40   *Mossley and Saddleworth Reporter*, 30 January 1915.

But some members opposed the war. In a debate on the theme *Is the Empire Worth Fighting For?* at the ILP club, Samuel Munns, claiming that he was speaking 'on behalf of the badly paid and sweated workers', argued that it was not worth fighting for. A 'large majority' disagreed.[41]

2 Mustering the Masses for War

labour movement opinion, either pro or anti-war, was not of course necessarily representative of mass opinion. Adrian Gregory[42] and Catriona Pennell[43] have both shown that contemporary press reports of wild patriotic fervour must be treated with some scepticism and that motives for supporting the war were decidedly mixed. There can though be little doubt that support for the war effort was solid, if not fervent. But the fundamental patriotism of most working class people was to be severely tested over the course of the war.

As nationally, the mass of Lancashire people supported the war. The ILP reported 'many signs of Jingo inoculation' in Failsworth, which adjoined both Ashton and Oldham.[44] In Ashton, according to the Liberal *Ashton Reporter*, there were 'thrilling scenes' in the town, the 'excitement' was 'as great, if not greater' than that allegedly shown 'during the Boer War'. At the Hippodrome, 'the audience sang Rule Britannia ... a foreign "turn" (said to be German) did not put in an appearance'.[45] The Tory *Ashton Herald* reported that 10,000 people watched as the local territorials started to march to Bury; 'cheer after cheer livened the men'.[46] In Mossley, the Tory *Ashton Herald* reported that in one day alone 80 men had volunteered and that on the next day crowds 'had gathered at the railway station to see them off'.[47] In Oldham, the mayor claimed that local people were 'responding splendidly': on Tuesday of that week, 37 men 'gave in their names', on Wednesday 29 'men volunteered' and on Thursday there were 31 'more aspirants'.[48] In late December, the *Manchester Guardian* (a liberal newspaper, the precursor of today's *Guardian*) published details of recruitment in various towns, occupations and industries and argued that 'whilst recruit-

---

41   *Mossley and Saddleworth Reporter*, 2 January 1915.
42   Gregory 2008.
43   Pennell 2012.
44   *Labour Leader*, 13 August 1914.
45   *Ashton Reporter*, 8 August 1914.
46   *Ashton Herald*, 22 August 1914.
47   *Ashton Herald*, 29 August 1914.
48   *Oldham Weekly Chronicle*, 15 August 1914.

ing for the army and navy has not been as strong generally around Manchester as in the city itself the response to the call of the country has been generous'.[49]

But these reports reflect the views of Liberal and Conservative town and regional notables committed to the war and anxious to boost support. While David Silbey has rightly argued that 'an enormous and unprecedented number of men'[50] volunteered, it is nevertheless true that even if most supported the war, only a minority were prepared to enlist. Moreover, as with attitudes to the war in general, those enlisting did so for a variety of motives.[51] Only 29.4 percent of the eligible national labour force of 1914 volunteered. Enlisting among textile and clothing workers was the lowest of all.[52] Contemporary union sources show that the majority of cotton workers did not volunteer. Though the leaders of the Spinners' Amalgamation argued in 1915 that the fact that 1,576 spinners and 3,400 piecers had enlisted 'goes to show ... that cotton workers are taking their fair share in the bearing of the nation's burden',[53] this represented only 10 percent of spinners. Probably though many spinners were too old for active service. A far greater proportion (35 percent) of members of the Weavers' Amalgamation, whose members would typically be younger than spinners, enlisted.[54]

Popular expectations of a swift British victory were punctured by reverses at Mons shortly after the declaration of war. Government disquiet at the shortage of volunteers led to various forms of encouragement and pressure to enlist. The Secretary of State for War, Lord Kitchener, launched his *Your Country Needs You* propaganda campaign. An *Ashton Reporter* editorial argued that many had not 'taken in' the graveness of the crisis. If not enough volunteered then conscription – 'a shadow that is dreaded in this land of freedom where willing defenders have never yet been wanting – will be inevitable'. Accordingly, 'Steps' were being taken (presumably by the town's millocracy) to call a town meeting 'in accordance with the suggestion of the Prime Minister whose idea is to rouse the country to a sense of duty during the present national crisis'. Under the headline 'Is Ashton doing its duty', the *Reporter* called on young men to ask themselves: 'Are you prepared to do your duty ... Never mind if you are wealthy or poor ... Put the question to yourselves'.[55]

---

49 *Manchester Guardian*, 22 December 1914.
50 Silbey 2005, p. 37.
51 See Gregory 2008, ch. 3.
52 Beckett and Simpson 1985, p. 9.
53 Spinners' Amalgamation, Quarterly Report of the EC for the quarter ending 31 January 1915, ACS/1/22 @ John Rylands University of Manchester Special Collections (JRSC).
54 *Ashton Reporter*, 16 April 1915.
55 *Ashton Reporter*, 5 September 1914.

Xenophobia (though it should be noted that in all three of our towns, letters protesting against ill-treatment of local aliens, including Germans, appeared) and peer pressure were used to encourage men to enlist. In Mossley, residents were urged to safeguard bridges and to 'keep an eye on foreigners, who are likely to be spies'.[56] The vicar of the parish church attacked Catholics and Dissenters: 'The Pope has been sitting on the fence ... and will no doubt continue to sit on the fence until the end of the war ... I say dissenting Protestantism is very much in the same box. The influence of dissenting Protestantism draws all inspiration from Germany – its home'.[57] In Ashton, the members of the local Congregational Church were told that the primary cause of the war was the 'truculence and overbearing ambition of the military caste in Germany'. If Germany were to win the war, 'Christian civilisation' would 'receive a setback from which it may take us centuries to recover'.[58]

A typical letter to the local press argued that it was 'lamentable to see the large numbers of able-bodied men and youths of fighting age who are prowling about the streets of Oldham with nothing to do ... Are they cowards or are they merely indifferent?'[59] Tardiness was manifest too in Mossley. In the spring of 1915, Alderman Bradbury presided over a Mossley recruiting meeting. Bradbury invoked the defeat of the Spanish Armada, noted that England 'was still the mistress of the seas' and called for a 'constant stream of volunteers'. Fred Brocklehurst, once a stalwart of Manchester ILP, but now a Tory, referred to the 'great debt' humanity owed to German writers, but in Germany now 'moral force had been crucified'. The Mossley men in the trenches, 'plain, ordinary sort of men', were wondering why Mossley men who had not volunteered weren't 'coming to help us'.[60]

But encouragement and propaganda failed to persuade sufficient men to volunteer. The innovation of 'Pal's' battalions was intended to overcome reluctance to enlist by allowing men to serve alongside men from the same occupation or locality. Many such battalions were created. General Rawlinson raised the first 'Pal's' battalion by appealing to London stockbrokers to set an example. Over a thousand men had enlisted in this 'Stockbrokers' Battalion' by the end of August.[61] One of the more bizarre episodes of the war came in June 1915

---

56 *Ashton Herald*, 22 August 1914.
57 *Ashton Herald*, 10 April 1915.
58 Church newsletter, September 1914. NC2/235 @ TLSAC.
59 *Oldham Weekly Chronicle*, 29 August 1914.
60 *Mossley and Saddleworth Reporter*, 24 April 1915.
61 Beckett and Simpson 1985, p. 39.

when an advertisement in Robert Blatchford's jingo-socialist organ, the *Clarion*, offered socialists the chance to serve in a socialist Pal's battalion.[62]

A 'Pal's' battalion (there called a 'Comrade's' battalion) was launched in Oldham with a great fanfare in the autumn of 1914. A page one banner headline in the *Chronicle* announced that 'a 1,000 men' were wanted. A packed Empire Theatre ('many had to stand') heard speeches by the Secretary to the Admiralty, T.J. MacManamen, the Mayor and other local dignitaries. MacManamen reminded the audience that Kitchener was 'asking for more volunteers ... A recruit today was worth more than a dozen three months hence'.[63] But recruitment was slow. 'It was discreditable' that only 200 men had responded in the first week, commented the *Chronicle*, 'out of the thousands of eligible young men who can be seen any evening parading the streets of the town and flocking to the places of entertainment'.[64]

By the summer of 1915, it was commonly assumed that conscription would sooner or later be introduced. The labour movement, both nationally and locally, was adamantly opposed. But it should be noted that opposition was not an expression of anti-war sentiments: the problem was compulsion. There was also a strong suspicion that military conscription would be followed by general industrial conscription, which would place labour under servitude to capital. A cartoon in the *Herald* illustrated this suspicion. A huge Kaiser-like figure addressed a fat, top-hatted, British capitalist: 'The German Prussian: "Ah! You admit you have to copy our method of conscription to beat Germany"'. 'The British Prussian – "Oh! You silly man to think we want conscription to beat Germany. We want it for the defeat of England"'.[65]

Oldham T&LC opposed conscription on liberal rather than class grounds: it would 'be contrary to the sentiments and principles of the British people, subversive of the free and democratic character of their institutions and involve a serious menace to the liberty and freedom of the Labour Movement'. But the council was careful to minute that it would continue to work to encourage volunteering for military service.[66] The council wrote to the WEWNC requesting 200 copies of their leaflet on conscription.[67] Stalybridge, Mossley and

---

62   Gregory 2008, p. 79.
63   *Oldham Weekly Chronicle*, 7 September 1914.
64   *Oldham Weekly Chronicle*, 14 September 1914.
65   *The Herald* (it had become a weekly for the duration of the war), 8 June 1915.
66   Minutes of Executive Committee of Oldham T&LC, 5 June 1915. M17/1/2 @ OLSA.
67   Letter of 13 October 1915. WNC/34/1/262 @ PHM. Indicative of the concern in the labour movement at the prospect of conscription there are in this file numerous requests for this pamphlet.

Millbrook Trades Council (hereafter referred to as Mossley Trades Council[68]) denounced conscription on similar liberal grounds as Oldham: it would be 'a violation of the principle of civic freedom hitherto prized as one of the chief heritages of British liberty'.[69]

Ashton Trades Council opposed conscription too, but its opposition was half-hearted at best, and certainly not based on a fundamental opposition to the war. A debate was marked by a furious row. For some time the council had been refusing to discuss an anti-conscription resolution submitted by Ashton's branch of the ILP ('an organisation not recognised by the council'), but in August 1915 an anti-conscription resolution submitted by the Railway Clerks was the subject of bitter debate. Lewis Watson of the Bricklayers – a self-styled 'pro-Briton equal to any of the German named [unintelligible] journalists who boomed the cry' – argued that conscription was unnecessary as there were sufficient volunteers. Conscription was being urged by 'the capitalist class and press to further enslave the workers'. Opposing the resolution, Charles Saxon of the Machine Workers asserted that the only issue was how to win the war: 'Young men were prating about peace principles who ought to be in the firing line ... as a socialist of many years standing he felt ashamed that any man calling himself an Englishman could throw cold water on the manifest duty of all men to go forward and help to crush the contemptible, cowardly Germans'. The resolution was carried by 23 to 22, but, the *Reporter* was careful to note, implying that the vote was not representative of majority opinion, 'a number of delegates had left the meeting when the vote was taken'.[70]

That same autumn 'heavy losses' in the Gallipoli Campaign, in which the Manchester Regiment was serving, and the continued low level of recruiting in Ashton and Oldham – in Ashton, in the summer, the Reporter had criticised young unmarried men who had not volunteered as 'shirkers who let married men fight for them', men 'who keep you safe in your little bed and keep your precious skin in one piece'[71] – led to a decision to give 'special attention' to recruitment campaigns in the two towns.[72] The 'special attention' seems to have consisted of the deployment of military bands to stir up martial sentiments. In Ashton, the band of the Manchester Regiment paraded 'the prin-

---

68   Mossley's delegates to the wider trades council seem frequently to have met separately and taken unilateral decisions.
69   *Ashton Herald*, 19 June 1915. A minority of delegates opposed the resolution or abstained.
70   *Ashton Reporter*, 15 August 1915.
71   *Ashton Reporter*, 12 June 1915.
72   *Manchester Guardian*, 13 September 1915.

cipal streets ... playing patriotic airs'.[73] In Oldham, bands played at 'open-air meetings' in various parts of the Borough. Various local dignitaries spoke at the meetings. W.C. Robinson, President of the United Textile Factory Workers' Association (UTFWA, an umbrella organisation of the main textile Amalgamations, the Cardroom, the Spinners and the Weavers) and prospective Labour candidate for Oldham, argued that it was 'the duty of every man of military age to join the army'. If they did not, then they 'must be prepared for conscription'.[74] The campaign hardly dented the reluctance of Ashton and Oldham men to enlist. In Ashton, for instance, it produced only 150 recruits; 'scarcely to be regarded as satisfactory [given that] there are 5,000 men of recruitable age in Ashton'. But such men were not attending recruiting meetings (presumably to avoid pressure to enlist), where audiences consisted 'almost entirely of women and children and men above the military age'.[75]

Continued reluctance to volunteer led to another innovation – the Derby Scheme. Lord Derby was made Director-General of Recruiting in the autumn of 1915. His eponymous scheme provided for all eligible men voluntarily to attend tribunals before which they could 'attest' their willingness to enlist if called upon to do so. Those who attested would be issued with armbands (doubtless intended to demonstrate that those who wore them were not 'shirkers'). Early in the campaign to promote attestation, the Local Government Board wrote to all local authorities urging them to do 'everything in their power' to assist. They should set up tribunals to overcome difficulties. 'It cannot be too much emphasised', the Board insisted, that 'there are at this moment a very large number of men who can be spared from their current occupations'.[76] But around the same time the well-connected *Manchester Guardian* (its editor, C.P. Scott, moved in high Liberal circles, including members of the government) reported that responses to the campaign were 'disappointing' and suggested that conscription was inevitable if the campaign failed.[77]

In both Ashton and Oldham though, the scheme was deemed by the press (which seems to have decided that denunciations of those not volunteering were counter-productive) to be a success. In Oldham, it was reported that so many had attested 'that there had been the utmost difficulty in coping'.[78] In

---

73 *Ashton Reporter*, 2 October 1915.
74 *Oldham Weekly Chronicle*, 9 October 1915.
75 *Ashton Herald* 9 October 1915.
76 Letter of 26 October 1915. Ashton Council, Minutes of General Purposes Committee, 15 November 1915, CA/ASH/111/27 @ TLSAC.
77 *Manchester Guardian*, 4 October 1915.
78 *Oldham Weekly Chronicle*, 22 October 1915.

Ashton, it was claimed that many men were enlisting without bothering to attest.[79] The trades council had held a special meeting at which the delegates had been addressed by Colonel Johnson and Colonel Winder. Johnson noted that 'we soldier chaps are not orators, it is up to you Labour men now to save the voluntary system'. Winder argued that if 'the eligible men of Great Britain would face this war as the union men faced a strike he would not have to be appealing for recruits'. There had been 'loud applause for his speech'.[80]

Towards the end of the campaign, attestation was still said to be going well:

> Gradually but surely the canvass of the eligible men of Ashton ... is approaching completion ... There has been a steady stream of recruits all week, the majority of whom attested under Lord Derby's Scheme ... Every day it has been a common spectacle to see men from the youth of 19 to the man of nearly 40 walk steadily up the town hall steps with an air of determination.[81]

At the climax of the attestation scheme, the main hall of the town hall was said to have been 'full to overflowing ... a cloud of tobacco smoke filled the room with a blue haze'. There had been 1,500 attestations by teatime.[82] In Mossley, too, many men were said to be attesting. But there were insufficient armbands; men were walking to Ashton or to Huddersfield to obtain them.[83]

But despite appeals, inducements (such as guarantees of reemployment at the end of hostilities – in Oldham, for instance, it had been reported that 'practically all' firms had given such guarantees),[84] threats (nationally, there were many cases of employers threatening dismissal of men who refused to enlist and some of fiancées threatening to break off engagements; in Ashton, it was suggested that the board of guardians should refuse relief to able-bodied paupers[85]), peer pressure, propaganda and innovations such as the Derby Scheme, insufficient men had enlisted by the end of 1915. The claim by the Chairman of Oldham's Recruiting Committee that out of the 30,000 eligible men at the start of the Derby scheme only 1,000 had not attested[86] cannot be true, given the failure of the scheme. Only 1,150,000 out of 2,179,000 single men appearing

---

79 *Ashton Herald*, 23 October 1915.
80 *Ashton Reporter*, 23 October 1915.
81 *Ashton Reporter*, 1 December 1915.
82 *Ashton Reporter*, 15 December 1915.
83 *Mossley and Saddleworth Reporter*, 15 December 1915.
84 *Oldham Weekly Chronicle*, 4 May 1915.
85 *Ashton Reporter*, 22 December 1915.
86 *Oldham Weekly Chronicle*, 8 December 1915.

before tribunals from October to December attested a willingness to serve.[87] The Derby Scheme had been a last attempt to avert conscription: its failure meant that conscription had become inevitable.

3 The End of the Road for Liberalism?

The Liberal government in power in 1914 had been still considerably in thrall to the nineteenth century doctrine of *laissez-faire*. True, it had introduced such measures as old age pensions and unemployment insurance, but these had more to do with heading off the challenge of the Labour Party than with a loss of faith in liberalism. But since August 1914 the pressing needs of war, labour movement demands for reform and working class unrest had combined to undermine liberalism and foster collectivism and statism. Conscription was the most radical breach with liberalism (what could be less liberal than coercing men into the army?) of a series of such breaches since the start of the war. The experience of war undermined not just liberalism but also the Liberal Party. The Conservatives and Labour became much more committed to social-imperialism. Working class people increasingly looked to the Labour Party as the party best suited to represent their interests. After the formation of a coalition government in 1915, the Liberals were never again the main governing party.

The Defence of the Realm Act (DORA), passed within days of the outbreak of war, was used to intern enemy aliens, to prohibit contact with the enemy and so on. The government used existing legislation to take control of the railways in order to ensure the efficient transport of men and munitions. The standard rate of income tax (a tax which most earned too little to be liable for) was doubled. These were measures to which even the most fanatical devotee of *laissez-faire* was unlikely to object in wartime. But a series of amendments to DORA gave the government ever wider powers over business. As early as August 1914 the export of such strategic war materials as nitro-toluene and phenol was prohibited. In December powers to take control of factories involved in the production of war materials were adopted. Little was done to regulate prices – an increasingly insistent demand from the trade unions – other than to regulate the price of coal.

More radical breaches with *laissez-faire* were facilitated by the formation in May 1915 of a coalition government. The new government included Conservat-

---

87 Beckett and Simpson 1985, p. 12.

ive and Labour ministers[88] and in consequence shifted the ideological balance of the government towards a greater acceptance of state intervention and control. The Munitions of War Act of 1915 was the work of Lloyd George, soon to replace Asquith as Prime Minister. Lloyd George was prepared to step on many toes in the interests of winning the war. The Act was passed in the wake of the shell crisis of the spring of 1915, which convinced the government that private companies could not be relied upon to supply sufficient shells of the requisite quality.

But probably a bigger spur to the passing of the Munitions of War Act was industrial unrest in munitions factories on the Clyde.[89] The Act prohibited strikes and lockouts in munitions factories and brought them under the control of the new Ministry of Munitions. It became a criminal offence to leave a job at such a factory without a leaving certificate, which was virtually impossible. The Act did not have a great impact on our three towns, given that the great majority of its workers continued to work in unmilitarised industries, but they were indirectly affected as the Act contributed to rising working class discontent and to the promises of reforms intended to contain it. The Clyde Workers' Committee (CWC), which was to sorely trouble the government during the rest of the war, was formed in response to the Act.

By 1915 the WEWNC had shed some of its early moderation[90] and hesitancy. It had never discussed whether or not Britain should participate in the war, discussing only 'the social consequences of the war'.[91] Initially, it took a purely defensive stance on these consequences. Its task, Henderson declared, was 'to mitigate the destruction which will inevitably overtake our working people while the state of war lasts'.[92] At the outbreak of war it anticipated that there would soon be widespread unemployment, but in fact the demands of war more than offset any disruption. More accurately, it anticipated that there would soon be rising prices and eventually food shortages. It therefore demanded that the government should take measures for the stockpiling and

---

88   Arthur Henderson, who had replaced the anti-war MacDonald as leader of the Labour Party, entered the cabinet as Minister of Education, but probably his main function was to act as the voice of labour in the cabinet.
89   See Marwick 1991, ch. 11, and Gregory 2008, pp. 187–91.
90   So moderate had the committee been that it received a letter from Buckingham Palace on behalf of the Queen, asking if it could suggest suitable women to 'advise and co-operate' with a sub-committee of a proposed 'Queen's fund for unemployed women'. Buckingham Palace to WEWNC, 15 August 1914. WNC/32/3 @ PHM.
91   Harrison 1971, p. 216.
92   Winter 1974, p. 186.

distribution of food and should set maximum prices for food.[93] Rather overestimating its authority and powers, the Committee gave itself the responsibility of maintaining food supplies and attempting to prevent 'unnecessarily high prices'.[94]

The committee soon adopted even wider perspectives and ambitions. It drafted an ambitious programme 'of such a character as will more completely arrest existing distress, and prevent as far as possible further distress and unemployment in the future'. It demanded, *inter alia*, a national system of relief for unemployment and distress, protection against rising prices, 'a comprehensive policy of national housing', the 'establishment of maternity and infant centres' and 'the continuance of national control over railways, docks and similar enterprises at the close of the war, with a view to the better organisation of production and distribution' and, extraordinarily for the time, that 'unmarried mothers should be given the full status of dependents'.[95]

But in the summer of 1915 it became clear that demands for reform then attracted little support from the wider labour movement. At the TUC's annual conference, a WEWNC inspired resolution calling for a 'new workers charter', including nationalisation of the mines, railways and land, an eight-hour day and a minimum wage failed to even get a seconder. In contrast, a resolution reiterating union support 'for final and complete victory' in the war passed easily.[96] But the hardships of war that were to come stimulated working class demands for reform and consequently support for the Labour Party, which in 1914 had been only a marginal player in national politics.

The formation of the precursor of the Labour Party, the Labour Representation Committee (LRC), in 1900 had not been a manifestation of a significant turn of working class men (women did not obtain the parliamentary franchise until 1918), who still overwhelmingly supported the Conservative and Liberal parties, towards the Labour Party: rather it signified primarily a belief of a minority of trade unions[97] that parliamentary representation was necessary in their struggle for better terms and conditions for the sale of labour power. Judicial attacks on the labour movement (the Taff Vale judgement of 1903 made trade unions liable for damages caused to employers during strikes, while the

---

93 Harrison 1971, p. 81.
94 Horne 1991, p. 229.
95 WEWNC, *The Workers and the War: A Programme for Labour*. The programme is undated, but internal evidence shows that it was published shortly after the start of the war.
96 Horne 1991, p. 220.
97 Minkin 1991, part 1, and Reid 2000. Only 17.4 percent of trade unionists were affiliated to the LRC on its formation. Thorpe 1997, p. 13.

Osborne judgement of 1909 made it illegal for trade unions to contribute to political parties) reinforced this stance.

At its founding conference the LRC rejected a proposal from the Social Democratic Federation (SDF) that the Marxist doctrine of the class struggle should be accepted. But the SDF might well have drafted the LRC's manifesto for that year's general election, which, as well as such moderate demands as 'Public Provision of Better Houses for the People', contained a call for the 'abolition of the standing army and the establishment of a Citizen Force' (a standard demand of the Marxist Second International, arising from the bloody suppression of the Paris Commune), all 'to enable the People ultimately to obtain the Socialisation of the Means of Production, Distribution and Exchange'. But, by 1906, probably due to the SDF's departure from the LRC in 1901 and an increasingly close Labour relationship with the Liberals (including the formation of an electoral pact in 1903), the LRC had come to accept capitalism. Its manifesto for that year's General Election demonstrated an implicit acceptance of capitalism in its call for the trade unions 'to have the same liberty as capital enjoys'.[98] As James Hinton argued, the formation of the Labour Party in 1906 (the LRC reconstituted itself as the Labour Party immediately after the election) 'represented, not a victory for the socialists, but the effective containment of the socialist impulse within older labourist traditions'.[99]

In Lancashire, working class support for Labour had begun slowly to grow around the time of the formation of the LRC. David Shackleton, a prominent weavers' official, was elected as Labour MP for Clitheroe in 1902. Through UTFWA, the main cotton unions became affiliated to the LRC in 1903. Lancashire labour was given a particular fillip in 1906, when the main issue in the general election of that year was free trade. Lancashire was traditionally Tory (Ashton, for instance, had been represented by a Tory for all but four years since the reform act of 1867), but the Tory campaign for tariff reform, which was seen as a threat to cheap food and to Lancashire's cotton exports, led to a sharp fall in working class support for the party. A deal with the Liberals, giving Labour a free-run against the Conservatives, allowed 30 Labour MPs to be elected, 13 of whom represented Lancashire constituencies (though our three towns remained loyal to the old parties).

A further boost for the Labour Party came in 1913 when the Liberal government legislated to again permit the use of union funds to finance political parties. All three cotton amalgamations balloted their members on whether or

---

98   LRC Manifestos for the 1900 and 1906 General Elections in Dale (ed.) 1962, pp. 9–11.
99   Hinton 1983, p. 24.

not to establish a political fund. It was understood that the issue was support for Labour, not merely a matter of principle. The members of all three cotton amalgamations voted in favour by large majorities (Ashton's spinners, for instance, voted 62 percent in favour, though Mossley's spinners recorded only 47.4 percent in favour).[100]

But, irrespective of what union ballots, conferences and leaderships might reveal and advocate, most trades councils continued to avoid 'politics' (even if in the past many of their members had campaigned for the Liberals[101]). One exception to this tendency was Oldham Trades Council. In the Oldham by-election of 1911, despite a dispute between the cotton unions over who should be the Labour candidate,[102] its members campaigned for the Labour candidate, Robinson of UTFWA. He won 24.65 percent of the vote.[103] In 1914 it was decided to establish a political section and become Oldham Trades and Labour Council.[104] But Ashton and Mossley trades councils continued to resist 'politics'. In these two towns it was, typically, the experience of war and, to a considerable extent, the influence of the WEWNC, which fostered a turn to the Labour Party.

In one attempt to forge links with the wider labour movement, the national committee of the WEWNC wrote to trades councils asking for details of local authority expenditure on free school meals. Oldham T&LC replied that in Oldham the town council provided free meals '6 days each week, 2 meals on Sundays'.[105] In Ashton, members of the Weavers' amalgamation, who had participated in a weavers' delegation to the inaugural meeting of the committee,[106] attended in 1915 a national conference convened by the Committee 'to protest against the high prices for food and fuel and the general increased cost of living'.[107] The Secretary of the local branch of the BSP wrote to the national committee asking for two dozen copies of its *Memorandum on Wheat and Coal*

---

100 White 1978, pp. 152–4.
101 In Ashton, for instance, according to the local newspaper, control of the council in the late nineteenth century had been contested by 5,000 ratepayers supporting the Tories and 6,000 Trades Council members supporting the Liberals (*Ashton Reporter*, 1 November 1891). In Rochdale, too, many members of the 'non-political' Trades Council had been 'privately Liberal' (Hill 1992, p. 52).
102 McHugh and Ripley 1987, p. 123.
103 *Oldham Weekly Chronicle*, 21 November 1911.
104 Oldham T&LC Minutes 1914–20. Special Delegate Meeting of Trades and Labour Council, 16 June 1914. M17/1/2 @ OLSA.
105 Reply to letter from Middleton, 22 December 1914. WNC.26/2/63 @ PHM.
106 Minutes of the Central Committee of the Weavers' Amalgamation, 4 August 1914. TU/Weavers/006 @ WCML.
107 Minutes of the Central Committee of the Weavers' Amalgamation 6 March 1915. TU/Weavers/006 @ WCML.

Prices.[108] The leaders of the Spinners' Amalgamation kept a file (a thin file) of WEWNC agendas, minutes and invites to meetings. There is no evidence of significant active participation in the organisation, though William Marsland, the Amalgamation's Secretary, seems to have attended several of its meetings at the House of Commons.[109]

The WEWNC was not content to simply issue policies and demands: it attempted, though with only limited success, to establish a network of local committees to act upon its policies and demands. Such committees were established in only a few localities, including Norwich and Walsall. Attempts were made in Manchester, Glasgow, Rochdale and one or two other places.[110] An Ashton Committee was inaugurated sometime in late 1914-early 1915. The trades council, the BSP and the ILP jointly agreed to set up a local committee and to ask the local co-operative society to join.[111] In the summer of 1915 the Committee's Secretary, Charles Griffiths, wrote to the national WEWNC requesting 13 copies of its *Memorandum on the Cost of Living*.[112] But there is no evidence that Ashton's Committee had more than a nominal existence. At a 1916 meeting of the trades council, a delegate from the bricklayers' union claimed that a branch had been formed in 1914, but there had been 'no interest'. Leaflets had been handed out in the town, 'but only twenty turned up'.[113]

After a year or so of war, rising prices and the threat of conscription were beginning to stir up working class discontent. For the WEWNC, the government had done nothing to alter a fundamental inequality between the 'sacrifices' of labour and those of capital: they did not 'interfere with the power of the idle, absentee owner of land or investments, to draw, year on year, an income in rent, interest or dividends from the labours of those who *are* rendering National Service'.[114] This theme struck a chord with many labour movement organisations. Sometime in 1915, for instance, Oldham T&LC wrote to the Committee, asking for 200 copies of its pamphlet on the 'conscription of riches'.[115] Several other labour movement bodies had called for general conscription. Poplar Trades and Labour Council, for instance, had resolved that 'in the event of the failure of the voluntary system, [the council] calls upon the government to introduce a true

---

108   Letter from Secretary of Ashton BSP, A.W. Humphrey, to WEWNC, 16 March 1915. WNC.33/1/111 @ PHM.
109   File on the WEWNC. ACS/6/10/9 @ JRSC.
110   Harrison 1971, p. 215.
111   *Ashton Reporter*, 6 February 1915.
112   Letter of 22 July 1915. WNC.33/1/153 @ PHM.
113   *Ashton Reporter*, 6 October 1916.
114   Horne 1991, p. 236 (emphasis in the original).
115   WNC/34/1/262 @ PHM.

national service, which should be ... that all people, rich and poor, should place all their resources in both labour and wealth at the disposal of the country'.[116] This sense of a greater sacrifice by labour than by capital stimulated working class unrest, which the government eventually felt constrained to respond to with promises of reform.

4   The Discontents and Demands of the Labour Movement

When referring to the 'sacrifices' of the labour movement, the WEWNC probably had principally in mind ending restrictions on overtime, eschewing strikes (at least in principle) and the acceptance of 'dilution' (the substitution of female for male and unskilled for skilled labour). There had been considerable resistance to changing long-standing practices. Even proposals that overtime should be worked had provoked controversy. Early in 1915 the quarterly meeting of Oldham members of the Weavers' Amalgamation had discussed working overtime, 'which was contrary to the rules of the society'. The weavers resolved that they should seek permission from the leadership before working overtime.[117] In March that year the spinners' executive council discussed the matter. They were 'not inclined to agree even temporarily' to overtime working, without 'first satisfying themselves that there was really some necessity for it in the interests of the country'. In fact, there was 'machinery standing idle' but the employers would not use it (implicitly because it was cheaper to pay for overtime than to employ additional workers).[118] In contrast, the leaders of the Cardroom Amalgamation, unapologetic in their support for the war effort and anxious to remove all obstacles to the production of war materials, asserted:

> of one thing, there can be no dispute, and that is that our men at the front must be kept well supplied with food and munitions of war ... If it is found that cotton goods are an absolute necessity and our members are willing to do a little extra time ... then it is our duty to place no restriction on them.[119]

---

116   *The Herald*, 9 October 1915.
117   *Oldham Weekly Chronicle*, 23 January 1915.
118   *Oldham Weekly Chronicle*, 6 March 1915.
119   Cardroom Amalgamation, Reports and Minutes March 1913–December 1916. Quarterly Report and Balance Sheet for the Quarter ending March 27th 1915, Report to District Officials from William Mullins, Secretary. TU/TEX/CARD/12 @ WCML.

Shortages of labour soon led to a relaxation of opposition to overtime. But overcoming rank-and-file resistance to giving up the strike weapon was considerably more problematic. By December 1914 the officials of the spinners union had agreed, after a series of meetings with George Askwith, a government official long experienced in negotiations with trade unions, that they would endeavour to ensure that there would be no strikes.[120] Talks were held in March 1915 between Arthur Henderson and a number of trade union leaders and Lloyd George, then Chancellor of the Exchequer, and Walter Runciman, the President of the Board of Trade. The union representatives agreed that for the duration of the war there would be no strikes in war industries – disputes would be resolved by arbitration.

Union discussions on 'dilution' with the Treasury's Committee on Production, headed by Askwith, led to the 'shells and fuses' agreement in which the unions accepted that in the interests of maximising production in the armaments and munitions industries, unskilled labour, including that of women, could be substituted for skilled labour. The agreement was to last only for the duration of the war.[121] But these agreements did not, could not, ensure industrial harmony and prevent strikes. Rank-and-file opposition to 'dilution' continued, notably on the Clyde, and in 1917 differing interpretations of the agreement by government and by workers was to cause serious unrest.

The traditional view – found, for instance, in the work of Bernard Waites[122] – namely that the outbreak of war brought an outbreak of industrial peace, needs some qualification, certainly as far as Lancashire is concerned. A more nuanced view is advanced by Adrian Gregory, but he too finds that a relative class peace descended on British industry, excepting only the South Wales Coalfield and the munitions industry on the Clyde.[123] It is true that the outbreak of war brought to a swift end the tumultuous class conflict of 1910–14.[124] After some initial dislocation at the start of the war (in Ashton, for instance, it was reported that 50 percent of cotton workers were unemployed and would soon have to seek public assistance),[125] the cotton industry enjoyed relative stability until 1917, when submarine warfare began to lead to severe shortages of cotton (all

---

120   Minutes of the Executive Committee of the Spinners' Amalgamation, 31 December 1914. ACS/1/21 @ JRSC.
121   Clegg 1985, p. 154.
122   Waites 1987, p. 22.
123   Gregory 2008, ch. 6.
124   In 1914, strikes accounted for 9,880,000 working days, but only 2,950,000 in 1915. Pelling 1987, p. 298.
125   *Ashton Reporter*, 26 September 1914.

of which, of course, was imported). Even so, though there was no major wartime strike in Lancashire until 1917, there was endemic low-level unrest over 'dilution', rising prices and the long-standing intractable problems of 'bad spinning'[126] and 'time cribbing'.[127]

In Oldham, for instance, workers at the Cheetham's and Roma mills, who had been on strike for some time, refused to return to work on the outbreak of war, despite appeals from the union.[128] A few days later, strikes commenced at Ashton's Bridge End and Tame Valley Thread mills.[129] The records of the Spinners' Amalgamation show that while there were very few strikes, the number of disputes involving spinners in the first year of war was more or less the same as in the last year of peace.[130] Clearly, many workers did not regard it as axiomatic that their support for the war effort should lead to a suspension of class conflict. Inflation, food and fuel shortages and a growing sense that the working class, in contrast to 'profiteers', was bearing an unfair share of the burden of war all stimulated unrest and strikes.

Though some workers experienced rising real wages, especially casual labourers, who were able to take advantage of labour shortages to remedy pre-war desperation, this was not true of workers in the cotton and engineering industries. By 1916 skilled engineers' wages had risen by only 11 percent,[131] spinners' wages by only 10 percent, compared with a rise in the cost of living of 46 percent.[132] Moreover, official inflation figures underestimated the effect of rising prices on working class incomes. Then, as now, food prices, which in the spring of 1915 had risen by 32 percent since the start of the war,[133] took up a

---

126 'Bad spinning' referred to the use of poor quality cotton for spinning, which led to frequent interruptions in the spinning process and thus to loss of production and lower wages. Ashton textile employers frequently reported such disputes. In January 1915, for instance, disputes were recorded at Cavendish, Tudor and Cedar mills. There were often short stoppages of work, but no strikes were reported. Minutes of Ashton and District Textile Employers Association 1912–16. ATEA/1/1/3 @ TLSAC.
127 'Time cribbing' referred to the practice of running machinery until the end of the working day. This meant that cleaning the machines had to be done by the workers in unpaid overtime. Though the practice was illegal, there had been many instances of the practice and some prosecutions. By 1914 the practice was less common, but there were some wartime instances.
128 *Oldham Weekly Chronicle*, 15 August 1914.
129 Minutes of the Central Committee of the Weavers' Amalgamation, 14 August 1915. TU/Weavers/006 @ WCML.
130 Minutes of the Spinners' Amalgamation. ACS/6/3/2 @ JRSC.
131 Winter 2003, p. 233.
132 Fowler 1987c, p. 148.
133 Clegg 1985, p. 146.

disproportionate share of working class income. That spring, the WEWNC convened a conference of trade unions to consider their response to rising food prices. The Weavers' Amalgamation was among those unions which accepted an invitation to attend.[134] It is not clear what decisions, if any, were taken at the conference. But in the case of the weavers it certainly did not lead to greater militancy: they were not involved in the cotton workers' strikes and threatened strikes of the spring and summer and in consequence did not receive a pay rise until January 1916.

The price of food was the principal cause of industrial unrest in 1915. In the Staffordshire coalfield, for instance, thousands of miners refused to await arbitration and went on strike in May, despite entreaties from their officials 'to be patriotic and remain at work'.[135] In February, Mossley Trades Council, claiming that the government had not 'anticipated the exploitation of the poor', demanded that it should 'acquire immediate powers to arrest and reduce the inflated prices being charged for all commodities'.[136] Mossley's town council also expressed its concern by urging central government to 'ensure a sufficient supply of foodstuffs at reasonable prices by accelerating transport and, if necessary, fixing official prices'.[137] In April, Ashton weavers, in response to their employers' refusal of a request for a wage increase, argued, clearly influenced by socialist ideas, that the government should 'take over the means of production, distribution and exchange so as to stop certain unscrupulous individuals from making profits out of the nation's misfortunes'.[138]

In March Oldham T&LC requested 200 copies of the WEWNC's *Memorandum on the Increased Prices of Wheat and Coal*[139] and organised a 'well attended' public meeting to protest over rising food prices. Labour's Councillor Frith presided over the meeting. He argued that the government should 'fix maximum prices' and alleged that food was being hoarded in the expectation of rising prices: the government should therefore 'acquire control of commodities that are or may be subject to artificial costs'. If 'workers and soldiers', Frith continued 'are to be asked to put country first … surely it was not too much to ask that employers and merchants ought also to be asked to put country first'.

---

134   Minutes of the Central Committee of the Weavers' Amalgamation, 6 March 1915, TU/Weavers/006 @ WCML.
135   *Times*, 17 May 1915.
136   *Ashton Reporter*, 20 February 1915.
137   *Mossley and Saddleworth Reporter*, 13 February 1915.
138   *Ashton Reporter*, 17 April 1915.
139   WNC/33/1/169 @ PHM. Oldham Co-operative Society also requested copies of the *Memorandum*. WNC/33/1/102 @ PHM.

The main speaker was George Barnes, Labour MP for Glasgow Gorbals, who argued that the government 'ought to take some drastic action to equalise the sacrifices made by the community'. If they did not, 'they would have a recurrence of what had taken place on the Clyde [where serious industrial unrest had erupted] up and down the entire length of the country'. If the government failed to act, 'the people will be justified in starting to enforce their demand that wages shall go up to something corresponding to prices'.[140] Tantamount to endorsing strike action, statements such as this, particularly by Barnes, known as one of the most right-wing of Labour MPs, could hardly fail to suggest to trade unionists that war or not, strikes were justified.

In April, representatives of Ashton, Dukinfield, Mossley and Stalybridge town councils met to discuss an application from council employees for a wage increase. Negotiations in progress at the start of war had been abandoned (presumably due to patriotic enthusiasm), but the Association of Municipal Employees now revived their application. The councils agreed to refuse the application. Negotiations dragged on for months. In August, the union threatened to call a strike. At a mass meeting, the employees were said to be 'unresponsive' to council leaders' appeals to their patriotism.[141] Strike notices were issued, but after arbitration a five percent increase was awarded.[142] In early June lockout notices were posted at Mossley's mills where spinners were threatening to strike for a 10 percent increase in wages; but the spinners agreed to accept arbitration.[143]

The most serious unrest in our three towns was among cardroom workers, who for a while in the spring of 1915 seemed likely to embark on an industry-wide strike. Trouble first erupted in Oldham. At the quarterly meeting of the cardroom workers it was alleged that 'certain firms' were 'making abnormal profits'. This was vehemently denied by the employers who were determined to 'unitedly resist' the workers' demand for a ten percent war bonus.[144] A week later, strike notices were posted at the centre of discontent, the Forge mill. Notices were also posted at several mills in neighbouring Rochdale.[145] Negotiations then started and collapsed. By the end of the month cardroom workers at the Forge and other mills were on strike. In response to the employers' threat to impose a general lockout, the spinners insisted that this would render any

---

140 *Oldham Weekly Chronicle*, 13 March 1915.
141 *Ashton Reporter*, 10 April 1915; 14 August 1915.
142 LAB/2/100/IC2566/1915 @ National Archives, Kew (NAK).
143 *Cotton Factory Times*, 12 June 1915; 19 June 1915.
144 *Oldham Weekly Chronicle*, 1 May 1915.
145 *Oldham Weekly Chronicle*, 8 May 1915.

existing agreement with them broken and they would 'immediately' put in a claim for a ten percent wage increase.[146]

Initial attempts at arbitration by the Board of Trade failed due to the employers' insistence that they would not accept arbitration unless the cardroom workers called off their strike. Given the obvious threat of an industry-wide strike, the government threatened to bring the cotton industry within the provisions of the Munitions of War Act unless the cotton unions accepted arbitration. Cardroom workers and spinners both buckled under this threat and accepted arbitration. They were awarded only five percent.[147] Unsurprisingly, resentment at rising prices continued to fester.

Rack-renting (profiteering landlords taking advantage of housing shortages) provoked much popular indignation in 1915. Rack-renting was particularly prevalent in Glasgow, where there was an acute shortage of working class accommodation and where there were particularly militant branches of the BSP and SLP. Working class women formed the Glasgow Women's Housing Association in order to organise a rent strike. Starting in May 1915, thousands of women refused to pay increased rents. There was frequently considerable disorder, sometimes involving members of the CWC, when evictions were attempted. The Glasgow rent strike was called off after the government, in another major breach with *laissez-faire* doctrine, passed in December 1915 the Rent and Mortgage Interest (War Restrictions) Act (commonly known as the Rent Restrictions Act), which restricted rents to a level no greater than that of August 1914.

Probably in response to the rent strikes on the Clyde, the WEWNC, which had been arguing for rent restriction for some time, had earlier in the year suggested that Tenants' Defence Leagues (TDLS) should be established throughout the country.[148] Rack-renting was not in our three towns the grave problem it was in Glasgow and thus these towns did not experience mass rent strikes. But the Glasgow events had suggested to labour movement activists that mass action could deter unscrupulous landlords from demanding excessive rents. Rather than organise a TDL, Oldham T&LC seems to have decided that it would itself take up the issue of rents. The council wrote to the WEWNC to inform it that 150 delegates had attended a conference on rents. A subsequent campaign led

---

146   *Oldham Weekly Chronicle*, 28 May 1915.
147   *Times*, June 17 1915.
148   Harrison 1971, p. 233. The importance attached to housing by the labour movement is indicated by the voluminous correspondence between the WEWNC and such organisations as TDLs, the Labour Housing Association, the Workmen's National Housing Council and so on. See, e.g., WNC/13/6 & WNC/13/7 @ PHM.

to several landlords refunding excessive rents.[149] In the summer the council decided to ask the WEWNC for information on rents.[150]

The most contentious – certainly among working class men – of the various 'sacrifices' which the labour movement had made to support the war effort was 'dilution'. Despite the agreements struck between government and union leaders, 'dilution' was vigorously opposed by many labour movement activists and not infrequently led to strikes. It is perhaps superfluous to state that opposition to 'dilution' was not, in the main, motivated by anti-war sentiments. Nor was it, in the main, motivated by a desire to defend the general interests of the working class (though this was probably the subjective motivation of many activists). Fundamentally, opposition to 'dilution' was motivated by a defence of the sectional interests of skilled workers, whose status, privileges and pay were threatened by an influx of semi and unskilled workers. This is a point made by James Hinton in his generally sympathetic account of the engineering shop stewards,[151] and in an unsympathetic study of the CWC by Ian McLean.[152]

Also at play, certainly in the Lancashire cotton trade, and doubtless elsewhere, was a defence of the privileges of male workers, threatened by an influx of women, and most men's ideological views on the proper role of women. The stance of the ILP that men should not oppose women 'dilutees' but should welcome them as sisters and fight for 'equal pay for equal work'[153] was shared by few male workers, or, for that matter, by few women. Though a majority of the cotton labour force was female (the vast majority in weaving), its labour movement was a male-dominated movement in which most men thought that women's role in the movement was at best secondary. Many men clearly objected to the employment of women in principle. It was the man's place to be the family breadwinner. Most women, though by no means all, would leave employment on marriage. In Oldham around the time of the First World War, only 24 percent of the town's women workers were married.[154] If a woman continued to work, then it was deemed to be for 'pin money', i.e., a supplement to the family income, not an essential part of it (though in practice it frequently was). Most men thought it axiomatic that many trades were unsuitable for women. Fears of sexual impropriety by women clearly underlay many men's objections.

---

149 Oldham T&LC to WEWNC, 14 May 1915. WNC/9/3/15/15 @ PHM.
150 Minutes of Executive Committee of Oldham T&LC, 3 August 1915. M17/1/2 @ OLSA.
151 Hinton 1973, p. 93.
152 McLean 1983, p. 47.
153 *Labour Leader*, 17 June 1915.
154 Winstanley 1996, p. 187.

5   'Dilution' and the Mobilisation of Women

There is a considerable literature on the experience of the women who moved into the labour force and into the labour movement before and during the war. The historiography is, unsurprisingly, dominated by feminist historians who have mostly been concerned to examine the difficulties faced by these women in a male-dominated movement.[155] But what of the impact of these women on the men in the movement?[156] In Lancashire the high proportion of working women doubtless accounts for the fact that the county was a stronghold of the National Union of Women's Suffrage Societies (NUWSS).[157] Many of these women were members of the cotton unions and some of them were active in the labour movement, but there is little evidence that they had had an ideological impact on the movement. Which may well be why, at the 1914 conference of the WLL, Ada Salter, its co-founder along with Margaret MacDonald, expressed the hope that the trades union movement would grasp 'that all workers, men and women, youths and maidens, were members one of another'.[158] It is suggested – no more, for it is more a matter of conjecture than of evidence – that improving links between the women's and labour movements and the more feminised wartime workforce contributed to at least some realisation of Salter's hopes. This transition and the part that women played in it will be discussed in the next two chapters.

There were many engineering factories in Lancashire, including in our three towns, but the 'shells and fuses' agreement allowed without much controversy the deployment of women in munitions establishments. We shall see though in the next chapter that this agreement came under severe strain in 1917. There was in the cotton trade no equivalent to the 'shells and fuses' agreement. Attempts to introduce women into spinning and card rooms provoked a great deal of resistance. There had been strikes on this issue for decades.[159] Considerable opposition was also generated against the employment of women as tram conductors.

---

155   It is clear that many had unpleasant experiences. See, for instance, Braybon 1981 and Thom 1998.
156   There has been some work on their impact on the political parties. See, for instance, Mayhall 2000 and Pugh 1974. See Hunt 2014 for the experiences of women trade unionists. But the impact of women on the male members of the trade union movement is unexplored.
157   Liddington and Norris 1978.
158   Cited in Collette 1989, p. 4.
159   As early as 1886 there had been a strike on the matter in Bolton. (McHugh and Ripley 1987, p. 123).

As a shortage of labour (caused mainly by piecers and cardroom workers volunteering for the armed forces) began to seriously hamper production of cotton goods, government, employers and, eventually, union officials began to try to persuade the spinners to accept female piecers in mule spinning rooms.[160] There were inconclusive discussions on the matter between the leaders of the Spinners' Amalgamation and government officials, headed by David Shackleton, who had become a senior civil servant. In its quarterly report to its members in the spring of 1915, the spinners' Executive Committee reported that it had been unpersuaded in its discussions with the government regarding the use of 'female piecers, working overtime ... etc., during the period of the war'. It had 'not yet seen the necessity for any of the Amalgamation's principles being temporarily suspended'.[161]

Despite the opposition of the spinners to the employment of women in spinning rooms, in January the Ashton Textile Employers Association (ATEA) had resolved that 'the question of employing female labour in the mule spinning rooms should receive the careful consideration of the Federation ... as the scarcity of male labour ... becomes more acute every day'.[162] In February a joint meeting of the ATEA and spinners' leaders met to discuss how to alleviate the shortage of labour. Edward Judson, President of the Spinners' Amalgamation and an Ashton town councillor, insisted that the most pressing matter was female labour: the spinners 'objected as a matter of principle to employment of females as spinners or piecers'.[163]

The Ashton employers solicited a lead on the matter from the Federation of Master Cotton Spinners' Associations. The Federation declined to pronounce on the matter, arguing that it was 'not expedient' to do so and it was left to each association or individual firm to deal with the question 'as they think proper'.[164] Despite the entreaties of employers and though many spinners complained that their lives became 'almost unbearable' when 'the piecers began to flock to the colours',[165] they mounted a dogged opposition to the employment of women in their spinning rooms until the end of 1915.

---

160 Mule spinning accounted for around 80 percent of spinning in Lancashire. (Fowler 2003, p. 29). There were also ring spinners. Many of these were women who, when organised, were members of the Cardroom Amalgamation. There was little ring spinning in our three towns.
161 Executive Committee of the Spinners' Amalgamation Quarterly Report 30 April 1915. ACS/122 @ JRSC.
162 ATEA, minutes of meeting 23 January 1915. ATEA/1/1/3 @ JRSC.
163 Minutes of Joint Committee, 11 February 1915. ATEA/1/1/3 @ JRSC.
164 ATEA, minutes of meeting 22 February 1915. ATEA/1/1/3 @ JRSC.
165 Spinners' Amalgamation annual report 31 December 1915. ACS/1/23 @ JRSC.

The *Cotton Factory Times*, while being careful not to be strident on the matter and to feature contrary arguments, was an early advocate of women replacing men who had gone to the front. Several articles on this theme appeared early in 1915 (though one argued that it would be 'grotesque' for women to 'go down the pit' or 'mount the footplate'[166]). A prominent article by Alice Smith, one-time worker in an Oldham spinning mill, but now a staff writer for the paper, criticised the 'backwardness of the [male] rank and file' in the labour movement. She praised capitalism for unwittingly educating women on the need to end capitalism: 'with her nose no longer to the domestic grindstone, the woman worker will realise that her interests are bound up with her fellow workers'. Smith, clearly a Marxist, presumably thought that these long-term prospects outweighed the matter of aiding the war effort. It is unlikely that many men were persuaded by Smith. Other articles opposed women working as piecers in spinning rooms. One argument was that while women were not as strong as men, it was also not 'considered desirable [implicitly on moral grounds] that young women should be introduced into spinning rooms'. Another correspondent opposed women working as piecers on the grounds that employers 'would take the opportunity to lower wages, but irrespective of that, women's clothing was unsuitable'.[167]

The WEWNC soon took up the question of the role of women in the war. A women's sub-committee, on which Bondfield and Phillips served, was quickly set up. Given the sensitivity of 'dilution' within the mainstream labour movement, it may have been external influences which prompted the committee to take a stance on the matter. Sylvia Pankhurst, the leader of the East London Federation of Suffragettes,[168] the trade union leader Ben Tillett,[169] Lansbury and others met in March 1915 and subsequently wrote to the committee urging it to convene a conference of interested parties to discuss 'the employment of women in the present war emergency'.[170] Probably around the same time, Ellen Wilkinson, future Minister of Education in the 1945–50 Labour Government, wrote to the committee in her capacity as the Secretary of the Women's

---

166   *Cotton Factory Times*, 19 February 1915.
167   *Cotton Factory Times*, 26 February 1915.
168   On the outbreak of war, the leaders of the WSPU, the autocratic arch-patriots Emmeline and Christabel Pankhurst, had suspended the WSPU's campaign for votes for women. Sylvia Pankhurst had split with them on this issue. She eventually became a communist and was prominent in the early attempts to establish a Communist Party in Britain. The NUWSS continued its lobbying of influential politicians.
169   Tillett was extremely influential in the labour movement as a result of his work in the great London dock strike of 1889.
170   WNC/20/1/1/45 @ PHM.

Emergency Corps (founded by the Women's Social and Political Union (WSPU) to co-ordinate women's military service activities) to inform them that she was organising a conference on the 'replacement of male by female labour'.[171] Whatever its genesis, the WEWNC issued a *Women's Appeal to Women* 'who are taking men's places during this period of national crisis'. It asserted that 'Never in the history of these islands has the work of women been recognised as of such high value to the nation as it is today', and urged them to fight for 'equal conditions and equal wages'.[172] But as with the arguments of the *Cotton Factory Times*, it is unlikely that many spinners or cardroom workers were then persuaded by the arguments of the WEWNC.

Mossley seems to have been particularly prone to disputes regarding 'dilution'. In February, there was a month-long lockout at Milton Mill, where spinners were opposing the promotion of little piecers to big piecers who were 'away owing to the war'. There was more trouble at the Milton Mill in April. Little piecers struck in protest at recently recruited piecers being promoted to spinners and thus being 'given precedence over piecers who had worked for the firm for ten years'. The dispute was resolved by the promoted piecers leaving. But the striking piecers went on strike again in response to being issued with summonses by the Employers' Federation for compensation for machinery allegedly damaged during the earlier dispute. How this matter was resolved is not recorded.[173] Earlier, spinners at several mills had struck for a few days in protest at piecers doing spinners' work.[174] As late as December, when opposition to the use of female piecers had largely been overcome, the *Cotton Factory Times* reported that some Mossley spinners were insistent that they '"want no females". Many of them regard the innovation as a menace to them and their sex after the war'.[175] But a majority of the town's spinners agreed at a special meeting to accept women piecers in the mule spinning rooms 'on the same terms as in Ashton and Stalybridge'.[176]

In March, Oldham's spinners had deprecated proposals to use women in mule spinning rooms as 'such work is totally unfitted for girls and women'.[177] But by the summer, no doubt in response to the pressing needs of the war and pressure from government and employers, the Spinners' Amalgamation's

---

171   Wilkinson to WEWNC, undated, but internal evidence strongly indicates that the letter was sent early in 1915. WNC/32/3 @ PHM.
172   The appeal is undated, but probably early 1915. WNC/29/5/16 @ PHM.
173   Various letters to spinners' headquarters from Wright Mosley. ACS/6/12/83 @ JRSC.
174   *Cotton Factory Times*, 7 May 1915.
175   *Cotton Factory Times*, 3 December 1915.
176   *Mossley and Saddleworth Reporter*, 5 December 1915.
177   *Cotton Factory Times*, 26 March 1915.

opposition to women working in spinning rooms had softened considerably. In its quarterly report the executive committee informed its members that it had held a joint meeting with the Employer's Federation at which it had told the employers that it 'would not interfere in any [local] arrangement during the war in regard to ... female labour'.[178] By the autumn, 'in three or four [Oldham] mills ... female labour had been introduced into the spinning room, as has long been allowed in Bolton, Ashton and Manchester'. Union officials were aware of this and 'no formal objection has been made to this innovation'.[179]

In discussions in the autumn between the spinners and the ATEA, an ATEA representative remarked that he had seen women in mule rooms 'working in a very efficient manner'. Judson still believed working in spinning rooms was not 'a fit job for females'. But he 'recognised something has to be done to keep the mules working'.[180] He subsequently told the ATEA that his committee had agreed to the employment of women as big and little piecers, 'but only until the end of the war. Women to be engaged on same terms as men, including equal wages'.[181] Judson told the *Cotton Factory Times* that 'we believe that where [women] have been employed as piecers they have on the whole acquitted themselves very well'.[182]

Around the time Judson was in discussions with the ATEA, Clynes, probably the most influential of Lancashire labour people, went to the works of Hall and Kay at Guide Bridge, on the outskirts of Ashton, where tins for tinned food for the armed forces were made, to make a rousing speech aimed at raising morale and winning conviction for greater sacrifices. Victory, he argued, depended upon the industrial population of the country. But now, while he had often 'stood up in defence of trade union rules and regulations ... there must be a relaxation of these rules to get the maximum output which was essential to victory'. Clynes made no specific proposals, but there would have been no doubt that he particularly had in mind the right to strike and opposition to dilution. In reply, Mr John Hague, one of the oldest employees, in proposing a 'hearty vote of thanks' to Mr Clynes, said 'his splendid address would be an incentive to all the workmen to put in all their energy for the benefit of the country'.[183]

---

178 Executive Committee of the Spinners' Amalgamation Quarterly Report 31 July 1915. ACS/122 @ JRSC.
179 *Oldham Weekly Chronicle*, 30 October 1915.
180 ATEA Special Minutes [minutes of meetings with trade unions] 1898–1917, 13 October 1915. ATEA/1/2/1 @ JRSC.
181 ATEA Special Minutes 1898–1917, 27 October 1915 and 10 November 1915. ATEA/1/2/1 @ JRSC.
182 *Cotton Factory Times*, 17 December 1915.
183 *Ashton Reporter*, 5 October 1915.

Despite the entreaties of Clynes and others, the Cardroom Amalgamation continued to resist 'dilution' by women. In December, an executive committee statement deprecated 'any attempt being made to introduce females to do male labour ... In the card and blowing rooms the work was quite unsuitable for women. In the blowing room it was too heavy and among the cards the dress of women would be positively dangerous'.[184] But in the spring of 1916 the amalgamation agreed that there could be a limited use of female labour.[185] Resistance to the employment of women 'dilutees' in the cotton trade had virtually collapsed.

In Oldham, much less so in Ashton and Mossley, tram conductors' resistance to the employment of women had been as stubborn as that of the spinners and cardroom workers. It was assumed (or at least asserted) that women would not be able to cope with the physical demands of the job. But in the spring of 1915, Ashton council began to discuss the possibility of employing women as conductors. There was some opposition from the trades council, but the Tramways Committee assured it that women would not be used on 'the hilly dangerous routes without two years training'.[186] A month or so later, the Committee decided that it would employ female conductors: because of 'the scarcity of [male] applicants ... female labour [can] be employed where such labour can be satisfactorily utilised'.[187]

Local opposition to the employment of women as tram conductors must have been strengthened when, against the advice of their executive, delegates at the annual conference of tramwaymen voted 'to protest vigorously against the employment of women'.[188] The vote was held at the height of a 19-day strike by London tramway workers. In Oldham, a tramways dispute around the same time was settled by arbitration.[189] In both cases, while the nominal cause of the dispute was a refusal by the employers to pay a war bonus, objections to the employment of women were clearly a major contributory factor. Lansbury was one of the most progressive of labour movement men on the 'woman question', but a *Herald* editorial on the tram disputes argued that the solution was for men to accept the employment of women for the duration of the war and afterwards insist that they return to the home. Union members should:

---

184 *Cotton Factory Times*, 3 December 1915.
185 *Cotton Factory Times*, 5 April 1916.
186 *Ashton Reporter*, 8 April 1915.
187 Ashton Council Tramways Committee Minutes, 19 May 1915. CA/ASH/111/27 @ TLSAC.
188 *Herald*, 29 May 1915.
189 LAB/2/100/IC2566/1915 @ NAK.

make the women who have been taken on members of the union, so that the conditions under which they work are fair, prevent the undercutting of men's rates and demand that women's labour be considered temporary labour. Otherwise, the country will be flooded with women working at scandalously low rates.

'Every union', the editorial continued, 'should open their ranks to women ... but at the same time, it should lay down quite definitely that where male labour has been displaced, women must give way when peace is declared and industry becomes normal again'.[190]

In September it was reported that in Ashton 'several young women have offered their services [as tram conductors] ... through the Labour Exchange'.[191] Women were taken on in both Ashton and Oldham. By then, most male tramway workers seem to have accepted the employment of female conductors, but not those in Oldham. Councillor Frith was one of those who objected because 'women conductors were keeping men out of jobs'. In a stunt aimed at demonstrating that female labour was unnecessary, he sent men too short for active service to apply for jobs as conductors. They had been refused employment, but according to the Tramways manager, they had applied for work as drivers and had turned down conducting work.[192]

As with the employment of women in spinning rooms, unspoken anxieties regarding the possibility of illicit sexual encounters probably played a part in male opposition to the employment of women. The manager of the Corporation Tramways wrote to the Tramways Committee to try to allay such anxieties. Declaring that he was 'quite satisfied with the experiment with women conductors', he added that:

> all the girls had been told that any familiarity with either side was to be dealt with properly, and if the girl was found to be getting too familiar with the men guards and if any of the passengers in any way interfered with them in the execution of their duty they were to be reprimanded at once and he would deal with it.[193]

Shortly afterwards, members of the union wrote to the *Manchester Guardian* to complain that the manager 'had suggested that women conductors were prefer-

---

190 *Herald*, 29 May 1915.
191 *Ashton Reporter* 11 September 1915.
192 *Oldham Weekly Chronicle*, 2 October 1915.
193 *Oldham Weekly Chronicle*, 9 October 1915.

able to male conductors'. How many 'trolley heads had been off' and how many times 'had the wires been down and how much mileage had been lost' since women conductors had been employed?, they asked, implying that such things had become more common since their employment.[194] But no more was heard of these implied deficiencies of female conductors. In Ashton, it was reported, in response to complaints of overcrowding on cars between Ashton and Oldham, that 'female labour is being introduced' on that route and that the service would improve.[195] Despite this being a 'hilly dangerous' route, there were no subsequent reports of problems. As in the cases of the spinners and cardroom workers, objections to the employment of women had virtually collapsed.

If, by the autumn of 1915, working class resistance to 'dilution' had mostly been overcome, there were signs that unrest over rising prices and the threat of conscription were threatening the unqualified support for war which the vast majority of the working class had so far exhibited. One manifestation of this was the attitude of Ashton Trades Council and Oldham T&LC to the Union of Democratic Control (UDC).[196] The UDC was not a pacifist organisation. But accepting a speaker from the organisation was problematic for both trades councils. Not only did it oppose the war, it was alleged by the right-wing press to be therefore 'pro-German'. Even so, as early as May 1915 the Executive Committee of the Oldham council had resolved that it was in favour of accepting an offer of a speaker (there is no record of whether the council was actually addressed by a UDC speaker).[197] For the 'non-political' Ashton council, but not for Oldham's united trades and labour council, the UDC's domination by leftish Liberal and Labour politicians presented a further problem. In the autumn of 1915, delegates heard a proposal to invite a UDC speaker. It was reported that in an 'exciting' (probably a euphemism for rowdy) discussion the UDC had been denounced as 'pro-German'. Though the proposal was defeated by 29 to 14,[198] it is highly unlikely that 14 votes, if any, would have been cast in favour a year earlier.

---

194 *Manchester Guardian*, 22 October 1915.
195 *Ashton Reporter*, 25 December 1915.
196 The UDC had been formed shortly after the outbreak of war. Its naïve belief was that the chief cause of the war had been the preceding secret diplomacy and that democratic control of foreign policy would prevent war. It argued that in future there should be parliamentary control over foreign policy and that negotiations should settle future conflicts. It further insisted that postwar peace terms should be just and there should be no 'artificial' postwar boundaries. (See Swartz 1971).
197 Oldham T&LC Executive Committee minutes 25 May 1915. M17/1/2 @ OLSA.
198 *Ashton Reporter*, 10 September 1915.

When in late 1915 it became clear that conscription would be introduced, the WEWNC convened an emergency national conference, attended by all three cotton amalgamations, which restated the labour movement's opposition to conscription,[199] but revealed its impotence in the face of government determination. Anti-conscription resolutions were passed by enormous majorities at emergency special conferences held by both the TUC and the Labour Party. Opposition was not unanimous though. A substantial minority – 541,000 to 2,221,000 – voted in favour of conscription at Labour's conference.[200] The executive of the Cardroom Amalgamation went against the tide and supported conscription.[201] Its President, James Crinion, denounced the TUC conference as a 'fake conference'. Present had been people such as Ramsay MacDonald and organisations such as the ILP, 'outside the pale of trade unionism'.[202] Opinion on Oldham T&LC had also swung in favour of conscription. A delegate from the Cop Packers said that 'he considered it a disgrace for married men to be fighting while single men were "swanking" about the streets'. Robinson of UTFWA, to 'applause', asserted that if young men 'would not go voluntarily ... they must be compelled to go'.[203]

A Military Service Bill introducing conscription was passed in January 1916. Conscription would begin in March, giving those who would rather volunteer time to do so. Despite their opposition to conscription, both sections of the labour movement continued to offer fundamental support for the war. But conscription was a watershed in the labour movement's attitude to the war. Previously, though there had been doubts and anxieties, worries regarding rising prices and occasional strikes, the movement's support for the war had been essentially unconditional. But conscription confirmed a rising suspicion that the working class was bearing an unfair share of the burden of war. If labour was to be conscripted, why not capital, as the WEWNC demanded? Resolving such matters was to prove extremely vexatious as the war progressed.

---

199   Minutes of the Central Committee of the Weavers' Amalgamation, 3 January 1916. TU/Weavers/006 @ WCML.
200   Ward 1998, p. 139. Obviously, there was not this number of delegates present. The votes were the block votes of the trade unions affiliated to the party.
201   *Cotton Factory Times*, 7 January 1916.
202   *Oldham Weekly Chronicle*, 8 January 1916.
203   *Oldham Weekly Chronicle*, 15 January 1916. Delegates to the T&LC were very likely to be middle-aged married men and these, the government had pledged, would not be subject to conscription while any eligible single men had not been conscripted.

CHAPTER 2

Labour's Unrest and Capital's Promises

The period after the passing of the Military Service Bill saw the foundations laid for a radical transformation in British society and politics which would be completed during the term of office of the Labour government of 1945–50. Opposition to the war, save for the possible exception of the Clyde, was confined to the margins of politics. But increasing working class unrest, stimulated not least by the elixir of Bolshevism, convinced the bourgeoisie that working class support for the war could no longer be taken for granted. The most serious unrest was in the munitions industry, where in May 1917 and again in January 1918 there were strikes and mass protests against conscription by skilled engineering workers previously exempt. The coalition's establishment of a Ministry of Reconstruction in 1917 was in part a response to working class unrest, an attempt to convince the working class that it would be rewarded for its sacrifices in war.

1   Conscriptions and 'Conchies'

Reactions to the passing of the Military Service Bill by labour movement activists varied, but probably the most common reaction was a resigned acceptance. At a meeting of the executive committee of Oldham spinners, for instance, the response of those present on learning that one of their number had been conscripted was to give him their 'best wishes' and their hopes that 'he would be successful and have a safe return'.[1] Presumably at least in part in order to ensure that their members obtained a fair hearing, labour movement organisations strived to obtain representation on military tribunals. In many cases employers joined unions in trying to gain exemption for valued workers. In late 1915, for example, Ashton textile employers' association, anticipating the introduction of conscription, had written to member firms giving advice on how to gain exemption, noting that 'Mr. Judson has promised to give all assistance possible'.[2]

---

1   Oldham Spinners EC Minutes 1917, Special executive committee meeting 22 January 1917. TU/1/1/33 @ OLSA.
2   ATEA Minutes 1916–19. ATEA/1/1/4 @ JRSC.

In the first year of conscription, Judson was nominated by Ashton town council to serve on the town's military tribunal[3] (he was to regularly preside over its meetings). William Marsland, Secretary of the Spinners' Amalgamation, accepted an invitation to serve on Lancashire's Appeal Tribunal.[4] S.T. Goggins, the Secretary of Ashton's Weavers, become a member of Ashton's military tribunal.[5] Frith and Farr too sat on tribunals. In Mossley, the hard line maintained by Farr on its military tribunal does not seem, as we shall see, to have affected his influence and popularity in the town.

But in Ashton, the presence of Judson on the town's tribunal did little to dispel the trades council's initial disquiet at its decisions. Early in February the council complained that one of their members had not been allowed to serve on the tribunal due to being of 'military age'.[6] Similar disbarments around the country contributed to an inevitable tendency for tribunal members to be older than the young men whose cases they were considering. Not only did they tend to be older, they tended to be local worthies assessing the cases of mostly working class supplicants. In Ashton's near neighbour, Hyde, for instance, the tribunal included 'the Mayor, a justice of the peace, a councillor, the chairman of the board of a local cotton mill and a businessman'.[7] It is not surprising that tribunal decisions provoked accusations of class bias. Ashton Trades Council wrote to the town council claiming that because most of those conscripted were working men, there should be more working men on the town's tribunal.[8] It was presumably in response to this and other representations that Goggins became a member of the tribunal.

But the trades council continued to maintain that a preponderance of businessmen and professionals on Ashton's tribunal led it to consistently make unfair decisions. At its August 1916 meeting, it 'deprecated' the 'unpatriotic' action of many of those who successfully appealed on grounds 'which ought not to stand'; it particularly objected to the number of publicans and shopkeepers who were allowed to masquerade on work of 'national importance'.[9] A few months later, at a meeting of Mossley Trades Council, Farr attacked middle class 'shirkers' for evading military service and condemned 'slackers', claiming that the sooner 'tribunals were done away with and compulsion brought in

---

3 Minutes of Ashton Council, February 1916. CA/ASH/100/25 @ TLSAC.
4 Spinners' Amalgamation Correspondence, September 1916. ACS/6/11/12 @ JRSC.
5 *Ashton Herald*, 9 September 1916.
6 *Ashton Reporter*, 5 February 1916.
7 Gregory 2008, p. 103.
8 *Ashton Reporter*, 11 March 1916.
9 *Ashton Reporter*, 5 August 1916.

properly the better it would be for everybody'. Tribunals, he claimed, benefited mainly 'the wealthy and those with influence'.[10]

In his survey of the work of various tribunals, Gregory argues that in the main tribunal members tried to be fair; the main problem was inconsistency and 'whimsicality'.[11] It is certainly hard to discern any consistent principle underlying the decisions of the Ashton tribunal, but it is also hard to see any consistent pattern of class bias. At a typical session in February 1916, exemption was not granted in most cases. Class bias was not perceptible in the tribunal's decisions when hearing several appeals by men who were only sons, the only support of widows. Exemption was not granted in the case of an appeal by the management of the Texas Mill Company, who argued that the work of a piecer was indispensable, nor in the case of a greengrocer who claimed that one son having enlisted, the labour of the other son was essential to his business. An appeal by the management of Charles Waterhouse, manufacturing chemists, on behalf of William Robinson MacDonald, their only qualified chemist, was successful. His work was seen as necessary war work.[12] It seems likely that the complaints of Ashton's trades council were a manifestation of an awareness of a much more fundamental problem – that the great majority of those who were sent to fight were working class and that those who benefited most were the employers – than of unfairness.

Another sign of increasing unrest in the labour movement, as in the case of the UDC, discussed in the previous chapter, was the attitude of trades councils towards conscientious objectors. Initially, there had been little sympathy. In the spring of 1915 Oldham's T&LC and Ashton Trades Council had both flatly refused to hear a speaker from the No-Conscription Fellowship, founded soon after the war to rouse opposition to conscription, expected to be inevitable, denouncing conscientious objectors as 'shirkers'.[13] But in 1916, probably due to the perceived unfairness of military tribunals, attitudes began to change. In the spring, despite the council's support for conscription, criticism at Oldham T&LC of Frith's sympathetic attitude to 'conchies' won virtually no support.[14] In the summer, Ashton Trades Council protested at the treatment of conscientious objectors and demanded the release 'of those who were being persecuted in the hands of the military'.[15] In the autumn though, a proposal that the Fel-

---

10 *Ashton Herald*, 7 April 1917.
11 Gregory 2008, p. 108.
12 *Ashton Reporter*, 19 February 1916.
13 *Oldham Weekly Chronicle*, 28 May 1915; *Ashton Reporter*, 21 April 1915.
14 Minutes of Oldham Trades and Labour Council 1916–18, 4 April 1916. M17/1/3 @ OLSA.
15 *Ashton Reporter*, 10 June 1916. By no means were all trade unionists sympathetic to 'con-

lowship should be allowed the use of the trades council's hall proved too much for most delegates to swallow.[16]

2   Social Patriots and (a Few) Internationalists

Perceptions of inequality of sacrifice did not, in most cases, undermine support for the war. Mainstream labour movement opinion became more and more pro-war as the war progressed. The *Herald's* denunciation of the Labour leaders – as 'the most pro-war of all the belligerent … nations. Mr Henderson and his colleagues are all for a fight to the finish, and at present their finish means carving up the Balkans, dividing Persia and sharing out the Turkish empire amongst the capitalist vandals' – was quite untypical of Labour opinion.[17] Much more typical was Marsland's reply to a letter from the International Arbitration League soliciting opinions on whether peace terms should be offered to Germany. Marsland insisted that the war was 'German-made' and that 'Until the objectives we set out to accomplish have been successfully attained the fight should go on. I believe the country generally would very strongly deprecate any premature sheathing of the sword'.[18]

In Lancashire, working class and labour movement unrest, manifest particularly in a national engineers' strike in 1917 and a cotton workers general strike in 1918, was caused by specific grievances arising out of the conduct of the war, not by opposition to the war. While the usual caution should be applied when considering the lack of evidence of opposition to the war, it is nevertheless striking how little such evidence there is. Certainly, there was increasing working class resentment at rising prices, food shortages, 'profiteers' and so on, but fundamental opposition to the war in our three towns, save for that of a small number of pacifists, was probably confined to the BSP and to the ILP.

Oldham branch of the BSP left no, and Ashton branch little, trace in the historical record. We saw that Ashton branch was involved in attempts to set up a local WEWNC. Whether Ashton branch was then part of the chauvinist majority or the internationalist minority of the BSP, it is impossible to say. But during a row on Ashton Trades Council in 1918, they were accused (as we shall see in the

---

chies'. According to a handwritten note filed with the minutes of the trades council, the credentials of H. Ashmore were rescinded by his union, the Cabinet Makers, for proposing the motion. DD310/4/15 @ TLSAC.

16   *Ashton Reporter*, 9 September 1916.
17   *Herald*, 24 March 1917.
18   Spinners' Amalgamation Correspondence 1916, Reply of 17 July 1916. ACS/6/11/12 @ JRSC.

next chapter) of having done 'their best to meet the enemies of this country'.[19] This was probably a reference to the Zimmerwald Conference of September 1915, convened by the Second International in the hope of building international left unity against the war. The BSP's decision to send delegates to the conference was a victory for the internationalist wing of the Party.[20] It therefore seems likely that whatever its initial stance, Ashton BSP was by September 1915 part of the Party's internationalist wing.[21] As we shall see in the next chapter, Harry Cocker, the branch secretary, was active in the early Communist Party (CP). It was the internationalists of the BSP who were to provide most of the founding members of the CP.

There is no evidence that Mossley ILP carried out anti-war activities. Indeed, in 1918 it was to claim that it had 'never agreed' with the ILP's opposition to the war.[22] Oldham ILP, on the other hand, did conform to the national anti-war line. As with Ashton BSP, the doings of Oldham ILP have left little trace. We saw that it mounted an anti-war demonstration at the start of the war. Perhaps the ILP had been the organisation responsible for anti-war speeches at the park gates. But probably not. In keeping with the party's reformist rather than revolutionary socialism, Oldham ILP had written to the town council at the start of the war urging it to establish schemes to find work for unemployed men (it was widely assumed that the war would lead to increased unemployment).[23] Later, the branch adopted a more robust anti-war stance. In early 1916 the branch resigned from the trades and labour council, probably in protest against its support for conscription.[24]

In the summer of 1917, a time, as we shall see, of political crisis, ILP speakers including their secretary Wilfrid Hill were 'mobbed' at an open-air peace meeting. Hill and other men 'dishevelled, sore and bleeding, found the police office at the Town Hall a haven of refuge, into which, rescued from a crowd of thousands, they were ushered by the police'.[25] According to the *Manchester Guard-*

---

19 *Cotton Factory Times*, 15 March 1918.
20 German socialists attended, but BSP and ILP members hoping to attend were denied passports. (Kendall 1969, pp. 62–6).
21 At its April 1916 conference the internationalists gained a majority. Early in 1917 the BSP's national treasurer, H.W. Alexander, visited all the Lancashire branches for an unspecified reason. CPA, Minutes of Openshaw Branch of BSP, 24 February 1917. CPA, CP/ORG/MISC/3/5 @ PHM.
22 *Mossley and Saddleworth Reporter*, 5 October 1918.
23 *Oldham Weekly Chronicle*, 19 September 1914.
24 Executive Committee of Oldham Trades and Labour Council, 16 February 1916, M17/1/2 @ OLSA.
25 *Oldham Weekly Chronicle*, 11 August 1917.

ian, the ringleaders of the disturbances were New Zealand soldiers who then proceeded to attack the headquarters of the ILP: 'they entered the premises and at once began to throw card tables, books and other small objects through the windows to the crowd outside'.[26]

Despite union membership of international workers' organisations (the first International Congress of Textile Workers, for instance, had been held in Manchester in 1894 and the last pre-war Congress in Blackpool), what was singularly lacking in the working class, even in the labour movement, was a deep conviction (not a mere formal recognition) of the working class as an international class with a common interest in overthrowing capital. The most obvious manifestation of this one-eyed class consciousness was of course support for the war effort of their 'own' bourgeoisie and a consequent failure to recognise that German workers were allies, not enemies. In March 1917, for instance, Ashton Trades Council protested against German prisoners of war being taught to make brushes for sale. The matter was raised by R. Hunt, the Secretary of the Brushmakers Society, who complained that 'After the war the men who were now learning the trade would become their competitors'.[27] But of course these were men of an enemy country. The Russian revolutions of 1917 did, as we shall see, stir up a sense of a common working class interest among a minority of workers.

But what was even more lacking than a sense of an international working class was any sense of a common anti-imperialist interest with the colonial peoples. The national struggle in Ireland, for instance, presented a virtually infallible ideological litmus test for distinguishing labour movement chauvinists from internationalists. Of course, there were those who were prepared to go against the prevailing chauvinist tide. The Workers' Socialist Federation (WSF) led by Sylvia Pankhurst was the only organisation of the British left to firmly support the Easter Rising of 1916. The *Herald* declined to support the rising, but did demand that the government should 'declare an amnesty for all those imprisoned' after the rebellion and 'allow all the Irish leaders to return to Ireland, withdraw the British garrisons and leave Ireland to be organised by the Irish for the benefit of their own country'.[28] But these were exceptional views. The ILP expressed the outlook of the mainstream of the labour movement in announcing that 'in no degree do we approve of the *Sinn Fein* rebellion'.[29] Even the BSP, while sympathising with 'the effort of the Irish people to throw off

---

26 *Manchester Guardian*, 8 August 1917.
27 *Ashton Herald*, 10 March 1917.
28 *Herald*, 24 March 1917.
29 *Socialist Review*, September 1916.

the alien yoke', disdainfully noted that 'in every demand made by the Sinn Fein movement there is the spirit of nationalism'.[30]

The national struggle in India presented another test. The Labour movement was generally, if only nominally, in favour of independence for India. The ILP's annual conference of 1911, for instance, had unanimously resolved that the 'immediate policy of the British government in India should be guided by ideas of self-government'.[31] But no protest was made when in 1914 the puppet Indian Government declared war on behalf of the Indian people. While the ILP and BSP offered occasional criticisms of the government's wartime colonial excursions, little came from the Labour mainstream and none from our local labour activists. Indicative of local labour movement indifference to colonialism was the response of the Executive Committee of Oldham T&LC to a letter from Bradford Trades Council urging support for home rule for India. The Committee resolved that it should 'lie on the table' (a euphemism for not responding to it).[32]

Here, racism probably played a part. We should be wary of the condescension of posterity. But even so, there was something shockingly egregious in the response of the BSP and the ILP to the plans of the British and French governments to use black colonials on the western front and in domestic industry. According to the BSP's *The Call*, they were 'poor simple blacks – the children of the planet'.[33] The ILP declared that the use of colonial labour in home industries would 'endanger the workers' standard of life and civilisation generally'.[34] The BSP declared that the plans presented a serious moral danger: with the men away at the front, 'the sex appetites of the women are being starved ... to dump thousands of negroes into the country under such conditions ... is asking for trouble'. Soldiers would naturally resent their women 'being delivered into the arms of the vigorous Othellos of Africa while they are in the trenches'. Similarly, the Party supported the 'white Australia' policy: the workers insisted upon this 'because they know a little of the blighting effects of "coloured" labour. The menace of the cheap Negro is here'.[35]

The 'threat' of 'cheap' foreign labour was a fairly consistent anxiety in trade union circles. In 1917, for instance, the cotton unions responded positively

---

30 *The Call*, 9 July 1916. The call was published after the BSP's anti-war wing won control.
31 Independent Labour Party, *Annual Conference Report 1911*, pp. 103–4.
32 Oldham T&LC Executive Committee Minutes 1913–16, Meeting of 28 November 1916. M17/1/3 @ OLSA.
33 *The Call*, 10 August 1916.
34 *Labour Leader*, 14 December 1916.
35 *The Call*, 25 January 1917.

to an invitation from the Anti-Sweating League[36] to attend a conference in Manchester. The League had greatly helped to promote public opinion against sweated labour and thus the passing of the Trade Boards Acts of 1909 and 1918, which set minimum wages for various trades.[37] But in this case (and doubtless other cases besides) the League acted as a pressure group for the British cotton industry. This was clearly the motivation – inspired by the 'desire of Commercial Attaches at the British Legation in Peking [Beijing] to meet representatives of the Cotton Trade to consider the position of the cotton industry in China and other Eastern countries' – of those calling the Manchester conference. According to a delegate from the weavers' union, a representative of the League had pointed out that the cotton being produced in China could be used to produce cotton goods suitable for the 'working class population of China'. The threat to Lancashire cotton was clear; but there were also opportunities in China. Britain had 'not penetrated as far into the country as we ought to and could do'. Other trades, notably the tobacco trade, had done so successfully. He proposed that a commission of employers and workers be formed 'with the objective of proceeding to China to make enquiries on the spot'. Trade union representatives, ignorant of or indifferent to the history of Anglo-Chinese 'trade',[38] had 'heartily' supported the appointment of a commission.[39]

Later that year, anxieties regarding Lancashire's cotton exports to India prompted further union collaboration with the millocracy. In an attempt to placate Indian nationalists and gain their support for the British war effort, the British government proposed to allow the Indian Government to impose duties on the import of Lancashire cotton goods.[40] The *Cotton Factory Times* criticised 'scandalous conditions in Indian cotton mills', in which children 'as young as nine years' were employed.[41] The Cardroom workers' union argued

---

36 The National Anti-Sweating League was formed in 1906. R.H. Tawney and Lady Astor were among two of its patrons.
37 Blackburn 1991; Hatton 1997.
38 China, of course, was not a formal British colony. But in the Anglo-Chinese wars (the so-called 'Opium Wars') of the mid-nineteenth century, Britain had forcibly opened up China to British exports. Hong Kong had effectively been annexed during these enterprises. By the turn of the century Britain and other imperialist powers had 'concessions' in Shanghai and elsewhere.
39 Letter of invitation from the Secretary of the National Anti-Sweating League to Weavers' Amalgamation, 20 February 1917; Report back from conference 6 March 1917. TU/Weavers/065 @ WCML.
40 Cain and Hopkins argue that the British government's policy was essentially economic: it 'sought to maximise [Indian] export earnings and to increase revenue by taxing imports and by promoting local industries'. Cain and Hopkins 1993, p. 173.
41 *Cotton Factory Times*, 16 March 1917.

that the government's proposals would benefit only 'a few wealthy Parsees and Anglo-Indian cotton spinners ... at the expense of injuring Lancashire's cotton trade ... and the poor Hindu serf'.[42]

However sincere this concern for working conditions in India, the cotton unions showed no sympathy for the national movement in India. The plight of workers in India's cotton mills prompted not attempts at forging international labour unity, but an ultimately futile united campaign of workers and employers against the government's proposals. William Mullins, the Secretary of the Cardroom Amalgamation declared that while it was 'very laudable' that the Indian government was prepared to make a war loan (the initial purpose of the duties was to raise money to fund the war loan) 'it seems that they want the cotton industry to pay the money for them'.[43] The *Manchester Guardian* argued that the proposed duties were 'something which touches all concerned, master and workman alike', they threatened 'the livelihood of a population as great as that which lives in the twenty-nine metropolitan boroughs'.[44] A joint deputation of cotton unions and employers' associations lobbied in vain Austen Chamberlain, the Secretary of State for India.[45]

Despite the palpable patriotism of most working class people, national and local government took care during the war to nurture patriotic sentiments and foster a sense of common class interest. Until 1917, the government took little interest in propaganda: it had little need to, given the barrage of anti-German propaganda from the national and local press. But by 1917 the strains and unrest generated by the war convinced it that public opinion must be shaped and managed. From 1917 onwards the government was keen to emphasise that the war was not only a matter of national defence, it was also being fought for a better future. Such were the themes of the propaganda generated and encouraged by the National War Aims Committee (NWAC), established in July 1917. Out of 528 constituencies 344 local committees were eventually established around the country.[46] Oldham T&LC was one body asked by the national committee to establish a local committee, but declined, claiming that there was 'no necessity for the formation in Oldham of a local War Aims Committee'.[47] There is no evidence that War Aims Committees existed in Ashton or Mossley.

---

42   *Cotton Factory Times*, 13 April 1917.
43   *Oldham Weekly Chronicle*, 3 March 1917.
44   *Manchester Guardian*, 7 May 1917.
45   Spinners' Amalgamation EC Minutes 1915–24. Undated minute. ACS/2/1/1/1 @ JRSC.
46   Monger 2012, p. 81.
47   Oldham T&LC Minutes 1916–18. Report of Council Meeting, 30 July 1917. M17/1/3 @ OLSA. A NWA Committee was established in Oldham in November 1917. (Monger 2012, p. 256).

While local ruling circles might not have been as effective as the NWAC desired, they were certainly zealous. Coverage by the local press of reconstruction themes commenced, as we shall see, even before 1917, as did local attempts to maintain and bolster patriotic sentiments and class harmony. In Mossley, for instance, the Vicar, C.H. Baggott, preached a sermon in which he argued that the war had been a 'great blessing'. It had rescued the nation from the threat of civil war which had seemed likely in 1914, but now the nation was united.[48] Possibly to stymy nascent anti-imperial sentiment, Empire Day[49] was promoted with greater zeal than in pre-war days. In Ashton, for instance, the Education Committee resolved in 1916 that school managers should 'be requested to make preparations for the proper observance … of Empire Day'.[50] The *Reporter* was concerned that the day was not much observed. The 'display of bunting was not great and most people wondered what it was all about', but was gratified that in the local schools things were different; 'National songs were sung, and teachers pointed out the meaning of the word Empire and all that it stands for … In some schools pupils were shown how to make paper Union Jacks'.[51] In Oldham, in 1917, the Mayor visited several schools on Empire Day. He urged pupils that they should feel that 'the Empire did in a very real sense belong to them'. He was happy to see a US flag in one school, because 'they were in the main our own stock and race'.[52] In 1918, the town's Education Committee resolved that Empire Day would be 'celebrated as usual' and, in response to a request from the Navy League, also resolved that schools would observe Trafalgar Day too.[53]

 Whatever activities this committee may have carried out have left no trace in the local press or archives.
48 *Mossley and Saddleworth Reporter*, 12 August 1916.
49 Empire day was established in 1904 to 'nurture a sense of collective identity and imperial responsibility among young empire citizens'. It was commonly observed in schools, where, as its founder, Lord Meath, intended, morning lessons which were 'directed towards exercises calculated to remind [the children] of their mighty heritage' were followed by a half-day holiday. English 2006, pp. 248–9.
50 Ashton Council Minutes 1915–16, Minutes of the Education Committee, 5 May 1916. CA/ASH 111/28 @ TLSAC.
51 *Ashton Reporter*, 27 May 1916.
52 *Oldham Weekly Chronicle*, 6 May 1917.
53 Minutes of Oldham Education Committee, Elementary Sub-Committee, 13 May 1918 and 12 October 1918. CBO/12/2/1/5 @ OLSA. The Navy League had been founded in 1895, when British naval supremacy seemed to some to be threatened by imperial rivals, chiefly Germany. It argued for strengthening the navy to ensure the security of the Empire. Trafalgar Day, a celebration of the defeat of the French and Spanish fleets in the battle of Trafalgar in 1805, doubtless seemed an ideal time to promote the aims of the League.

What effect such endeavours had, it is impossible to say. Working class unrest mounted steadily from 1916, but the vicissitudes of war did not significantly undermine the fundamental patriotism of the great majority of British workers. This was to be demonstrated, as Bernard Waites observed, in the spring of 1918, when German advances on the Western front led to a revival of working class patriotism 'highly reminiscent of the early months of the war', marked by a precipitous fall in strikes.[54] What the trials of war did do was to foster class antagonism and an increasing sense, particularly among labour movement activists, that the working class had distinctive class interests which would be best served by the Labour Party. A minority of activists, especially after the Russian Revolutions of 1917, developed revolutionary inclinations.

3   Labour Unrest and (Eventual) Government Response

Working class unrest was fuelled primarily by inflation, food shortages and the deplorable treatment of discharged or dead members of the armed forces and their dependents. Righteous indignation at this last matter shines out of bulging files of the WEWNC at the People's History Museum. In contrast to the miserly pension of 7/6d. (37.5p) provided by the government, the Committee insisted that one pound was necessary.[55] Committees, clearly the antecedents of the National Federation of Discharged and Demobilised Sailors and Soldiers (NFDDSS),[56] began to spring up around the country as more and more men were killed or discharged. In Bradford, for instance, a Soldiers, Sailors and Dependents Protection Association was founded and in South Wales a Campaign to Demand Adequate Public Maintenance for Disabled Soldiers and Sailors.[57] Oldham T&LC wrote to the WEWNC stating that it was taking up the matter with the town council.[58] It was also in correspondence with Labour's NEC on the matter.[59] In 1917 the T&LC reported that it had 'assisted in forming a discharged soldiers and sailors association'.[60]

---

54   Whereas in both December 1917 and in January 1918 about 250,000 working days were lost in strikes, in April 1918 only 15,000 day were. Waites 1987, p. 232.
55   WNC/24/1/119–290 @ PHM.
56   See Burnham 2014 for an account of the origins and later history of the NFDDSS. See also Wooton 1956.
57   WNC/24/1/119–287 @ PHM.
58   Oldham T&LC to WEWNC, 15 March 1916. WNC/24/1/131 @ PHM.
59   Oldham T&LC to NEC, 14 May 1915 and 21 May 1915. WEWNC, WNC 15/1 @ PHM.
60   *Oldham Weekly Chronicle*, 21 July 1917.

In Ashton, a *Reporter* editorial in the autumn of 1916 argued that armed forces' pensions were grossly inadequate: the 'attitude of the responsible authorities cannot be described as other than mean and parsimonious'. The public were said to be 'strongly agitating for more generous treatment'. There were a number of people in Ashton who were 'compelled to lead an existence of anxiety'.[61] Early in 1917 the trades council took up the matter. They had received a letter from the Lancashire Federation of Trade Councils referring to the 'great dissatisfaction which prevailed in connection with the inadequate payments to wholly and partially disabled soldiers, and to the widows and mothers of men lost in the war'. The Federation had suggested that local associations of 'discharged sick and wounded soldiers' be established. Though an Ashton committee clearly had been founded by 1918, in 1917 the Council resolved to leave the matter 'in abeyance'.[62]

Perhaps council delegates recognised that they had no power to directly affect pensions: wages were a different matter. Inflation, particularly of food prices, continued to stimulate industrial unrest. By 1917 the government's Committee of Enquiry into Industrial Unrest reported that food prices had risen by 102 percent.[63] Stephen Jones contends that a year later average real wages of cotton workers were only 75 percent of pre-war levels.[64] But many contemporaries argued that many, if not most, working class people were enjoying an improved standard of living. In appalled middle class circles, apocryphal stories that munitions workers were buying such luxuries as pianos spread.[65]

Most labour movement people though, certainly those working in cotton and engineering, thought that their wages were being rapidly eroded by inflation. But in contrast to later in the war, in 1916 and early 1917 most wage disputes in Lancashire – for instance, of engineers in Oldham in 1916 and of drivers and carters in Mossley in 1917[66] – were quickly settled by arbitration. Even threatened strikes were usually eventually called off. A ballot of spinners in the spring of 1916 on whether or not to strike for a 10 percent increase in wages won, in a harbinger of much more serious unrest to come, 96.67 percent in favour.[67] After the failure of initial negotiations led to the issuing of strike notices, government intervention and protracted negotiations involving Askwith led to the

---

61   *Ashton Reporter*, 16 September 1916.
62   *Ashton Reporter*, 13 January 1917.
63   Gregory 2008, p. 197.
64   Jones, 1987, p. 37.
65   See Gregory 2008, ch. 6 for a survey of the literature and the evidence.
66   Ministry of Labour LAB2/4/IC/640J/1916 and LAB2/143/IC3313/1917 @ NAK.
67   *Cotton Factory Times*, 12 May 1916.

union reluctantly accepting a five percent increase.[68] In Mossley, dissatisfaction with the increase led to spinners at the Britannia Mill giving a week's strike notice. The notices were withdrawn after an intervention by the union head office at the behest of the employers.[69] Cardroom workers too deemed insufficient a wage increase awarded after arbitration by Askwith. According to Oldham and Rochdale employers, a threatened strike was called off only when the government threatened to bring cotton workers within the purview of the Munitions of War Act.[70]

Rising prices also boosted sentiment that working class people were bearing an unfair share of the burden of war, in contrast to the 'profiteers' held to be making vast profits at the public expense. In the summer of 1916, the TUC held a special congress which in effect adopted the 'conscription of riches' agenda which the WEWNC had been promoting ever since the government had first mooted conscription.[71] Such sentiments gradually spread throughout the labour movement. In the autumn, for instance, Judson complained that wage increases were being greatly outstripped by price increases and that in consequence 'the very class of men which has provided 95% of the brave men fighting or in training is being ground under the heel of men who are growing enormously wealthy at our expense'.[72] Shortly afterwards, food prices were the principal matter on the agenda of Ashton Trades Council. Booth Wimpenny (who in 1919 was to become a communist town councillor) of the Brasiers and Sheetmetal Workers claimed that prices had increased by 65 percent while wages had increased by only 11 percent. No doubt reflecting on the slaughter on the Western Front (1916 was the year of the Somme), Wimpenny noted that those most affected were 'the dependents of those who had offered themselves to their country'. The Council passed a resolution urging the government to mobilise and 'ultimately conscript' wealth.[73]

In the autumn, delegates to Oldham's T&LC debated a resolution on the 'cost of living' which insisted that the government had 'failed to give proper attention to the serious grievances the mass of people are suffering by reason of the enormous and unjustifiable increase in the cost of coal, food and all other

---

68   *Manchester Evening News*, 16 June 1916.
69   July 1916 Correspondence between Master Spinners and Operative Spinners head offices. ACS/6/3/5 @ JRSC.
70   Oldham and Rochdale Textile Employers Association (OTREA) Annual Reports 1916–20. 1916 report, pp. 7–8. AAN/1/1/2/3 @ OLSA.
71   Harrison 1971, pp. 246–7.
72   *Ashton Reporter*, 16 September 1916.
73   *Ashton Reporter*, 7 October 1916.

necessaries of life' and called for price controls 'in order that further exploitation, may be brought to an end, and the exorbitant profits now being made out of the needs of the nation thereby prevented'. An angry Grinders and Glaziers delegate declared that it was a 'waste of time to further appeal to the government' and moved an amendment that the miners' demand for 'urgent and drastic action to compel the government to take the matter up'[74] should be supported, but agreed to withdraw the amendment in order to give the Labour Party time to pressurise the government.[75]

Government control was an obvious response to working class resentment over rising prices, but, certainly until the formation of the Lloyd George coalition in December 1916, *laissez-faire* ideology still tended to trump interventionism. Runciman, as President of the Board of Trade, was the Cabinet minister primarily responsible for prices, but he generally resisted demands for price controls. A September 1916 report from a Board-appointed Committee on Prices found no case for price controls. In response to a circular from Runciman, the *Oldham Chronicle* conceded that 'controlling prices is difficult, far more difficult than some imagine', but noted that 'Mr. Runciman tells us nothing about profiteering, about which we have heard so much from the Labour organisations'. Surely, the *Chronicle* argued, the government 'might fairly step in for the regulation of prices [which] might be done without disturbance of the world's markets'.[76]

By the autumn of 1916, labour movement unrest was beginning to cause concern in some bourgeois circles. Promises of postwar reform were beginning to be made. Neville Chamberlain, the future Prime Minister, but then the Conservative Lord Mayor of Birmingham, argued, in his address of welcome to the delegates assembled at the TUC's annual conference, that after the war the worker 'must get a larger share of the wealth he helps to create'.[77] In referring approvingly to his speech, the *Ashton Reporter* editorially insisted that the 'overwhelming majority of the vast armies at the front are men who worked for a weekly wage, and have to come back and get a living in the ordinary way

---

74   It is unclear precisely what this delegate had in mind, but the miners, particularly in South Wales, proved troublesome to the government throughout the war. In July 1915 the government had brought a five-day strike to an end by threatening the miners with imprisonment under the Munitions of War Act but also by conceding a pay increase. Continuing trouble led to the government taking control of the South Wales coalfield in December 1916. Francis and Smith 1998, pp. 22–7.
75   Oldham T&LC Minutes 1916–18, Quarterly meeting, 3 November 1916. M17/1/3 @ OLSA.
76   *Oldham Weekly Chronicle*, 30 September 1916.
77   *Manchester Guardian*, 5 September 1916.

when the war is over. The future interests of these men have to be considered'.[78] But it was not until the summer of 1917, after strikes in the munitions industries which threatened the prosecution of the war, that such expressions of concern were translated into firm promises of reform.

By the end of 1916, German submarine warfare was threatening food supplies. Doubtless reflecting anxieties in Ashton's millocracy, a *Reporter* editorial on 'The People's Food' asserted that 'All over the country meetings are being held to protest' against rising food prices. 'Indeed in many localities workmen are threatening more drastic action. Scottish miners are calling for a national Labour conference, while the South Wales miners threaten a national strike'. 'It is difficult', the editorial continued, 'to eradicate the suspicion in the minds of the people that there is a good deal of manipulation and exploitation in connection with our food supply. The Government must put an end to this ... if they are to avert a national calamity'.[79] What the calamity might be was not stated, but the *Reporter* was clearly concerned that working class unrest was threatening national unity and thus the prosecution of the war. The paper was unimpressed when the government appointed a food controller (it was 'not likely to reduce prices'), though it conceded that the imposition of controls on the price of milk was a 'step forward'.[80]

Shortly afterwards, a special national labour movement conference on food prices welcomed the appointment of a food controller, but insisted that more radical action was needed. The government should purchase 'all imported essential foodstuffs', commandeer 'home products such as meat, wheat, oats, barley, potatoes and milk', commandeer ships and control 'freights and freight rates' and 'place on the retail market all supplies so obtained and controlled at prices which will secure the full benefit of Government action to the consumer'.[81]

It was extremely unlikely that any conceivable British Government would take such étatist steps to interfere with private enterprise, but general ruling class dissatisfaction with the conduct of the war, including the handling of working class unrest, led to the collapse of the Asquith administration and the formation of the Lloyd George coalition on the 7th of December, the day of the labour conference. The new regime did not, as A.J.P. Taylor once argued, introduce 'war socialism',[82] nor did it signify the final defeat of *laissez-faire* ideology,

---

78   *Ashton Reporter*, 9 September 1916.
79   *Ashton Reporter*, 4 November 1916.
80   *Ashton Reporter*, 18 November 1916; *Ashton Reporter*, 25 November 1916.
81   *Manchester Guardian*, December 8 1916.
82   Taylor 1965, p. 46.

which, Dracula-like, was merely slumbering. It did, however, mark a decisive shift towards interventionism, at least for the duration of the war. A flurry of interventionism followed the formation of the new government. Of symbolic significance was the Public Meals Order of December 1916 which (slightly) curtailed the amount of food which could be consumed in restaurants and thus forced the better off to (slightly) share the privations of the working class. Of much more than symbolic importance was the formation of the new Ministries of Food and Labour. It was intended that the Ministry of Food would keep food prices under control and ensure adequate food supplies. The Ministry of Labour would, it was hoped, integrate labour more fully into the war effort and mitigate industrial unrest. Labour's more prominent role in the new government was doubtless intended partly to more firmly anchor the labour movement in the war effort. Henderson became a member of the newly formed War Cabinet. Two trade unionists – George Barnes of the Engineers and John Hodges of the Steel Smelters – became members of the full Cabinet in the highly sensitive posts of, respectively, Minister of Pensions and Minister of Labour.

But unrest over food prices, profiteering and food supplies continued to mount. Early in the New Year, Oldham T&LC convened a conference of 'organised workers, co-op societies and women's co-op societies' to discuss the rising cost of living. Councillor Frith asserted that 'if the people did not know that huge profits were being made they might be satisfied in the crisis, but it was because they did know that it was the work of exploiters that they were kicking the government'. The appointment of a food controller would do little: the conference resolved that the government should 'either fix prices or [in response to submarine warfare] take full control of the shipping trade'.[83] The council claimed that many local shopkeepers were petty profiteers exploiting food shortages. Grocers wouldn't sell sugar unless tea costing 'ten times as much' was also bought.[84] Mossley's spinners condemned rising prices in biblical terms: 'capitalists have waxed fat, profiteers have wrung out a golden harvest'[85] while Lancashire's weavers believed that 'profitmongers' had exploited food shortages while 'some six million men have been giving their blood on the battlefields'.[86]

---

83   *Oldham Weekly Chronicle*, 10 February 1917.
84   *Oldham Evening Chronicle*, Letter from Oldham T&LC, 10 April 1917.
85   *Mossley and Saddleworth Reporter*, 2 February 1917.
86   Weavers' Amalgamation, *Annual Report 1917*, DDX 1123/1/12 @ Lancashire Record Office, Preston (LROP).

In April the WEWNC urged the government to allow local authorities to assume control of food supplies and to set up municipal restaurants and suggested that labour movement organisations should establish Food Vigilance Committees to expose and root out profiteering. Committees were established in Hull, London, Scarborough, Edmonton and no doubt other places.[87] But if one were established in any of our three towns, no trace has been left. Oldham T&LC continued to campaign on food prices and against profiteering by other means. It held a second conference in May. A public meeting at which Clynes argued for criminalisation of food speculators was held on the same day. A resolution, clearly based on the recent labour movement special conference demanded, *inter alia*, government 'purchase of all essential imported foodstuffs, commandeering and control of all homegrown foodstuffs ... price controls'.[88]

Oldham T&LC started a new campaign on rack-renting in 1917. It was reported that it was taking steps to help tenants faced with illegally raised rents. It had taken legal advice and written to landlords. It had held a public meeting presided over by Councillor Frith.[89] A year or so later, at its annual meeting, the Council again discussed rents. A 'large number of landlords ... had illegally raised rents ... Some of them were very abusive when their attention was called to the illegality'. The Council had helped many tenants and 'over £300' had been 'got back'.[90] Always less militant than its Oldham counterpart, Ashton Trades Council did not form a TDL until 1917.[91] There is no evidence to suggest that Mossley Trades Council set up a TDL.

Probably, the new government's more energetic prosecution of the war ensured or at least hastened victory and thus also ensured the continued fundamental loyalty of the great majority of the working class. But the new Ministries of Food and Labour were not notably successful in their allotted tasks. Inflation and food shortages stoked up greater working class unrest and no doubt fostered the support given to the two Russian Revolutions of 1917 by some labour movement activists. The wider influence of revolutionary ideas was manifest in an upsurge of unofficial strikes and in the emergence of an influential shop stewards movement in the cotton industry. Lancashire was the fulcrum of a shop steward-led national engineering strike in the spring of 1917. In the cotton trade, shortages of cotton caused by intensified submarine

---

87 WEWNC circular 21 April 1917. WNC/12/73/1–21 @PHM.
88 *Oldham Weekly Chronicle*, 19 May 1917.
89 *Oldham Weekly Chronicle*, 17 May 1917.
90 *Oldham Evening Chronicle*, 19 January 1918.
91 *Ashton Reporter*, 5 May 1917.

warfare (in January the German government had ended all restrictions on submarine warfare) and the attempts of the Cotton Control Board (CCB) to deal with these shortages, which led to short-time working, caused serious unrest.

4 Strikes, Shop Stewards and Revolutionaries

The Russian revolutions were not the cause of the strike wave of 1917. We have seen that working class discontent had been mounting since the start of the war in one way or another. Industrial unrest had been fermenting from the very beginning of 1917 (in 1917 there were 5,650,000 days of strikes, compared with 2,450,000 in 1916).[92] In but one case, union officials were able to end a 12-day unofficial strike of Spinners at the Shiloh Mill in Oldham only after an intervention by Askwith.[93] But the revolutions undoubtedly affected the particular form – a rapid growth of shop steward influence and initiative – assumed by industrial conflict in the last years of the war and in the early postwar period.

The *Herald* was elated by the February Revolution in Russia. Below a front page banner headline, 'Russia', were joyful celebrations of revolt by Lansbury and the veteran socialist Henry Brailsford. Both argued that social reform was urgently needed in Britain.[94] While only a few enthusiasts claimed that revolution was necessary in Britain, 1917 stimulated class consciousness and fostered a general and, for a while, an industrial revolt that in its emphasis on rank-and-file control and decentralised leadership showed the influence of the CWC and the Soviets established by Russian revolutionaries.[95]

The cause of the most critical unrest, that impacting on war industries, was the demands for more and more men by the Molochs of the Imperial General Staff. For British imperialism, the main theatre of war was France. In 1917 a stalemate, a bloody war of attrition with opposing armies bogged down in trenches, had existed there since the end of 1914. Of the 2,300,000 or so men conscripted into the British armed forces, most were sent to the abattoirs of France. By November 1918, when Germany sought an armistice, nearly one million men from Britain and its colonies and dominions had been killed or were missing in action.

---

92 Pelling 1987, p. 298.
93 Oldham Spinners Executive Committee Minutes 1917. Undated minute. TU/1/1/33 @ OLSA.
94 *Herald*, 24 March 1917.
95 See Kendall 1969, chs. 6 and 7. Despite some questionable political judgements, Kendall's is still the best account of this movement. See also Macintyre 1980, ch. 1.

As in Russia, the military situation inevitably impacted on the domestic front. In November 1916, in response to industrial unrest among skilled engineering workers, the government had introduced the 'trade card' scheme, which guaranteed that skilled men in munitions factories would not be conscripted. The government also undertook that dilution would only be applied in munitions works.[96] The *Herald* had denounced the agreement, arguing that the reprieve given to the skilled men would inevitably lead to discontent among the greater numbers of the semi- and unskilled being conscripted: the 'sense of betrayal' of unskilled workers would 'never be appeased'.[97]

Despite the government's pledges, the demand for more men at the front meant that skilled men had eventually to be conscripted. The government's introduction of a Manpower Bill to rescind its concessions led to widespread engineering strikes in the Manchester conurbation in May. Lancashire, and the Manchester area in particular, was the heart of the textile engineering trade, which would inevitably be affected by the government's new view on dilution. The engineers' mass strike was sparked by the attempt of the management at Twedales and Smalley's in Rochdale to transfer 30 women dilutees from an expired shell contract to private work. Within days 30,000 engineering workers were out on an unofficial strike.[98] In Ashton and Oldham several factories were on strike. The *Ashton Reporter*'s insistence that the strike did not aim 'to cripple war work, but to force the government to keep its pledge to the engineering trade'[99] is borne out by Hinton's analysis of the strike.[100]

But what particularly alarmed the government, and union officials for that matter, was the growing influence of shop stewards (and the consequent erosion of the influence of union officials), which suggested that revolutionary ideas from the Clyde and Russia were gaining ideological traction. In March, a 'special meeting' of 'representatives of districts covering the United Kingdom' had been held in Manchester to discuss the Manpower Bill. Though it was not an official meeting called by the union, those present denied that it was a meeting of shop stewards.[101] It is hard to avoid the conclusion that it was indeed a meeting of shop stewards. At the start of the strike, the District Committee of the Amalgamated Society of Engineers (ASE) heard a report of a meeting at the Star and Garter pub in Manchester between representatives of the Committee

---

96 Grieves 1988, pp. 57–8.
97 *Herald*, 27 January 1917.
98 *Manchester Evening* News, 4 May 1917.
99 *Ashton Reporter*, 5 May 1917.
100 Hinton 1973, pp. 196–212.
101 *Manchester Guardian*, 25 March 1917.

and the Shop Stewards: 'our advice and efforts to induce a return to work had no effect, they exhibited a very determined attitude. We were treated courteously and have nothing to complain of regarding our reception, with the exception that our efforts were fruitless'.[102]

Conscription of many militants and the arrest of several strike leaders under DORA brought an end to the Manchester strikes by the end of May. Shop Stewards from the greater Manchester area met and recommended a return to work, but many workers, including from Ashton and Oldham, stayed out, and new strikes erupted in Liverpool, Birkenhead and Preston.[103] Stewards from both Ashton and Oldham attended a further meeting in the township of Audenshaw, midway between Ashton and Manchester, which agreed to recommend a return to work.[104] The strikes were finally settled when the government dropped the charges under DORA and the shop stewards agreed to abide by decisions made between the Ministry of Munitions and union officials. Plans to reverse the trade cards scheme and to extend dilution into non-munitions work were quietly shelved. But the problem of manpower for the front was daily becoming more acute: the horrendous casualties on the western front led to a new assault on the privileges of the ASE early in the New Year.

But before then the government turned its attention to trying to fathom the causes of industrial discontent. In June the government appointed a Commission of Enquiry into Industrial Unrest, which quickly reported and claimed that:

> Hostility to capitalism has now become part of the political creed of the majority of trade unionists in the mining, if not in other industries ... Nearly all the movements initiated by the South Wales Miners' Federation ... are directed towards the overthrow of the present capitalist system.[105]

While the commissioners had not found that such attitudes were present in all the industrial areas of Britain, they clearly thought that they were contagious. The Commissioners for the North-West (one of whom was Clynes) were keen to stress the essential 'patriotism' of the workers in the area. Even so, they reported deep and widespread resentment over such matters as food prices, profiteering, dilution and liquor restrictions (supplies and the alcoholic content of beer had

---

102   Minutes of Manchester District Committee of ASE, 4 May 1917. TU/ENG/7/24/1 @ WCML.
103   *Manchester Guardian*, 15 May 1917.
104   *Manchester Evening News*, 21 May 1917.
105   *Industrial Unrest. The Report of the Commissioners (July 1917) Collated and Epitomised*, London, 1917, p. 16.

been severely curtailed). Further, they had found 'abundant evidence that the real hope of the workers of this area is not a restoration of pre-war conditions but a far better thing'.[106]

Fears and hopes that British workers would emulate the Russians were both exaggerated. Presumably, the events in Russia had some influence on the shop stewards, but most labour movement activists, while welcoming the revolution, seem to have had little inclination to emulate it. Some of those who attended the Leeds 'Soviet Convention' organised by the ILP and BSP in June 1917 indulged in wild talk of revolution, but few of them fought for revolution afterwards.[107] Even the BSP could not anticipate a more radical turn than the election of a majority of 'direct representatives' of the working class at the next general election.[108]

The revolutionary events in Russia did not intrude into the politics of our three towns until July. Early that month, a meeting at Oldham's Weaver's Institute was held 'under the auspices of the Anglo-Russian Workers' League' (probably an ILP front, given that the principal speakers were from the ILP) to 'hail the revolution in Russia'. Only 29 people were sufficiently interested in that momentous event to attend. Despite the fact that the provisional government in Russia had made clear its determination to remain allied with Britain and France in their war with Germany, the ILP speakers claimed that the revolution had increased the chances of a peace settlement. Though the ILP had not suggested such a thing, a T&LC member present was adamant that he 'was not going to say "put down your arms and go home"'.[109] The council was clearly wary of being too closely associated with revolution. In late July, it discussed whether or not to hold a demonstration to congratulate 'the working people of Russia' on their revolution. It was decided that 'the time was not yet opportune'. Instead, a resolution congratulating 'the Russian democracy' was passed.[110]

Lancashire's trade unionists were lukewarm in their responses to attempts by the International to convene an international conference of socialists from all combatant countries. The government became deeply hostile to such a conference being held, especially after the St. Petersburg Soviet had endorsed the idea and the All-Russian Soviet of Workers and Soldiers had sent revolutionary greetings to John MacLean, one of the principal architects of the trouble

---

106   *Report of the Commissioners for No, 2 Division, the North-West Area*, London, 1917, pp. 53 and 61.
107   See White 1974 for an account of this event.
108   *The Call*, 28 June 1917.
109   *Oldham Weekly Chronicle*, 4 July 1917.
110   Oldham T&LC Minutes 1916–18, Minutes of Meeting of 30 July 1917. M17/1/3 @ OLSA.

on the Clyde. The *Manchester Evening News* claimed too much when asserting 'Textile workers are rather suspicious. The great majority of them want to see Germany severely beaten, and they do not like the idea of intercourse of any kind with men from enemy countries while the war is in progress'.[111] In our three towns, only Mossley's spinners were definitely opposed.[112] Ashton Trades Council decided 'not to express an opinion'.[113] Oldham's spinners decided to attend a special Labour Party Conference convened to discuss whether or not to send delegates to Stockholm.[114] Labour's conference authorised Henderson to attend. Lloyd George considered this incompatible with membership of the government. Henderson accordingly resigned but assured Lloyd George that he continued to share his 'desire that the war should be carried to a successful conclusion'.[115] Labour's commitment to the war effort and the necessity of its direct representation in government was recognised by the appointment of Barnes to replace Henderson in the War Cabinet. Barnes was replaced by another trade unionist, G.J. Wardle.

The most militant of those who had attended the Leeds Convention, mostly shop stewards organised as the Workers and Soldiers Council, many of them members of the SLP, decided upon a new convention, to be held in Manchester. Ashton Trades Council declined to attend.[116] Oldham T&LC too decided 'by a large majority' not to attend.[117] It is very probable that most council members anticipated that revolutionary sentiments of a kind that they would not want to hear would be advanced at the meeting. It is also very probable that the minority were either members or sympathisers of the militant Oldham shop stewards movement which rapidly grew in influence over the next few months.

Historians of the Communist Party record that the new convention was held in Manchester on the 5th of August, as planned and advertised.[118] But, unable to find a hall in Manchester willing to hold the new convention, the organisers held it in Stockport, a few miles south of Manchester, on the 10th of August. Arthur MacManus of the CWC presided and hailed the strike wave then convulsing the country as 'a symptom of the beginnings of revolutionary developments in this country'. Those attending were threatened by members

---

111 *Manchester Evening News*, 1 August 1917.
112 *Mossley and Saddleworth Reporter*, 3 August 1917.
113 *Cotton Factory Times*, 10 August 1917.
114 Oldham Spinners EC Minutes 1917, Special EC, 13 August 1917. TU/1/1/33 @OLSA.
115 Labour Party, *Report to the Seventeenth Annual Conference of the Labour Party*, London, 1918, p. 6.
116 *Cotton Factory Times*, 10 August 1917.
117 Oldham T&LC Minutes 1916–18, Minutes of Meeting of 30 July 1917. M17/1/3 @ OLSA.
118 Kendall 1969, p. 164; Challinor 1977, p. 159.

of the British Workers League (BWL) who had gathered outside. One of these shouted, 'Look at them, they won't fight because they can't. They cannot fight big dinners, people like them, yet they profess to represent the British working man'.[119] MacManus and his comrades were not deterred: they continued to attempt to build a revolutionary movement in Britain, culminating in the formation of the Communist Party in 1920.[120]

Mounting industrial unrest and the report of the commissioners into that unrest were instrumental in the formation of the Ministry of Reconstruction and the publication of a reforming Education Bill in August 1917. Reconstruction, the government insisted, meant not so much the 'rebuilding of society as it was before the war, but of moulding a better world out of the social and economic conditions which have come into being during the war'.[121] The 'better world' the government had in mind was one with a modest improvement, particularly in housing and education, in social conditions, an improvement that did not require a revolution.

5   A Better World Coming?

The parameters and content of reform were largely determined by government, the civil service and the labour movement's leadership. With the notable exceptions of electoral reform and nationalisation (both discussed in the next chapter), and housing, the role of the rank-and-file of the labour movement in shaping postwar policy was largely reactive. Class antagonism co-existed with deference towards the men in government and the civil service who 'knew best' (some of whom, Christopher Addison[122] for instance, were shortly to join the Labour Party) and such bourgeois intellectuals as Sydney Webb. Though there was substantial postwar reform, notably in the franchise and the creation of

---

119 *Manchester Evening News*, 11 August 1917. The proto-fascist BWL was founded as the Socialist National Defence Committee in 1914 by right wing socialists who supported the war effort. It soon attracted support and finance from Lord Milner's National Service League. It was renamed the BWL in 1916. Ward 1998, p. 125.
120 The origins of the CP can arguably be traced back to the meeting in Stockport. Such prominent future leaders of the party as MacManus, Tom Bell, J.T. Murphy and Willy Gallacher were present and thereafter fought collectively in the revolutionary movement.
121 Cited in Marwick 1991, p. 279.
122 As Minister without Portfolio in the Lloyd George coalition, the Liberal Addison was the main intellectual and ideological inspiration behind plans for postwar reconstruction. Dismayed by the postwar reaction, he joined the Labour Party and served as Minister of Agriculture in the 1929–31 Labour Government.

a Ministry of Health, a conservative postwar reaction, prompted by interwar slump and depression, meant that much reform, especially regarding the poor laws and housing, was not delivered. Nevertheless, proposals for reform were not forgotten and were to be resurrected in 1940.[123]

It was not until 1916 that the labour movement as a whole began to seriously consider the question of postwar reform. We have seen that early in the war, probably in late 1914 or early 1915, the WEWNC published *The Workers and the War*, its programme for postwar reform. We have seen also that this programme failed to attract support from the labour movement. In January 1916 too, the movement had been cautious. Labour's special conference adopted a *First Report on Labour after the War* which assumed that there would be an economic crisis after the war and thus advocated mainly defensive measures, such as planned demobilisation, work creation and a reform of the poor laws.[124] But later that year, Sydney Webb, the likely author of *The Workers and the War*, addressed the question of postwar reform in a series of influential articles in the *Daily News and Leader*. Webb was the principal intellectual influence in the shaping of Labour's programme for postwar reconstruction. He sat on the WEWNC and the Reconstruction Sub-Committee of Labour's NEC, both of which were involved in shaping the movement's postwar policy. In the *Daily News and Leader*, Webb reprised many of the themes of *The Workers and the War* and anticipated some of the reforms demanded in Labour's final programme for postwar reform,[125] which we will consider in the next chapter.

But before then, the labour movement had to consider and respond to the government's proposals for reform. The dreadful state of much working class housing – damp, inadequate ventilation, overcrowding, vermin infestation, poor sanitation – determined that it was housing which eventually became the principal element of the offer of reform to the working class. In our three towns, the state of working class housing, though shocking, did not compare with the dreadful conditions in many working class areas of Glasgow, Belfast, London, Liverpool or Manchester.

Mossley's housing was in a poor state, but calls for social reform there were much more muted, no doubt the consequence of continuing deference, than in the other two towns. Ashton's working class housing was in a much worse state than Oldham's. Moreover, it had a town council dominated by Conservatives far more concerned to keep the rates down than to improve the town's hous-

---

123   See Marwick 1991, Cronin 1989, Orbach 1977, Reid 1988 and Sherington 1981, for some aspects of reconstruction policy and postwar retreat.
124   Horne 1991, pp. 225–6.
125   See, for instance, *The Prevention of Unemployment. Daily News and Leader*, 3 August 1916.

ing stock. Shortage of building land exacerbated these factors. Oldham's town council in contrast was much more responsive to calls for housing improvement than Ashton's. For all these reasons, working class unrest in Oldham found its main outlet in the shop stewards' movement, while demands for housing reform were much more insistent in Ashton than in the other two towns.

In August 1917, Oldham's town council responded positively to a Local Government Board circular, one of the first fruits of the government's attempts to bolster working class support for the war effort, on the 'provision of houses for the working classes at the conclusion of the war' which 'intimated' that central government would be prepared to offer the necessary funds.[126] A few weeks later, the council noted that good houses were the 'foundation of a healthy nation' and that houses would be 'urgently required after the war'. Shortly afterwards, the Borough Surveyor presented a report on postwar housing to the Surveyors and Buildings Committee (a Housing Committee had not yet been established). According to the Surveyor, 'very few dwelling houses for the working class' had been built since 1910. But the town had few cellar dwellings, back-to-backs or 'slum' houses. It was said that 500 houses should be erected in the first postwar year and 250 in each of the three succeeding years. Noting the Chair of the Committee's caveat that people 'could not expect the same sort of cottage in Oldham as in Somerset', the Committee accepted the Borough Surveyor's recommendations.[127]

In Mossley, despite Alderman Farr's insistence that the town's housing stock was poor, the town council responded to the Local Government Board's circular with prevarication and procrastination. In April, Farr had attended (as a delegate of the Cardroom Amalgamation, not the council) a Manchester conference of the National Housing and Town Planning Council. At the conference, Farr militantly argued that 'if we could spend seven or eight million a day upon the destruction of life it would be a standing disgrace if we could not provide £20,000,000 or even £25,000,000 to provide sanitary and healthy houses. The people would have to realise that there was no one to look after the interests of the workers but the workers themselves'.[128]

In a discussion of the Local Government Board's circular Farr pressed the town council to draw up a scheme for the building of council houses, but, despite the *Reporter*'s comment that the issue was of the 'utmost importance', had little response.[129] On the day in October that the question of housing came

---

126 *Oldham Weekly Chronicle*, 8 August 1917.
127 *Oldham Weekly Chronicle*, 6 October 1917 and 13 October 1917.
128 *Ashton Reporter*, 7 April 1917.
129 *Mossley and Saddleworth Reporter*, 1 September 1917.

up at a meeting of the General Purposes Committee, the *Reporter* denounced the poor state of the town's housing: six percent were back-to-backs or 'underhouses' (cellar dwellings) and 25 percent had no through ventilation. Farr's insistence at the committee meeting that over 1,000 houses were unfit to live in, that it would be 'a black crime' if the serving soldiers had to return to the 'pigsty homes they left behind them', were met with cries of 'no no'. Councillor Taylor said the council 'had enough to do without building houses that were not required'.[130]

A week later, the town's acting surveyor presented the survey of housing requested by the Local Government Board. He reported that 79 percent of houses had only four rooms. Hardly any houses had a bathroom, indoor lavatory or pantry or other suitable food store. There was much overcrowding.[131] Though the meeting of the General Purposes Committee had resolved that the Local Government Board should be informed that the council was prepared to build 200 houses, subject to 'satisfactory financial arrangements' (i.e. with central government funding), no firm plans were made. As we shall see in the next chapter, the town's labour movement did little to challenge the council's complacency and sloth on the matter. Farr's militancy did not survive into the peace.

Even before the start of the war, the state of Ashton's housing had promoted tension. In the 1913 municipal elections, the Liberal candidate for Market Ward knew of a case where the rent had been raised three times and the tenant told that if he didn't like it 'he could clear out'.[132] Fred Smales, the trades council candidate for St. Peter's Ward, criticised the 'great dearth of houses in Ashton, and the consequently abnormally high rents and the overcrowding'. But Ashton's workers were still wedded to the parties of the millocracy: Smales came bottom of the poll.[133] The difficulties faced by those seeking reform are shown by the reception given by the council's Health Committee to a deputation from the trades council laying their case for building housing for the working class. They were told by Alderman Shaw, the chairman of the committee, that to build such houses would be a 'burden on the rates'.[134]

Ashton's trades council was but one of several labour movement organisations represented at the National Housing and Town Planning Council's con-

---

130 *Mossley and Saddleworth Reporter*, 13 October 1917.
131 *Mossley and Saddleworth Reporter*, 20 October 1917.
132 *Ashton Reporter*, 1 November 1913.
133 *Ashton Reporter*, 25 October 1913 and 8 November 1913.
134 Ashton Council Minutes, 1914–15. Minutes of the Health Committee, 21 October 1914. CA/ASH 111/27 @ TLSAC; *Ashton Herald*, 28 November 1914.

ference which Farr had attended.[135] Delegates urged the government to adopt a national 'after the war housing policy which should, at the same time, provide healthy housing and avert any crisis of unemployment which might arise in the building trade at the end of the war'. It also urged local authorities to establish Housing Committees.[136] After the conference, in reply to a circular from the council asking for financial help for its work 'to secure that adequate preparation shall be made to deal on national lines with the great problems of housing and unemployment at the close of the war', the spinners sent a cheque for 15 guineas, noting that to let 'servicemen come from the horrible waterlogged trenches to something little better than a pigsty would indeed be criminal ... and would be a negation of all we have said during this war, that we can never repay these men for what they have done for us'.[137]

The conference invigorated Ashton Trades Council. It seems unlikely that it was a coincidence that it was shortly after the conference that a local tenant's defence league was established. In June, the TDL held a public meeting at Ashton Trades Club. A report to the trades council noted that threats of eviction after the war had been made. Already a number of illegally raised rents had been repaid.[138] Another public meeting attended by various dignitaries, including Manchester Labour Councillor Mellor, President of the Manchester Tenants Defence Association, was held in August. James Massey (a future town councillor, Mayor, alderman and freeman of the borough) insisted that the role of the TDL was not just to defend tenants; one of its aims was 'to provide more and better homes for the workers, and it was for them to get the Corporation to take up the question'.[139] What may have been the final meeting of the TDL was held in January 1918. Complaints were made regarding the partiality of magistrates. In a particularly egregious case brought by the league, a landlord was fined 10/- (50p), but £5.0.0 in costs was awarded against the complaining tenant.[140] The TDL seems to have become inactive after this meeting. It is probable that the trades council decided that lobbying the council and contesting municipal elections was a better way to fight to improve the town's housing.

---

135 The spinners, represented by Marsland, were members of the council. A year or so earlier the Spinners had agreed to pay an annual subscription of 10 guineas. Spinners' Amalgamation, EC Minutes 1916, meeting of 8 April 1916. ACS/2/1/1/1 @ JRSC.
136 *Ashton Reporter*, 7 April 1917.
137 National Housing and Town Planning Council to Spinners' Amalgamation, 14 June 1917; Spinners' Amalgamation to National Housing and Town Planning Council, undated. ACS Correspondence 1917. ACS/6/10/10 @ JRSC.
138 *Ashton Reporter*, 9 June 1917.
139 *Ashton Reporter*, 4 August 1917.
140 *Ashton Reporter*, 26 January 1918.

For most of the summer of 1917, Ashton's council and people were understandably preoccupied with the consequences of a colossal explosion at a local munitions factory. 46 people were killed and around 400 were injured, 120 of them requiring hospital treatment. The explosion was so great that around 2,000 became homeless.[141] Until August not much attention was paid to other matters. That month the *Reporter* commented on the Local Government Board's circular. The paper welcomed central government's plans for 'taking in hand the question of the housing of the working classes and that a much-needed stimulus is to be given to local authorities to provide a programme of housing'. Few towns, the *Reporter* claimed, 'are so badly off as Ashton for suitable dwellings in sufficient numbers ... For years scarcely any new houses have been erected, and there is a great deal of overcrowding and the health of the community suffers'.[142]

A week later, under the heading 'Why a Housing Scheme is needed in Ashton', the *Reporter* linked poor public health with poor housing. The Medical Officer of Health's (MOH) report for the past year had shown that infant mortality in Ashton was 116.7 per thousand compared with a national average of 91.0.[143] One in four children in Ashton, the MOH had reported, died before they reached the age of five. Overcrowding, insanitary conditions and damp were major factors. The *Reporter* had solicited the views of Judson, 'who can claim to speak for a large number of working men in the town'. Judson had spoken of a great deal of overcrowding. He 'knew of a case where 17 persons were living in a house with two bedrooms'. The town council, the *Reporter* argued, should take up the responsibility for housing since 'nothing is to be expected in this direction from private enterprise for some years to come'.[144]

The question of housing brought a great deal of heat to the town council, as Liberals, backed by Judson and the trades council, fought for reform and Conservatives resisted. In September, Liberal Councillor Dr Crawshaw moved

---

141   See Billings and Copland 1992 for a full account of this event.
142   *Ashton* Reporter, 4 August 1917.
143   In a recent Local Government Board circular, Ashton had been identified as a town with a much higher than average infant mortality rate. *Ashton Reporter*, 21 April 1917. Infant mortality and overall death rates were generally significantly higher in working class than in middle class areas. Manchester and Salford Trades Council noted that the death rate in inner-city Ancoats was 27.9 per 1,000, but only 11.39 in suburban Withington, and argued that 'house building must no longer be a private speculation, it must be Public Service, a means of developing healthy citizens, not a source of private profit'. Manchester and Salford Trades and Labour Council, *Housing Conditions of Some of the Working Class in the City of Manchester* (Manchester, 1917).
144   *Ashton* Reporter, 11 August 1917.

a resolution that a committee should be set up to investigate Ashton's high infant mortality. He had compared Ashton with Nelson, a similar place, but with much better working class housing and a significantly lower infant mortality rate. In Nelson, there were 'no alleys, courts or slums'. The resolution was seconded by Judson, but opposed by Alderman Shaw, who claimed that the problem 'was not so much insanitary conditions as the habits of the people'. In reply, Crawshaw quoted a report of the Local Government Board which said that 'sometimes pockets are considered more than lives'. He 'did not know how far that applied to Ashton'. The resolution was lost, all the Conservatives voting against. Crawshaw raised the question of infant mortality again at the October council meeting, to 'the laughter of some members of the council' and Shaw's remark that he was a 'bore'.[145]

Probably essentially a placatory gesture to central government, the council decided in September that the health committee would be reconstituted as a housing committee. The duties of the new committee would include, 'if thought desirable' (a crucial caveat), to 'bring forward a scheme to meet the shortage of dwelling houses which undoubtedly exists in the borough'. It was agreed to co-opt as members of the committee representatives of the trades council and of Ashton Property Owners Association.[146] The committee met for the first time in December, but appears to have been virtually inactive thereafter.[147] The committee's claim that while the council wanted to build 1,000 houses, the cost of land would lead to 'prohibitive rents for most working class people' and its invitation to Boothman, the local secretary of the Spinners Amalgamation, to join a deputation to government on the housing question, offer some evidence that the committee was not completely inactive.[148] But the minutes are strongly suggestive of procrastination, which was, as we shall see, to be a major factor in the Labour Party's spectacular progress in the municipal elections of 1919. Before then, criticism did surface from time to time (the Reverend Cummings, the 'communist vicar' of Hurst,[149] regularly attacked the council and 'slum landlords' and in October 1918 was to argue that the fundamental problem was 'private ownership'),[150] but the decision to set

---

145 *Ashton Reporter*, 15 September 1917; *Ashton Reporter*, 13 October 1917.
146 *Ashton Herald*, 29 September 1917.
147 Ashton Town Council Minutes 1917–18, Housing Committee Minutes, 18 December 1917. CA/ASH/111/30 @ TLSAC.
148 *Ashton Reporter*, 20 July 1917 and 26 July 1918.
149 Hurst was a neighbouring township of Ashton. In the 1930s it was assimilated into Ashton. See Locke 1997 for an account of the activities of the Reverend Cummings. See also Poole 2014, pp. 29–58.
150 *Ashton Reporter*, 19 October 1918.

up a housing committee had served to temporarily mollify most critics of the council's housing policy.

Second only to housing, education was another government priority for reform. The low educational level of many volunteers and conscripts for the armed forces had provoked nearly as much alarm in bourgeois circles as had their poor physical state. The main elements of the Education Bill of August 1917 (or least of those enacted in the 1918 Education Act – the so-called Fisher Act, after H.A.L. Fisher, the President of the Board of Education) were raising the school-leaving age from 13 to 14, ending the system of half-time education (12 and 13 year olds were permitted to work half-time and attend school half-time) and allowing local authorities to offer scholarships for secondary education. The bill was broadly supported by the labour movement, though the Labour Party argued that fees for secondary education should be abolished.[151] Due to these fees, few working class children attended secondary schools. In Ashton, for instance, in 1912 only eight percent of the town's schoolchildren (hardly any of whom, we can safely assume, were working class children) attended a secondary school.[152] But raising the school-leaving age and, especially, ending half-time education provoked considerable opposition among some of the trade union leadership and most of the rank-and-file of the trade union movement, due to the threat these measures posed to household income.

Educational reform was widely anticipated even before the publication of the bill. Local authorities tended to philistinism on this matter. Oldham's education committee, the *Chronicle* claimed, opposed raising the school-leaving age because most councillors 'are simply concerned with the provision of cheap and abundant labour for Oldham's mills and factories'.[153] Later that year, in a debate on the provision in the bill for compulsory post-school day-release for education up to the age of 18, Alderman Ashworth declared that 'we were not only interested in education, but also in the industry of the town and, if the industry of the town was cut off, what was the good of education' (cries of 'Hear! Hear!' were heard). Despite Ashworth's objections, the education committee supported the provision, only for the full council to water this down, indeed to sabotage it, to support for provision of voluntary evening classes, rather than compulsory day release.[154]

---

151 Labour Party, *Report to Eighteenth Annual Conference of the Labour Party* (London, 1918), pp. 71–3.
152 Lancashire County Council Board of Education Inspection of Ashton Secondary School September 1912. CC/EV/21 @ LROP. (As Ashton was a municipal, not a county borough, Lancashire County Council was ultimately responsible for education in the town).
153 *Oldham Weekly Chronicle*, 20 January 1917.
154 *Oldham Weekly Chronicle*, 8 December 1917.

In contrast, perhaps more aware of the needs of British imperialism than the town's millocracy, the T&LC welcomed educational reform on impeccably social-imperialist grounds. A council speaker at a public meeting claimed that 'our greatest enemy in the war is the superior scientific research and methodological arrangement of the Germans'; another asserted that 'if we are to take our place among the countries of the world, we must keep foremost in our minds the need ... for continual education beyond the elementary stage'.[155] Such sentiments were widespread among the trade union leadership. In 1916, for instance, the report of the executive council of the UTFWA had been insistent that 'if this country is to succeed as a nation we shall have to make up our minds to increase and improve the opportunities for the workpeople to gain a good commercial education'.[156] But some in the labour movement took a wider, Deweyist view of the purpose of education. In 1918, Mullins would assert that 'we may rest assured a measure [raising the school-leaving age] will be passed giving the youth of this country an education, making them better and more enlightened men and women, and making the democracy of this country superior to that of any other country on the face of the globe'.[157] And in 1920, Fred Smales, a Labour member of Ashton's Education Committee, objected to the assertion that the objective of education was 'to turn out a better workman'. Rather, Smales argued, it should 'turn out people with a "broader outlook"' and 'improved mental capacity'.[158]

But such views and, even more so, those on ending half-time education were not shared by most cotton workers. Half-time education had been in decline for some time. In Ashton, for instance, only eight percent of school children were half-timers in 1914.[159] Even so, most working class families lived from one week's pay packet to the next. Sending children to work half-time in the mill was something to fall back on if necessary. This is undoubtedly why in 1908 rank-and-file cotton workers had overturned a vote at UTFWA's annual conference in favour of raising the minimum age for half-timers from 12 to 13.[160] During the war, the household income of many families declined sharply when men joined the armed forces: pressure for children to work as soon as they leg-

---

155 *Oldham Weekly Chronicle*, 5 March 1917.
156 *Cotton Factory Times*, 28 July 1916.
157 Cardroom Amalgamation, Reports and Minutes January 1917–December 1920. Quarterly Report and Balance Sheet for the Quarter ending March 23rd 1918. Report to District Officials from William Mullins, Secretary, p. 6. TU/TEX/CARD/13 @ WCML.
158 *Ashton Reporter*, 7 February 1920.
159 Ashton Council Minutes, Minutes of Education Committee, 5 October 1914. CA/ASH/100/26 @ TLSAC.
160 McHugh and Ripley 1987, p. 142.

ally (or illegally)[161] could do so increased correspondingly. It was hard to give priority to education when struggling to feed a family and pay the rent.

Shortly after the start of the war, the Central Committee of the Weavers' Amalgamation had discussed a letter from the Society for the Abolition of Half-Time Labour. The Society considered that 'more stringent bye-laws' were necessary to protect children. The Amalgamation replied that it did not consider this appropriate 'at the present time'.[162] Raising the school-leaving age proved equally problematic. In evidence given to the Department of Education in September 1916, Marsland claimed that there was 'a strong and widespread objection among cotton operatives to a leaving age of 14 … however, he and a majority of local committees are not in accord with the workers'. Further, they thought that 'children [were] not likely to become good workers if entry to the mill is postponed till 14'.[163]

In 1917, as speculation regarding the shape of postwar education increased, the *Cotton Factory Times*, after publishing many letters and resolutions from unions and trades councils arguing against an increase in school-leaving age and ending half-time education, countered the arguments of the objectors to reform. On child labour, for instance, readers had been urged to 'think of the widow. What will happen to her if her girl can't go to the mill at 12?' But, the paper argued, 'the misfortunes of parents do not give them a vested interest in the misfortunes of their children'.[164]

But most cotton workers were not convinced. Rank-and-file opposition mounted after the publication of the bill, especially after UTFWA's legislative council resolved to support ending the half-timer system.[165] Rather late in the day, almost on the eve of a ballot of all cotton workers on the Education Bill, UTFWA organised a conference of textile workers and MPs on the bill's proposals on half-timers.[166] But it was too late. Goggins clearly spoke for the majority of textile workers, when stating that he agreed with the bill in general but to prohibit half-time working would be 'the height of folly': it would 'feed the mind and starve the body'.[167] Only 32,392 cotton workers voted in favour of ending

---

161   In 1917 it was reported that in the first three years of the war 600,000 children had been put to work 'prematurely'. Marwick 1991, p. 157.
162   Minutes of the Central Committee of the Weavers' Amalgamation, 31 October 1914. TU/Weavers/006 @ WCML.
163   Spinners' Amalgamation File on Juvenile Employment. ACS/6/9/3 @ JRSC.
164   *Cotton Factory Times*, 13 April 1918.
165   Legislative Council of UTFWA to Spinners' Amalgamation, 12 February 1918. ACS/6/3/14 @ JRSC.
166   UTFWA circular, 4 April 1918. DDX/1123/4/7 @ LROP.
167   *Ashton Herald*, 27 April 1918.

half-time education compared to 81,449 who voted against.[168] In Oldham, 75 percent of spinners voted in a ballot in which only 1,663 voted in favour compared with 3,166 against.[169]

6   More Strikes, More Shop Stewards and Some Revolutionaries

By the end of 1917, labour movement discourse on postwar reform was beginning to become tinged with class antagonism. In a letter to the local press, S. Bradbury, the Secretary of the Stalybridge, Dukinfield and Millbrook branch of the Labour Party, attacked a speech by Sir Hugh Bell, the 'well known North Riding Ironmaster'. Bell had argued that those who expected radical change in relations between capital and labour after the war were 'living in a fool's paradise'. So, asked Bradbury:

> no interference with the dividend to the capitalist. No increases in the reward to the worker. That is what we are to offer to the men who return from the war. It is not to be wondered that there are rumours of possible revolution even in this easygoing country.[170]

Similarly, W.H. Carr, the Secretary of the South East Lancashire Association of the Cardroom Amalgamation, based in Ashton, angrily noted

> that for the fourth time we have to take stock of our position as an association in the midst of a great and bloody war ... Just how long the people will allow the mad passions of the handful of men who claim to be their rulers to go on laying waste and soaking the earth with the best blood of all lands it is impossible to say ... The indications are quite unmistakeable that when peace becomes once more established the people in all civilised countries will take a much larger share in shaping their own future destiny than they have ever previously had ... there is a much better way of dealing with ... adverse conditions than the 'every man for himself and the devil take the hindmost' style of policy which has always been adopted in the past.[171]

---

168   *Cotton Factory Times*, 12 April 1918.
169   Oldham Spinners EC Minutes 1918, Special EC 9 April 1918. TU/1/1/34 @OLSA.
170   *Ashton Reporter*, 17 November 1917.
171   South East Lancashire Association of the Cardroom Amalgamation, *Annual report for 1917*. TU13/2/3 @ TLSAC.

Bradbury's and Carr's outbursts had probably been provoked by widespread opinion that the hardships caused by intensified German submarine warfare were not being equally shared. Supplies of food and cotton had been gravely affected. Food prices had increased sharply in the first half of the year. Lord Rhondda, a businessman and Liberal politician, was appointed Food Controller in July, with a brief to ensure supplies and control prices. Fixed prices for certain essential foods were set: but the task of policing prices and allocating supplies was devolved to local Food Control Committees appointed by local authorities. The composition and decisions of these Committees intensified class antagonisms.

In Mossley, the structure and decisions of the Committee (on which Alderman Farr and Wright Mosley sat)[172] seem not to have initially provoked dissent. But in both Ashton and Oldham seeds of conflict were being sown. Ashton's Committee met for the first time on the 30th of August. Most members were town councillors and aldermen[173] (though the trade council's James Massey was also a member), prompting immediate suspicions. The *Reporter* gave considerable prominence to a letter claiming that the town council had 'packed the committee in the interest of the tradesman not the consumer ... out of the eight members, seven are members of the Conservative Party, and the other is a Liberal and Secretary of the Traders' Association'. It noted that in Salford and Liverpool it had been decided that 'no interested person' should be on the food committee. The trades council unanimously passed a model resolution received from Retford Trades Council claiming that as 'labour represents the greatest proportion of the population, it is entitled to at least half the representatives on each committee'.[174] Shortly afterwards it was reported that Lord Rhondda was to investigate the composition of the committee.[175] During his investigation, complaints mounted. The *Reporter* asked if there was 'any justification for milk selling at 7d. a pint in Ashton when it is 5½d. in Hyde ... Many poor people have had to curtail their milk supply ... and children have gone short'. It implied that the reason was composition of the committee 'which includes ... a strong retail trading interest'.[176]

In June 1917, the Board of Trade had established the Cotton Control Board (CCB) which attempted to deal with shortages by rationing supplies. Other than tighten their belts, working class people could do little in response to the

---

172   *Mossley and Saddleworth Reporter*, 1 September 1917.
173   *Ashton Reporter*, 1 September 1917.
174   *Ashton Reporter*, 8 September 1917.
175   *Ashton Reporter*, 15 September 1917.
176   *Ashton Reporter*, 6 October 1917.

decisions of Food Control Committees. They could do something about the decisions of the CCB: they could go on strike. The EC of the Spinners' Amalgamation sent several of its leading members, including Judson and men from Mossley and Oldham, to a conference called by the Board of Trade to discuss how the CCB might operate.¹⁷⁷ Judson, Crinion and two other union officials became members of the Board. But according to the Secretary of the Board, H.D. Henderson, they 'at no time [played] an equal part in the determination of policy'.¹⁷⁸ Certainly, textile workers came to see the CCB as a tool of government and employers. A one-day protest strike of piecers at the Britannia Mill in Mossley signalled that the establishment of the CCB would lead to trouble.¹⁷⁹

The delegates to Oldham's T&LC were in a sour mood when they met in November. The government's failure to control food prices was contrasted with 'the assistance which the working class movement has always given the government during the war'. The delegates feared that 'the unrest which is growing will assume such a character that it will be difficult to control'.¹⁸⁰ The delegates were doubtless influenced by the considerable 'unrest' stirred up by Oldham's young and militant shop stewards over the previous few months, which they clearly disapproved of. For quite some time Oldham's textile employers had been complaining that their employees, especially younger employees, had been disruptive. In 1916 they had reported 'difficulties' in 'controlling operatives' who had 'taken advantage of the shortage of labour to make extravagant demands. The younger generation have been more active ... than their elders. It is extraordinary to find wages paid to boys of 14 and 15 which previous to the war were very good for adults'.¹⁸¹ Industrial strife, occasionally leading to strikes, had been endemic in Oldham's mills since the beginning of 1917. At the Shiloh Mill, for instance, spinners had struck for nearly a fortnight in February. The cause is unknown, but it had taken an intervention from Askwith, pointing out that the spinners were engaged in government (presumably war) work, with the clear threat of bringing spinners within the ambit of the Munitions of War Act to end the strike.¹⁸²

In October 'the younger generation', who were the backbone of the Oldham shop stewards movement (as they had been on the Clyde and in the May

---

177   *Manchester Guardian*, 25 June 1917.
178   Cited in Fowler 1987c, p. 149.
179   Minutes of the EC of the Spinners' Amalgamation, 23 June 1917. ACS/2/1/1/1 @ JRSC.
180   Oldham T&LC Minutes 1916–18, Special EC Meeting 14 November 1917. M17/1/3. @ OLSA.
181   ORTEA Annual Reports 1916–20. Report for 1916, p. 10. AAN/1/1/2/3 @ OLSA.
182   Oldham Spinners EC Minutes 1917, Disputes Committee, 1 February 1917. The strike had ended by the 12th of February. TU/1/1/33 S @ OLSA.

engineering strikes), led a major strike in the Oldham area in protest at the decisions of the CCB. Rationing of cotton meant that machines were periodically idle. Whereas piecers had previously been able to exploit labour shortages to increase their pay, their pay now fell. Moreover, the CCB insisted that staff should not be laid off when their machines were idle, but should be utilised on other machines. Doubtless intensifying the resentment of the piecers was that the spinners' leadership, mostly indifferent to piecer grievances, was co-operating with the employers in implementing the decisions of the CCB and had told the piecers that they would 'get no help from the union'.[183]

The strike started on the ninth of October when piecers at several mills refused to start work. The piecers went from mill to mill and 'brought out those who were at work ... Persons have been assaulted and mill windows broken'. A mass meeting was held 'on the market ground and subsequently a great crowd marched to the offices of the union ... A small deputation went inside to see the Secretary'.[184] According to the employers, 170 mills stopped work. 'Boys and youths' had started the strike, 'but there is no doubt the spirit of revolt was assisted and fomented, both openly and secretly, by a section of the minders [spinners] ... For a time it seemed that an attempt was going to be made to rule by mob law. The feelings of the men were inflamed by self-constituted oratorical leaders who sprung up from outside and inside the district'.[185]

The strike lasted for six days. No doubt threats from the CCB that summonses for damages would be issued played a part in the decision to resume work. But the strike had clearly boosted the prestige of the shop stewards, the 'self-constituted oratorical leaders'. The decision to resume work was taken at a mass meeting addressed by a 'self-appointed' strike committee. The meeting agreed that in future disputes would be put to a committee of shop stewards, rather than involve union officials. A return to work was agreed only after the employers agreed that there would be no victimisation of strike leaders.[186] Rising prices and food shortages combined with the refusal of union officials to sanction strikes served to increase the influence of shop stewards in both the cotton and engineering industries. Early in the New Year they would become prominent in new waves of industrial strife.

By the end of 1917 the national food situation had become critical. There were many prosecutions of traders for violating food control orders. Supplies had virtually dried up. In January 1918 there were, for instance, only 5,725 cattle

---

183 *Manchester Guardian*, 4 October 1917.
184 *Oldham Weekly* Chronicle, 13 October 1917.
185 ORTEA Annual Reports 1916–20. Report for 1917, pp. 11–12. AAN/1/1/2/3 @ OLSA.
186 *Cotton Factory Times*, 20 October 1917.

at markets surveyed by the Ministry of Food, compared with 18,509 in January 1916.[187] In Ashton, it was reported that housewives were 'scouring the town for staples ... only to be met by notices such as 'no tea, no bacon no butter''.[188] Rationing schemes for sugar, butter and margarine were introduced in various localities in response to shortages. Over the next few months, meat and such staples as tea and lard were rationed. A not very effective national rationing scheme was introduced in July 1918.[189]

In December dissatisfaction with Ashton's Food Control Committee led to the appointment of a new Executive Officer, Harold Hyde, who, at a meeting of Ashton traders, 'agreed that traders must make a fair profit, but stressed the need for fairness to the public'.[190] There is no evidence that he met with representatives of the town's labour movement or of consumers. Rationing of tea, butter and margarine was started in all three of our towns in January 1918, but was seen by many, especially in the town's labour movement, as a system which favoured traders. In Oldham, Clynes had told a public meeting that rationing would inevitably have such an effect.[191]

In January, the *Reporter* expressed concern regarding an increasingly angry working class and labour movement: the 'working people, of which this district is mainly composed, are becoming very restless'. The trades council had called upon the Food Control Committee, which it claimed was favouring traders, to co-opt trade unionists. It had demanded that the government establish a national scheme. Ominously, for the Liberal millocrats that the *Reporter* represented, a 'large section' of the council meeting had argued that the working class should 'down tools' unless a national scheme was introduced and had resolved (here, the influence of Bolshevism and the CWC was palpable) to itself adopt, if necessary, 'other measures to secure to the workers the necessary supply of food essential to their needs'. Urgent action was necessary. There was a serious shortage of meat. Currently, only 50 percent of that which had been consumed the previous October was available. Many butchers were closed most of the week. It was 'Pitiable to see women and children queuing in the falling snow and biting east wind'.[192]

In Oldham, there were many shortages: in one week there had been 'no margarine in Woodhouses', in another, 'no meat' in Oldham. But the leaders

---

187 Gregory 2008, p. 214.
188 *Ashton Reporter*, 6 December 1917.
189 Gazeley and Newell 2013.
190 *Ashton Reporter*, 15 December 1917.
191 *Oldham Weekly Chronicle*, 15 December 1917.
192 *Ashton Reporter*, 5 January 1918.

of the town's trade unionists, depending on their view on the matter, seem to have been concentrating on either developing or containing the shop stewards movement. Even so, the trades and labour council did discuss the food situation. In a much more moderate stance than Ashton's, perhaps reflecting the influence of its political section, it urged a public inquiry into 'profiteering' and 'heavier taxation on profiteers and the restitution of their profits to the state'.[193] Probably in an attempt to placate the council, Oldham's Food Control Committee co-opted four members from it.[194]

In the engineering trade, anger at food shortages was exacerbated by the government's response to another manpower crisis. The slaughter on the western front in 1917, culminating in the capture of the village of Passchendaele,[195] led the War Cabinet to decide that a further 450,000 men must be conscripted: some of them would have to be skilled men currently with exemptions. Sir Aukland Geddes, the Minister of National Service, attempted to win over trade union leaders at a Manpower Conference in January 1918. There were follow-up Conferences dealing with the particular problems of each industry. The ASE refused to participate in the munitions conference.[196]

It was just before and at the Manpower Conference that Lloyd George made the first explicit statement of the government's war aims, partly intended to reassure the labour movement, the trade unions in particular, that the war was indeed a just war.[197] Prompted by the Bolshevik's November *exposé* of the Sykes-Picot Agreement and by the clearly impending victory of the British army over the Turkish forces in Palestine (British troops had just entered Jerusalem), the Labour Party and the TUC had held in late December a special conference on British war aims.[198] In a *Memorandum on War Aims* which was essentially a summary of UDC policy and an endorsement of President Wilson's demand for a postwar international organisation of states, the labour movement disclaimed 'all sympathy with the Imperialist aims of Governments and capitalists who would make of ... territories now dominated by the Turkish hordes merely instruments either of exploitation or militarism'.[199]

---

193 *Oldham Evening Chronicle*, 12 January 1918.
194 *Oldham Evening Chronicle*, 16 February 1918.
195 822,000 men were killed, wounded or missing in action on the Western Front in 1917. Grieves 1998, p. 166.
196 Grieves 1998, pp. 181–3.
197 *Times*, 7 January 1918.
198 *Manchester* Guardian, 29 December 1917.
199 Labour Party and Trades Union Congress, *Memorandum on War Aims* (London, 1918), p. 5.

Given that the special conference had rejected all anti-war resolutions and endorsed Labour's participation in the government,[200] Lloyd George could with impunity have ignored the labour movement's oblique criticism of Anglo-French policy, but presumably considered it unwise to, given the sensitive manpower situation. 'We are not fighting a war of aggression against the German people', Lloyd George declared. The government was essentially fighting for self-determination for all peoples, including the Belgians, recently subject to aggression by Germany and those of Alsace-Lorraine, 'torn from the side of France' during the Franco-Prussian War of 1870. As for the subject peoples of the Ottomans, they were entitled 'to a recognition of their separate national conditions'.[201] The trade union leaders were reassured by this no doubt deliberately ambiguous statement, either not noticing or, more likely, indifferent to Lloyd George's conspicuous failure to include the subject peoples of the British Empire among those whose rights of self-determination were affirmed.[202]

The *Memorandum* too had failed to assert a right of self-determination for the peoples of the Empire. The labour movement's continuing commitment to the war effort was made clear by including in the published version of its *Memorandum* the sophistries by which the left of the allied nations had in 1914 justified their support for war. After piously declaring that the war was a 'monstrous product of the antagonisms which tear asunder capitalist society and of the policy of Colonial dependencies and aggressive Imperialism, against which International Socialism has never ceased to fight, and in which every Government has its share of responsibility', these parties had nevertheless declared that the 'invasion of Belgium and France by the German armies threatens the very existence of independent nationalities ... In these circumstances a victory for Germany would be the defeat and the destruction of democracy and liberty in Europe'.[203] There was more than a hint of disingenuousness in reprinting this statement, when such episodes as the recent bloody suppression of the uprising in Ireland[204] had made very clear indeed the hypocrisy of British claims to be fighting for the right of nations to self-determination.

In the winter of 1917–18, trade union leaders were far more troubled by militant shop stewards than by the question of war aims. In Mossley, 'bad spinning'

200 Bridgen 2009, p, 101.
201 *Manchester Guardian*, 7 January 1918.
202 Lloyd George, *Prime Minister Lloyd George on British War Aims* (London, 1918).
203 Labour Party and Trades Union Congress, *Memorandum on War Aims* (London, 1918). Appendix, pp. 7–8: Declaration of Conference of Socialist and Labour Parties of Allied Nations, 14 February 1915.
204 In the immediate aftermath of the Easter Rising several of its leaders, including James Connolly, had been executed.

led to an unofficial strike at the Brunswick Mill, attributed to the influence of shop stewards. The workers were said to have 'ignored the instructions of their local secretary'.[205] Oldham and Rochdale textile employers' claim that minders as well as piecers were involved in the shop stewards movement was confirmed when they met to discuss strategy and tactics. There was a 'good attendance'. The Chairman, Heys of Middleton, insisted that there must be a 'reconstruction' of the union. The shop stewards' movement had arisen because officials did not respond to rank-and-file grievances. But the shop stewards were 'not out to smash the union'. There 'must be co-operation with officials'.[206] Early in the New Year, at the same time that engineering workers in Manchester voted by 16 to 1 in favour of 'including shop stewards among trade union officials',[207] Oldham spinners had voted 2 to 1 'in favour of the shop steward principle'. Soon after, a conference of shop stewards adopted proposals on the functions of shop stewards which would inevitably lead to conflict with officials. In particular, it was resolved that officials should be involved in disputes only when stewards could not resolve them. The shop stewards' secretary, Wilde of Stockport, clearly far more militant than Heys, denounced union officials as 'Kaisers'. There must be a 'parting of the ways … It was time the new unionism was applied in place of the old unionism'.[208] Oldham in particular was to experience a robust fight for a 'new unionism' later that year.

January saw a new wave of militancy among engineering shop stewards, who met in Manchester immediately following the Manpower Conference to discuss 'food and manpower'.[209] A mass meeting of members of the ASE and other skilled engineering unions was held in Oldham to consider the government's threat to their exemption from conscription. A resolution was passed which stressed their patriotism – the matter should be dealt with in 'such a manner as will cause the least friction at home and avoid any delay in providing supplies to those fighting at the front' – but which also complained that the government had not made 'every effort … to comb out of munitions and engineering shops those men of military age who have sought such havens of protection with a view to escaping military service'.[210] In other words, 'dilutees' should be conscripted before skilled men. As James Hinton argued, 'because of the issues

---

205   Mossley Head Office Master Spinners to Head Office Spinners' Amalgamation, 14 December 1917. ACS/6/3/6 @ JRSC.
206   *Cotton Factory Times*, 22 December 1917.
207   *Manchester Evening News*, 7 January 1918.
208   *Times*, 27 February 1918.
209   *Ashton Reporter*, 5 January 1918.
210   *Manchester Guardian*, 7 January 1918.

over which it was fought', the engineering shop stewards movement 'tended to reinforce the craft character of the movement, and thus to prefigure its final defeat'.[211]

By now, the influence of the October Revolution in Russia was evident. One delegate at the Manchester meeting rhetorically asked the delegates: 'Who can say that this conference may not start a revolution? ... There is going to be a revolution in this country within a week or two'.[212] There was some justification for this delegate's excitement. In Manchester, a demonstration of striking munitions workers 'two miles' in length marched to the city hall to protest at the food situation.[213] Shop stewards in many parts of the country (though there is no evidence of such activity in our three towns) had organised mass meetings and demonstrations in support of the Bolsheviks and against continuation of the war.[214]

Ashton's weavers, alarmed by a report by a member who had probably been present at the January conference of shop stewards, resolved at their annual meeting that 'the civil population, particularly the poorer classes, are feeling the effects and horrors of war more and more every day, and unless there is an improvement in the supply and distribution of food there will be a revolt'. But this was no expression of revolutionary defeatism. The weavers hoped that 'authority will take steps to avoid such a "calamity" '.[215]

The engineering shop stewards were not able to rally support to resist the government. At their conference they had declared that they would 'actively resist the manpower proposals of the government'. Delegates were asked to find out what action workers in their districts would be prepared to take.[216] But to 'actively resist' would be to impede the war effort: thus, when testing opinion in Manchester and Sheffield, the delegates found that most 'were opposed to strike action'.[217] Confident that there would not be mass opposition to their manpower proposals, the government introduced a new Military Service Bill on the 14th of January. Crucially, the bill would give Geddes the power to cancel exemption certificates if he thought it necessary. The Bill received royal assent on the 6th of February.[218]

---

211   Hinton 1973, p. 212.
212   Kendall 1969, p. 165.
213   *Manchester Guardian*, 21 January 1918.
214   Hinton 1973, pp. 256–62.
215   *Ashton Reporter*, 26 January 1918.
216   Kendall 1969, p. 165.
217   Hinton 1973, p. 262.
218   Grieves 1988, p. 182.

The food crisis too was overcome without a 'revolt'. At the start of the year shortages – cheese consumption, for instance, in January was only 37 percent of what it had been in October 1916[219] – led to serious discontent. In Luton and Bedford in late January there were major protests against the decisions of local Food Control Committees. In Bedford 10,000 munitions workers protested.[220] In Ashton the food supply was only 'fifty % of normal'. There was 'no mutton, no rabbits, the supply of fish and fowl is small. English onions seem to have disappeared and there are only the higher priced foreign varieties. But rationing would ensure that everyone has some margarine'.[221] Men and women from Ashton and Oldham were among thousands of striking munitions workers who in the greater Manchester area 'downed tools for several hours' in a protest over food prices.[222] But consumption of most staples, bread in particular, stabilised in January and had begun to recover by the end of February.[223] There were still many complaints regarding shortages and prices. In Mossley (where the Food Control Committee had merged with Ashton's) there was 'considerable dissatisfaction' with the meat ration. It was said that the ration in the town was only half that in Oldham.[224] As late as July the decision of Ashton's Food Control Committee to succumb to pressure from farmers to increase the price of milk had 'to say the least, caused much dissatisfaction among consumers'.[225] But a national food crisis had been averted.

We noted earlier that the number of days lost in strikes had fallen sharply in the wake of the initially successful German offensive of spring 1918. But once the military situation had stabilised, underlying working class discontent led to renewed industrial unrest, notably in cotton general strikes in September and November. Industrial relations in the cotton trade had become volatile. Many workers were angered by falling real wages and apprehensive regarding the proposals of the CCB. By June, despite a 25 percent pay increase agreed in May, workers were worse off, due to working fewer hours. There were several disputes at Oldham mills regarding the application of the pay awards. At several mills cardroom workers had tendered strike notices 'without the authorisation of their officials'.[226] In Mossley, the employers at the

---

219   Gregory 2008, p. 214.
220   Waites 1987, p. 230.
221   *Ashton Reporter*, 26 January 1918.
222   *Cotton Factory Times*, 19 January 1918.
223   Gregory 2008, p. 215.
224   *Mossley and Saddleworth Reporter*, 16 March 1918.
225   *Ashton Reporter*, 13 July 1918.
226   *Cotton Factory Times*, 22 June 1918.

Atlantic Mill capitulated after a two-week strike caused by their refusal to honour the 25 percent increase.[227]

More ominously, from a government and employer point of view, there were signs of mounting shop steward influence. The Cardroom Executive passed a resolution 'denouncing and repudiating ... a few members who would injure the reputation, influence and power of the Amalgamation in future negotiations with the employer's associations'.[228] In their report for 1918, Oldham textile employers claimed that the 'extraordinary conditions created by the war furnished the man "agin" the government with plenty of opportunities for displaying his power'. Among the Operative Spinners 'the malcontents [were] strongly in evidence ... they have attempted to usurp among some sections of their members the functions of their accredited representatives'.[229] There is considerable evidence to support the employers' contention. The Spinners Shop Stewards met in conference in Manchester on the 20th of July and resolved (presumably in order that workers could go to where work was available) that 'official agreements' that do not 'recognise the right of every spinner to decide for himself the factory and district in which he shall work' should be rejected.[230] Shortly afterwards, a postcard was sent to the Spinners' Head Office urging officials to attend a meeting of Shop Stewards at the Star and Garter, threatening that 'if you are not there we shall most certainly oppose your committee man ... and mind you we shall beat him too. So beware if you don't come'.[231]

September's spinner's strike was caused by the decisions of the CCB.[232] When accepting May's pay increase, cotton workers had assumed that the CCB would continue to make payments for short-time working, as it had since taking the responsibility for allocating supplies of cotton. However, the CCB insisted that such payments could no longer be made. Further, the rota system would be abolished, raising the possibility that some workers would become permanently unemployed. In August, UTFWA accepted essentially unchanged proposals, but a spinners ballot produced an 81 percent vote in favour of a strike. In

---

227 *Mossley and Saddleworth Reporter*, 26 July 1918; *Mossley and Saddleworth Reporter*, 6 August 1918.
228 *Cotton Factory Times*, 22 June 1918.
229 In other words, the shop stewards had been attempting to bypass the union officials and appeal directly to the rank-and-file. ORTEA Annual Reports 1916–20, Report 1918, OLSA, AAN/1/1/2/3.
230 *Oldham Evening Chronicle*, 27 July 1918.
231 Filed with Oldham Spinners EC Minutes 1918, Meeting of 5 August 1918. TU/1/1/34 @ OLSA.
232 The analysis of the cause of the strike presented here is based on that in Fowler 1987c, pp. 151–2.

Oldham, the district which would be most affected by the new proposals, voting was nine to one in favour of a strike to 'enforce the continuation of the rota system ... and the payment of unemployment benefit'.[233]

When the War Cabinet discussed the unrest in the cotton trade it was with the belief that the Oldham shop stewards were responsible. Rather than use DORA to make the strike illegal, they forbade providing strike pay, assuming that this would lead to a swift return to work.[234] As governments and employers usually do, the Cabinet underestimated the importance of underlying causes and overestimated the influence of militants, preferring to believe that without the malign influence of the latter there would be peace and harmony in industry. The shop stewards, in Oldham in particular, but in other places too, were certainly a major factor in the unrest, but the fundamental cause was the privations of four years of war, exacerbated by the continued perception of an inequality of sacrifice. As Mullins rhetorically asked, could it be 'wondered that grave unrest exists amongst the operatives when it is seen reported in the public Press the princely dividends being paid to shareholders'.[235]

The CCB itself and the clearly widespread perception that union officials were more government agents than servants of the membership were also major factors stirring discontent. Judson, for instance, had told the influential *Manchester Evening News* prior to the August ballot of spinners that 'there would be no stoppage of work if he could help it'.[236] F.W. Birchenough, the Secretary of the Oldham branch of the spinners publically denounced the stewards for taking advantage of the 'high nervous tension created by the war to create revolt, discontent and disunity and taking advantage of every opportunity to improve their position economically'.[237]

The spinners' ballot was followed by notice that a strike would begin on the seventh of September. A deputation headed by Judson met the poacher turned gamekeeper David Shackleton in London on the 31st August. Shackleton had nothing to offer but bluster and threats. He pointed out 'in unmistakeable terms some of the powers the Government possessed and the penalties attaching to those who undertook to push the government too far'.[238] These threats prompted a week's postponement of the strike to seek further approval of strike action

---

233   Oldham Spinners EC Minutes 1918. Special EC 19 August 1918. TU/1/1/34 @ OLSA.
234   War Cabinet minutes, 13 September 1918. CAB 21/97 @ NAK.
235   Cardroom Amalgamation, Reports and Minutes January 1917–December 1920. Quarterly Report and Balance Sheet for the Quarter ending September 28th 1918. Report to District Officials from William Mullins, Secretary, and p. 5. TU/TEX/CARD/12 @ WCML.
236   *Manchester Evening News*, 17 August 1918.
237   *Manchester Guardian*, 31 August 1918.
238   Ibid.

from a Special Representative Meeting. Approval won, the strike began on the 14th of September.[239] It was solid; in Mossley, for instance, 'Not a single spindle has been running in the town this week'.[240] The usual condemnations of strike action were forthcoming, including from Annie Kenney, the prominent suffragette and former weaver, who endorsed Emmeline Pankhurst in attacking the strike and the shop stewards movement as the work of 'Bolshevism'.[241]

Strikers were generally indifferent to condemnations such as these. But what prompted a return to work after one week? Possibly it was an appeal from the Prime Minister. Lloyd George had written to the spinners' leadership beforehand to argue that a strike 'would severely interfere with the production of war material'. He appealed 'in the interests of the men who are fighting' that there should not be a strike. He offered an enquiry into the spinners' grievances and finally appealed to the 'patriotism of Lancashire men [which] has been tested in many fields, and has never yet failed'.[242] The appeal was referred to District Committees.[243] It may have been the appeal to the 'patriotism' of the spinners or the implication that the men at the front were being let down that did the trick. But no doubt an injunction forbidding, under the provisions of DORA, the payment of strike pay, played a part.[244] The enquiry sat in Manchester in early October, but was unable to resolve the spinners' grievances. A further, nine-day, strike in November was settled by a 50 percent increase in piece rates offered after management and employers were received by Lloyd George at 10 Downing St.[245]

One consequence, certainly in Oldham and doubtless more widely, of the handling of the unrest regarding the work of the CCB was profound distrust between the union officials and the shop stewards. Oldham's union officials met in between the two strikes of 1918. The 'Question of disloyal members [the shop stewards] was considered'. It was argued that the stewards 'were in many instances acting unconstitutionally ... It was in the interests of the association for there to be no creeping in at the back door ... concocting proposals in secrecy and springing them on the monthly meeting'. Some of those present 'wanted the shop stewards put in their place'. It was resolved to recommend to the membership 'not to elect any official of the shop stewards society to the

---

239 Spinners' Amalgamation Quarterly EC Report 31/10/18. ACS/1/26 @ JRSC.
240 *Mossley and Saddleworth Reporter*, 21 September 1918.
241 *Cotton Factory Times*, 20 September 1918.
242 Cited in Fowler 1987c, p. 153.
243 Spinners' Amalgamation, EC Quarterly Report 31/10/18. ACS/1/26 @ JRSC.
244 *Manchester Guardian*, 12 September 1918.
245 Spinners' Amalgamation, EC Minutes, undated. ACS/1/26 @ JRSC.

membership of any committee within this association'.²⁴⁶ We shall see in the next chapter that these unresolved antagonisms were to play a major part in the cotton general strike of July 1919.

Towards the end of the war, Tom Mann, veteran Marxist and leader of the great London dock strike of 1889, and soon to become a founder member of the Communist Party, spoke at an Oldham street meeting. He exhorted his listeners to emulate the Bolsheviks who were 'setting an example to the world. The capitalists of this county feared that if the Russians succeeded we would want to copy them'.²⁴⁷ But the evidence strongly shows that far more representative of the temper of the great majority of British working class people in 1918 were W.C. Robinson and Oldham's T&LC. Shortly before the end of the war, Oldham ILP had written to Robinson, arguing that the government should respond positively to Austria-Hungary's peace overtures. Robinson was not in favour: he wanted 'complete victory for the allies, such as will crush militarism for ever'. He was opposed to any 'patched-up solution'.²⁴⁸ When it had become apparent that Germany was on the verge of collapse, the delegates to OT&LC congratulated the 'magnificent achievements on sea and land' of the armed forces 'in the fight for world-wide freedom and for the crushing of militarism'.²⁴⁹

The ambition of the great majority of Britain's workers was to obtain a bigger slice of the capitalist cake. The war had done little, in the vast majority of cases, to foster a wider ambition than that expressed in 1916 by Mullins: 'now is a time that employers can show they mean what they say, that in times of prosperity the operatives should share in that prosperity'.²⁵⁰ By the end of 1918 such a share, as much in social reform as in wages and conditions, was on offer. But the semi-settlement between labour and capital which emerged from the First World War was fragile and shallow, and was threatened by a grave postwar crisis, notably in the 'Red Year' of 1919.

---

246 Oldham Spinners EC Minutes 1918. Yearly conference of District Chairmen, Secretaries and EC delegates 26 October 1918. TU/1/1/34 @ OLSA.
247 *Oldham Weekly Chronicle*, 10 August 1918.
248 *Oldham Weekly Chronicle*, 5 October 1918.
249 Trades and Labour Council Minutes 1918–21. Representative Meeting, 15 October 1918. M17/1/4 @ OLSA.
250 Cardroom Amalgamation, Reports and Minutes March 1913–December 1916. Quarterly Report and Balance Sheet for the Quarter ending 25 March 1916. Report to District Officials from William Mullins, Secretary, p. 5. TU/TEX/CARD/12 @ WCML.

CHAPTER 3

1919: a 'Red Year'?

The First World War came to an abrupt end in November 1918. Neither imperial alliance had been able to militarily defeat the other. Germany had been compelled to seek an armistice after the collapse of its allies, Austria-Hungary and Turkey, and when it seemed that German workers might do in 1918 what Russian workers and peasants had done in 1917. Mass social unrest, and divisions in Germany's rulers, had sparked a democratic revolution which by early November had forced the abdication of the Kaiser and the proclamation of a republic. The armistice commenced on November the 11th. An unsuccessful attempt at proletarian revolution in Germany swiftly followed.[1]

In Britain, in contrast to these tumultuous and momentous events, the armistice was greeted and followed with jubilation. The suffering and deprivations of four years of war had not undermined the fundamental patriotism and moderation of most members of the labour movement or of the working class. A general election called shortly after the armistice returned a huge majority for the coalition (which Labour had left). Much more significant than the coalition's victory is that the 'coupon'[2] general election was fought on a greatly expanded electorate, the result of that year's Representation of the People Act. This was perhaps the most significant reform of the early twentieth century. By greatly increasing the political competition for working class votes it ensured that henceforth social-imperialism would become much more fundamental to British society and politics. All the main parties offered substantial social reform during election campaign. But the interwar period saw a persistent tension between the attempts of the bourgeoisie to ensure social peace at home and their efforts to resolve at the expense of the working class the series of economic crises which followed the end of a short-lived postwar economic boom.

---

1 For a vivid, if contentious, account of these events, see Haffner 1973.
2 Authorised coalition candidates were issued with a letter (dubbed by Asquith as a political 'coupon') signed jointly by Lloyd George and Bonar Law, the Conservative leader, that they were the recognised government candidates.

1 A Revolutionary Situation in Britain?

But what of the serious social unrest – mutinies in the army, mass strikes by railway workers, cotton workers, miners and even police, and troops on the streets of Glasgow – of the 'Red Year' 1919? Had Britain been on the cusp of revolution? Some contemporaries certainly thought so. Walter Long, for instance, the First Lord of the Admiralty, sent Lloyd George a series of alarmist memos. One such, based on a report from an anonymous secret service agent, claimed that in 1919 there were 'more Bolsheviks per head of population in Britain than there had been in Russia'.[3] Even if this highly dubious claim had been true, one crucial factor differentiating Britain from both Russia and Germany was the absence of a revolutionary crisis in the ruling class. The situation in Britain was not remotely comparable to the political tempests which had forced the abdications of the Tsar and the Kaiser. Britain had emerged from war victorious, if weakened and heavily in debt, especially to the United States of America, but with a stable and tempered ruling class and sufficient resources to allow the concessions to the working class discussed here.

The evidence from Lancashire strongly suggests that those historians sceptical of revolutionary possibilities are correct.[4] Which is not to say that there were no revolutionaries in Lancashire. We have seen that in Manchester, Oldham and Ashton and doubtless other places, some militants, especially among the shop stewards, responded to revolutionary ideas emanating from such places as Moscow and Glasgow. Such ideas continued to resonate among some enthusiasts in the early postwar period. In Oldham, for instance, an 'extremist' minority on the T&LC refused to participate in the town's 'Peace Day' celebrations, held to celebrate the signing of the Treaty of Versailles. They thought these celebrations inappropriate while the army was 'fighting in Russia' (presumably a reference to Britain's anti-Bolshevik intervention there).[5] A fiery

---

3 Wrigley 1993, p. 262.
4 Perhaps taking their inspiration from the recollections of Willy Gallacher (1936), Red Clydesider and founder member of the Communist Party, historians of a leftist outlook have argued that the unrest on the Clyde posed a revolutionary challenge to capital. See (e.g.) Foster 1993. Sceptics such as Ian McLean (1983) disagree, arguing that the great majority on the Clyde were not opposed to the war and did not aspire to overthrow the social order. Hinton (1973), while supportive of the argument that unprecedented levels of unrest existed on the Clyde, argues that nationally only a small minority of industrial workers had revolutionary ideas.
5 *Oldham Weekly Chronicle*, 18 July 1919. This may well have been part of the 'hands off Russia' campaign organised by the BSP and other Marxists. Many of them, such as William Paul, became founder members of the CP. But how militant was the typical BSP member? If the

by-election leaflet circulated in Hurst in 1919 (its biblical imagery suggestive of the hand of the Reverend Cummings) claimed that the election involved 'the preaching of the Kingdom of God ... the end of the injustice of landlordism, and the fraud of capitalism; the putting down of the mighty from their seats and the exalting of the humble and weak' and denounced the 'political terrorism' of the mill-owners on their workers.[6]

But such people were part of a small minority. While militants had some influence, the unrest of 1919, certainly in Lancashire, did not signify a mass desire to overthrow capitalism. When the Labour candidate in an Oldham municipal by-election meeting argued that 'the methods adopted' in such places as the Clyde 'were not the methods calculated to give to the working classes those reforms for which they were asking' his remarks were greeted with applause.[7] Almost certainly more representative of labour movement opinion in Lancashire than the 'extremists' was the refusal of spinners at the Commercial Mill in Oldham to work with a piecer because he had been a 'conchie'. The piecer was sacked.[8] Similarly, there were disturbances in Greenfield, midway between Ashton and Oldham, when it was thought that members of Greenfield Socialist Institute were to welcome home in procession released conscientious objectors. Members of the NFDDSS organised a counter-demonstration. According to the *Chronicle*, 'Conchies' and their supporters bearing 'red flags' were 'pelted with eggs'. Some were 'seized and ducked in the river'.[9] The NFDDSS, singularly unappreciative of the social advances made by women in the course of the war, also agitated in Oldham for the dismissal of women tram conductors: its members had a 'great grievance with the number of girls at present working on the Oldham tramways. In other towns lady conductors had died out and they ought to do so in Oldham'.[10]

---

    minutes of the Openshaw branch are any guide, not very. The minutes for 1919 contain no reference to strikes in this year of serious industrial unrest. The activities most mentioned are dances, whist drives and so on. CPA, CP/ORG/MISC/3/5 @ PHM.
6   *Hurst Election Gazette*, April 1919. DD94/8 @ TLSAC.
7   *Oldham Weekly Chronicle*, 15 March 1919.
8   Oldham Spinners EC Minutes 1918, Special Meeting of 27 January 1919. TU/1/1/34 @ OLSA.
9   *Oldham Weekly Chronicle*, 4 May 1919. The paper subsequently published a letter from the Institute saying that it was a May Day meeting, which had had 'absolutely no connection' with conscientious objectors, which had been attacked. *Oldham Weekly Chronicle*, 11 May 1919. 'Ducking' seems to have been a common tactic of the Federation. 'Stop the War' hecklers were threatened with such at its inaugural meeting In Victoria Park, East London. Burnham 2014, p. 31.
10 *Oldham Weekly Chronicle*, 2 August 1919. A marked feature of the early postwar period was a campaign to pressurise women, having done their duty in wartime industry, to go back to the home and make way for the men returning from the war. See, for instance, Bed-

Even allowing for probable exaggeration by the local press, the 'dense crowds' which in the spring of 1920 lined the streets of overwhelmingly working class Ashton to welcome home from the war the 22nd. Battalion of the Manchester Regiment were probably representative of working class opinion. The soldiers marched in procession through the town led by Hurst brass band.[11] The war had produced a sea change in the ideology and politics of many working class people. But the change was not a turn to revolution;[12] it was a turn away from the old parties of the bourgeoisie, the Tories and the Liberals, to the emphatically constitutionalist Labour Party, to a party which offered, as we shall see, substantial social reform. After the General Election of 1918 Labour became the main opposition party. In 1924 it took office for the first time. In the first postwar municipal elections, those of 1919, it made major gains.

Before considering the general election and postwar events, we should consider why Labour's electoral prospects had been so transformed since 1914. In the December 1910 general election, the last before that of 1918, the party had won 42 seats, an improvement on 1906, but there was little to suggest that Labour, especially given its dependence on Liberal patronage (under the terms of the electoral pact concluded with the Liberals in 1903, of the 50 Labour candidates of 1906, 31 were unopposed by the Liberals[13]) could break out of its third-party status.

2   Expanding the Franchise: Suffragettes, Suffragists and the Labour Party

In the first half of the nineteenth century the British bourgeoisie had fiercely and forcibly resisted demands that working class people should have the vote. But since then a combination of working class agitation and an increasing con-

---

doe 1989. The continued employment of women as tram conductors led to serious unrest in several towns and cities in 1920. In Bristol, for instance, discharged and unemployed soldiers and sailors threatened the women. Trams were vandalised. All the women were sacked. Kelly and Richardson 1996, p. 220.

11   *Ashton Reporter*, 24 May 1920.
12   That the postwar unrest in Britain was not to be compared with that in revolutionary Germany is demonstrated by the failure of the British Communist Party to attract more than a tiny number of adherents. On its foundation in 1920, the party claimed 5,125 members. In February 1922, at the end of the postwar crisis, it had 3,970 members. Thorpe 2000, p. 284. In sharp contrast, the German Party at the end of 1919 had 106,656 members, 449,700 members at the start of 1921, and 218,195 members in September 1922. Fowkes 1984, p. 204.
13   Pugh 1993, p. 122.

fidence among the ruling class that workers would use their vote 'responsibly', in other words not significantly encroach on the rights of property, had led to reforms which had given the vote to the 'respectable' majority of working men, the householders.[14] After these reforms in Ashton and Oldham, for instance, still only around 60 percent of adult men had the vote.[15] No women had the parliamentary franchise. But the pre-war campaign of the WSPU, continued campaigning by the NUWSS and the contribution of working class men and women to the war effort, made universal adult suffrage a cause whose time had come.

The pre-war labour movement had been relatively unconcerned by the restricted franchise, doubtless because the typical activist was a male householder who had the vote, tended to assume that excluded men, lacking his own assumed enlightenment, would vote Tory, and who was opposed to votes for women. Ashton Trades Council, for instance, had been for many years unresponsive to appeals for support from the local women's suffrage society. Many Labour women too, Margaret Bondfield for instance, had either opposed or been indifferent to reform, assuming that the most probable reform would enfranchise middle class but not working class women, and thus bolster the Conservative and Liberal parties. Of course, not all members of the movement were indifferent to the cause. The ILP had long been committed to universal suffrage. In Manchester, for instance, the Party campaigned with the NUWSS on the matter.[16] And in 1910, the Labour Party, in response to the constitutional crisis of that year, which we shall consider later, and fearful that the Liberals might accede to the WSPU's demand that the parliamentary franchise be extended to women on the same basis as men, included a demand for adult suffrage in its manifesto for that year's January General Election.[17]

In 1912 the NUWSS decided to support Labour, as the party most likely to deliver votes for women. But suffrage reform remained a low priority for most labour activists.[18] There is relatively little on the matter in the voluminous files on the WEWNC at the PHM. Though, as we have seen, the committee raised various matters of concern to working women, it seems to have initially assumed that to campaign for votes for women would be diversionary.

---

14   See Conacher 1971.
15   Clarke 1977, p. 427. Mossley was part of the Prestwich constituency: discrete figures are not available, but it can be assumed that roughly the same proportion of men had the vote as in Ashton and Oldham.
16   Liddington and Norris 1978, pp. 189, 213.
17   Labour Party 1910 General Election Manifesto in Dale (ed.) 1962, p. 14. The 1900 manifesto had included this demand, but the 1906 manifesto had not.
18   In Holmfirth, in the West Riding of Yorkshire, for instance, the 'local Labour Party was reluctant even to share committee rooms with NUWSS organisers'. Liddington 2006, p. 264.

Middleton claimed as much in a letter to Sylvia Pankhurst. 'I hold very strongly', he insisted, 'that no move should be made at present to renew the public aspect of the suffrage agitation. Such action would, I think, be very premature, and would have exactly the contrary effect to that which we all desire'.[19]

But the demand for suffrage reform was gaining support. The Women's International League for Peace and Freedom claimed that thousands of men and women attended a Glasgow pro-adult suffrage open air rally in July 1916 and that in Oldham two open-air meetings were to be held in September and a public meeting in October.[20] A year or so later, Ashton and Stalybridge Women's Suffrage Society, resumed its activities after three years dormancy. At a works meeting of women munitions workers held by the Society, nearly all declared themselves 'in favour of women's suffrage'.[21]

Support for an extension of the franchise must have been bolstered by the considerable wartime increase in the number of women working in industry and joining unions. The number of women in trade unions increased from 357,956 (288,630 of them in the cotton trade, where even before the war, the NUWSS had built up substantial support for votes for women) in 1914 to 1,086,000 (423,000 in cotton) in 1918.[22] Perhaps responding to this influx of women, Robinson of UTFWA argued at its 1916 conference that in his view there should be 'manhood and womanhood suffrage. If these young men and women workers are ready to sacrifice their all for their country, then they should have the full right of citizenship in the country they have so splendidly defended'.[23]

Bowing to the prevailing wind, Middleton, along with George Lansbury and Margaret Bondfield, joined the leadership of the National Council for Adult Suffrage on its formation in October 1916. Rank-and-file labour movement activists also began to declare in favour of an extension of the franchise. In February 1917 the EC of Oldham T&LC resolved to be represented at a conference on electoral reform and to support reform. In December the same year, in response to a letter from the Manchester & District Federation of Women's Suffrage Societies on the municipal franchise, the T&LC resolved that women should have this franchise.[24] In the summer the Weavers' Amalgamation agreed to a request from

---

19   Middleton to Pankhurst, 13 December 1915. WNC/32/7/8 @ PHM.
20   *Women's International League Monthly Newssheet September 1916.* WEWNC ephemera. WNC/32/7/8 @ PHM.
21   Report of Annual meeting of Ashton and Stalybridge Women's Suffrage Society. DD18/2 @ TLSAC.
22   Drake 1920, p. 89.
23   *Ashton Reporter*, 4 August 1916.
24   Oldham T&LC Minutes 1916–18. ECs of 27 February 1017 and 29 October 1917. M17/1/3 @ OLSA.

the Labour Party to attend a conference 'to consider the new law relating to the enfranchisement of women'.²⁵

Parallel with and clearly influenced by mass sentiment, a ruling class consensus that there should be franchise reform emerged during the war. It began to become unthinkable that the young working class men who had demonstrated their patriotism at the front should not have the vote – as many, perhaps most of them would not under the existing property qualification – at the first postwar election. By extension, an assumption grew that women's participation in war work should qualify at least some women for the vote. In early 1917 a 'memorial' (a petition) supporting women's suffrage, signed, the organisers were anxious to stress, not by the 'general public' but by 'representatives and influential people' from many Lancashire, Cheshire and Derbyshire constituencies, including Ashton and Oldham, many of them 'before the experience of war ... indifferent, even hostile' to women's suffrage, but now in favour, was being prepared for submission to the Prime Minister. As well as businessmen, university professors, clergymen, lawyers, doctors and the like, the petition was endorsed by '341 officials of trade unions and trades councils ... all the trade unions representing organised women munitions workers and the most important trades in this area affected by women's labour'.²⁶

Responding to public opinion and sensing political advantage, the coalition parties established a Speaker's Conference on franchise reform, which reported to parliament in January 1917. The consequent Representation of the People Act of January 1918 gave the parliamentary franchise to men at 21 and women who were ratepayers or the wives of ratepayers at 30 years of age (this leap towards universal adult suffrage was completed in 1928 when further legislation gave the vote to women at 21).

By 1918 Labour's electoral prospects had been transformed. Nearly all main trade unions were affiliated to and providing funds for the party. The enormous increase in the mostly working class parliamentary electorate from 8 to 21 million (in Ashton, for instance, it had increased by 163.4 percent, from 7,913 to 20,839²⁷) and the growth of wartime radicalism were two major factors in Labour's advance.²⁸ A split Liberal Party, which divided the Liberal vote between the Lloyd-George Liberals within the coalition and the Asquithian Liberals without, was another factor. Perhaps most importantly, the labour

---

25   Minutes of the CC of the Weavers' Amalgamation, 29 June 1917. TU/weavers/070 @ WCML.
26   *Manchester Guardian*, 25 January 1917.
27   Calculation based on statistics in *Ashton Reporter*, 22 June 1918.
28   See McKibbin 1994 and Turner 1992 for discussions of the relative importance of these two factors.

movement's wartime transition, enshrined in a new political platform ('programme' is something which doctrinaire continental socialists had), from a movement mainly concerned with the narrow interests of trade unionists to one which aimed to fight for the interests of all working class people, male and female, skilled and unskilled, organised and unorganised, meant that Labour was able to take advantage of pent-up working class demands for social reform in the General Election of 1918. On the eve of the election the cotton unions succinctly expressed Lancashire labour opinion: 'The Labour Party is the only party which knows and understands the needs of labour [it stands] for the abolition of the Poor Law and the creation of a Ministry of Health'.[29]

3 Labourists, Feminists and Socialists: Labour's New Platform

For a short while after its conferences of February 1918, adjourned from January, and June 1918, Labour was arguably a socialist party, or at least a party with a socialist platform. Socialism had burst out of the labourist bonds which had contained it since 1906. But this socialist impulse did not last long: by the time of the general election it had been swamped by familiar Fabian and labourist perspectives. The winter conference had adopted a new constitution, clause four of which committed the party to fighting for the 'common ownership of the means of production, distribution and exchange'.[30] The summer conference adopted *Labour and the New Social Order*, a radical programme for postwar reconstruction. The tone of the conference was captured in the demand of an UTFWA delegate who argued that postwar reconstruction should not be a 'patchwork gerrymandering of the anarchic individualism and profiteering of pre-war time' but the 'gradual building up of a new social order based ... not on the domination of subject classes, subject races or a subject sex but on cooperation'.[31] Of course, implementing Clause Four could mean nothing more than state capitalist ownership of key industries in a capitalist economy, which is what Labour advocated in the election of 1918 and was to introduce between 1945 and 1951.

To what extent was the wartime transformation of the labour movement – a question raised in Chapter 1 – due to the wartime influx of women into industry and the labour movement? To what extent did this influx change men's

---

29 UTFWA circular of 1 December 1918, DDX/1123/4/7 @ LROP.
30 Thorpe 1997, p. 44.
31 Labour Party, *Report to the Eighteenth Annual Conference, June 1918* (London, 1918), p. 43.

views on the proper role of women? And what role did women already in the labour movement play?

We should not ignore though that majority of women who did not enter the industrial labour force and were not part of the labour movement. It is usual in left circles to regard such women as a drag on progress, and no doubt some of them were. But it must be assumed that many of these women were affected by the wartime mood that there must be social improvements after the war. There would have been innumerable political conversations and discussions involving women in industry, the labour movement and the home.

Nor should we forget that some Labour women – in the ILP[32] and particularly in the WLL – had helped to lay the foundations for change even before the war. By 1914 the WLL (which was particularly active in Lancashire[33]) had had some moderate success in persuading trade unionists to take more seriously questions of social reform. Though the national LP had refused affiliation to the Women's Labour League until 1908, 'locally, *de facto* recognition had [already] been achieved. The League sent delegates to local party meetings, arranged joint events, shared platforms at public meetings'.[34] No doubt helped by such activities as making collections in Oldham (where the League had held its district conference) and elsewhere to aid those locked out in the great Dublin lockout of 1913–14,[35] it was able to report at its annual conference of 1914 that 245 labour movement organisations had adopted a model resolution in favour of baby clinics sent to them by the League.[36]

Probably to avoid a split in its ranks, when war erupted the WLL nationally declined to take a stance. But the Oldham branch (where a prominent member was Mary Clynes, the wife of J.R. Clynes) seems to have taken a pro-war stance. Early in 1915, its Secretary, Miss Chefflin, participated in an unsuccessful deputation of women from a broad spectrum of opinion, including the arch-imperialist Primrose League, to press on Oldham Council's Health Committee their case for the provision of a maternity centre. Chefflin adopted an impec-

---

32 The WSPU had emerged from the ILP. See Liddington and Norris 1978.
33 No doubt a consequence of the disproportionate number of women working in industry in Lancashire, the WLL had 32 branches in the county, compared to 28 in London. Collette 1989, p. 61.
34 Collette 1989, p. 38.
35 From August 1913 to January 1914, Dublin's employers locked out thousands of transport and general labourers trying to organise in the Irish Transport and General Workers Union. The TUC in Britain refused to organise sympathetic strikes. The labourers were driven back to work by hunger.
36 Women's Labour League, *Report of Annual Conference of Women's Labour League, Glasgow, 16 February 1914* (London, 1916), pp. 8, 27, 11.

cably social-imperialist case for reform: she insisted that 'the whole thing is a history of a military problem. We cannot get soldiers readymade ... at the time of the South African War, the number of men who presented themselves and were suffering from the effects of rickets in infancy were so large'.[37]

During the war approximately 1,600,000 women had joined the national labour force,[38] mainly to replace men on active service. In consequence, women had begun to play a greater role in the labour movement. We have seen that there was an influx of women into trade unions. In our three towns, women began to take up official positions in the labour movement. In the first year of war, for instance, Ashton weavers appointed the first woman collector of dues. Edith Riding was reported to be 'giving every satisfaction'. Several other women had applied to become collectors.[39] In 1917, Ashton Power-Loom Weavers elected the first woman member of their committee and reported that it 'is expected that several others will be appointed to fill up the vacancies caused by the male members enlisting'.[40] The number of female delegates to Ashton Trades Council increased. One of these delegates, Miss Thompson of the Railway Clerks, frequently expressed opinions which probably would not have endeared her to the more staid members of the council. In response to a letter from the Workers Educational Association (WEA) inviting the Council to affiliate, a request which evinced little enthusiasm from most, Thompson declared that while through state education the workers were given 'the governing class point of view' the purpose of the WEA was to teach the workers 'how to look after their own interests'.[41]

It is impossible to quantify the effect these women had on the wartime labour movement, but they, and such women as Alice Smith of the *Cotton Factory Times*, Margaret Bondfield, Marion Phillips and Ellen Wilkinson, would surely have shifted the centre of gravity of the movement towards reform, would surely have chipped away at the movement's economism, as would have

---

37 *Oldham Weekly Chronicle*, 23 January 1915. Women's Labour League, *Report of Annual Conference of Women's Labour League* (Bristol, 1915), p. 10.

38 See Braybon and Summerfield 1987 and Thom 1988. An unknown number of women moved from one occupation to another, particularly from domestic service to munitions. In Ashton, the number of women employed in domestic service declined from 11 percent of the female labour force in 1901 to 1.6 percent in 1921. Almost certainly, this decline mostly occurred in the war years. 1901 Census, Table 35A, Grouped Occupations (His Majesty's Stationery Office (HMSO) 1903) and 1921 Census. Table 16, Occupations by Sex of Urban Areas with more than 20,000 Population (HMSO 1923).

39 *Cotton Factory Times*, 25 June 1915.

40 Minutes of Ashton Power-Loom Weavers, 9 February 1917. TU/Weavers/070 @ WCML.

41 *Ashton Reporter*, 16 October 1915.

many of the hundreds of thousands of unknown women newly working in spinning rooms, munitions factories and on trams.

If such influence is impossible to quantify, it is nevertheless discernible. Oldham T&LC, for instance, impressed by the work of the WLL in fighting rent increases,[42] unanimously adopted in 1916 a WLL model resolution on the provision of child welfare clinics, arguing that it was 'convinced that we ought to do everything in our power to preserve the child life of the borough'.[43] Later in the war, after the Local Government Board offered funds to local authorities to provide such facilities, Farr cited the work of the WLL in urging Mossley Council to open a maternity clinic. Twenty-three mothers and their babies – one of whom said she would not have missed it 'for a sovereign' – attended the first session, held in November 1917.[44]

It is discernible also in a report by the *Joint Committee* [of the TUC and the Labour Party] *on Labour Problems after the War*. The report implicitly assumed that many women would not resume their old primarily domestic role by advocating equal pay and a unionisation drive among women workers.[45] In March 1916, similar conclusions emerged from a conference on *The Position of Women in the Readjustment of Labour after the War*. The conference, chaired by Margaret Ashton,[46] was convened by the Manchester Women's War Interests Committee, which, according to Alison Ronan, had had some success in changing labour movement attitudes.[47] ASE delegates present – one of whom stated that after the war the engineers were going to 'weed out the women' – insisted that women 'dilutees' would have to leave the engineering trade at the end of the war. Most (but implicitly not all) of the male delegates were said to share this view.[48] But the *Herald*'s assumption of 1915 that all women would have to 'give way' to returning men was beginning to be replaced by an acceptance that some women would be retained. The conference resolved that women kept on should receive equal pay and that those who were laid off should receive

---

42 Women's Labour League, *Report of Annual Conference of Women's Labour League, Glasgow*, 25 January 1916 p. 15.
43 Oldham T&LC Council Minutes 1916–18. Representative Meeting, 4 April 1916. M17/1/3 @ OLSA.
44 Mossley and Saddleworth Reporter, 17 November 1917.
45 Horne 1991, p. 230.
46 Ashton was a prominent women's suffragist. In 1908 she had become the first female councillor on Manchester City Council. In 1914 she had resigned from the NUWSS in protest at its pro-war stance.
47 Ronan 2013.
48 *Manchester Guardian*, 20 March 1916.

'adequate out of work benefit',[49] implicitly rejecting the orthodox view that married women should be maintained by their husbands.

Equally suggestive of a change in the attitudes of many working men is the discussion at Ashton Trades Council in the spring of 1917 of a conference held in Manchester on women war workers. One delegate, Albert Taylor, revealed his prejudices by claiming that the women present had not been 'of the working classes, but faddists and feminists who were concerned only as to how they could get women into comparatively well-paid jobs and were unconcerned as to how the men fared when the war was over'. Taylor reported approvingly that many men present at the conference had said that while they would teach women skilled work, they 'would not tolerate them at all after the war'. Taylor's remarks were greeted with 'Cries of "shame"'.[50] We also have Judson's rebuke of Clynes in 1919, a rebuke he almost certainly would not have made in 1914. Clynes had recently asserted that women didn't eat as much as men and therefore should not get equal pay. Presiding over a meeting of the Ashton Women's Citizens Association on the issue of equal pay, Judson said that Clynes should tell the women of Lancashire 'who had to toil in the factories from 6 am to 5.30pm, that they did not need to eat as much as a clerk who worked six or seven hours a day'.[51] Finally, a suggestive piece of evidence is the correlation between the comparative absence of women in Mossley's spinning rooms (15 percent) compared to those of Ashton and Oldham (58 percent and 52 percent respectively[52]) and the unreconstructed economism, discussed below, of that town's spinners, manifest in the municipal elections of 1919.

In summary, the evidence is thin and largely circumstantial. It certainly does not indicate that male chauvinism in the labour movement had withered in the course of the war (rather, the determined attempts in 1917–19 of Bolton's male weavers to prevent Alice Foley from becoming their Assistant Secretary suggest that male chauvinism was still entrenched in the movement).[53] It is merely

---

49 The resolutions are in the files of the WEWNC, as are letters from local Labour parties informing the committee of resolutions passed modelled on the resolutions of the conference. WNC/15/1 @ PHM.
50 *Ashton Reporter*, 8 April 1917.
51 *Ashton Reporter*, 22 February 1919.
52 The data for Oldham are taken from Oldham Spinners EC Minutes 1919, Special Meeting, 5 August 1919. TU/1/1/35 @ OLSA. For Ashton and Mossley they are taken from the 1921 census Table 16, Occupations by Sex of Urban Areas with more than 20,000 Population and Table 17, Occupations by Sex of Urban Areas with less than 20,000 Population (HMSO 1921). The proportion of women would almost certainly have been higher in 1919, given postwar pressures on women to return to the home.
53 Whitehead 1987. See Foley's autobiography (Foley 1973) for an account of her early life.

suggested that women probably did play a significant role in shaping Labour's postwar programme and that more men than in 1914 accepted a greater role for women outside the home.

In *Labour and the New Social Order*, Labour asserted that its proposals for reconstruction were proposals which recognised 'in the present world catastrophe ... the collapse of a distinctive industrial civilisation, which the workers will not seek to reconstruct'. It was not a programme for the reconstruction of 'this or that piece of social machinery', but of 'society itself'. Based on an assumption that the ills of society were due to the 'individualist system of capitalist production, based on the private ownership ... of land and capital',[54] it demanded the 'progressive elimination from the control of industry of the private capitalist'[55] and that the 'surplus' arising from production should be used for 'the common good'.[56] The millenarian, anti-capitalist perspectives of the 'collapse' of existing society, to be replaced by socialism, were patently a product of the unprecedented upheaval and carnage of 1914–18, a reflection of the radical wartime mood of many labour movement activists. They did not survive into the peace.

The anti-capitalism of *Labour and the New Social Order* was in any case one of tone more than content. Even for 1918, the specific proposals of the programme were not especially radical. But to many they doubtless appeared to be so. They represented a more fundamental break with *laissez-faire* ideology than the reforms of earlier decades, but were – except for proposals for nationalisation – recognisably in that tradition, more particularly of the reforms of the pre-war Liberal administration. Among Labour's demands were: that government should find work 'for every willing worker' or, in the absence of work, 'adequate maintenance'; proportional representation and the 'complete abolition of the House of Lords'; the 'immediate nationalisation' of the railways, the mines and electricity generation; the abolition of fees for secondary education; and that a million houses with 'four or five rooms, larder, scullery, cupboards and fitted bath' be built by local authorities in the first two-to-three years of peace 'with capital supplied free of interest' by central government.[57] When enacted, as they mostly were in one way or another over the next 40 years,

---

54 Labour Party, *Labour and the New Social Order a Report on Reconstruction* (London, 1918), p. 3.
55 Labour Party, *Labour and the New Social Order a Report on Reconstruction* (London, 1918), p. 12.
56 Labour Party, *Labour and the New Social Order a Report on Reconstruction* (London, 1918), p. 21.
57 Labour Party, *Labour and the New Social Order a Report on Reconstruction* (London, 1918), pp. 9–10, 12, 15–16.

by governments of various political hues, these reforms resulted in a reformed capitalism, a more humane and ordered capitalism, but capitalism nevertheless.

4 The Labour Movement in the General Election of 1918

The net effect of Labour's new-found socialism on the activists of 1918 is impossible to calculate. We must assume that it inspired and attracted socialists and those radicalised by the war: on the other hand, it must have repelled many of the old hands. Unlike Oldham T&LC, until 1918 Ashton's trades council had maintained a persistent, if weakening, anti-socialist, anti-politics stance. In 1900, it had received a circular from the newly-formed LRC inviting affiliation. The council's Secretary replied that he would 'raise the matter at the next meeting' and asked for 50 copies of the LRC's conference report. The committee's invitation and several others over the next few years were declined.[58] In 1905, a mild pro-Labour wind was suggested by a letter from the council to the Labour Party asking for a list of parliamentary labour candidates to include in their yearbook, stating that 'socialist candidates are included in the word Labour'.[59] But even as late as 1918, advocates of affiliation to the Labour Party had to overcome bitter opposition.

According to the *Reporter*, the meeting in 1918 which finally decided to support Labour was 'stormy'. The 'discussion became so lively that the chairman had the greatest difficulty in conducting the business'. So stormy was the meeting that it led to the resignation of Edgar, the council's Secretary.[60] There were two extremely contentious issues confronting the delegates. A decision had been taken earlier in the year to field a candidate in the next general election, but should the candidate be a Labour Party candidate or a trades council candidate? Secondly, should the local branches of the anti-war ILP and the BSP be invited to the April conference which would decide on the nature of the candidate? Delegate Saxon declared that he was 'an Englishman before he was a socialist', a socialist candidate would lose a hundred votes for every one gained because of the socialists' record on the war.

Edgar was firmly of the old school. He maintained that the candidate must be a trades council candidate. His (almost certainly it would be a male candidate) politics – whether they be socialist, Liberal or Conservative – didn't matter.

---

58   Labour Party Archive (LPA), LRC.1/8; LRC.3/6; LRC.3/7; LRC.17/22 @ PHM.
59   LPA, LRC.25/5 @ PHM.
60   *Ashton Reporter*, 9 March 1918.

Only trade unionists should take the decision – admission to the conference should be by union card. As for the BSP and the ILP, well, he had been to a recent meeting attended by 'long-haired gentry' at which the *Red Flag* had been sung.[61] These people had opposed the war. Before associating with such people the delegates should look at Russia, 'bleeding and torn, cursed by the very men who should have been her saviour'. Edgar must have had considerable support given the 'stormy' nature of the proceedings, but it was decided to invite the BSP and the ILP to attend the conference, whereupon Edgar resigned. He refused a request to withdraw his resignation, stating that he would not write to the BSP or the ILP 'under any circumstances'.[62]

Organisations (including delegates from Ashton Co-operative Society, the ILP and the BSP) interested in forming an Ashton Labour Party attended the April conference. Several contributions demonstrate the distance travelled since 1914. Judson welcomed the extension of the franchise and 'hoped no steps would be left untaken to induce the women to throw in their lot with the Labour Party'. Temple of the National Union of Railway Workers (NUR) criticised the 'craft mentality' of many trades council members and urged it to organise all workers.[63]

Further meetings decided that the 'objectives' of Ashton Labour Party should include Clause Four of Labour's new constitution and a commitment 'to promote the political, social and economic emancipation of the people, and more particularly of those who depend directly upon their own exertions by hand or by brain for the means of life'.[64] It was also decided, perhaps a concession to the old school, that rather than found a separate Labour Party branch, the council would become a trades and labour council (hereinafter referred to Ashton T&LC).[65]

A branch of the Labour Party was founded in Mossley too in 1918. There had been a branch of the ILP in the town since 1893. But, even allowing for Farr's work on the town council, it had been more a social club than a political party.

---

61 Such suspicion of intellectuals was common among trade unionists. At the February 1918 special conference of the Labour Party, which adopted a new constitution permitting individual membership, it was said that there were 'too many cranks' in the party already. Shaw of UTFWA said that he didn't want to see 'every disgruntled Liberal and Tory they could find' joining the party. McKibbin 1974, p. 100. The new constitution also established, doubtless to the dismay of Shaw and others, a women's section. The WLL dissolved itself, many of its members joining the new women's section.
62 *Cotton Factory Times*, 15 March 1918.
63 *Ashton Reporter*, 13 April 1918.
64 *Ashton Reporter*, 11 May 1918.
65 *Ashton Reporter*, 6 July 1918.

The meeting which had discussed the empire in 1915 had been an exceptional event. Indicative of changing times and attitudes, such meetings became less unusual from late 1917. Farr gave a speech at the ILP Club on housing and town planning. Such was the interest that there was 'talk of engaging a larger hall and calling a public meeting'.[66] A few months later, members heard 'a speaker from Ashton' denounce 'private ownership of land'.[67]

The *Reporter* had claimed in December 1917 that 'public feeling in favour of Labour Representation [i.e., the formation of a branch of the Labour Party] is gaining ground rapidly' and that 'a local minister' had said he would vote Labour.[68] Over 30 societies attended the meeting which founded Mossley Labour Party in June 1918.[69] It is not clear what role, if any, Mossley ILP, or Mossley's delegates to Ashton Trades Council[70] played in these proceedings, though local spinners and cardroom workers affiliated to the branch.[71] In August, Farr, perhaps encouraged by Labour's adoption of a 'socialist' constitution, spoke on the need for a Labour government at a demonstration. 'Unless', Farr claimed, working class people were 'strong enough after the war, unless they obtained political control by returning their own Labour candidates, the workers would find their standard of living reduced to a bare pittance'.[72] In October, it was reported that Mossley ILP had dissolved itself in favour of the Labour Party.[73]

The general election of 1918 illustrates the ideological and political journey travelled by Labour since 1910, when a General Election had last been held. In 1910 there had been two general elections, fought over the constitutional issue of whether or not the hereditary, unelected and permanently Tory-dominated House of Lords could legitimately thwart the will of the democratically elected House of Commons. Labour saw this constitutional crisis as evidence of an anachronistic constitution, an uncompleted democratic revolution. Arguing that domination of large landowners had 'crippled capital and impoverished labour', the party insisted that 'the Lords must go', and demanded payment for MPs and, as we saw earlier, adult suffrage. It stood also for moderate reforms

---

66   *Mossley and Saddleworth Reporter*, 8 December 1917.
67   *Mossley and Saddleworth Reporter*, 23 February 1918.
68   *Mossley and Saddleworth Reporter*, 22 December 1917.
69   *Mossley and Saddleworth Reporter*, 22 June 1918.
70   In 1917 there had been a reorganisation of two of our trades councils. Stalybridge, Millbrook and Mossley Trades Council merged with Ashton, Dukinfield and District Trades Council to form Ashton, Stalybridge, Dukinfield and District Trades Council. *Ashton Reporter*, 6 July 1917.
71   *Cotton Factory Times*, 15 November 1918.
72   *Ashton Reporter*, 24 August 1918.
73   *Mossley and Saddleworth Reporter*, 5 October 1918.

favourable to working class people, notably for the poor law 'to be broken up' and for the repeal of the Osborne Judgement. There was nothing in either of Labour's election manifestos that Liberal MPs could have objected to.[74]

In contrast, Labour's election manifesto for 1918 called for the 'immediate nationalisation and democratic control of vital public services, such as mines, railways, shipping, armaments and electric power'.[75] This, clearly based on the wartime experience of state control, was a major line of demarcation with the other two main parties, who saw state control as a temporary wartime expedient. By the end of the war, support for nationalisation had grown in all three strands of the labour movement.

But the anti-capitalist vision of earlier in the year was no longer in evidence. Labour's socialist impulse had waned. Labour demanded 'nationalisation', not 'socialisation', the term generally preferred by Marxists. The Marxist case for state ownership of the means of production – that it was an initial step towards ending the exploitation of the working class by the capitalist class and paved the way to communism – had, as we saw in Chapter 1, been adhered to by only the socialist fringe of the movement. In 1918, Labour argued that state ownership was a matter of the national interest and that it would improve working conditions. The Fabians had long been keen advocates of nationalisation on the grounds of 'national efficiency'. Those trade unionists who supported nationalisation had tended to do so on pragmatic grounds of safety and working conditions – it was widely assumed that removing the 'profit motive' would lead to improvements in both.

Clynes was a great enthusiast for nationalisation. In the autumn of 1915 he had given a lecture on land nationalisation at Oldham's Co-operative Hall. He later gave lectures on rail and mine nationalisation. In general he argued for nationalisation on Fabian premises. In the case of land nationalisations he presented an argument designed to appeal to Oldham's millocracy rather than its working class. He asserted that private ownership of land had 'cost the community a great deal'. Current high taxation to finance the war could have been avoided if the 'hundreds of millions of pounds which had been paid out in rent by the industrious classes to the owners and commanders of land had been paid into the coffers of the country'.[76]

---

74 General Election manifestos of January 1910 and December 1910, in Dale (ed.) 1962, pp. 12–15. Much of this programme was introduced in the new parliament in which the Liberals governed with the support of Irish MPs. The Lords was not abolished, but a Parliament Act severely curtailed its ability to obstruct the Commons. Payment for MPs was introduced and the Osborne Judgement repealed.
75 *Labour's Call to the People* (London, 1918), p. 6.
76 *Oldham Weekly Chronicle*, 23 October 1915.

Only a year after the 1915 rejection of a pro-nationalisation resolution, the TUC's annual conference of 1916 had resolved that the railways and mines should be nationalised after the war. Displaying Fabian influence, the mover of the resolution argued that vital industries 'should no longer be left in the hands of capitalists whose object is profit, and workers whose first object is wages. Such industries should be regulated by the State in the national interest'.[77] Around the same time, the WEWNC adopted Sidney Webb's proposal for post-war nationalisation of all those industries currently under government control (which then included the mines and the railways).[78]

Trade unionists in Ashton and Oldham had seen no need to wait for the peace. As early as 1915 the quarterly meeting of Ashton's Weavers' Association had demanded that the government should 'take over all means of production and distribution so as to stop certain unscrupulous individuals from making profits out of the nation's misfortunes'.[79] By 1917 Ashton's trade council was in favour of nationalisation. A public meeting was held to argue for nationalisation of the railways. Councillor R.J. Davies of Manchester City Council moved a resolution calling for nationalisation and 'for the trade unions to have such a share in the management of the railway system as would enable the workers to have a real voice in the control of the conditions of their life and work'. The resolution was carried.[80] Later that year Oldham T&LC resolved that the 'control' which the government is now assuming over 'capitalist interests' ought now be converted 'into government ownership in order that [industry] henceforth be administered with the utmost efficiency and without opportunity for profiteering'.[81]

By 1918, nationalisation was not the only matter on which Labour was outflanking the two other parties in trying to appeal to the working class. In contrast to the vague aspirations of the coalition, it called for a million homes 'let at fair rents' to be built 'at once', opposed 'every attempt to place burdens upon the poor by indirect taxation', that those 'who have made fortunes out of the war must pay for the war', and for 'equal pay' for women. Labour's manifesto of 1918 also insisted, while affirming that it had had 'no mean share' in victory in the war, that it stood for a 'peace of reconciliation', 'freedom for Ireland and India'

---

77 Trades Union Congress, *Trades Union Congress 48th Annual Conference Report, Blackpool, 4th September 1916* (London, 1916), p. 76.
78 Winter 1974, p. 215.
79 *Ashton Reporter*, 17 April 1915.
80 *Ashton Reporter*, 27 January 1917 and 3 February 1917.
81 Oldham T&LC Minutes 1916–18. EC 20 November 1917. M17/1/3 @ OLSA.

and the right of self-determination for 'all the subject peoples' of the Empire.[82] But how was this nominal commitment to be reconciled with the interests of British capital? Cotton masters and unions began to press once more for the ending of duties on cotton exports to India. An UTFWA circular urged Labour candidates to refer 'in your speeches ... to the Indian import duties and the necessity of their repeal'.[83] The Oldham Master Cotton Spinners Association solicited views from employers and trade unionists on the matter. All, including Robinson, expressed their opposition to the duties.[84]

The coalition parties fought the election on a brazenly social-imperialist platform. Slogans designed to rally support for policies directed against Britain's principal imperialist rival Germany (one of Lloyd George's last election manifestoes 'opened with the slogans "Punish the Kaiser", "Make Germany Pay"')[85] were combined with an offer of social reform to the working class. It was immediately prior to the campaign that Lloyd George famously declared that it was his aim 'to make Britain a fit country for heroes to live in'. Even the King had begun to favour reform. At Buckingham Palace in 1918 he told representatives of local authorities that 'it is not too much to say that an adequate solution of the housing question is the foundation of all social progress'.[86] The joint election manifesto of Lloyd George and Bonar Law declared that

> the principal concern of every Government must be the condition of that great mass of the people who live by manual toil. The steadfast spirit of the workers, displayed on all the wide fields of action ... has left an imperishable mark on the heart and conscience of the nation. One of the first tasks of the Government will be to deal on broad and comprehensive lines with the housing of the people.[87]

Organisationally, Labour had had the support of few labour activists and fewer still working class people in 1910. By 1918 it had built up considerable support among both. The peculiar circumstances of the General Election concealed this reservoir of support, but it burst out in the municipal elections a year later. But Labour faced considerable organisational difficulties in 1918. Until a few

---

82   Labour Party, *Labour's Call to the People* (London, 1918), pp. 7, 9.
83   UTFWA Central Committee Circulars 1918, Circular of 9 December 1918. DDX 1123/4/7 @ LROP.
84   *Oldham Evening Chronicle*, 12 December 1918.
85   Wilson 1968, p. 138.
86   Burnett 1978, p. 216.
87   *The Manifesto of Lloyd George and Bonar Law* (London, 1918).

months prior to the election there had been no constituency parties and no individual membership, and thus, except in places where the trades council was affiliated, no reliable mechanism for mobilising pro-labour voters. Many branches of the party had only recently been formed. Probably, as in the case of Ashton, many of them were merely renamed trades councils.[88]

At the meeting of Ashton Trades Council, which had decided to establish a branch of the Labour Party, Harry Ford, its new secretary, complained that the local labour movement had shown little interest in the project. Only two of the trade unions presently affiliated to the council had indicated that they would affiliate to the new T&LC. The Conservatives and the Liberals were said to be 'working hard on the new registration, but the Labour element was conspicuous by its absence'.[89] At the inaugural meeting of Ashton T&LC in July, only seven trade unions, the BSP and a few individuals were present. Several unions were said to be discussing whether or not to affiliate.[90] Insufficient support had been mustered by November to allow a Labour candidate to be nominated for the general election. The T&LC probably supported Lister, the NFDDSS candidate.

Mossley Labour Party too failed to field a Labour candidate. The Party lacked confidence in its ability to win support. It tailed behind the Co-operative Party, as, in the 1919 municipal elections, it would tail behind the Liberals. Shortly after the formation of Mossley Labour Party it was reported that there was ill-feeling between the party and the Co-op Union over the latter's decision to contest Mossley. The Labour Party considered that there should have been consultations. Co-operative societies had been invited to the meeting which established Mossley Labour Party, but none had attended.[91] In December, the *Reporter* claimed that Mossley Labour had 'done very little' in the election and that the party had decided unanimously to support the co-op candidate.[92]

Oldham T&LC was of course able to field Robinson. The problem here was that Robinson was essentially a Liberal. In September he addressed a special conference convened by the council. Robinson did not refer to the socialist platform adopted by Labour in the summer; he preferred to emphasise his

---

88　In the first six months of 1918, the number of local parties affiliating to the national Labour Party nearly doubled (from 215 to 397). But when Henderson went to Widnes in 1919, 'he found the Widnes divisional party merely a renamed trades council'. Cited in McKibbin 1974, pp. 136–40.
89　*Ashton Herald*, 6 July 1918.
90　*Ashton Reporter*, 27 July 1918.
91　*Mossley and Saddleworth Reporter*, 19 October 1918.
92　*Mossley and Saddleworth Reporter*, 7 December 1918.

admiration for the radical John Bright, one of the founding fathers of Liberalism (Bright's son John Albert Bright had been a Liberal MP for Oldham from 1906 to 1910). War had not changed his view that free trade was 'the broadest and surest foundation for world prosperity'. War was the result of antagonism between democratic and autocratic states, not of imperialist competition.[93] The fiercely Liberal *Chronicle*, which knew a Liberal when it saw one, urged 'progressives', those in favour of 'liberty' and 'progress' to vote for Robinson and the Liberal candidate (Oldham was a two-member constituency).[94] Robinson enthused few Oldham electors. The electors much preferred the two Conservative coalition candidates, who outpolled the two 'progressive' candidates by a margin of over three to one.[95]

In Mossley, Austen Hopkinson, a coalition Liberal, was issued with the 'coupon'. In a town where the influence of local employers was to linger for decades, his status as a local employer (he was the owner of the Delta engineering works in Audenshaw, part of the new Mossley constituency) was doubtless a major asset. His war record was a further asset. He had, according to his election address, equipped Ryecroft, his house in Audenshaw, as a 50-bed auxiliary military hospital. He had served as an officer in the army. More than that, after being discharged due to a severe injury in 1915, he 'enlisted again as a private in the crisis of 1917'.[96] Given these credentials, the Co-operative candidate had virtually no prospect of success, despite (or perhaps because of) Hopkinson's blunt and robust right-wing views. At the hustings, he opposed nationalisation of the railways, expressed scepticism regarding a possible state health service and said Germany should be 'squeezed' for reparations.[97] Hopkinson won the election by the overwhelming margin of 16,188 votes to 5,227.[98]

Ashton's electors were presented with a straight fight between Sir Albert Stanley, President of the Board of Trade, a 'coupon' Unionist (Conservative), and Lister, the national chair of the NFDDSS. The Ashton branch of the NFDDSS had been established in September. It was reported that it had 600–700 members in the town and that it insisted that the care of its members should be the responsibility of the state. They should not be dependent on charity.[99] Stanley, following the national coalition lead, adopted Hun-bashing, reform and labour

---

93   *Oldham Weekly Chronicle*, 28 September 1918.
94   *Oldham Weekly Chronicle*, 13 December 1918.
95   *Oldham Weekly Chronicle*, 4 January 1918.
96   Election ephemera. Hopkinson's 1918 election leaflet. DD293/1 @ TLSAC.
97   *Mossley and Saddleworth Reporter*, 30 November 1918.
98   *Mossley and Saddleworth Reporter*, 4 January 1918.
99   *Ashton Reporter*, 28 September 1918.

matters as his main themes. An enormous press advertisement urged Ashton's electors to 'Vote for Stanley. Justice for our Sailors and Soldiers! Make Germany Pay!'[100] At a public meeting Stanley said that more and better working class housing was urgently needed and that nothing had given him 'greater satisfaction' than while at the Board of Trade the recently concluded agreement with the railwaymen for an eight-hour day.[101]

Lister too spoke on anti-German themes (though less so than Stanley) and reform. At a public meeting he spoke on 'pensions, reconstruction … the exploitation of labour and the housing question, laying special stress on the latter'.[102] Lister's campaign lends some support to the claim of the official historian of the British Legion that the Federation had left-wing inclinations and had close contacts with the Labour Party.[103] The Federation's activities in Greenfield and Oldham, outlined earlier, suggest a fundamental social-patriotism, as does Lister's attempts to smear Stanley for having connections with a firm that had traded with the 'Huns'.[104]

The *Reporter* had opposed the election, claiming that calling it was 'sinister', timed 'so as to disenfranchise' large numbers of the newly enfranchised, the 'very men who have helped us to win the war'.[105] When reporting the election result it would claim that there had been over 4,000 'absent voters', nearly all sailors and soldiers serving overseas in places other than France and Belgium (votes from these places were said to have 'come in fairly satisfactorily').[106] The paper gave implicit support to Lister (who was an ex-chairman of Lancashire Young Liberals) in the absence of a Liberal candidate. His meetings were usually chaired by local Liberals. Ashton Labour too seems to have supported Lister. Crinion spoke at one of his meetings.[107] Though Stanley won with relative ease, winning 10,261 votes, Lister's poll of 7,334, probably an expression of support for his advocacy of much better treatment for ex-servicemen, was a remarkable performance for an outsider.[108] Alderman Coop claimed, in an aside typical of the arrogance of Ashton's Conservatives, an

---

100   *Ashton Reporter*, 7 December 1918.
101   *Ashton Reporter*, 14 December 1918.
102   Ibid.
103   Wooton 1956, pp. 1–5.
104   *Ashton Reporter*, 14 December 1918.
105   *Ashton Reporter*, 23 November 1918.
106   *Ashton Reporter*, 4 January 1918.
107   *Ashton Reporter*, 7 December 1918.
108   Out of 19 Federation candidates standing, 11 came last. But Ashton was not the only place where a NFDDSS candidate did well. In Everton, Liverpool, the Federation's candidate lost by only 592 votes. Swift 2014, p. 146.

arrogance that was to prove costly to them in the municipal elections later that year, that Stanley's victory was a victory for the 'people who count' in Ashton.[109]

Though the election turnout was low, and many serving soldiers were not enrolled on the new registers, it is unlikely that these factors substantially affected the result. Given that the armistice was widely perceived as a British victory and a vindication of the decision to go to war with Germany, it is unsurprising that the coalition decisively won the election. Nor is it surprising that the Conservatives, the party of crown, country and empire, won by far the most seats (379 to the Lloyd George Liberal's 127).[110] Labour candidates who had opposed the war, such as the ILP's Ramsay MacDonald and Philip Snowden, were crushed. On the Clyde, the main centre of wartime working class unrest, the ILP's Neil Maclean narrowly beat the Unionist candidate in Govan; but a truer test of working class opinion took place in the Gorbals, where the robustly right-wing MP George Barnes, who had been recently expelled from the Labour Party for continuing to support the coalition and who had thus received the 'coupon', beat John MacLean, veteran anti-war agitator and leading member of the BSP by a margin of 2 to 1.[111]

But Labour was not crushed. After finally breaking the electoral pact with the Liberals, Labour won 57 seats. Admittedly, this was a mere 15 seats more than in 1910. But the party was now the largest opposition party, with around 20 percent of the vote (compared with 7 percent in 1910)[112] and was poised to make rapid advances in general and municipal elections in the next decade.

5   1919: a Tumultuous but Not 'Red Year' in Lancashire

The victory of the coalition had demonstrated the patriotism of the overwhelmingly working class electorate and the willingness of the bourgeoisie to concede reforms to the working class. It did not herald an end to class conflict. But, certainly in Lancashire, this conflict was economic conflict which did not challenge the rule of capital. Some limited reform, notably in social insurance and housing was enacted or proposed, not as much as labour movement activists had hoped for, but not as little as they would eventually claim. The new

---

109   *Ashton Reporter*, 4 January 1919.
110   The Asquithian Liberals, denied Lloyd George's support, won only 36 seats. This election marked the beginning of the Liberal's precipitous decline.
111   MacFarlane 1966, p. 42.
112   Thorpe 2000, pp. 48–9.

government was anxious that social unrest should not impede a smooth transition from war to peace. Accordingly, social legislation was introduced early in the new parliament and a National Industrial Conference, the first of several interwar attempts to promote co-operation between employers and the unions, was convened in February 1919 to provide a forum in which capital and labour might discuss matters of assumed mutual interest.

Indicative of the class collaborationist ideology dominant among the trade union hierarchy, 600 leading trade unionists attended the inaugural meeting of the National Industrial Conference in 1919. A Joint Committee of 30 employer and 30 trade union representatives, including one from UTFWA, was established.[113] The Committee's report to government, signed by Arthur Henderson and, for the employers, Sir Alan Smith, recommending such measures as a maximum working week of 48 hours and more generous pensions, was adopted in April. But government inactivity, increasing working class militancy and the end of a postwar boom in 1921 combined to ensure that the report stayed in the government's in-tray. The Conference collapsed in July 1921, when the trade union members resigned.[114]

The departure of the trade unionists came after a long period of social unrest. Soon after the General Election there was a great outpouring of class antagonism, which had undoubtedly been kept in check by the ideological pressures of war. January 1919 saw mutinies in the army and navy in protest against delays in demobilisation and against the British intervention in Russia. The 35 million days lost in strikes that year, in, for instance, national rail and bakers' strikes, was the highest so far in the twentieth century.[115] Glasgow saw a mass strike and mass demonstrations inspired by the Clyde Workers Committee. Troops, arrests and imprisonment quelled the unrest. Nationally, miners voted for a strike by a margin of 5 to 1 after the government rejected its demands for a six-hour day, a 30 percent increase in wages and the nationalisation of the mines. The government referred the matter to a commission, the Sankey Commission. Further government manoeuvring, and procrastination by trade union officials, averted a national strike until 1921; when this strike ended in defeat and savage wage cuts.

All three of our towns (Mossley much less so than the other two) and many other towns in Lancashire were affected in one way or another by these and other strikes, notably the near three week's general cotton strike. From the beginning of the year local worthies were anticipating unrest. The Tory *Ashton*

---

113   *Times*, 28 February 1919.
114   Lowe 1978, p. 673.
115   Clegg 1985, p. 121.

Herald urged continued co-operation between labour and capital in several editorials on the 'industrial situation'. A prominent article reported on a public meeting convened by the Church of England Men's Society on 'industrial problems'.[116] The *Oldham Chronicle* warned of the 'dangers of Bolshevism [if] there be gross mishandling of the after-war problem'.[117] The Annual meeting of Oldham's Chamber of Commerce heard a warning that 'labour unrest [was] the rock ahead'. Typically, agitators, were blamed: a 'large number of workers ... instead of being guided by the experienced and responsible leaders of trade unionism ... are being led away by agitators, whose chief object seems to sow seeds of discord'.[118]

Unrest in local bourgeois circles was justified. In January, Ashton T&LC had discussed a report on problems of demobilisation. A representative of the Cardroom Amalgamation had 'toured the battlefields' and found 'a great deal of unrest'. Soldiers believed that the government was deliberately holding back demobilisation in order that laid-off munitions workers would get the 'pick' of other jobs.[119] In February, Judson warned of deepening unrest. He hoped that strikes would not be necessary in Ashton, but there was 'trouble ahead'. Lloyd George had 'promised them a new world, but the employers were getting ready to reduce wages'. The workers 'had won the war, while others had made profits. Now it was the workers' turn'.[120]

Earlier that month 3,000 Ashton miners had struck in a one-day unofficial strike in protest against the government's pay offer[121] and weavers at three Ashton mills had struck 'in protest at intense cold' in the factory.[122] In Oldham, teachers had given in strike notices in a dispute over salary structures.[123] In March, miners at New Moss colliery, Ashton, struck for one day in protest over procrastination by the Sankey Commission.[124] In May, the Ashton branch of the Police Union unanimously passed a resolution demanding a national ballot on strike action (a limited police strike in June seems not to have affected our three

---

116 *Ashton Herald*, 19 January 1919.
117 *Oldham Weekly Chronicle*, 25 January 1919.
118 *Oldham Weekly Chronicle*, 8 February 1919.
119 *Ashton Reporter*, 11 January 1919.
120 *Ashton Reporter*, 15 February 1919.
121 *Ashton Reporter*, 15 February 1919. There had been other local miners' strikes. In Yorkshire, for instance, 150,000 had struck in January for 13 days. Clegg 1985, pp. 269–70.
122 *Ashton Herald*, 15 February 1919.
123 *Oldham Weekly Chronicle*, 1 February 1919. The strike was called off when a new salary structure was agreed just before the expiration of the strike notices. *Oldham Weekly Chronicle*, 1 March 1919.
124 *Manchester Evening News*, 28 March 1919.

towns).[125] In July, hatters in Denton, Hyde and Romiley struck.[126] In August, there was 'little or no bread baked' in the Manchester area for several days. The striking bakers were demanding an increase in pay but, like the cotton workers, seem to have been more concerned with their hours of work: they wanted a reduction in hours from 50 to 44, an end to night baking and a week's holiday with pay.[127] In the same month co-op employees in Ashton and Oldham struck in protest against the refusal of local co-operative societies to recognise their union.[128] During the national rail strike of the autumn Farr addressed Mossley's railwaymen, who later 'marched in procession' to the market ground. At a mass meeting, members of the National Union of Railwaymen (NUR) 'were enjoined to remain firm, not to act in any riotous or illegal manner'. 'All four stations in Ashton' were closed, as were those in Oldham and Hyde.[129]

The most serious dispute in Lancashire was the nearly three-weeks long cotton general strike of June–July. Interestingly, though this strike involved more people and led to more lost days than any other strike of the time, it has received far less attention from historians than the other major disputes, such as those of the miners and railwaymen. Perhaps this lack of attention is because most cotton workers were women. Marwick claimed, quite erroneously, that 'a Lancashire cotton-workers' strike ... passed off without great incident'.[130] In March UTFWA had put in a claim for a reduction in the working week from 55 to 44 hours and for the working day to start at 7am, not 6am (a small improvement only to those who do not have to rise at 5am and, in winter, break the ice in an outside lavatory, six days a week). Employers and government began to anticipate a strike. At the annual meeting of the Ashton textile employers, the Chairman observed that 'the operatives are very aggressive on the question of hours. They want shorter hours and higher wages'.[131] The Ministry of Labour's weekly report to the Cabinet noted that 'the workers in the [North West] are recorded as "jumpy" under the shadow of the anticipated crisis in the cotton trade'.[132]

---

125   *Ashton Reporter*, 31 May 1919. In August 1918 there had been a mass police strike. The strike of 1919 led to the passing of the Police Act, which made it illegal for police to form a trade union.
126   *Manchester Evening News*, 19 July 1919.
127   *Manchester Evening News*, 9 August 1919; *Ashton Reporter*, 9 August 1919; *Oldham Weekly Chronicle*, 9 August 1919; *Manchester Evening News*, 16 August 1919.
128   *Manchester Guardian*, 23 August 1919.
129   *Mossley and Saddleworth Reporter*, 27 September 1919; *Manchester Evening News*, 27 September 1919; *Ashton Reporter*, 4 October 1919; *Oldham Weekly Chronicle*, 4 October 1919.
130   Marwick 1991, p. 314.
131   ATEA special minutes 1917–21, Minutes of ATEA Annual Meeting, 26 May 1919. ATEA/1/2/2. @JRSC.
132   Report for week ending 4 June 1919. CAB/24/81 @ NAK.

The employers responded to UTFWA's claim with an offer of a reduced working week of 49½ hours.¹³³ Protracted negotiations failed to produce an improved offer. Confirming Judson's remarks on the mood among Lancashire's workers, cotton workers responded by voting overwhelmingly, 267,650 to 6,347, in favour of a strike. In Oldham, the spinners voted 6,949 to 156 in favour.¹³⁴ The strike began on the 23rd June. That same day, negotiations resumed under the chairmanship of Sir Herbert Dixon, the chair of the Cotton Trade Reconstruction Committee (CTRC), resulted in an improved offer of a reduction in hours to 48, accompanied by an increase in piece rates to compensate for the effect of the reduction in hours. The Legislative Council of the UTFWA accepted this offer and recommended a return to work, to be followed by a branch ballot on the employers' offer (there is no evidence that a ballot was actually held).¹³⁵

But the spinner's leadership broke ranks with UTFWA and rejected the improved offer. Allan Fowler argues, almost certainly correctly, that this 'was clearly an attempt by the leadership to regain its credibility among the membership and to head off the growing influence of the shop stewards movement'.¹³⁶ We noted in the previous chapter the growing influence of the shop stewards, especially in Oldham, and the determination of the officials to curb their influence. For the strike of 1919, we have the testimony of the *Manchester Guardian's* 'special correspondent', who seems to have been singularly well-informed. According to this person:

> the rejection by the spinners of the terms negotiated by [UTFWA] is due to the activity of the shop stewards, especially in the spinning mills of Oldham ... As the shop stewards are now banded together they are a menace to the discipline of the union ... It is their influence which is directing the present revolt against the proposed terms of settlement of the strike. They captured the district meetings, and as matters stand the council of the union has little more than a titular leadership.¹³⁷

The dominance of spinning in and around our three towns meant that the strike in these places was fairly solid. Even so, many – presumably mainly

---

133 Circulars of Central Committee of Weavers' Amalgamation, circular of 20 March 1919. DDX 1123/4/8 @ LROP.
134 *Cotton Factory Times*, 27 June 1919.
135 UTFWA Legislative Council letter to union branches, 27 June 1919. ACS/3/6/14 @ JRSC.
136 Fowler 1987b, p. 159.
137 *Manchester Guardian*, 1 July 1919.

weavers, cardroom workers, non-unionists and, no doubt, strike-breaking spinners – went back to work or had never struck in the first place. A furious reaction erupted among those on strike. There were 'disorderly scenes' in Hyde. Strikers gathered at the mill of Edward Hibbert and Co. (where a majority of the workers had gone back) and 'demanded that the operatives cease work'. The management, fearful of more disorder, closed the mill. There were similar scenes at Ashton Brothers, one of the biggest mills in Hyde, where 'stones were thrown'.[138] In Stalybridge, a hosepipe was turned upon protesters who had attempted to storm the back entrance of a mill.[139] In Oldham, those weavers who had returned to work had to come out again, not only 'because of attacks on those who went back', but also because of the 'impossibility of the weaving departments carrying on for long without the spinners'. Cardroom workers were also said to have come out again 'because of the spinners' attitude',[140] but this may actually have been due to the influence of a newly-formed shop stewards movement among these workers.[141] The disturbances do not seem to have spread to Mossley (a rumour spread that women from Ashton were *en route* to demand that Mossley workers come out, but none seem to have arrived), where only 3 or 4 mills out of 30 were running.[142]

Ashton saw the most disturbances, in which, according to the *Reporter*, the 'ringleaders seemed to be women, girls and irresponsible youths'. A crowd gathered in the centre of Ashton and then went along the river Tame valley to neighbouring Droylsden, visiting several mills *en route*. There were a 'number of discharged soldiers along the route' who were 'egging on the some of the bolder spirits among the women out of sheer mischief'. Particular anger was directed by 'a crowd of over 1,000 women and girls' at non-unionists who had returned to work at Oxford Mills.[143] Windows were smashed at one mill. At another, the manager was attacked by women, one of whom 'plastered a piece of bread and margarine over his face'. A 'crowd of 1,000 appeared at the Tame Valley Mill, demanded that the workers come out and then smashed the windows'. At yet another mill, when 'the operatives came out at dinner [lunch] time they were surrounded by a crowd of angry women'. In response to these commotions the

---

138   *Manchester Evening News*, 30 June 1919.
139   *Manchester Guardian*, 2 July 1919.
140   *Oldham Weekly Chronicle*, 5 July 1919.
141   *Manchester Guardian*, 7 July 1919.
142   *Mossley and Saddleworth Reporter*, 5 July 1919.
143   *Cotton Factory Times*, 4 July 1919. A persistent complaint among union members was that non-members paid no dues but enjoyed the improved wages and conditions won by the unions.

majority of mills along the route were closed down in order to prevent 'damage to property or injury to persons'.[144]

The opposition of the spinners' shop stewards to the proposed settlement prolonged the dispute for nearly three weeks. If there was a shop stewards movement among the weavers, it seems to have had little influence. At a meeting of delegates to the Amalgamation in Manchester, held shortly after it had become clear that the spinners had rejected the proposed settlement, it was reported that the leaders of the Amalgamation claimed that 'the general body of delegates is satisfied with the work of the executive' and that 'the meeting decided to leave the further conduct of the dispute in the hands of the Legislative Council' of UTFWA.[145] Further negotiations failed to gain any further concessions on the matter of hours, but an agreement, which the spinners' shop stewards do not seem to have opposed,[146] that the wages element would last only nine rather than eighteen months, led to a general return to work on the fourteenth of July.[147]

Fowler claims that 'the shop stewards movement within cotton spinning represented a conservative rather than a radical force within cotton', arguing that 'they wanted to maintain their privileged position and their differentials in wage agreement'.[148] This is a rather one-sided assessment. There is certainly ample evidence of conservatism. But we have seen evidence that some shop stewards were inspired by the Russian Revolution (it would be extremely surprising if that were not the case) and that at least some cotton workers regarded the shop stewards movement as a progressive revolt against conservative officials, an attempt to make their union more receptive to the rank-and-file and to upset the cosy relationship which many officials had with the employers. Several contributions in a *Cotton Factory Times* discussion on the positive and negative aspects of the shop stewards movement made this point. Other contributors – for instance, one who had been present at a spinners' meeting where the resignation of the local spinners' president had been demanded[149] – regarded such demands as evidence of 'extremism'. In reply, Alice Smith, who had been present at the meeting which had demanded the resignation, and who was clearly supportive of the shop stewards, pointed out this demand was in conformity with the Spinners' rule book.[150]

---

144 *Ashton Reporter*, 5 July 1919.
145 *Manchester Guardian*, 1 July 1919.
146 *Manchester Guardian*, 11 July 1919.
147 ORTEA Annual Reports 1916–20. Report for 1919, p. 15. AAN/1/1/2/3 @ OLSA.
148 Fowler 1987b, p. 160.
149 *Cotton Factory Times*, 25 July 1919.
150 *Cotton Factory Times*, 1 August 1919.

Though a connection is not suggested, the cotton general strike of 1919 ended around the time the Housing and Town Planning Act (the 'Addison Act') of July 1919 was ending its passage through parliament. The act may have inspired local labour movement activists to agitate for housing reform in the local elections that autumn. The act envisaged that 500,000 houses – houses which, according to a Local Government Board *Housing Manual*, should have a bathroom and inside lavatory (a radical proposal for working class housing at the time)[151] – were required more or less immediately. Crucially, in order to overcome anticipated resistance from local authorities, the cost was to be subsidised by central government. The spur for local activists was that the act also required local authorities to report within three months to central government on the state of the housing stock in their areas together with plans for improving it.[152] By the time of the municipal elections in November, only Oldham of our three councils had so reported.

6 Housing Reform and the Municipal Elections of 1919

The Labour Party made spectacular gains in the municipal elections in, to note only a few places, London, Manchester, Blackburn, Hull, Colne and Leeds.[153] Doubtless, these gains were the fruits of the expanded electorate, the still not spent wartime radicalism and the militant working class mood of 1919. The municipal franchise was a householder franchise, which had fewer electors than the parliamentary franchise. Even so, the municipal electorate, in, for instance, Ashton was 84.8 percent greater than in pre-war days.[154] In the municipal elections, a majority of the newly enfranchised municipal voters were women.[155] In our three overwhelmingly working class towns, the great majority of these women would have been working class women. Working class support for Labour's stance on housing reform, particularly among women, was probably the main factor in Labour's greatly increased support. In our towns the local press noted that women particularly responded to demands for housing reform. In Ashton, for instance, Labour's stance on the matter was reported

---

151 Burnett 1978, p. 221.
152 Malpass 2005, p. 40.
153 *Manchester Guardian*, 3 November 1919.
154 Calculation based on statistics in Ashton Reporter, 22 June 1918.
155 Female householders had had the municipal vote since 1869, but now the wives of male householders too could vote. A significant difference with the parliamentary franchise was that the voting age, 21, was the same for women as for men.

to be 'especially' appreciated by women, as was a claim that if the Liberals and Tories had lived up to their promises, 'the people's houses and education would be better'.[156]

In Oldham, housing was the most prominent issue in the election. Oldham council had its share of utilitarian Bounderbys. During a debate on the high death rate in the borough, Conservative Alderman Simister had asserted in 1914 that 'it is the individual and you must ... let the people know that they are responsible for their own salvation'.[157] In 1917, completely unswayed by the growing wartime demand for social reform, Simister demanded to know why the council should provide homes for working class people: 'as people had to feed and clothe themselves ... why should they not house themselves'.[158]

But Simister was not typical of opinion on Oldham council. The Liberal *Chronicle* had consistently campaigned for better working class housing: it was a 'vital problem ... in Manchester alone 5,000 [houses are] urgently needed'.[159] We saw in the previous chapter that in 1917 the Liberal-dominated council had undertaken to provide council houses. Early in 1919 a more concrete promise to build 1,200 houses was made, giving priority to returning soldiers.[160] In a council by-election in March, the Labour candidate insisted that 'It was the duty of the municipality, quite apart from private enterprise, to see that every household or family was housed in a proper building ... Every working man's house should have a bathroom'.[161] No doubt anticipating a strong Labour challenge, the Liberal election manifesto included such 'progressive' demands as 'a plentiful supply of pure water; Cheap Electricity ... A comprehensive housing scheme ... Medical attention for school children; Municipal bathhouses'.[162]

Labour campaigned mainly on the housing question. One candidate insisted that every house should have a 'bath and three bedrooms. The time of the four-roomed house was gone'.[163] The *Chronicle* had urged the 'progressive' parties, Labour and the Liberals, to form an electoral pact against the Conservatives. The paper's advice was spurned. Labour did well in the four wards it contested, coming second in each. But, the *Chronicle* lamented, the 'Large progressive vote [was] divided',[164] allowing the Conservatives to win the most wards.

---

156   *Ashton Reporter*, 11 October 1919.
157   *Oldham Weekly Chronicle*, 8 August 1914.
158   *Oldham Weekly Chronicle*, 17 February 1917.
159   *Oldham Weekly Chronicle*, 18 January 1919.
160   *Oldham Weekly Chronicle*, 15 February 1919.
161   *Oldham Weekly Chronicle*, 15 March 1919.
162   *Oldham Weekly Chronicle*, 30 October 1919.
163   *Oldham Weekly Chronicle*, 8 November 1919.
164   *Oldham Weekly Chronicle*, 3 December 1919.

Mossley's reactionaries had considerable influence. In 1915, Conservative Alderman Sykes had complained that legislation meant that they were 'not allowed to keep young children in the workhouse. Scattered homes had been established so that children could be brought up in ordinary homes. This entailed considerable expense'.[165] In response to a Local Government Board circular, the council's General Purposes Committee had resolved in 1917 that 200 council houses could be built, despite the protests of Tory councillor Rhodes, who thought that the council 'had enough to do without building houses that were not required'.[166] But the Liberal-dominated council made no concrete plans to improve the town's housing stock. In 1919, Sykes, whose parsimony had not been moderated by the experience of war, advocated at the full council caution in proceeding with the building of council houses. The Committee agreed.[167]

The Labour Party therefore had an excellent opportunity to exploit the housing issue. But the opportunity was spurned. After Farr, Wright Mosley, the spinners' secretary, was probably the most influential figure in Mossley's labour movement. But his mental world was that of the pre-war Labour Party, a party then still struggling to emerge from a trade union chrysalis. He was out-of-step with the party's new socio-economic programme. Though nominated as a Labour candidate, he fought Yorkshire Ward as a 'trade union' rather than Labour candidate. At his adoption meeting he had been insistent that he was 'the nominee of the operative spinners' and declared that those present at the meeting (only 50 or so) were a 'small band of missionaries who ... would help to spread the gospel of trade unionism'.[168]

Farr, who, as we saw in the previous chapter, had during the war been a keen advocate of radical housing reform, seems to have lost his ideological bearings in the peace. He and his party had failed to sever the ideological and political umbilical cord connecting them to the Liberals. Far from campaigning on the issue of housing, Labour fought the election in an anti-Tory alliance with the Liberals. A joint Labour-Liberal 'progressive' election appeal to the electorate, which owed much more to the millocracy's Liberal, non-conformist tradition than to Labour's new postwar programme, failed to mention housing reform. Remarkably, it asserted that all the 'progressive' candidates stood for 'temperance'.[169] This was a stance guaranteed to mobilise many working men for con-

---

165   *Mossley and Saddleworth Reporter*, 10 April 1915.
166   *Mossley and Saddleworth Reporter*, 13 October 1917.
167   *Mossley and Saddleworth Reporter*, 10 January 1919.
168   *Mossley and Saddleworth Reporter*, 25 October 1919.
169   Ibid.

servatism, but might well have mobilised many Methodists and women for the alliance. Labour's joint campaign with the Liberals could only have helped the established parties. No seats were won by Labour.

In Ashton, housing reform became the key election issue. In marked contrast to the Liberal *Reporter*, the Tory *Ashton Herald* had consistently sneered at local reformers' 'utopian' views and complained that the impact on the rates had not been considered. Though occasional nods in the direction of reform were made – for instance, the Conservative-controlled council had in 1918 instructed the Borough Treasurer to consider the financial implications of the Local Government Board's proddings on housing reform[170] – by the end of 1919 no concrete plans to improve the borough's housing stock had been made.

Especially given that Ashton Labour Party had been founded only the year before, the scale of the party's victory in the municipal elections is astonishing. It only just failed to beat the Liberals (34.7 percent to 34.8 percent) in the popular vote; 5 of the 8 councillors elected were Labour councillors.[171] Labour's victory was the result of Labour agitation and a working class revolt against an obdurately reactionary council dominated by such Tory backwoodsmen as Alderman Shaw (who we met in the previous chapter). During the election campaign, Tory Councillor John Andrew had claimed that the Labour Party 'could not point to a town in the whole of England where the council had done more to put the houses in a better sanitary condition than they had in Ashton'.[172] But Labour's Edward Meeks had insisted that Ashton workers 'did not deserve the conditions they were forced to live under'.[173] Echoing Lloyd George, Labour's James Massey insisted that he was 'determined that Ashton ... should be made fit for heroes to live in. The greatest heroes they had in Ashton were the poor people'.[174]

Ashton Labour Party began to make advances too in parliamentary politics. Early in the new year, Stanley went to the Lords, precipitating a by-election. It came during a local strike of foundry workers. A procession of strikers and supporters marched to support a Labour election meeting attended by thousands and addressed by 'Jimmy' Thomas, the leader of the NUR. In contrast, a NFDDSS (by now firmly in the right-wing camp) meeting called to support the Unionist coalition candidate, Sir Walter de Freece (a 'music hall proprietor and the

---

170 Ashton Council, Minutes of the Housing Committee, 18 August 1918. CA/ASH 111/31 @ TLSL.
171 *Ashton Reporter*, 8 November 1919.
172 *Ashton Reporter*, 25 October 1919.
173 *Ashton Reporter*, 11 October 1919.
174 *Ashton Reporter*, 1 November 1919.

husband of music hall star Vesta Tilly'),[175] attracted only 50 people.[176] The Tories tried to portray Labour as extremists, as quasi-Bolsheviks. A Unionist press advertisement claimed that the Labour candidate, Robinson (W.C. Robinson of UTFWA), belonged to a 'party that stands for revolution' and was 'supported by the type of men … who welcome Lenin and Trotsky in the streets of Ashton … who would make us slaves of a state managed by one class only'.[177] Despite (or because of) such wild and palpably false claims, Robinson attracted a great deal of support, polling 39.6 percent to the 43.3 percent of the Unionist candidate (the Liberal candidate came third).[178]

7 The Post-war Crisis, the Working Class, and the Empire

The only significant working class gain arising from the militancy of 1919 (as opposed to reforms initiated by the wartime coalition) was the Unemployment Insurance Act of 1920, the result of bourgeois fear of the consequences 'if something were not done to provide economic security for the British working man'.[179] This reform, building on the provisions of the 1911 National Insurance Act, meant that many more people, if only temporarily, were covered by an insurance scheme,[180] rather than having to hope for a sympathetic hearing by the Poor Law Board of Guardians.[181]

Within months of the Ashton by-election the short-lived postwar inflationary economic boom began to crumble. A Government and Parliament dominated by Tory businessmen – a 'lot of hard-faced men who look as if they had done very well out of the war', according to Stanley Baldwin – were determined to lay as much of the burden of an economic crisis on to the working class as was consistent with minimising or at least containing social unrest. The government rapidly tightened fiscal and monetary policy. Unemployment began to

---

175   *Times*, 16 November 1922.
176   *Ashton Reporter*, 24 January 1920.
177   *Ashton Reporter*, 24 January 1920.
178   *Ashton Reporter*, 14 February 1920.
179   Anonymous minister cited in Gilbert 1970, p. 66.
180   Payments under this Act began in November 1920. Virtually all manual workers, except for those working in agriculture and domestic service and those deemed to be free of the risk of unemployment, such as railwaymen, and non-manual workers not earning more than £250p.a., were covered. Payments were initially fairly generous. Up to 15 weeks benefit, at a rate of one week's benefit for six weeks' contributions, was payable. Garside 2002, p. 37.
181   Croucher 1987, pp. 19–20, argues that members of local Boards of Guardians were susceptible to pressure to be more sympathetic to claimants whereas state officials were not.

rise rapidly. In Oldham, for instance, the number of men registered as unemployed rose from 494 in October 1920 to 2,706 in September 1921.[182] Nationally, the unemployment rate rose from 3.1 percent of the workforce in 1920 to 13.5 percent in 1921.[183]

Rising unemployment aided employers in a general attack on working class wages and conditions. In April 1921 the miners were locked out for refusing a wage cut. They held out until July, when semi-starvation forced them back to work and to accept an even more vicious wage cut. That summer, Lancashire's cotton workers were locked out by employers trying to enforce what would effectively have been a 30 percent cut in wages. The lockout was settled after two weeks when the unions accepted a staged slightly smaller cut in wages.[184] By the end of 1921, the wages of over 8 million workers had been cut.[185]

In August 1922, the Government established the Committee on National Expenditure, chaired by a businessman, Sir Eric Geddes. When later swinging the 'Geddes Axe', the government cut public spending by a sum considerably less than that recommended by the Committee, but even so, by around £52 million.[186] For the working class, the most serious of these cuts were that new approvals under the Addison Act were immediately stopped[187] and that expenditure on unemployment benefit under the Act of 1920, despite the sharp rise in unemployment, was reduced over the next year from £205.8 million to £181.2 million.[188]

One reason for the defeat of the miners in 1921 had been that on 'Black Friday', the 15th of April 1921, the leaders of the transport and rail unions had reneged on a promise to join a general strike with the miners (probably though, by now dispirited rank-and-file trade unionists would have had little appetite for a sympathy strike). Many other examples could be given of the invaluable assistance given by the leaders of the labour movement to capital in its efforts to resolve the postwar economic crisis. Here we will consider only the *cordon sanitaire* they attempted to construct around the Communist Party (CP), founded in July 1920, mainly by members of the BSP, and their support for and at times active participation in the suppression of movements for colonial freedom.

---

182 *Manchester Guardian*, 8 September 1921.
183 Marwick 1991, p. 323.
184 Fowler 1987b, pp. 171–3.
185 Marwick 1991, p. 323.
186 Peden 2000, p. 169.
187 Burnett 1978, p. 221.
188 Peden 2000, p. 171.

Many criticisms can and have been made of the Communist Party (the present writer has made quite a few[189]), but nonetheless there now existed a working class party committed to the revolutionary overthrow of capitalism. This was not at all to the liking of the Labour Party. Soon after its foundation, the CP decided to seek affiliation to and give electoral support to the Labour Party. Perhaps unsurprisingly, given that Lenin advised at that summer's Second Congress of the Communist International (Comintern) that Labour should be supported like 'a rope supports a hanged man', Labour rejected in September the CP's request for affiliation.[190] But the fundamental problem was that Labour wished to reform capitalism and the CP wished to overthrow it. The resultant fractious relationship between the two parties can be seen in microcosm in developments in Ashton Labour Party.

Two of the five new Labour councillors elected in 1919 – Harry Cocker and Meeks – were members of the BSP. Shortly after the elections, Booth Wimpenny, also of the BSP (in 1918 he had spoken as a BSP member at a public meeting alongside the Reverend Cummings).[191] These three were too far to the left for the comfort of Ashton Labour Party. Cocker became a founder member of the CP.[192] Meeks and Wimpenny presumably did. Though town hall politics in Mossley and Oldham changed little as a result of the municipal elections, Cocker, Meeks and Wimpenny took their Marxist convictions into the council chamber. At the count, Cocker had declared that 'Labour would fight to the full length of their power for the benefit of the working classes'. Their opponents spoke of 'all pulling together for the benefit of the whole community', but Labour councillors could not 'serve two masters ... those who own their own property and those who own nothing but their labour power', while Meeks had insisted that he and Cocker 'had fought the election as rebels to the present system, and they went to the council chamber as rebels'.[193] Wimpenny had promised to 'carry the class war [to] the council chamber'.[194] There were several

---

189   Redfern 2005.
190   Thorpe 2000, pp. 47–51.
191   *Labour Leader*, 21 December 1918.
192   Delegates from Ashton attended the founding convention of the CP. One of them, Harry Webb, 'loudly proclaimed the need for men with guns in their arms'. Klugman 1969, p. 4. Cocker presided over the inaugural meeting of the Lancashire, Cheshire and North West District Council of the CP, held in Openshaw, Manchester. *The Communist*, 16 September 1920. In 1921, according to state surveillance of the CP, he and Webb were then members of that committee. Report on Revolutionary Organisations in the United Kingdom, 23 November 1921. CAB/24/25 @ NAK.
193   *Ashton Reporter*, 8 November 1919.
194   *Ashton Reporter*, 22 November 1919.

stormy meetings of the new council. At the first, Cocker insisted, amid uproar, that there should be Labour members on the Watch Committee.[195] The Watch Committee, claimed Cocker, was used by capital to suppress labour. During a recent tram strike, cars 'had run with a policeman at either end'; on another occasion, the police 'were sent to help the proprietors' break a strike at Curzon Mill.[196]

It was presumably members of the BSP who early in the new year disrupted a public meeting at the Co-operative Hall. Russian trade union leaders spoke on the 'horrors' of Bolshevism. It was alleged that 'Gatherings of trade unionists' had been broken up and 'women killed'. When questions were put, 'Many of the answers did not seem to please some of those present and when the meeting ended several mounted the platform and attempted to address the audience'.[197]

In August, at a meeting of the T&LC, Massey criticised 'people in the Labour Party' (presumably Cocker, Meeks and Wimpenny), who were 'prepared to risk all in a mad gamble which could only bring reaction and disaster in its train'. But Labour only had 'to go forward in the same manner as they had been going forward for the past two to three years'.[198] In September, Cocker and co. were said to have been 'shouting and screeching' in open council meetings and 'flouting the authority of the chair'. The Mayor had had to suspend one meeting.[199] Judson, who was on friendly terms with employers and with councillors of other parties, condemned the militant behaviour of Cocker and co. in the council chamber.[200] Earlier that month, 'Little Red Flag wavers' and communists 'in [the] guise of Labour' were attacked. There were claims that speakers in the market place 'connected' to Cocker had advised people not to vote Labour.[201]

Massey complained that the local Unemployed Workers Committee – probably led by Cocker as part of the embryonic National Unemployed Workers Movement (NUWM) – had refused to co-operate with the T&LC on 'unemployment Sunday' and had organised a separate event.[202] The fundamental problem was that the Committee wanted to campaign on the streets, while the

---

195   *Ashton Reporter*, 15 November 1919.
196   *Ashton Reporter*, 22 November 1919.
197   *Ashton Reporter*, 10 January 1920.
198   *Ashton Reporter*, 7 August 1920.
199   *Ashton Herald*, 25 September 1920.
200   *Ashton Reporter*, 30 October 1920.
201   *Ashton Reporter*, 2 October 1920. This is quite possibly true. Many CP members did not support the leadership's attitude to the Labour Party.
202   Minutes of Ashton, Stalybridge, Mossley & Dukinfield T&LC, 8 November 1920, TLSL, DDTC/5.

Labour majority organised only a lobby of the Board of Guardians.[203] Like the Labour Party nationally, Ashton Labour was unsympathetic to the increasingly militant tactics of the NUWM.[204] A year later, the T&LC organised another lobby of the Board of Guardians. Against the wishes of the council, 'hundreds' of the unemployed organised by the Unemployed Workers Committee attended carrying a banner with a skull and crossbones and the slogan 'Death better than starvation'.[205] By then, Cocker had been expelled from the Labour Party.

At Ashton Unionist Association's annual dinner in the autumn of 1920, De Freece attacked 'Cocker and others' who, though 'working under the guise of Labour', were actually members of the BSP, which was 'allied to the Third Moscow International'. De Freece anticipated later conflations of Bolshevism and Judaism: Zinoviev, the Jewish President of the Comintern, was said to be 'a Russian Jew with German tendencies'.[206] The *Herald* claimed that the BSP had 'become' the Communist Party and asserted that Cocker and Meeks were members.[207] In the new year, anticipating Labour's annual conference of June 1922, which ruled that members of other parties were not eligible to stand as Labour candidates,[208] Ashton Labour resolved that the CP was not eligible for affiliation. Deeming Cocker to be a member of the CP, he had been invited to 'explain his position'. Following his refusal to do so, Labour announced that Cocker had been expelled, was 'not recognised as a Labour councillor, and is not entitled to speak' for Labour. Meeks resigned from the Labour Party in protest.[209]

In November 1922, Meeks and Cocker stood as 'Independent Labour' candidates in the municipal elections. According to the *Herald*, Labour election meetings were 'sparsely attended', but 'Communist' [Independent Labour] meetings attracted 'as usual, a large following from miles around'.[210] Their uncompromising class struggle rhetoric over the past three years had increased their support. They increased their average share of the vote from 39.3 percent to 46.2 percent. This was not enough. Presumably in order not to split the vote against Cocker and Meeks, the Labour Party did not field candidates against them. But

---

203 Unemployed people with insufficient contributions to the insurance scheme had to apply to the Board of Guardians for relief.
204 Croucher 1987, ch. 3.
205 *Ashton Reporter*, 8 October 1921; 15 October 1921.
206 *Ashton Reporter*, 2 October 1920. 'German tendencies' was presumably a reference to the canard that during the war the Bolsheviks had been in receipt of funds from Germany.
207 *Ashton Herald*, 5 October 1920.
208 Klugman 1969, p. 174.
209 *Ashton Herald*, 15 January 1921.
210 *Ashton Herald*, 28 October 1922.

at a time when the pro-Labour tide was rapidly receding, Cocker and Meeks won a bigger share of the vote than Labour candidates in other wards.[211]

Were these votes for Communism (though Cocker and Meeks stood as Independent Labour candidates, most would surely have known that they were members of the CP)? Almost certainly not. The Ashton branch of the CP built only minimal support after the departure of Cocker and Meeks from the Labour Party. In 1922, most workers probably saw Cocker, Meeks and Wimpenny simply as uncompromising working class militants. As the militant working class mood of the early postwar period continued to evaporate in the wake of defeat, the more class conscious working class people mostly turned to Labour,[212] not communism.

What of Labour and the Empire? In principle the labour movement was committed to colonial freedom. In its *Labour and the New Social Order* of 1918, for instance, Labour had repudiated 'the imperialism that seeks to dominate other races'. As for that 'great Commonwealth of all races, all colours … that we call the British Empire, the Labour Party stands for its maintenance and its progressive development, the fullest respect for the rights of each people, whatever its colour, to all the Democratic Self-Government of which it is capable'. The paternalist assumption here of course was that it was for the British to decide which peoples were 'capable' of self-government and when they were capable. A racial hierarchy was usually deployed to determine this. The white settler colonies already had control of their affairs under dominion status; India and Ireland were assumed to be ready for a limited degree of self-government; while the black 'children of the planet' we met in the previous chapter would eventually attain self-government under British tutelage.[213] Even in the much less radical election manifesto of that year, the party had, we saw earlier, called for the right of self-determination for 'all the subject peoples' of the Empire. But could a party committed to fighting for the national interest, as Labour was, reconcile such principles with the needs of British capital, considerably dependent on tribute from the empire?

---

211 *Ashton Reporter*, 4 November 1922.
212 Cocker too returned to the Labour fold. According to his obituary, he rejoined Labour shortly after his election defeat in 1922. *Ashton Reporter*, 5 May 1934. This seems unlikely, but it is clear that he was readmitted some time in the 1920s. Many of those who joined the CP in the heady days of 1920–22 quickly left to join Labour. One such was Wilkinson ('Red Ellen', as she came to be known), who unsuccessfully contested Ashton for Labour (while still a member of the CP) in the General Election of 1922. As we shall see, Meeks eventually became a prominent member of the Labour Party. Wimpenny disappears from the historical record in 1922.
213 *Labour and the New Social Order*, p. 22.

The deeds of the labour movement, with one or two notable exceptions, failed to live up to its words. Those in labour movement circles who wish to affirm the internationalist credentials of the movement frequently cite the case of the *Jolly George* (Pollitt became very prone to this). In the summer of 1920, a threat by the British and French imperialists to intervene on the side of Poland in their war with Russia stimulated a renewed 'hands off Russia' campaign. British dockers refused to load the *Jolly George* with armaments destined for counter-revolutionaries in Russia.

But it is much more characteristic of that time that dockers and other transport workers did not even consider thwarting the sending of troops and supplies to India, Ireland, Iraq or Egypt, to name just a few places where the British army was engaged in the early postwar period in repressing anti-colonial movements. Around the time of the *Jolly George* incident, a British delegate to the Second Congress of the Comintern of 1920 remarked, in attempted justification for the British labour movement's failure to support anti-colonial movements, that the mass of British workers would have regarded such support as treasonable. This is almost certainly true, but as the Bolshevik Karl Radek retorted, 'we have a right to demand this difficult work of the British comrades'.[214]

In the 'difficult' cases of India and Ireland, little support from any part of the British labour movement was forthcoming. In 1919 the Labour Party had given critical endorsement to the Government of India Act, passed in the wake of the Amritsar Massacre.[215] The Act was a classic example of changing things in order that they should not change. It made some concessions to middle class nationalists but introduced a highly restricted franchise and contained nothing that would undermine British rule.[216] At the founding congress of the CP, held only a few months after the massacre at Amritsar, the delegates had failed to even discuss the colonial question.[217]

Due to anti-Catholic and anti-Irish prejudice in a fiercely Protestant society and to the great number of Catholics (almost all of Irish descent) and Irish in Lancashire,[218] matters Irish could very easily stir up sectarian divisions in the county (Ashton, where the Orange Order[219] had had much support, had

---

214 Redfern 2005, pp. 53–9.
215 In April 1919, between 300 and 400 people participating in a nationalist demonstration at Amritsar had been killed by the British army.
216 Ahmed 1987, pp. 30–40.
217 Communist Party, *Communist Unity Convention Official Report* (London, 1920).
218 In Ashton, for instance, ca. 9 percent of the town's population in 1921 was Catholic. Diocese of Salford, *Salford Diocesan Almanac 1921* (Salford, 1921).
219 The Orange Order (properly called the Loyal Orange Institution) is a sectarian Protestant organisation based in Northern Ireland and dedicated to the defence of the union with Bri-

been the scene of the worst disturbances of the anti-Catholic Murphy Riots of 1867).[220] Labour had of course been a participant in the government which had ruthlessly suppressed the Easter Rising of 1916. After leaving office, the party did offer some criticism of the increasingly sanguinary methods used to suppress the national struggle in Ireland, but was prepared to support only constitutional nationalism.

Probably due to a desire not to provoke sectarian tensions, labour movement activists in our three towns tended to avoid speaking out on the situation in Ireland. In Mossley though, as the general election of 1918 approached, the Co-operative Party candidate W.H. Brown, who was supported by the newly-founded Mossley branch of the Labour Party, had spoken at the Co-operative Hall in favour of home rule for Ireland. He clarified his views at a later election meeting, declaring that he was in favour of home rule for the whole of Ireland, including the province of Ulster[221] (which the locally dominant Presbyterians, descendants of Scottish settlers, and the Tories demanded should remain part of the United Kingdom).[222]

In February 1921, during the Anglo-Irish War,[223] Irish Republican Army (IRA) attacks on several towns in Lancashire, including Oldham, Rochdale and Stockport,[224] stirred up intensified anti-Irish and anti-Catholic feeling, part of a general upsurge of racism in Britain in the early 1920s. In Oldham, there were frequent letters in the *Chronicle* objecting to unspecified 'aliens' setting up stalls in the market.[225] There were attacks on West Indians and Arabs in Glasgow and Cardiff and against black people in Salford.[226] In Stalybridge, IRA 'outrages' stirred up near-hysteria, culminating in a farce. Armed guards were sent to the

---

tain and to defending the Protestant Ascendancy. It has offshoots in Britain, particularly in Glasgow and Liverpool, cities with large numbers of people of Irish Catholic descent, where it has consistently promoted sectarian divisions among the working class.

220 Herbert 2001, p. 39.
221 *Mossley and Saddleworth Reporter*, 16 November 1918 and 30 November 1918.
222 In 1920, the Labour Party opposed the Government of Ireland Act on the grounds that it imposed partition of the protestant-settler dominated province of Ulster from the rest of Ireland. Gibson 2013, p. 507.
223 In January 1919, after Sinn Féin had won the majority of Irish seats in the General Election of 1918, the party illegally summoned the Dáil (the Irish Parliament) and issued a declaration of independence. The Anglo-Irish war which followed ended in December 1921 when, faced with the threat of an 'immediate and terrible' escalation of the war, Irish negotiators accepted partition of six counties of Northern Ireland and Free State status for the rest of Ireland within the Empire.
224 Herbert 2001, p. 109.
225 See, for instance, the *Oldham Weekly Chronicle*, 9 November 1920.
226 See Kirk 1994 and Jenkinson 2009.

Calico Printers factory. As they arrived, members of the Coal Committee, who had been checking coal stocks, were departing by taxi. Assuming them to be IRA men, the guards fired. Police and local special constables were summoned. An extensive search for supposed 'Sinn Feiners' failed to find any.[227]

Local Labour politicians refused to support the armed independence struggle in Ireland, but condemned Britain's repression of the national movement there. It is perhaps overly cynical to wonder if these sentiments were motivated partly by a desire to appeal to Irish and Catholic voters at a time when the traditional allegiance of such to the Liberals was being eroded by that Party's complicity in the Anglo-Irish war.[228] Farr, presiding over a public meeting convened by Royton and Shaw Trades Council declared that it was 'a disgrace to the people of this country that such harsh and horrible deeds should go on as was the case in Ireland today'.[229] T.W. Gillander, the prospective parliamentary Labour candidate for Ashton, condemned at a public meeting the British government's policy in Ireland. Another Labour speaker claimed that 'the blackest crimes alleged against Germany were as nothing to the crimes perpetrated in Ireland' by the Black and Tans.[230]

But for most labour movement activists and the mass of workers in our three towns, the most pressing matter of international relations was the prospects of the cotton trade: it was this which dominated press and trade union discourse. Early in 1919, for instance, Canon Parfitt of Jerusalem, who had just returned from Salonika (now Thessaloniki), where many troops from the Manchester Regiment were still stationed,[231] expressed these concerns when giving a lecture in Ashton's neighbour, Dukinfield. Parfitt spoke on the importance of Palestine for the cotton trade. 'Let no one think Palestine a sideshow', he declared, the Middle East was crucial for Britain. The fall of Baghdad[232] had meant the end of Germany's attempts to control the area, which was crucial for the 'supply of the cotton mills with materials and wages for the people of Lancashire'.[233]

The cotton unions' leaders shared Parfitt's concerns: the war had not changed their fundamental social-chauvinism. We saw that the question of the

---

227   *Ashton Herald*, 19 February 1921.
228   Fielding 1993, pp. 84–6.
229   *Oldham Weekly Chronicle*, 2 February 1921.
230   *Ashton Reporter*, 12 February 1921. The Black and Tans were irregular British soldiers.
231   British troops had been stationed in Greece since 1915 to help defend it and Serbia against German's ally Bulgaria.
232   Baghdad had been captured from Turkey in 1917.
233   *Ashton Reporter*, 1 February 1919. Cotton was grown in several parts of the Middle East, notably in British-controlled Egypt.

duties on Lancashire's exports to India had surfaced during the general election. Later, the annual report of the Weavers' Amalgamation complained that 'during the past year [the government] had increased the duty on cotton goods imported into [India] from Lancashire'.[234] Mullins of the Cardroom Amalgamation complained that the poor wages and conditions of workers in the Indian cotton trade gave their employers an unfair advantage: 'In India the native has to work more hours per week than is allowed to be worked in this country, whilst the Hindu workers' wages are a mere pittance. The wealthy cotton spinner and manufacturer has his trade protected by a tax on imported cotton goods ... These are matters well deserving the attentions of our legislators'.[235]

Mullins had a point. But he sought not solidarity with Indian cotton workers, rather co-operation with the millocrats in seeking new markets in the Empire. At the end of the year Mullins turned to the matter of the long-term development of the cotton trade, seeing in the economically underdeveloped African colonies of Britain an opportunity for the expansion of Lancashire's cotton trade: 'those countries in which cotton ... can be grown are largely yet in their natural state ... it now remains with Lancashire to rise to the occasion and give the help the Empire Cotton Growing Association of the Board of Trade are going to ask, to get the government to open out and develop ... Africa. By doing so it will be beneficial to the African natives, to this country and to Lancashire especially'.[236]

Underlying the general indifference of the labour movement towards class struggle in the colonial world and towards anti-colonial movements was Eurocentrism. It was assumed that that the workers and peoples of the colonial world were simply too immature in their outlook, too backward, to strike serious blows at capital. It would be in the advanced capitalist countries of Europe and its outposts in the Americas and elsewhere that capital would be overthrown. Accordingly, it had long been assumed by those few who reflected on the matter that colonial freedom would be given to the colonies by the proletariat of the advanced capitalist countries when power was won. But the anti-imperialist movements which emerged after the war in such countries as Egypt and India were early indications that the centre of world revolution was

---

234 Weavers' Amalgamation Annual Report for year ending 12 April 1919. DDX 1123/1/14 @ LROP.
235 Cardroom Amalgamation, Reports and Minutes January 1917–January 1920. Quarterly Report and Balance Sheet for the Quarter ending 28 June 1919. TU/TEX/CARD/13 @ WCML.
236 Cardroom Amalgamation, Reports and Minutes January 1917–January 1920. Quarterly Report and Balance Sheet for the Quarter ending 27 December 1919. TU/TEX/CARD/13 @ WCML.

moving to the East. Even the communists, who became far more supportive of anti-colonial movements than most, were slow to recognise this. The manifesto on the colonial question of the First Congress of the Comintern showed the persistence of Euro-centrism when proclaiming 'Colonial slaves of Africa and Asia: the hour of proletarian revolution in Europe will also be the hour of your liberation'.[237]

Of course, we have the benefit of hindsight. In 1919 it was not at all clear that the revolutionary movement in Europe had passed its zenith. We should not be overly critical of those who failed to recognise this. But the Comintern soon did. Out of the debates on the colonial question at the First and Second Congresses of the Comintern in 1920 there emerged a conviction that there was little prospect of proletarian revolution in the imperialist countries while those countries extracted superprofits from their colonies and semi-colonies. There emerged too a corresponding appreciation of the revolutionary potential of national liberation movements and a clear recognition that such struggles and the struggle of the working class of the imperialist countries formed a common front against imperialism.[238]

After the Second Congress of the Comintern, the British CP's publications did now begin to more firmly support revolutionary national movements, including that in Ireland. A long article combatted indiscriminate anti-nationalism by insisting that there was 'a vast difference between the nationalism of a dominant nation and that of an oppressed nation'.[239] Shortly afterwards an announcement that Wilkinson had been to Ireland 'on a mission of investigation' was accompanied by a denunciation of the activities of the British army and the Black and Tans.[240] An article on the Empire in 1921 was unequivocal on the importance of the anti-colonial struggle. Indeed, it went so far as to say:

> Unless we grasp the imperial character of our struggle, as something more than a subject for perorations, we shall meet with unexpected difficulties, both at present and in the future, and we shall run the risk of tripping over the same obstacle that has stood in the way of socialist development in this country from the beginning. That obstacle is the British Empire. The British Empire is the knot which socialism in this country will have to unravel if it is to succeed.[241]

---

237 Riddell 1987, pp. 227–8.
238 See Redfern 2005, ch. 2, for a discussion of these debates.
239 'Communism and Sinn Fein', *The Communist*, 7 October 1920.
240 *The Communist*, 28 October 1920.
241 'Our Imperial Responsibilities', *The Communist Review*, June 1921.

This knot has never been unravelled. It might have been if the adherents of the new line on the colonial struggle had, like Alexander, severed the knot rather than trying to unravel it. There must have been much active and passive opposition to the new line in the party, for the present writer found no evidence in its archives that practical solidarity with the national struggle in, for instance, Ireland was embarked upon. In its report to the annual conference of 1922, the Party's Executive Committee had nothing to say, nor did any branch submit a resolution, on imperial matters. It seems clear that little importance was attached to anti-colonial work generally. Though various committees were set up in 1921 to direct the Party's practical activities, a colonial committee was not established until 1924.[242] Thereafter, while the CP did carry out sporadic anti-colonial activities – for instance, 'Down with Empire' demonstrations on Empire Day 1930 – they were always a very subordinate aspect of the party's practice.

Such activities were virtually non-existent in the wider the labour movement. In 1919 the Labour Party's annual conference had heard an appeal for solidarity from B.P. Wadia, President of the Madras Labour Union and a 'fraternal' [sic] delegate to the conference. Wadia had reported on conditions in the Indian textile industry: many workers had to rise at 4am to walk to the mill by 5.45, and had a similar journey after work. They 'reach home merely in time to eat their food and go to bed'. Wadia noted that employers claim that they cannot improve wages and conditions in India because of competition between British and Indian workers, but 'both you and we suffer because we are divided. The cause of Labour is one. Give us your help'. A delegate from the Spinner's Amalgamation reported on the appeal to the leadership. The report was filed away to gather dust.[243]

In 1921, William Thomasson, the new Secretary of the Cardroom Amalgamation, met with the Secretary of State for India at a time when Lancashire's cotton trade was entering its terminal decline. Thomasson met the Secretary of State 'with the object of either getting the import duty [on cotton imports to India] repealed or a corresponding excise duty put upon cotton goods manufactured in India'. But he had 'held out no hope'. The matter was extremely serious: 'All that we ask is to be allowed to compete fairly'. But, perhaps recognising that it would, at least strategically, be better to unite with Indian workers than to compete with them, Thomasson then argued that 'What is needed is that we and the Indian people shall come closer together and then we shall

---

242   Redfern 2005, pp. 58–62.
243   Spinners' Amalgamation files on Indian Textile Industry. ACS/6/3/14 @JRSC.

probably find that our interests are identical, and that we can each help the other to attain a better standard of living'.[244] But such sentiments and such appeals as that of Wadia had no concrete effect. This writer found no trace of attempts to build international unity against capital in the records of any of the cotton amalgamations.

On Armistice Day 1922, according to Wal Hannington, the chief organiser of the Communist-led NUWM, 25,000 unemployed Londoners, mostly ex-servicemen, took part in the ceremonies. Their banners had hundreds of First World War medals pinned to them. As they approached the cenotaph, many of the men took pawn tickets from their pockets and pinned them to their coats. The marchers at the front of the procession carried a wreath with an inscription which read 'From the living victims – the unemployed – to our dead comrades, who died in vain'.[245] We cannot but be angry in response to the suffering of the unemployed in interwar Britain, many of whom had been pressganged by capital to fight in the war and then cast aside like so much rubbish. But the implication of the inscription is that these ex-soldiers and sailors should have been better rewarded for their participation in an imperialist war, and that if they had been so rewarded their support would somehow have been validated.

Hannington, writing in 1936, did not draw his readers' attention to the reforms which had been enacted by 1922. It does not belittle the anguish of the unemployed to insist that there had been reform. As we have seen, even the unemployed were treated far less harshly than in pre-war days. The franchise had been greatly extended, the Education Act of 1918 had raised the school leaving age, abolished half-time education and provided for scholarships for secondary education, and a start had been made on providing decent houses. Further reforms in the immediate post war period, notably the establishment in 1919 of the Ministry of Health, led to much greater state responsibility for public health. By 1936, as we shall see in Chapter 5, there had been further and substantial social reform. Even so, the postwar settlement between labour and capital was flimsy and shallow. It took another world war – in which the social-chauvinist trope of 'broken promises' was used by the labour movement to obtain from capital further and ample reward for working class support for another imperialist world war – to produce a firm and deep, if temporary, settlement between labour and capital.

---

244   Cardroom Amalgamation, Reports and Minutes January 1921–December 1924. Quarterly Report and Balance Sheet for the Quarter ending 24 September 1921. TU/TEX/CARD/14 @ WCML.
245   Hannington 1936, p. 77.

CHAPTER 4

Rallying Round the Flag Again

Few would dissent from the view that the war of the allied imperialist powers of Britain, France and the USA against the axis imperialist powers of Germany, Italy and Japan was the 'good war'. Many of those who regard the First World War as an imperialist war believe that the Second World War was qualitatively different. It was a progressive anti-fascist war. But had anything fundamentally changed since 1914? True, in both Italy and Germany acute class struggle, popular resentment against the Treaty of Versailles and ruling-class fear of Bolshevism had led to the imposition of fascism by the most reactionary and expansionist sections of capital. True too, Japan was ruled by an expansionist military dictatorship. But British, French and US imperialism were essentially no less reactionary than German, Italian or Japanese imperialism. From an orthodox Marxist point of view there could be no doubt that the Second World War was an imperialist war. The main enemy of the working class of the imperialist countries was still 'at home'. True, liberal democracy was threatened in Britain and France. True also, there was the socialist Soviet Union to defend against its most bitter enemy, Nazi Germany. In 1939, in a euro-centric rationalisation – which ignored or glossed over the fact that Britain and France were both far greater international exploiters and oppressors than Germany – many of the left argued that these latter aspects of the Second World War justified support for war against Germany.

1   An Imperialist War in Anti-fascist Clothing

A general European war erupted after Germany invaded Poland in September 1939. This was regarded by both Britain and France as an expansionist step too far: an ignored ultimatum to Germany was immediately followed on the 3rd of September by a British declaration of war. Labour's National Executive Committee (NEC) and the leadership of the Parliamentary Labour Party (PLP) met immediately after Britain's ultimatum and decided that while the Party would not join a coalition government, it would give full support to war with Germany (though a minority of MPs opposed the war on pacifist grounds) and would join an electoral truce for the duration of the war.[1] The *Daily Herald*, the voice

---

1   Brooke 1992, pp. 34–7.

of mainstream Labour opinion (it had long since broken with the left), offered unequivocal support for war.[2]

It is not in the least surprising that the great majority of the deeply social-chauvinist British labour movement supported the British war effort. But the capitulation of the once-revolutionary Communist Party,[3] the British section of the Comintern, to social-chauvinism in the 1930s illustrates the depth of penetration of bourgeois ideology into the labour movement. At its Seventh Congress of 1935 the Comintern had adopted a reformist strategy of trying to build the broadest possible front against fascism. Eventually, it was argued that such countries as Britain and France should be defended against the challenge of Nazi Germany.[4]

The CP declared in favour of war against 'the mad dogs of Europe – Hitler and his Nazi government' who had 'set out on their last bloody adventure'[5] – on the outbreak of war. Its *New Propeller*, aimed at engineering shop stewards, declared 'we are out to win the war'.[6] But a *volte-face* was imposed by the Comintern. A Soviet-German non-aggression pact concluded just before the start of the war required an adjustment in communist politics. Stalin now instructed the Comintern to inform the British and French parties that the war was an imperialist war which could not be supported. After much agonising, the British Party accepted this edict. But, greatly relieved, the CP was freed to once more support the war effort after the German invasion of the Soviet Union

---

2 *Daily Herald*, 3 September 1939. Between 1922 and 1929 the Herald had been the paper of the TUC. Since then it had been published by Odham's Press, but continued to voice mainstream labour movement opinion.
3 The British Communist Party is given more attention in our last two chapters than its size and influence perhaps merits, but because it organised on a mass, rather than primarily electoral, basis it has left far richer sources of rank-and-file attitudes and activism than has the Labour Party.
4 It is usual to argue that Comintern policy was essentially an adjunct of Soviet foreign policy, a view I have tended to (Redfern 2005, pp. 72–3). But I now think this is misleading. For communists, the Comintern was not simply defending a state; it was defending the socialist Soviet Union, the perceived bastion of world revolution. But whatever the subjective view of communists, Comintern subordination of the general revolutionary interest to the defence of the Soviet Union helped imperialism to survive the crisis of 1929–45 and usher in the long postwar boom. Arguably, it fostered the forces which eventually overthrew socialism in the Soviet Union. See Morgan 1989 and Redfern 2005 for discussions of communist politics in the period 1935–41.
5 *Daily Worker*, 2 September 1939.
6 *New Propeller*, 3 September 1939.

in June 1941. On the left, only the largely irrelevant Trotskyist sects[7] and the pacifist ILP[8] now opposed the war.

The trade unions too had no qualms in offering support for the war. Addressing the annual conference of the TUC shortly after the start of the war, Walter Citrine, its General Secretary and probably the most right-wing of trade union leaders, argued that the war had been caused 'by the rise of a new menace to human liberty. Step by step, a deliberate policy of aggression has been developed. One act of lawless violence has led to another. The unrestrained policy of the Aggressor Powers broke the League of Nations as an instrument of collective security'.[9] 'Collective security' was of course a policy intended to preserve the existing domination of the international order by Britain and France. This aspect of the matter was not addressed. In early October the Prime Minister, Neville Chamberlain, was assured by the TUC that the trade union movement was 'wholeheartedly behind the Government in the prosecution of the war against Hitlerism'.[10]

Quite what the TUC meant by 'Hitlerism' is unclear. Was it merely a rationalisation of support for war? Probably not. Understandably, given that the first victims of Nazi power had been the German Communist and Socialist Parties and the trade unions, the labour movement had become intensely concerned with the threat of fascism. But as the inter-imperialist antagonism between Germany and Britain grew ever sharper, so the labour movement began to see German fascism as primarily a threat to British national independence rather than as a threat to the working class.

Earlier that summer, members of the Weavers' Amalgamation had attended the 16th Congress of International Federation of Textile Workers in Stockholm, where the delegates had dressed up support for the looming war with anti-fascist sentiments:

---

7   Trotskyists played an insignificant part in the matters discussed here and are therefore not discussed. See Callaghan 1984 and Upham 1980, for the activities of British Trotskyists in the Second World War. See also Challinor 1995 for a Trotskyist historian's perspectives on the war.
8   By 1939, the ILP had virtually no influence in Lancashire (with the exception of Scotland's industrial belt, its influence everywhere was negligible). By then the ILP had been eclipsed by the CP as the main force to the left of the Labour Party. In 1932 the ILP had had 16,673 members to the CP's 5,600, but by 1939 it had only 2,441 members to the CP's 17,756. McIlroy and Campbell 2011, p. 878.
9   Trades Union Congress, *Trades Union Congress 71st Conference Report* (London, 1939), p. 76.
10 Clegg 1994, p. 259.

> Throughout the world the working class must always remember that the possessing classes are prepared to sacrifice even the liberty of the peoples … the working class is the safest and most important rampart against the advances of fascism. It protects the democratic constitution of the state and also fights for the realisation of democracy in every sphere of life.[11]

In similar vein, the leaders of the Amalgamated Engineering Union (AEU)[12] were doubtless quite sincere in declaring that the problem was not the German people – it had to be assumed that 'the great majority of Germans want peace'.[13] But there was no dissent from the AEU when Britain attempted to terrorise the German people into defeatism through saturation bombing of their cities. Given the 'Christmas blitz' of 1940 over Manchester (where hundreds were killed and thousands injured), it is perhaps unsurprising that when an officer of the RAF visited an aircraft factory in the 'North West' a few months later and told the workers there that the war would be won by bombing 'until the Germans yell for mercy' and that he could 'assure them that the mess we made of [Kiel] was absolutely grand', his remarks were greeted with 'laughter and cheers'.[14] Very little criticism of mass bombing was offered from the labour movement. One exception was the Labour MP for Ipswich, Richard Stokes, who courageously denounced the fire-bombing of Dresden in 1945, in which tens of thousands died, as a 'war crime'.[15]

The Executive Committee of the Spinners' Amalgamation claimed that the 'outbreak of hostilities immediately brought into prominence the supreme necessity of doing everything possible to aid the war's prosecution'. The Amalgamation's opposition to overtime was suspended because 'it is quite unthinkable that our soldiers and sailors should be denied materials urgently necessary'.[16] The leaders of the Weavers' Amalgamation clearly considered it self-evident that the war against Germany was just, for no attempt at justification was made. A circular to the membership made no reference to the politics of

---

11   Delegate's report filed with the Annual Report for the year ending 31 March 1940. DDX 1123/1/35 @ LROP.
12   The AEU was formed in 1922, when the ASE merged with several other unions.
13   *Amalgamated Engineering Union Monthly Journal*, December 1939, p. 414.
14   *Ashton Reporter*, 4 July 1941.
15   Roberts 2009, p. 456.
16   Quarterly Report of Executive Committee of the Spinners' Amalgamation, 31 October 1939. The EC had already agreed with the employers that overtime could be worked on 'government orders of an urgent character which might necessitate the working of overtime'. EC meeting of 19 October 1939. ACS/1/46 @ JRSC.

war, merely informing them that the employers had given permission to collect dues 'inside the mill during the present emergency'.[17] They too were prepared to relax restrictions on overtime. A Joint Emergency Committee of union and employers was established, which 'agreed to oversee overtime working: applications were received from a number of firms desiring to operate overtime ... Permission was granted in a majority of cases and others were refused for various reasons'.[18]

Prompted by the government, trade unions and employers quickly established mechanisms to foster co-operation in the war effort. A Joint Advisory Council of employer and trade union representatives was established, with the remit of dealing with 'all matters in which employers and employees have a common interest'.[19] The introduction for cotton workers of a week's holiday with pay[20] (engineering workers had enjoyed holidays with pay since 1937)[21] no doubt smoothed the path to wartime co-operation. At the end of 1943, agreement was reached that from the following year paid holiday weeks would be increased to two.[22]

In October, the National Committee of the AEU concluded with the Engineering and Allied Employers' National Federation (EAENF) a 'Temporary Relaxation of Existing Customs as to Employment of Skilled Men'. The central issue, as in the First World War, was 'dilution'. It was agreed that dilutees 'must be paid the skilled men's rate'.[23] As in the First World War, the point of insisting on equal pay, was, for most, not that women should on principle be paid the same as men, but that men's wages should not be driven down. On the other hand, the ingrained male assumption that women should not get a man's wage undermined the agreement,[24] as we shall see.

In Oldham, the town's spinners had considered it necessary to assert that the 'outbreak of hostilities immediately brought into prominence the supreme

---

17 Weavers' Amalgamation, circulars 1939, circular of 20 September 1939. DDX/1123/4/28 @ LROP.
18 Weavers' Amalgamation Annual Report for the year ending 31 March 1940. DDX 1123/1/35 @ LROP.
19 Clegg 1994, pp. 166–7.
20 The cotton unions had first put in a claim for holidays with pay in 1920, but the employers had resisted until 1939, when agreement was reached that from 1940 workers would have six days paid holiday. Spinners' Amalgamation quarterly representative meeting, 25 March 1939. ACS/1/46 @ JRSC.
21 Croucher 1982, p. 16.
22 Spinners' Amalgamation circular, 2 December 1943. ACS/6/5/6(1) @ JRSC.
23 *AEU Monthly Journal*, October 1939, p. 414.
24 See Smith 1981.

necessity of doing everything possible to aid the war's prosecution',[25] but more typical of the response of Lancashire's trade unionists was that of the committee of Ashton's weavers and winders who in their first meeting after the declaration of war discussed merely the practical question of air raid shelters.[26] Similarly, Ashton's cardroom workers' committee merely resolved that 'in view of the new situation [the war] all members called up to serve under the military service act be excused payment of all contributions for the period which they serve'.[27] Mossley's spinners felt no need to record their support for war.[28]

Labour Party organisations in our three towns seem to have similarly simply assumed that the war must be supported. In Oldham, the T&LC indulged in an unseemly squabble with the Conservatives over which party should preside over the local Food Control Committee.[29] In Royton and Shaw there were squabbles over who should be appointed as air raid wardens.[30] In Ashton, the Labour Party[31] participated in a local electoral truce. After the death of F.B. Simpson, Labour MP for Ashton, the Conservatives and Liberals agreed not to oppose the candidature of Labour's Sir William Jowitt. Organisations to the left of Labour were rather timid. Ashton's branch of the ILP wrote to the Reporter not to denounce the war but to feebly record its opposition to the electoral truce: it reserved the right to field a candidate, arguing that it was 'essential for the maintenance of democracy that the opportunity to test public opinion should be preserved'.[32] In Mossley, Farr was elected as a vice-president of the board of Ashton and District Infirmary and noted with pride that he was the first 'representative of the working classes' and the first from Mossley to be so elected.[33]

---

25 Spinners' Amalgamation, Quarterly Executive Council Report, 31 October 1939. ACS/1/46 @ JRSC.
26 Minutes of Ashton District of South East Lancashire and Cheshire Weavers and Winders Association, undated, but clearly September 1939. TU/6/18 @ TLSAC.
27 Minutes of Ashton district of the South East Lancashire Cardroom Amalgamation, 20 September 1939. TU/12/5 @ TLSAC.
28 Minutes of Mossley Spinners' Amalgamation, 8 September 1939. ACS/6/2/88 @ JRSC.
29 *Oldham Evening Chronicle*, 12 September 1939.
30 Members of Oldham T&LC argued that as wardens received a small payment, preference should be given to the unemployed. *Oldham Evening Chronicle*, 28 September 1939.
31 At an undetermined time in the interwar period, Ashton T&LC had split into a separate trades council and a branch of the Labour Party.
32 *Ashton Reporter*, 6 October 1939.
33 *Mossley and Saddleworth Reporter*, 8 March 1940.

Ashton's branch of the CP was clearly affected, like most branches, by the Party's change of line. Nationally, the CP probably lost several thousand members.[34] Many more would have been deeply unhappy, given the anti-fascist politics promoted by the CP since 1935. Communists had for years, with some success, sought influence in local League of Nations Unions in which they had promoted popular front politics. Prior to the change of line, Ashton CP had announced a public meeting to be held in late October in support of the war. But then Frank Cropper, the Secretary of Ashton League of Nations Union and presumably a member of the CP, wrote to the *Reporter* to promote the CP's stance that Britain should accept Germany's peace proposals:[35] 'faced with the might of the Soviet armies in the East ... Hitler has been forced to consider offering peace proposals to the Governments of France and Britain' and urged that any proposals should be 'seriously considered'.[36] The public meeting was cancelled. Shortly afterwards, the Party's branch secretary apologised for the cancellation. No explanation was offered.[37]

In January 1940 Citrine presided over a Manchester conference of Lancashire and Cheshire trades councils convened to discuss the 'trade union movement and war problems'. Communists present were rebuffed when moving a resolution objecting to the government's support for Finland in its 'Winter War' with the Soviet Union.[38] 'Dilution' was the main matter to be addressed. (In Mossley, a 'grave' shortage of labour had already led to a swift agreement on 'the employment of female piecers in the mule spinning rooms').[39] Ashton Trades Council sent delegates to the conference, some of whom had reservations on the question of 'dilution'. One delegate thought that the TUC was not 'active enough in the interests of labour'. Another insisted that though there was a severe shortage of engineers they would not 'take any Tom, Dick or Harry into the union'.[40] Though reciprocity was expected, there seems to have been general agreement among the delegates that dilution would have to be introduced. Following the lead of the TUC, which in a meeting with the government shortly after the declaration of war had sought as a *quid pro quo* for its support for the

---

34 See Morgan 1989, *Appendix*.
35 Germany's proposals included British acceptance of the *casus belli*, Germany's conquest of Poland.
36 *Ashton Reporter*, 13 October 1939.
37 *Ashton Reporter*, 3 November 1939.
38 *Daily Worker*, 31 January 1940.
39 Mossley Committee of Spinners' Amalgamation, Annual Report, January 1940. ACS/6/2/88 @JRSC.
40 *Ashton Reporter*, 9 February 1940.

war the repeal of the Trade Disputes Act of 1927,[41] the delegates supported a resolution of the Union of Clerks and Administrative Workers demanding the repeal of the Act.[42]

Simple patriotism rather than anti-fascist sentiments probably provided for most people the motivation for support for war. The prevailing popular mood – insofar as this can be established with any certainty – was one of resignation and determination. Probably the consequence of popular memory of the slaughter and suffering of 1914–18, there was in 1939 little of the jingoism – even if manufactured, stimulated and exaggerated – which had accompanied the outbreak of war in 1914. Opposition was much more tolerated.[43] Conscription, which had stirred up such hostility in 1916, was fully introduced at the start of the war of 1939–45[44] and provoked little opposition. In Ashton, by the end of October, 400 young men between the ages of 20 and 22 had registered for military service. Only two registered as conscientious objectors.[45] Critical replies to letters in the local press from members of the pacifist Peace Pledge Union tended to be conciliatory rather than hostile.[46] In Oldham, conscientious objectors appearing before military tribunals were treated with forbearance. A member of the Holiness Tabernacle Church who asserted that he was not 'prepared to use force' even on behalf of 'victims of aggression', had his name removed from the register but was warned that he must expect to be called up for 'non-military duties'.[47]

By-election results in the first few months of the war suggest negligible anti-war sentiment. Harry Pollitt, who we met in Ashton's market place in 1914 and who was now the leader of the CP, fought Silvertown, London, in February 1940. Only 966 electors voted for him, in contrast to the Labour candidate's 14,343. Given that the election took place at the height of the 'Winter War' between Finland and the Soviet Union, a conflict used to stoke up anti-communist sentiment, the result was perhaps more the result of anti-communist rather than pro-war sentiment, especially as Pollitt did not usually directly raise the matter of either war.[48] The voters of Prestwich and Middleton in Lancashire sent pack-

---

41 Pelling 1987, p. 181. The Act, passed in the wake of the General Strike of 1926, had made sympathetic strike action illegal.
42 Minutes of Central Committee of Weavers' Amalgamation 1939–45, January 1940. TU/weavers/019 @WCML.
43 See Gardiner 2004 for an excellent discussion of popular sentiment.
44 Limited conscription had been introduced earlier in the year.
45 *Ashton Reporter*, 27 October 1939.
46 *Ashton Reporter*, 6 October 1939; 13 October 1939.
47 *Oldham Weekly Chronicle*, 1 January 1940.
48 Morgan 1989, pp. 158–61.

ing a fascist who had denounced the war as a 'Jewish swindle'. He was trounced 32,036 to 418 votes.[49] Stephen Brooke provides several other instances of the poor showing of anti-war candidates.[50]

The outbreak of war the previous September had been followed by several months of 'phoney war' in which hardly a shot had been fired (at least not on land – there had been some engagements at sea). But in the spring of 1940 the 'phoney war' ended when a spectacularly incompetent British campaign in Norway (intended to prevent Swedish iron ore being transported to Germany) was met with a swift German occupation of Denmark and Norway and an evacuation of British forces. This catastrophic defeat of British arms – to be shortly followed by another in France – led to the forging of even closer unity of purpose between labour and capital.

2 The Crisis of 1940

A debate in the House of Commons on the debacle in Norway led to Chamberlain's resignation and the formation on the 10th of May of a coalition led by Winston Churchill. Clement Attlee, the leader of the Labour Party, joined the coalition as Lord Privy Seal and later became Deputy Prime Minister. A politically adroit appointment by Churchill, clearly intended to foster and boost trade union co-operation in the war effort, was that of Ernest Bevin, the leader of the Transport and General Workers Union (TGWU), as Minister of Labour. Another crucial appointment was that of Labour's Herbert Morrison, a man of working class origins who had come up through the ranks of London Labour politics, initially as Minister of Supply, but shortly afterwards as Home Secretary.

Clearly written in anticipation of the debate in the Commons, *The Tribune*, the paper of the Labour left, denounced Chamberlain and advocated an openly social-imperialist policy. Germany, argued *The Tribune*, must be defeated, and out of the war must come social reform:

> [Chamberlain's] incompetence appals even his own followers. Knowledge of it has now penetrated to the mass of normally indifferent citizens. From [Labour's] ranks alone can alternative leadership come. Our responsibilities and our opportunities are very great ... we can turn the

---

49   *Oldham Weekly Chronicle*, 25 May 1940.
50   Brooke 1992, pp. 35–7.

present disaster into the greatest victory for peace, freedom and social equality the world has ever known.[51]

On the morning of the formation of the coalition came news that the German imperialists had invaded the Low Countries. A successful German *Blitzkrieg* in Holland, Belgium, Luxemburg and France followed. France concluded an armistice with Germany, which occupied the north of France. A nominally independent extreme right-wing French government was established at Vichy. Italy entered the war as an ally of Germany.

The bulk of the defeated British Expeditionary Force (BEF) was evacuated from the beaches of Dunkirk. The British imperialists eventually resolved to fight on. This decision gave rise to the myth that Britain fought on 'alone'. But Britain was not 'alone': it had the resources of its Empire. At the start of the war the white settler dominions of Australia, Canada, New Zealand and South Africa had declared war on Germany. The other peoples of the Empire had not been consulted: Britain declared war on their behalf, an act of typical imperialist arrogance which was to create considerable difficulties for British imperialism, especially in India. From the spring of 1941, when 'lend-lease' was agreed with the USA, American aid was provided.

Defeat in France was followed by expectation of a German invasion. From right and left came excitement – Orwell thought that 'in a year's time we shall see red militias billeted in the Ritz'[52] – and demands for emergency measures. Churchill's crony Robert Boothby argued for the establishment of a Committee of Public Safety.[53] *The Tribune* published an edition in which the entire front page was devoted to a call for a 'People's Army'. Inside, the prominent Labour Left MP, Aneurin Bevan, who was to lead an unofficial left parliamentary opposition throughout the war, argued that 'Mr Churchill ennobles retreat and can rally the nation ... but he cannot unfold for us the plan for victory, because there is not another victory left in the order to which he belongs and of which he is the last distinguished representative'.[54] In its next issue, anxious Tribunites called for workers' control of industry:

> If the ruling class is too decadent or corrupt to organise a proper war economy, the working class certainly is not. The effect of having elected workers' control committees in all vital factories would be tremendous. If

---

51 *The Tribune*, 10 May 1940.
52 Angus and Orwell 1970, p. 400.
53 Boothby 1962, p. 74.
54 'End of Retreat', *The Tribune*, 21 June 1940.

they had been there since the beginning, the present shortage of supplies would have been impossible.[55]

The CP's leaders were extremely alarmed by the capitulation of France and the defeat of the BEF. On the 11th of July, Willy Gallacher, the CP's sole MP, met with 'Rab' Butler, then a Foreign Office minister, to ask if Pollitt could go to Moscow 'in order to use the party's influence with the present leaders of the Soviet Union in order to enlist the aid of the Soviet Union in the great struggle in which we are engaged'.[56] The CP cannot have believed that a mission to Moscow would have influenced Soviet foreign policy. What then was the purpose of the proposed trip? Monty Johnstone plausibly argued that the Party hoped for party-to-party discussions on the 'momentous developments' in the war.[57] But was this the real reason for the meeting with Butler? The phrase 'the great struggle in which we are engaged' might have been intended to convey to the government that a fundamental reappraisal of the CP's stance on the war was underway (verbal assurances might have been given). As indeed it was. By June 1941, when Germany invaded the Soviet Union, the CP had come close to open support for the war.[58]

The Tribunites underestimated Churchill. He was an archetypal social-imperialist. Though now a Tory, Churchill had been a prominent member of the reforming 1906–15 Liberal governments which had introduced such reforms as old age pensions and unemployment insurance. Fiercely committed to Empire, he had worked closely with Manchester cotton magnates opposed to further measures of self-government for India. In 1933, they had founded the Cotton Trade League, which campaigned, without success, for a repeal of the tariffs imposed on Lancashire cotton exports to India.[59] Churchill now presided over a government in which Labour combined with such reforming Tories as Harold MacMillan, later to be Prime Minister, 'Rab' Butler, responsible for the 1944 Education Act and Henry Willink, who drafted the proposals for a postwar health service, and the influential Liberal intellectuals Keynes and Beveridge, came to dominate the domestic political agenda. Churchill's establishment in the summer of a War Aims Committee was a symbolic (the Committee never seriously got down to business) first step towards a domestic social reform programme.

---

55 *The Tribune*, 28 June 1940.
56 FO/371/24856 @ NAK.
57 Johnstone 1997, pp. 38–9.
58 See Redfern 2005, pp. 102–8, for an analysis of the CP's reaction to the crisis of 1940, and Morgan 1989, ch. 7, for a discussion of its politics between then and June 1941.
59 Cain and Hopkins 1993, pp. 192–3.

In an almost teleological process, the British defeat of 1940 was the spark for the coalition's proposals for reform, Labour's landslide victory in 1945 and the postwar construction of the 'welfare state'.

3 Building a Labour-Capital Pact

For some decades after the Second World War there was a consensus among historians that, give or take some subordinate differences, a political consensus emerged in the wartime coalition that there should be comprehensive postwar social reform. Not coincidentally, a revisionist critique of the historiographical consensus emerged after the postwar political consensus collapsed in the 1970s. Paul Addison's *The Road to 1945* was particularly criticised by, for instance, Kevin Jefferys and Stephen Brooke.[60] Consistent with a renewed historiographical stress on so-called 'high politics', Brooke and Jefferys concentrate on parliamentary and Whitehall discussions, debates, arguments and intrigues. But whether or not there was an elite consensus (the present writer believes that there was a consensus, albeit a limited and strained one), a concentration on 'high politics' is to miss the most crucial aspect of wartime and postwar politics. The cement which shaped and sustained these politics was a pact and then a settlement between labour and capital. This is a crucial point, which as Richard Croucher argued, Addison himself missed.[61]

Leading Labour politicians insisted throughout the war that there must be postwar reform. In November 1939 Attlee had told a special conference of MPs and prospective parliamentary candidates that the war would inevitably lead to radical social and economic change and therefore a new society. After the war, he had insisted, there must be no return to 'economic anarchy'.[62] During the parliamentary debate on the King's Speech in December, Hugh Dalton moved a motion which regretted the Government's failure to consider a solution 'on the basis of social justice of the problems which will arise on the return of peace'.[63] In the New Year, the Lancashire and Cheshire Regional Conference of the Labour Party organised a series of public meetings, including one in Oldham, to discuss the party's 'peace aims'.[64] The AEU insisted at the conference that there must be 'resolve to abolish all … causes of international friction …

---

60   Addison 1977; Brooke 1992; Jefferys 1991.
61   Croucher 1982, p. viiii.
62   Attlee, 'Labour's Peace Aims', in Attlee 1940, pp. 234–50.
63   Clegg 1994, p. 259.
64   *Manchester Guardian*, 4 January 1940.

Instead of competition, co-operation. Instead of privilege, equality. Instead of tyranny, democracy and freedom'.[65] In January, the president of Ashton Trades Council doubtless spoke for many when asserting that working class people would not be '"led up the garden path" after this war like they were after the last'. The TUC was 'watching the workers' interests at the same time as they were backing the country 100%'.[66] In the spring of 1940, just before the defeat of the BEF, Labour had argued in *Labour's Home Policy* that 'we may yet use this war to lay the foundations of a juster and more generous life'.[67] Shortly afterwards, just before joining the government, Attlee declared at Labour's annual conference that 'the world that must emerge from this war must be a world attuned to our ideals'.[68]

A crucial difference between the ruling class politics of 1914–18 and those of 1939–45, one which was instrumental in ensuring that postwar social reform was delivered, is that the labour movement's leaders were becoming fully incorporated into bourgeois power structures. The knighthood given to Citrine perhaps best demonstrates this incorporation. Two Labour Governments in the interwar period had confirmed the Party's commitment to the capitalist order, even if it still aspired to make it more responsive to working class needs and aspirations. Locally, Labour was, as Mathew Worley has shown in his aptly titled *Labour inside the Gate*,[69] making steady inroads into municipal power, while demonstrating its inherent moderation and respectability. In Ashton, for instance, the leaders of the Trades Council had accepted an invitation to meet the King and Queen on the occasion of their visit to the town in 1938,[70] an episode which inevitably brings to mind Engels's remark that Tom Mann's fondness 'of mentioning that he will be lunching with the Lord Mayor' demonstrated the 'bourgeois respectability' of British labour leaders.[71] And in 1939, Edward Meeks, the Ashton town hall rebel of 1919–22, had been made the town's Mayor.[72] Demonstrating starkly the role of trade unions in maintaining state power, by 1940, six of 16 District Secretaries of the Cardroom Amalgamation were magistrates.[73]

---

65   *Amalgamated Engineering Union Monthly Journal*, December 1939, p. 498.
66   *Ashton Reporter*, 9 February 1940.
67   Brooke 1992, p. 43.
68   Labour Party, *Labour Party Annual Conference Report 1940* (London, 1940), p. 125.
69   Worley 2005.
70   Ashton Trades Council Minutes, meeting undated. DDTC/7 @ TLSAC.
71   Engels to Sorge, 7 December 1889. Marx and Engels 1971, p. 351.
72   *Ashton Reporter*, 13 October 1939. Meeks must have been readmitted to the Labour Party fairly soon after his resignation, for he had again become a Labour councillor in 1928. In 1938 he had become an alderman.
73   Cardroom Amalgamation, Reports and Minutes January 1936–December 1940. Quarterly

The greatly increased power of the labour movement in 1940, compared to 1914, allowed the movement's leaders to play a vital role in the wartime coalition, compared to their marginal role in 1915–18. Such Labour bourgeois politicians and intellectuals as Clement Attlee, Hugh Dalton and Douglas Jay – who, famously, had argued not long before the war that people like him knew 'better what is good for people than the people know themselves'[74] – formed an organic link between the bourgeoisie and the organised working class in the trade unions, as had, though much less effectively, Sidney Webb in the earlier war. Such links helped to determine the content of postwar reform and to foster a growing working class confidence that its support for the war effort would be rewarded.

But in 1940 the key link in forging co-operation between the labour movement and the government was Bevin. While the labour movement's co-operation with the war effort had not so far been fundamentally jolted by the events of that year, who knew what might happen as the war developed? Popular support for war is given in expectation of victory: defeat can easily precipitate social unrest. The memory of 1917–21 in continental Europe must have been vivid in bourgeois circles in Britain in 1940.

The reviving fortunes – membership and sales of publications had both revived after an initial decline[75] – of the CP since it had begun to denounce the war as an imperialist war showed that there was a potential constituency for anti-war politics. Though, as in Pollitt's campaign in Silvertown, the CP's anti-war politics were pacifist and economist, not revolutionary. At a conference of engineering shop stewards held in April 1940, which had 'discussed a broad range of issues, including ... the control of overtime and better working conditions',[76] the party's stewards had made no attempt to raise anti-war sentiment. But that was then. After the military disasters of 1940 in France, who could afford to be complacent regarding the potential for disruption of the CP's highly influential shop stewards? But the government need not have been unduly alarmed. Croucher and Nina Fishman[77] have both shown that while the CP's industrial militants were involved in some strikes, the Party did not aim to disrupt the industrial war effort.

Report and Balance Sheet for the Quarter Ending, 23 March 1940. Report to District Officials from Alfred Roberts, General Secretary. TU/TEX/CARD/17 @ WCML.

74 Cited in Thompson 1990, p. 104. Educated at Winchester and New College, Oxford, Jay had in 1937 been an Oxford University academic economist.
75 The Party claimed that sales of *Labour Monthly* had increased from 10,469 in August 1939 to 14,500 in May 1940. *Labour Monthly*, 23, 1 January 1941.
76 *New Propeller*, 15 April 1940.
77 Croucher 1982; Fishman 1995.

Whatever the threat from the CP, Bevin moved swiftly to bring the trade unions, or at least their leaders, into the imperialist tent alongside the Labour Party's leaders. Immediately after his appointment Bevin gained the agreement of employers and unions to establish a Joint Consultative Committee (JCC) of seven employers and seven union leaders to collaborate on maximising production of war materials. On the same day, engineering unions agreed to relax for the duration of the war all customs impeding war production. Later, the members of the JCC agreed that employers and unions would abide by the decisions of a newly established National Arbitrations Council.[78] Neither unions nor employers objected to the passing of Order 1305, which made strikes and lockouts illegal where collective bargaining structures, more or less universal in the main war industries, existed. Potential labour movement objections were probably neutralised by an Emergency Powers Act which applied salve to a running sore from the earlier world war by allowing the conscription of property as well as labour.

The immediate and spontaneous response of trade union leaders and many ordinary workers to the national crisis of 1940 had been to pledge to work harder to meet the needs of the war effort. The Executive Committee of the Spinners' Amalgamation met with the employers and agreed that those 'engaged in the production of yarns and cloths for barrage balloons' should work two shifts, six days a week for the next four weeks. It was noted that the Cardroom Amalgamation had agreed that a 60-hour week could be worked.[79] The leaders of Oldham's spinners met at the height of the crisis. The government's appeal for 'full speed ahead in industry' was met by a decision to increase their working week from 48 to 55½ hours. 'It is not easy', the spinners' Secretary reflected,

> for men and women to give up the privilege and advantage of a 48 hour week, which was really the only improvement our members received out of the chaos, suffering and tragedies of the last war, but when it is necessary to ease the suffering of our troops and provide them with all the necessary fighting material, I know that none of us will complain.[80]

In Manchester, workers involved in the production of radar at the Metropolitan-Vickers factory worked for 48 hours without a break to complete urgently

---

78   Pelling 1987, pp. 202–6; Weiler 1993, pp. 142–5.
79   Minutes of the Executive Committee of the Spinners' Amalgamation, 17 June 1940. ACS/1/47 @ JRSC.
80   *Oldham Weekly Chronicle*, 15 June 1940.

needed equipment.[81] Such Stakhanovite efforts were common, but could not be maintained for long. Within a few weeks national production levels were back to normal.[82] In response, Bevin toured the country urging industrial workers to maximise production. In Ashton, a week before he was due to speak, interest was 'said to be so great' that the capacity of the 1,000 seat cinema was insufficient. It was arranged for his speech 'to be relayed to the Theatre Royal, where 2,000 can be seated'. On the day both venues were full.[83]

Government measures to boost working class support and morale had soon emerged after Dunkirk. The decision to raise the excess war profits tax from 60 percent to 100 percent was, so 'the official historian of financial policy' claimed, 'essentially a political decision, hastily taken in the heat of the new political climate'.[84] In June, the Food Policy Committee, chaired by Attlee, decided that mothers and their children under five could have free or subsidised milk. In July, the Board of Education decided that all children could have free school meals.[85] An editorial in the Conservative Party's house journal the *Times* (though written by the left-leaning E.H. Carr, the future eminent historian of the Soviet Union), insisted that:

> If we speak of democracy, we do not mean a democracy which maintains the right to vote but forgets the right to work and the right to live. If we speak of freedom, we do not mean a rugged individualism which excludes social organisation and economic planning. If we speak of equality we do not mean a political equality nullified by social and economic privilege. If we speak of economic reconstruction, we think less of maximum production ... than of equitable distribution.[86]

By no means would all Conservatives come to subscribe to such views. We shall see later that the Beveridge Report, the foundation of the postwar 'Welfare State', provoked a great deal of Conservative misgivings and some outright opposition. In early 1943, 116 Tory MPs, clearly believing that they were faced with a modern peasants' revolt, would oppose Bevin's Catering Wages Bill which aimed to enforce minimum wages for catering staff, including those in parliament.[87] But such backwoodsmen were fighting a rearguard action against

---

81 Rowlinson 1949, pp. 39–40.
82 Calder 1969, p. 136.
83 *Ashton Reporter*, 11 October 1940; 18 October 1940.
84 Cited in Addison 1977, p. 116.
85 Addison 1977, p. 116.
86 *Times*, 1 July 1940.
87 Calder 1969, pp. 353–4.

growing sentiment in government and bourgeois circles generally that in 1940 it was not only the army but prevailing socio-economic assumptions which had been found wanting, and that reform, or at least promises of reform, were essential to the successful prosecution of the war and to postwar reconstruction.

In August 1940, Sir Raymond Streat, the Chairman of the Cotton Control Board, heard 'at lunch today' a speech by Bevin (broadcast to the USA) in which he addressed the American Chamber of Commerce. 'His goal is what he calls "Social Justice". If we win the war he will see to it, I fancy, that a social revolution will take place'.[88] A few months later, Streat expressed an increasingly widespread sense of optimism for the future when opening a Cotton Industry War Exhibition designed to show the trade's contribution to the war effort (typical of British indifference to the interests of the colonial peoples, the *Manchester Guardian*, reporting Streat's speech, remarked that the 'Mosquito and sandfly nets, camouflage coverings for tanks, guns and lorries' on display showed the debt which our armies in Africa may owe to Lancashire). Commenting on the postwar prospects for cotton, Streat spoke of his 'confidence', based on his belief that the industry and its workers

> would be definitely more versatile, resourceful and generally effective ... after the war by reason of their wartime experiences. He could see these qualities growing by leaps and bounds in his daily work ... Progress was in the air, and millowner, merchant and operatives could all benefit from it.[89]

While few concrete proposals emerged before the turn of the war at El Alamein in late 1942, three momentous developments before then were heralds of the postwar world, the first concrete and significant signs that postwar politics would rest on a pact between labour and capital. In the spring of 1941, in response to TUC concerns regarding health insurance, the Ministry of Health announced the formation of a committee to undertake a comprehensive survey of social security and to make recommendations for the future. William Beveridge, he of the eponymous Report, chaired the committee.[90] The spring of 1941 also saw a major step towards the postwar policy of full employment. The budget for that year signified the ideological defeat (until comparatively recently) of the 'balanced budget' approach of the interwar years and the

---

88   Sir Raymond Streat, Diaries 1939–45. Entry for 20 August 1940, GB133=133ERS @ JRSC.
89   *Manchester Guardian*, 19 March 1941.
90   Jefferys 1991, pp. 112–13.

triumph of Keynesian deficit financing.[91] In the autumn the government announced that 'as soon as may be possible after the war' it intended to 'ensure that by means of a comprehensive hospital service, appropriate treatment shall be readily available to every person in need of it'.[92]

4   Never Again! The Early Growth of Popular Reform Sentiment

From early in the war, particularly after the crisis of 1940, there had emerged a rapidly growing, if inchoate, movement for reform, an insistence that out of the war there must emerge a better world, a world much more responsive to the needs of working class people. In Lancashire, local politicians, business people, churchmen, journalists, labour leaders and so on articulated and disseminated such ideas. In February 1940, Gwyn Thomas, the newly elected President of Oldham's branch of the National Union of Teachers (NUT), insisted that the war must lead to a radically new concept of both education and democracy. In the postwar world, Thomas insisted, the 'mass of the people' will have to be assured of an 'education which will give them a sense of power and a sense of responsibility'. As for democracy, he was 'convinced that democracy is a dangerous delusion, unless the people have, and know that they have, the power to realise their dream of a good society'.[93]

During the battle for France, the Dean of Manchester, F. Garfield Hodder-Williams declared at a conference in Ashton that 'A new England will come after this war. What kind, God only knows, but it will be new from top to bottom. Every kind of condition … will be new … Economically the thing is obvious. The whole country will be new … We are in one of those great moments in history when you can hear the old things passing and the new inevitably coming'. Demonstrating that these were not just the views of a wild visionary churchman, the *Reporter* devoted a complete and prominent column to this speech.[94] This mood accelerated after Dunkirk. It was noted that at Ashton's mayor-making ceremony of 1940 (probably indicating a loss of confidence among the town's affluent citizens), far fewer top hats than usual were being worn, and women ambulance drivers in the procession daringly wore 'blue slacks'.[95]

---

91   Brooke 1992, pp. 245–50.
92   Thane 1996, p. 187.
93   G. Thomas, 'Education in Wartime and Afterwards', *Oldham Weekly Chronicle*, 2 February 1940.
94   *Ashton Reporter*, 17 May 1940.
95   *Ashton Reporter*, 22 November 1940.

A discordant note had been struck in Oldham, where the Libraries Committee had banned from the town's libraries the *Daily Worker, Tribune, Peace News* and the fascist paper *Action* on the grounds that they were 'seditious' publications.[96] More typical of Oldham opinion was a resolution passed by the Women's Citizens Association, who called for the introduction of family allowances and 'family income insurance'.[97] In the autumn, George Tomlinson, the Labour MP for Farnworth, addressed a Labour Party conference in Greenfield, near Oldham. He was sure that out of the war would emerge 'a new world, a kind that the people would find to their liking. The war would ... open the eyes of the people'. If labour people 'kept their movement intact the future would undoubtedly be theirs'.[98]

At Ashton Labour Party's annual fair and sale of work in the autumn of 1940, Councillor William Andrew, the party's President, referred to that year's events on the 'continent'; 'it was not members of our class who betrayed the continent. It was the Lavals [Pierre Laval became a leading figure in the Vichy government] ... who let the people down. I ask you to keep our organisation intact, so when the time comes we shall be able to speak for England, for social justice and security'.[99] In December, at a CP public meeting, Sam Wild (a CP member who had been the commander of the British battalion of the International Brigade in the Spanish Civil War) argued, at a time when the CP still nominally regarded the war as an imperialist war, that a man from an officer training corps was not necessarily better equipped to lead the defence of his country than a man 'who came from a workshop and factory and had led his trade organisation'.[100]

But in Mossley, the crisis of 1940 seems to have done little to undermine the prevailing stuffiness and conservatism of the town's millocrats and their representatives. The vicar of St James's church thundered from his pulpit that he had been 'appalled' to have 'seen with his own eyes ... brazen women' going straight from the mill to the pub. He had 'been told', but hoped it was 'not true', that there are 'women who drink at dances'. Women 'who drink with men are brazen and have lost all sense of shame and decency'.[101] Alderman Farr's (the same Farr we

---

96 The *Chronicle* criticised the decision to ban these papers. It published a letter of protest from *The Tribune*'s editor, who insisted that the paper 'is, and has been, for the relentless prosecution of the war against Nazism. We have ceaselessly pointed out to the workers that nothing could be more disastrous for them and their liberty than a Hitler victory'. *Oldham Weekly Chronicle*, 21 August 1940.
97 *Oldham Weekly Chronicle*, 6 July 1940.
98 *Oldham Weekly Chronicle*, 7 September 1940.
99 *Ashton Reporter*, 29 November 1940.
100 *Ashton Reporter*, 6 December 1940.
101 *Mossley and Saddleworth Reporter*, 12 August 1940.

met in earlier chapters) attempts to get appointed as a spinners' representative on the town's food committee were rebuffed.[102] The *Reporter's* regular columnist *Pennine*'s complaints regarding unwarranted informality during council meetings were answered in November: it was announced that in future, on the announcement '"the Mayor approaches", all will stand until the Mayor is seated'. *Pennine* was satisfied: 'this is as it should be ... Civic dignity must be upheld'.[103]

In this early phase of the war, support for 'British Restaurants' epitomised a growing belief that Britain must become a much more collectivist society. Autumn 1940 saw the beginning of the Blitz, the German imperialists' campaign to bomb Britain into submission. It had been assumed that aerial bombing would leave tens, if not hundreds, of thousands of people homeless and in need of emergency accommodation and feeding. After the 'Christmas Blitz' over Manchester, Ashton and Oldham councils moved quickly to establish communal feeding centres. Oldham council was preparing to set up centres to feed thousands.[104] A special meeting of Ashton council's Economy Committee agreed that such centres should be set up. Committee members planned to inspect a centre at Ardwick, a district of Manchester a mile or so outside the city centre.[105] But damage caused by German bombing, though severe, was much less than had been anticipated. Moreover, it soon became clear that bombing would be concentrated on major cities and that most other places would be little affected (our three towns endured little bombing, though 27 people were killed in Oldham by a V1 missile (the so-called 'doodlebug' or 'flying bomb') late in the war[106]). In many places plans for communal feeding were with government encouragement adapted to set up British Restaurants. Nationally, 2,500 had been set up by September 1943.[107]

The *Ashton Reporter* supported the decision to establish British Restaurants, but acknowledged that some had misgivings – would it be like a 'glorified soup kitchen' which people would associate with the depression? Others were sceptical that there would be a demand for it.[108] But in Ashton and Oldham, enthusiasts for British Restaurants soon emerged.[109] It was argued that they

---

102 *Mossley and Saddleworth Reporter*, 23 August 1940.
103 *Mossley and Saddleworth Reporter*, 17 November 1940.
104 *Oldham Weekly Chronicle*, 28 December 1940.
105 Ashton Council, Minutes of the Economy Committee, 13 January 1941. CA/ASH 111/53 @ TLSAC.
106 *Manchester Guardian*, 27 April 1945.
107 Field 2011, p. 132.
108 *Ashton Reporter*, 14 February 1941.
109 See Price 1988 for a fuller discussion of British Restaurants.

would to some degree socialise one of the main conventionally accepted social responsibilities of women, i.e., the provision of family food, and thus allow women to play a greater role in the war effort. Further, by providing modestly priced nourishing food, they would give working class people access to food 'off the ration', previously the prerogative of those who could afford to patronise private restaurants.[110] In Ashton, Labour's Councillor Mrs Mamourian argued that a British Restaurant would 'free many women from household cooking and enable them to take part in work of national importance'.[111] Early in 1941 the *Oldham Chronicle* devoted half a page to a speech by Margaret Bondfield at Failsworth Co-operative Hall. The war, she said, had 'led to a much more collective spirit'. After the war, there must be built 'a world system of trade that would really put service before profit, just as a teacher or doctor does'. Bondfield lauded British Restaurants as a practical example of this spirit. Moreover, in order to curtail the practice of the better-off eating 'off ration' in conventional restaurants, only British Restaurants should be allowed to serve meat.[112]

In April 1941, Oldham's 'Churchill' Municipal Restaurant (a British Restaurant in all but name) was opened. The considerable importance with which the *Chronicle* regarded this event was demonstrated by the half page devoted to it, accompanied by a prominent photograph of local worthies, including the Mayor, in attendance. A three-course meal of lentil soup, roast beef, carrots and potatoes, apple sponge and custard could be had for 6d. Alderman Buckley emphasised what a 'boon' the restaurant would be for many people. 'Women who have been asked to go into industry', for instance, would be able to 'obtain a really first class meal for a nominal sum'. Perhaps to emphasise that in the *Chronicle's* view there was no need to impose restrictions on what private restaurants could offer, it was reported that the Churchill Restaurant 'was full of people eager to try it and it is difficult to imagine anyone going away disappointed'.[113]

---

110 The ability of the better-off to supplement rations by eating in restaurants caused considerable resentment among working class people. The influential columnist, 'Cassandra' of the *Mirror*, called for this (probably deliberate) loophole to be closed. 'Stop this food scandal', *Daily Mirror*, 8 January 1941.

111 *Ashton Reporter*, 28 February 1941.

112 *Oldham Weekly Chronicle*, 15 March 1941. In the Labour Government of 1929–31, Bondfield had become the first ever female Cabinet Minister. She had been one of the minority of ministers who argued for severe cuts in unemployment benefit following the Wall Street crash of 1929. Bondfield's case might not then have carried much weight with members of Oldham's labour movement.

113 *Oldham Weekly Chronicle*, 19 April 1941. By November 1943, six British restaurants had opened in Oldham. *Oldham Weekly Chronicle*, 20 November 1943.

In August a British Restaurant was opened at Ryecroft Hall, in Audenshaw. Many travelled there from Ashton. Many employees from local factories 'appreciated the comfort of the dining room ... and the excellence of the food'.[114] In September, Ashton's first British Restaurant was opened by Lady Jowitt (the wife of William Jowitt). Jowitt described the restaurant as 'a first line of defence' which would prove a 'blessing to many war workers' and referred to the benefits of 'communal feeding'.[115] A second British Restaurant opened in September 1942. At the opening ceremony Councillor Ratcliffe remarked that the success of the restaurants 'answered those who questioned the wisdom of communal feeding ... the restaurants were patronised by people from all walks of life, not merely artisans'.[116]

In keeping with its general conservatism and stuffiness, Mossley council stoutly resisted pressure to establish a British Restaurant. In September 1941, various councillors raised blinkered objections: food consumed would not be cooked in Mossley and therefore would not benefit local businesses; Councillor Heap claimed that 'many a good meal came from a chip shop – people did not appreciate how nutritious potatoes were'; others spoke of the value of 'tu'penny pies' and 'steak puddings'; 'many would think themselves lucky if they could get a pie for dinner'. Rather than agree to the opening of a British Restaurant, the council decided to approach the Food Control Committee to see if chip shops could be provided with extra fat to allow more fish and chips to be cooked.[117] In 1942, the council, skilled in procrastination, referred a letter from the Ministry of Food 'urging the establishment of a British restaurant' to the General Purposes Committee.[118] Despite an agreement in principle in 1943 to open a British Restaurant,[119] there is no evidence that one was ever provided.

Dissent from the emerging consensus was to be found on the left as well as on the right. A symptom of submerged unrest had been the relative success of the CP-inspired People's Convention of January 1941. It was intended that the Convention would launch a mass movement for the formation of a People's Government, deemed to be the precondition for a just war against Nazi Germany. The CP's desperate desire to be able to join the defence of Britain was made very clear indeed by the Convention's programme, which prominently

---

114 *Ashton Reporter*, 15 August 1941.
115 *Ashton Reporter*, 19 September 1941.
116 *Ashton Reporter*, 18 September 1942.
117 *Mossley and Saddleworth Reporter*, 18 September 1941.
118 Mossley Council Minutes 1941–42, meeting of full council, 21 July 1942. CA/MOSS 101/20 @ TLSAC.
119 Mossley Council Minutes 1944, Minutes of Special British Restaurant Committee. 5 January 1944. A meeting of 15 November 1943 had approved plans. CA/MOSS 101/22 @ TLSAC.

featured a long quotation from the Digger Gerrard Winstanley's *Appeal to all Englishmen* of 1650: 'This Commonwealth's freedom will unite the hearts of Englishmen together, so that if a foreign enemy endeavours to come in, we shall all, with joint consent, rise up to defend our inheritance'.[120] 2,234 delegates attended the inaugural meeting of the Convention.[121] Further evidence that the CP was successfully tapping into currents of unrest came a month later, when the party won 15 percent of the vote at the Dumbartonshire by-election (the Labour vote increased by 43 percent[122]). A Home Office observer reported that the communists had 'succeeded in mobilising more goodwill than was reflected in the actual vote'.[123]

5 Dissent and Discontent in the Working Class and in the Labour Movement

The CP had campaigned vigorously to build labour movement support for the People's Convention, but had faced implacable opposition from the movement's leadership. In December 1940, at the height of the campaign for the Convention, the TUC had withdrawn recognition from Manchester and Salford Trades Council, due to its 'toleration' of communists. Delegates had been 'regularly seen taking part in Communist meetings or in meetings of variously named bodies whose active spirits are mostly Communists'.[124] Shortly afterwards, ten members of the CP were 'removed from the list of delegates' to the council.[125] Nationally, six people were expelled from the Labour Party for working on the People's Convention campaign and, following 'representations made to them', 40 people withdrew from the party.[126] Suspicion continued. In 1942, Labour Party headquarters warned local parties that their party's campaign to help the Soviet Union was the *Help for Russia* fund. Other committees had been set up by the CP 'to lure all and sundry into their net'. Party headquarters should be consulted before taking part in public meetings on Russia or should

---

120 *Programme and Agenda* for the People's Convention (London, 1941). On the front of the *Programme* was printed Pollitt's favourite quote, 'rise like lions from slumber', from Shelley's *Masque of Anarchy*, written in denunciation of the Peterloo Massacre of 1819.
121 *The People Speak* (Report of the People's Convention) (London, 1941). The success of the Convention led to a ban on the *Daily Worker*, in place until September 1942.
122 Jefferys 1991, p. 223.
123 'Dumbartonshire by-election', Home Intelligence Report, 5 March 1941. INF 1/2/492 @ NAK.
124 *Manchester Guardian*, 21 December 1940.
125 Minutes of Manchester and Salford Trades Council, 16 February 1941 @ WCML.
126 Labour Party, *Labour Party Annual Conference Report 1941* (London, 1941), p. 51.

take part only in such meetings as were organised by their own Party, the Ministry of Information or local authorities.[127] As late as 1943, when the CP had more than established its patriotic credentials, the nomination of the prominent engineering shop steward Eddy Frow[128] as a delegate to Manchester and Salford Trades Council was not accepted 'as the rule in relation to members of the Communist Party is still in operation'.[129]

The moderate line pursued by the CP since 1935, even in 1939–41, was presumably instrumental in building sufficient support in Ashton to allow a party bookshop to be opened there. By September 1942 Ashton CP had 130 members and Oldham 109.[130] But, assuming that local recruitment patterns followed national and regional trends,[131] the great majority of these members would have been recruited since June 1941, when the Soviet Union had entered the war, and would not have been very active members.[132] Another major problem for the Party in Lancashire was its comparative weakness in the cotton trade. Only 10 of the delegates to the Lancashire and Cheshire District Congress in 1945 had a background in textiles, compared with 73 in engineering.[133] It is unsurprising then that the CP had little success – certainly in our three towns – in building a mass Convention movement in Lancashire. The Ashton CP meeting at which Sam Wild had spoken had been convened to elect a delegate to the inaugural Convention meeting (initially intended to be at Manchester's Free Trade Hall because of the city's historic associations with Chartism, but was switched to

---

127 Labour Party, *Labour Party Annual Conference Report 1943* (London, 1943), p. 16.
128 In later years, Eddy Frow was mainly responsible for building the collection of labour movement archive material now held at the WCML.
129 Minutes of Manchester and Salford Trades Council, 19 September 1943 @ WCML.
130 *Lancashire News*, September 1942. By 1945, Ashton and Oldham branches had, respectively, 139 and 116 members. *Lancashire and Cheshire News*, 3 December 1945. A reorganisation had led to the formation of a Lancashire and Cheshire District of the CP. *Lancashire News* and *Lancashire and Cheshire News* were both district committee publications for members only.
131 Of the CP's 56,000 members at the end of 1942, at least 65 percent had been recruited since June 1941 (calculation based on membership statistics in Thorpe 2000, Appendix II); in the first quarter of 1942, the Lancashire District's membership increased by 202 percent. *World News and Views*, 18 April 1942.
132 Many new members found it too taxing even to read the *Daily Worker*: 'Approximately 50 percent' did not, according to a complaint of the leadership in the spring of 1943. *World News and Views*, 17 April 1943. The Lancashire and Cheshire DC complained later in the war that apart from the factory groups 'the Party only lives through the Branch Committee. There is little or no organised life in the form of active area and ward groups', *Lancashire News*, 15 January 1944.
133 *Lancashire and Cheshire News*, February 1945. It is unlikely that these proportions had been significantly different earlier in the war.

London due to the Manchester hall sustaining bomb damage). From the floor, Labour's Councillor Ratcliffe asked how a People's Government was to come into being. The CP speaker disingenuously replied that such questions should not be addressed to the CP, as the Convention was not a CP organisation. Nominated, Ratcliffe declined to attend the Convention.[134]

Early in 1941 a Convention meeting, presumably organised by the CP, was held in Ashton. The main speaker was William Blackwell, who had attended the inaugural meeting of the Convention with two other delegates from Ashton. Blackwell spoke mainly on the banning of the *Daily Worker*. Accusations that the *Worker* was hindering the war effort were met not with a denunciation of the war as an imperialist war but by affirming the paper's attacks on 'profiteers' and its demand for deep shelters 'instead of shelters such as those recently demolished in Ashton'. At a meeting of the trades council, where a CP circular asking for support for a campaign to end the ban on the *Worker* was discussed, it was argued that the paper should have been banned 'long ago'. The meeting resolved that the issue should 'lie on the table and that they take no further notice of it'.[135]

According to a Mass Observation reporter present, 'the vast majority' of those present at the inaugural meeting of the convention had been 'ordinary trade unionists, etc., of very varying shades of left-ish opinion'.[136] Those attracted to the convention were, presumably, mostly those who were supportive of the war but did not consider that the class struggle should be put in abeyance for the duration of the war. In preparation for the Convention, no attempt had been made to raise anti-war sentiments. The two main demands raised at the convention were 'defence of the people's living standards' and 'defence of the people's democratic and trade union rights'.[137]

Working class support for the British war effort, whether motivated by patriotism or anti-fascism, should not be mistaken for support for the employers. Though it has been argued that 'most of industry remained essentially peaceful',[138] antagonism and mutual suspicion between employers and workers did not evaporate simply because war had been declared. A Mass Observation report from the North of England around the time of Dunkirk argued that 'the most striking feature of the industrial situation here is the survival of strictly

---

134 A Mr D. Goodwin (presumably a CP member) was to attend the Convention. *Ashton Reporter*, 6 December 1940.
135 *Ashton Reporter*, 7 February 1941.
136 Cited in Morgan 1989, p. 204.
137 Ibid.
138 Fielding et al. 1995, p. 31.

peacetime procedures in the conflict between employers and men, which is still today the predominant conflict here'.[139]

After Dunkirk, no doubt mindful of the rapid inflation and severe food shortages which had caused so much working class unrest in World War I, the government imposed increasing and effective controls on the economy. In the first few months of the war, a reluctance to introduce rationing had led to rapidly increasing food prices. Rationing was introduced in January 1940 and then gradually extended, so that by the war's end most basic foodstuffs were rationed. By the middle of 1941 inflation had been stabilised. On average, due to controls, full employment and overtime, working class real wages rose by 25 percent in the war years.[140] Workers in the cotton trade probably enjoyed an increase in real wages.[141]

The number of strikes fell sharply in the period immediately following Dunkirk (though even then the secretary of Ashton's Spinners reported that he 'had attended to conflicts and disputes' at 15 Ashton mills),[142] but began slowly to rise again once the immediate invasion scare was over. In the cotton trade, a lockout of spinners in 1929[143] and the 'more looms' disputes of 1931 and 1932,[144] had both generated much ill will towards employers, even if economic decline and unemployment had served to undermine militancy. Antagonism between employers and workers persisted throughout the war. ORTEA frequently reported disputes of one sort or another, though few led to strikes. In the spring of 1940, for instance, spinners at the King Mill in Royton did strike, due to the cold, but disputes at the Fir Spinning Mill in Royton over 'time crimping' and at the Granville Mill over 'bad spinning' did not lead to strikes.[145]

But between Dunkirk and El Alamein, the hinge of the war, there were few serious strikes in Lancashire. In and around our three towns, as in most places, there were occasional strikes of a short duration. In Royton, for instance, spinners at the Park Mill struck for a week in January 1941 in protest at the management's refusal to honour a pledge to reinstate a man temporarily laid off. The dispute threatened to spread to other mills.[146] This strike was illegal under the provisions of Order 1305. But six men were charged instead under the

---

139   Cited in Calder 1969, p. 299.
140   Field 2011, pp. 119–21.
141   Fowler 1987a, p. 198.
142   Minutes of Ashton Amalgamation 1939–43, Minutes May–June 1940. ACS/1/47 @ JRSC.
143   Fowler 1987a, pp. 169–72.
144   Employers had tried to force weavers to operate six or even eight looms rather than the traditional four. See Bowden and Higgins 1999.
145   ORTEA Letter Book 1940. AAN/1/1/8/1 @ OLSA.
146   *Oldham Weekly Chronicle*, 11 January 1941.

archaic Master and Workmen's Act of 1875 with leaving work without giving a week's notice. After the men gave pledges not to do so again, the charges were dropped.[147] In the spring, Bevin obtained more power to deal with disputes. Essential Work Orders (EWOs) prevented, without the authority of a Ministry of Labour National Service Officer, employers sacking workers or workers leaving their post in any establishment deemed to be a place of essential work.

EWOs and Order 1305 were used in April 1941 to end a potentially serious strike of engineering apprentices.[148] The dispute began on the Clyde and then spread to several other towns and cities, including several in Lancashire, where apprentices in the poorly paid textile machinery trade went on strike. The strike – over low pay and the failure of the AEU to take the apprentices' grievances seriously – at one point involved 25,000 young men. The AEU in Lancashire accepted that the apprentices had a case, but insisted that 'there must be no interference with production'. They had been told to return to work. The union suspected that 'there is some subversive influence at work. We have reason to believe that a deputation from Glasgow has been going round the shops in this district trying to persuade the youths to strike'.[149] The Lancashire apprentices began to return to work when threatened with prosecution under Order 1305. One strike leader, William Bennison of Ashton, was among six men charged at Manchester Police Court under the provisions of an EWO.[150] By the 7th of April 'nearly all' had returned to work.[151] In Oldham, only 5 percent or so of 500 apprentices who went on strike were still out.[152]

But prosecutions and hard work can achieve only so much. A much more sophisticated means of maximising production and incorporating workers more firmly into the war effort was that of Joint Production Committees (JPCs). Bevin, impatient with production log-jams and what he saw as management dilatoriness and incompetence, and believing that plant-level co-operation of employers and workers was essential, had first floated the idea of JPCs, in which managers and workers would together seek ways to improve production, in October 1940.[153]

---

147   *Oldham Weekly Chronicle*, 18 January 1941.
148   See Croucher 1982, pp. 127–81, for an account of the strike.
149   *Manchester Guardian*, 1 April 1941.
150   *Manchester Evening News*, 4 April 1941.
151   *Manchester Evening News*, 7 April 1941.
152   *Oldham Weekly Chronicle*, 5 April 1941.
153   Field 2011, p. 92.

6 Joint Production Committees: a 'Nazi System of Labour Organisation'?

Though co-operation between employers and workers may well have boosted the government's willingness to concede reform, it is unclear whether JPCs had a significant impact on production.[154] Due to resistance from managements suspicious that JPCs would encroach on management prerogatives and from union leaders concerned that they would usurp the functions of their officials, it was several months before Bevin's ideas took off, and then, at first, only in the Communist Party. The CP too had for some time opposed JPCs: they would 'closely [resemble] the Nazi system of labour organisation'.[155] But from June 1941 the CP desisted from comparing JPCs with Nazi methods, though in truth there was some validity to the comparison. JPCs were effectively plant-level organs of state used to boost production and discipline workers.

Now that the war was no longer to be denounced as an imperialist war, the CP's energies were switched to campaigning for the speediest, more or less immediate, opening of a second front in Europe and, in industry, the sweeping away of all obstacles to the maximum possible production of war materials. While basic working class conditions and rights had to be defended, strikes in vital war industries had to be avoided at all costs. Pollitt denounced the 'total time' strike on Tyneside, which took place during the battle for Stalingrad, as 'a disgrace to all concerned'.[156]

The CP was not completely inflexible on the matter and did from time to time decide that it might be judicious to support, or at least not oppose, a strike. Nina Fishman deploys the oxymoronic concept of 'revolutionary pragmatism' to describe this flexibility in the CP's post-June 1941 industrial policy.[157] Semantic quibbles apart, there was nothing at all revolutionary in this policy: fighting for JPCs and supporting or participating in the occasional strike (to have rigidly opposed them would have been counter-productive) were both essential aspects of the CP's determined support of the British mobilisation for war. Bert Williams, a CP member and shop steward at the Metro-Vickers plant in Manchester, remembered that CP members had participated in strikes called when employers, knowing that their employees could not legally strike, took

---

154   See Hinton 1994 and Fishman 1995 for full discussions of JPCs, their effectiveness and the CP's role in them.
155   *Daily Worker*, 28 December 1940.
156   *Daily Worker*, 6 October 1942. See Croucher 1982, pp. 180–7, for a discussion of this strike.
157   Fishman 1995, p. 12.

advantage of Order 1305 and EWOs to attack working conditions.¹⁵⁸ Hugh Scanlon, the future President of the AEU, was also then a communist shop steward at Metro-Vickers. He remembered that CP members had succeeded in 'squeezing little bits here and there' from management.¹⁵⁹

The CP's extensive network of influential shop stewards, built up in pre-war days to wage the class struggle in the factories, was now being turned into its opposite. The Party organised several successful production conferences, attended by many delegates from Lancashire.¹⁶⁰ Announcing a conference to be held in October 1941, Walter Swanson, the CP convenor at Napier's aircraft factory in Acton, west London, insisted that workers should 'demand the right to play their part in solving production problems as they arise, through the means of Joint Production Committees'.¹⁶¹ At this conference, a Blimpish outburst from a delegate from Merseyside – that not all workers were 'pulling their weight, if a man doesn't pull his weight he should be put in the army' – had drawn applause. After the conference, lest any delegates had had revolutionary objectives in mind, the CP stressed that the conference had been 'useful in clearing up confusion on the role of production committees'. They were *not* to be confused with workers' control of industry (as *The Tribune* had advocated).¹⁶² Similarly, Allan Hutt argued against those in the movement, including some who had attended the conference, who 'clung to ... shibboleths'. He had in mind 'the suggestion that total war could not be waged unless capitalism had been swept away'.¹⁶³

The CP's enthusiastic support for JPCs was probably the principal factor impeding official support for them. Government, employers and trade unions must have been apprehensive at the prospect of Communist shop stewards gaining control of such potentially powerful workplace organisations. The AEU's concern was sufficiently great for it to write to the Prime Minister expressing concern at rumours that the government was going to hold discussions with the shop stewards. The union was adamant that it 'knows nothing of a National Shop Stewards Movement. It gives recognition for no such body as a National Shop Stewards Council'.¹⁶⁴ But soon after the union claimed at a meeting of the JCC that unofficial production committees were being established and that in the absence of official approval they were falling under commun-

---

158 Interview with the author, 1997.
159 Fishman 1995, p. 315.
160 Fishman 1995 pp. 297–8.
161 'How to Increase War Production', *Labour Monthly*, October 1941.
162 *World News and Views*, 25 October 1941. Emphasis in the original.
163 'Production – Key to Victory', *Labour Monthly*, November 1941.
164 *AEU Monthly Journal*, December 1941, p. 286.

ist control.¹⁶⁵ It was this which prompted official sanction for JPCs. In March, engineering employers and unions agreed to their formation. The AEU argued that JPCs were clearly a CP initiative aimed at giving aid to the Soviet Union. But the union supported this objective and also the formation of JPCs. In a sally aimed at the CP, it insisted that 'if such bodies were necessary now, they were certainly not less so at the time of Dunkirk'.¹⁶⁶

Once sanctioned by unions and employers, JPCs sprang up in many engineering factories. By 1944 around 4,500 had been created.¹⁶⁷ In September 1942, the 'first birthday of JPCs was being celebrated by workers at a North West airplane factory ... During the year they claim to have increased production by 250 %'.¹⁶⁸ In the spring of 1944, the CP reported on a campaign 'at a factory in the Oldham area against management attempts to sack a well-known communist' which resulted in management agreement to set up a JPC.¹⁶⁹ In Ashton, a JPC was formed at the factory of the National Gas and Oil Engine Company. The company's work's journal reported in 1944 that the JPC had received 'over 100 suggestions' since it had been formed. In June 1945, just after the war in Europe had ended, it boasted that the 'Shop Stewards Committee has played a vital role in keeping the wheels of production running smoothly ... and we are proud of the fact that there has not been one prosecution for absenteeism or failure to perform Civil Defence duties, nor have we had any strikes'.¹⁷⁰

But the frequency with which members of JPCs felt it necessary to admonish, chivvy and even refer for prosecution laggard workers strongly suggests that many workers did not share their enthusiasm for class collaboration. At the Vickers-Armstrong factory in Manchester, the shop stewards, led by the future Labour MP Frank Allaun, kept a close eye on absenteeism. In November 1942 they insisted that 'the figures shown for absenteeism on the works board are disgraceful and can be altered'. They 'had a word' with persistent offenders.¹⁷¹ CP members working as Manchester tram and bus conductors worked on a joint management-union Absentee Committee which had been 'able to separate those absent with real reason and the deliberate slackers'. The Committee had 'found it necessary to prosecute [presumably under EWOs] only seven cases in the past two months. These were the really bad cases of persistent

---

165   Weiler 1993, p. 126.
166   *AEU Monthly Journal*, April 1942, p. 87.
167   Croucher 1982, p. 155.
168   *Daily Worker*, 8 September 1942.
169   *Lancashire and Cheshire News*, 1 April 1944.
170   'National News', October 1944; June 1945. DD64/9 @ TLSAC.
171   *Factory News* [a publication of the Manchester and Salford branch of the CP], November 1942.

absentees who had not responded to the appeals of the Committee'. By concentrating on such cases, 'absenteeism had been reduced from 15% to 3½%'.[172] There were many other such cases in Manchester's factories and depots.[173]

Calls to set up JPCs in cotton mills seem to have fallen on stony ground. One was presumably set up at Whitehead and Sons (probably the Whitehead mill in Wigan), for a handbill propagating the demands of the Lancashire Women's Parliament of 1942 (which is discussed below) urged that 'Production Committees as in Whitehead and Sons' should 'be set up in mills'.[174] But this was probably an isolated case. Early in 1943, the Lancashire District of the CP noted that 'few' mills had JPCs and argued that 'the question of JPCs for the cotton industry is the next big job to be faced'.[175] Later in the year it urged that 'hostility' to JPCs 'must be overcome'.[176] Alfred Roberts (later to become Sir Alfred Roberts), the General Secretary of the Cardroom Amalgamation was probably a supporter of JPCs. His union had sat on the fence – it 'officially decided not to object to the establishment of works councils' – but Roberts argued that 'we must either reverse this decision and fight the whole works council conception (a dangerous step to take) or make up our minds that this is going to be a valuable adjunct to our movement'.[177] There is no further reference to JPCs in cotton mills in the Cardroom archive. Nor do we find mentions of them in TUC annual conference reports[178] or in the *Trade Letters* of the Cotton Board, which was always anxious to promote innovations and initiatives on production.[179]

---

172 *Lancashire News*, 10 April 1943.
173 Crowley 1998.
174 *Report of the Lancashire Women's Parliament*. This (CP/CENT/ORG/MISC/01/03) and other reports, pamphlets and ephemera from the Women's Parliament movement can be found in the CP archive at the PHM.
175 *Lancashire News*, 2 January 1943.
176 *Lancashire News*, 11 September 1943.
177 It is clear from the context that by 'works councils' Roberts was referring to JPCs. Cardroom Amalgamation, Reports and Minutes January 1941–November 1945. Quarterly Report and Balance Sheet for the Quarter ending 27 June 1942. Report to District Officials from Alfred Roberts, General Secretary. TU/TEX/CARD/18 @ WCML.
178 In the 1944 report, for instance, there are several mentions of engineering JPCs, but no mention of any in cotton mills. Trade Union Congress, *Trade Union Congress 76th Annual Conference Report* (London, 1945).
179 The Cotton Control Board's *Trade Letter* for March 1942 reported on the efforts of 'Lancashire Stakhanovites' working at a mill which had daily production targets. Workers with good and/or improved output wore badges with the legend 'war production workers'. To help boost production, 'weekly five minute pep-talks are being given through microphones while the workers have meals in the canteen'. Whether this boosted or hindered production must be moot.

One probable reason for the apparent failure of JPCs to take root in the cotton trade is that communists, who had provided the ideological and political impetus for their take off in engineering, were rare birds in the cotton mills. The militant cotton shop stewards movement which had emerged towards the end of the Great War, and which might well have provided militants for the infant Communist Party, did not survive the severe interwar decline of the trade. Oldham, which had been the centre of the movement, was particularly badly hit by the interwar depression. The number of spindles in its cotton mills fell from 19,651,081 in 1925 to 10,917,661 in 1940.[180] Ashton too, was badly hit. There, the membership of the Weavers' amalgamation fell from 6,500 in 1920 to 1,400 in 1940.[181]

With union collaboration, a new CCB set up by the Cotton Industry Act of 1938 had acted to concentrate production in fewer, larger mills. But the continued decline of the cotton trade (to some degree abated by the demands of the war effort) and a high turnover of workers would have militated against the formation of JPCs. Many workers were conscripted. Others left for better paid and more congenial employment. Though an EWO was applied to the spinning trade, by 1941 a labour shortage had begun to threaten production of war materials. The exhibition which Streat had opened that year had been partly designed to boost recruitment. Appeals, especially to women, to return to the trade became common. A large advertisement in the *Oldham Chronicle* appealed to 'Cotton Operatives – Machines are Idle, Waiting for You! Russian women are fighting in the frontline – they know what it means to them if Hitler Wins'.[182] But the inexorable decline of the industry continued. Between 1939 and 1944 the membership of the Spinners' Amalgamation virtually halved.[183]

As in the First World War, labour shortages due to the large number of men serving in the armed forces affected most industries. There were considerable problems in persuading women to replace men. Doubtless this was the result of capitalism's social conditioning of women. Probably too, many women remembered or were aware of the 'back to the kitchen' campaign which had followed the end of the First World War. A survey in October 1939 suggested that 32 percent of women were unwilling to do any sort of war work. A survey of housewives in 1941 found that around 46 percent of them were unwilling to

---

180   ORTEA Annual Reports 1939–42, Report for 1940, p. 4. AAN/1/1/2/8 @ OLSA.
181   Central Committee of the Weavers' Amalgamation, Annual Report for year ending 31 March 940. DDX 1123/1/35 @ LROP.
182   *Oldham Weekly Chronicle*, 23 December 1941.
183   Fowler 1987a, p. 197.

work in factories and that 43 percent were only willing to engage in war work if such domestic obstacles to participation as childcare and shopping were overcome.[184]

7   Out of the Kitchen Again: Mobilising Women to 'Do Their Bit'

By July 1940 only 320,000 additional women had moved into the labour force, strongly suggesting that the government's Manpower [sic] Requirements Committee target of an additional two million industrial workers to replace men moving into the armed forces would not be met.[185] In March 1941 a system of voluntary registration for war work was set up. Women aged 19–40 were encouraged to register with their local labour exchange. By August only 2 million out of approximately 10 million eligible women had registered. The National Service Act of December 1941 then introduced conscription for single women and childless widows between the ages of twenty and thirty inclusive. The maximum age was increased to 40 in January 1943. By 1943, due to persuasion and coercion, 7.5 million women were in employment, compared to 6.25 million in 1939. The greatest increase, presumably accounted for by women in munitions, was in engineering, up from 97,000 to 602,000.[186] It is highly likely that this increased participation in industry was a significant factor in the substantial wartime increase in support for the Labour Party among women, a matter explored in the next chapter.

The much greater acceptance of 'dilution' in World War II compared with World War I suggests that the male chauvinist attitudes discussed in Chapter 1 had been undermined to some extent. In Oldham, where the employment of women as tram conductors had provoked so much opposition from men in the earlier war, one newly appointed woman bus conductor claimed, a little implausibly, that 'all the men have been very kind and helpful, and will do anything they can to make things easy and pleasant for us'.[187] There was no opposition in Ashton either.[188] By the summer of 1941 more than half of the town's bus conductors were women. The council was to discuss whether they should wear skirts or slacks.[189]

---

184   Field 2011, p. 129.
185   Ibid.
186   Calder 1969, pp. 308–10.
187   *Oldham Weekly Chronicle*, 29 June 1940.
188   *Ashton Reporter*, 9 August 1940.
189   *Ashton Reporter*, 29 August 1941.

But male chauvinist attitudes had certainly not been vanquished. While Ashton's council was happy to employ women as bus conductors, employing women as police officers was another matter: 'there is no possibility of policewomen being seen in Ashton … there is ample provision for female prisoners, as there are already two police matrons'.[190] In 1941 some Ashton shopkeepers tried to resolve cigarette shortages by refusing to sell them to women.[191] Objections were raised against women carrying out fire-watching duties. In Oldham, for instance, cardroom workers claimed, in what was very likely in reality a fear of illicit night-time sexual encounters, that such duties were 'not conducive to the smooth running of the war effort as many husbands and sweethearts in "HM Forces" will resent such an order which places their wives and sweethearts in dangers which should be borne solely by men'.[192] Underlying such attitudes were of course ideological assumptions that whatever they might do in the war, women's role was still primarily domestic. Moreover, it was precisely factors arising from this role, such as inconvenient shop opening hours, which, as the women responding to the survey of 1941 well knew, which would present considerable difficulties for working women and prevent them from realising their full potential in war work.[193]

The cotton unions, despite their many female members, furnish many examples of male chauvinism. In July 1940 Henry Boothman, the Secretary of Ashton's spinners wrote to the President of the Board of Trade expressing 'much concern' at the substitution of ring spinning for mule spinning at the Texas Mill, 'which throws males out of work and permanently substitutes females'.[194] That autumn, Roberts of the Cardroom Amalgamation gave a warm welcome to legislation which, after a long campaign by the amalgamation, had finally recognised Byssinosis (a disease, similar to Pneumoconiosis, caused by inhaling cotton particles) as an occupational disease and provided for compensation for those suffering from it. Roberts failed to mention that although c. 80 percent of cardroom workers were women, the legislation applied only to men.[195] The Secretary of the Oldham District of the amalgamation wrote

---

190   *Ashton Reporter*, 13 September 1940.
191   *Ashton Reporter*, 27 September 1941.
192   Cardroom Amalgamation, Minutes of Oldham district of South East Lancashire Cardroom Amalgamation, Minutes of 24 October 1942. TU/12/5 @ OLSA.
193   See Braybon and Summerfield 1987, Summerfield 1989, and Williams 2002, for general discussions of women in industry in World War II.
194   Spinners' Amalgamation, Ashton file, 1936–56. Ashton Association to President of Board of Trade, 12 July 1940. ACS/6/2/6 @ JRSC.
195   Cardroom Amalgamation, Reports and Minutes January 1936–December 1940. Quarterly

to protest that 'steps should be taken to include females under the Byssinosis legislation',[196] but there is no evidence that steps were taken.

For some male trade unionists, boosting production was the main consideration. In Ashton, a joint meeting, chaired by Goggins, the retired secretary of Ashton's weavers, was held late in 1940 to discuss the 'urgent need for recruits in connection with munitions work, especially for women'.[197] The meeting seems to have been productive, for a few weeks later Goggins and others wrote to the *Reporter* to inform its readers that 'fifty women from Ashton and district are training at the Ministry of Labour centre near Manchester'. But there was still an 'urgent' need for both men and women to train for 'work connected with the war effort'. The *Reporter*, keen to do its bit, featured a major article and a photograph of women training in Salford. Ashton was said to be the first town to send a contingent: 'the general opinion of the women' was said to be 'I'd sooner do this than housework'.[198]

Many of those women who did move into industry faced considerable difficulties. Locally, disputes on the issue of 'dilution' erupted from time to time. In the autumn of 1940, there was a brief strike on the issue at a factory in Guide Bridge, near Ashton. And in the winter, skilled men at Northern Aircraft objected to an attempt 'to use semi-skilled labour [of women] on a particular job [which] our steward claimed ... should be done by skilled labour'.[199] The agreement between engineering employers and unions that women should enjoy equal pay with men was regularly flouted. A notable strike on this was that of 16,000 women (and a fair number of men) in 1943 at the Rolls-Royce engineering plant at Hillington, Glasgow. In a victory of sorts, it was agreed that the rate for the job would be determined by the machine being operated, not the gender of the person operating it.[200]

In principle, women started on the women's rate (typically 50 percent) and moved incrementally to the full rate as they showed they could work without supervision. Even so, many employers evaded the 1940 agreement. A shop stewards survey of 58 engineering factories found that only 31 percent of women

---

    Report and Balance Sheet for the Quarter ending 26 December 1940. Report to District Officials from Alfred Roberts, General Secretary. TU/TEX/CARD/17 @ WCML.
196 Cardroom Amalgamation, Executive Council Meeting 6 March 1941. TU/TEX/CARD/18 @ WCML.
197 *Ashton Reporter*, 27 December 1940.
198 *Ashton Reporter*, 24 January 1941.
199 Ashton AEU District Committee Minutes, 13 October 1940 and 1 December 1940. TU/ENG /7/2/3 @ WCML.
200 Croucher 1982, p. 285.

doing equal work with men were getting equal pay.[201] In Ashton in 1941, the District Committee resolved, in reference to another dispute at Northern Aircraft, that it objected, 'to our members working with women who are not receiving the conditions as laid down in the [1940] Agreement'.[202] This dispute highlighted a fundamental problem with the agreement. Only members of the union were eligible for the full men's rate, but it was not until 1943 that the union decided to allow women to join. By the end of the war 138,717 women had joined the AEU. But women were not admitted to full membership – their membership cards were stamped 'Temporary Relaxation Agreement', reflecting an assumption that women would not be working in engineering after the war.[203]

Difficulty in shopping was but one aspect of a double burden of work and domestic responsibilities afflicting working women. Absenteeism was twice as high among women as among men,[204] partly due to women attempting to get their shopping done in working hours. There were sporadic and ineffectual attempts by the government to persuade shop owners to be more flexible in their opening hour.[205] In Oldham, where the Cardroom Amalgamation argued that 6pm closing meant that women workers could not get to the shops before they closed, the town council agreed, with the support of the shop assistants union and the Chamber of Commerce, that shops should open until 7pm on most days and until 7.30 on Fridays.[206]

In Ashton and in Mossley there had been frequent reports of shop assistants resisting staying open later. A frequent complaint in all three of our towns was that there was nothing left in the shops after the 'stay-at-homes' had done their shopping. In late 1941, Emily Hector, the president of Ashton and District Weavers Association, pleaded for improved shopping facilities for women workers. 'As a trade unionist', she argued, 'I am prepared to stand up to the shop assistants and say they must do more for the war'.[207] In the autumn of 1942, Oldham's Health Committee was urged by the T&LC to win more concessions from shopkeepers. They should be reminded of the 'importance of shops remaining open at midday in order to give women shoppers the opportunity of doing their shopping during the lunch-hour interval'. Why, the council asked, does the gov-

---

201   Croucher 1982, p. 211.
202   Ashton AEU District Committee Minutes, 1914 (undated). TU/ENG/7/2/4 @ WCML.
203   Summerfield 1989, p. 143.
204   Field 2011, p. 142.
205   Gardiner 2004, p. 518.
206   *Oldham Weekly Chronicle*, 30 November 1940.
207   *Ashton Reporter*, 5 December 1941.

ernment 'constantly overlook' this question which is so important if women are to play 'an ever-increasing part in the war effort?'[208]

It was in an attempt to resolve such problems that in 1941 the Women's Parliaments movement had been launched. According to Noreen Branson, house historian of the CP, the idea for Women's Parliaments came out of discussions between Ted Bramley, the London District Secretary of the party and Tamara Rust, a London District Committee member 'responsible for women's work'. A suggestion was 'passed on to the organisation known as the People's Convention'.[209] The name chosen for the movement was probably intended to invoke memories of the pre-1914 Women's Parliaments set up by the WSPU. But the wartime Women's Parliament movement was not a feminist movement. The role of women in capitalist society was not challenged. At Lancashire Women's Parliament, held in Manchester in April 1942, where, as we saw earlier, there was a call for JPCs to be established in cotton mills, a member of the NUT insisted, to 'applause', that 'wartime work must be made to fit in with women's jobs as mothers'.[210]

The first Women's Parliament met in London in July 1941. The opening address was by the actor Beatrix Lehman. She was not a Communist, but she moved in left-wing circles. The main business was a 'bill' to 'safeguard the health and well-being of women in industry'. Demands were made, *inter* alia, for equal pay, that women should join unions, for extended shopping hours and for communal restaurants.[211] There is no record of further sessions of the Lancashire parliament, but sessions of the London parliament continued to 1945, when 771 delegates attended, compared to 346 in 1941.[212] Other parliaments met in Bradford, Newcastle, Glasgow and South Wales. They attracted support of one sort or another from such disparate characters as Lady Astor, Megan Lloyd George and Eleanor Rathbone.[213]

Colonial freedom had been a notable absence in the demands of the Women's Parliaments. Probably, in keeping with the determinedly moderate

---

208 *Oldham Weekly Chronicle*, 23 October 1942.
209 Branson 1997, p. 45.
210 *Report of the Lancashire Women's Parliament*; CP/CENT/ORG/MISC/01/03 @ PHM. There is a PhD or at least an MA dissertation yet to be written on the Women's Parliament movement. The collection of reports, pamphlets and ephemera in the CP archive would be a good place to start.
211 *Report of the First Session of the London Women's Parliament*. CPA, CP/CENT/ORG/MISC/01/03 @ PHM.
212 *Report of the Second Session of the London Women's Parliament*. CPA, CP/CENT/ORG/MISC/01/03 @ PHM.
213 Field 2011, p. 318.

stance adopted by the CP since 1935, it had been deemed too controversial. In the autumn of 1936, for instance, shortly after the Comintern's Seventh Congress, Pollitt had met with Bevan and other members of the Labour left to discuss the prospects for anti-fascist unity. Pollitt asked Bevan why there was not a demand for colonial independence in a draft of a proposed joint manifesto, but did not press the matter.[214] Similarly, when challenged on why there was no demand for colonial freedom in the programme of the 'People's Government' which the People's Convention of January 1941 had called for,[215] the CP had replied that such a demand was 'implicit'.[216] The CP itself remained nominally committed to colonial independence, but, like the rest of the labour movement, regarded this as conditional on defeating Britain's imperial rivals.

8 Not Counting the Colonies: the Labour Movement and the Empire

If Churchill's main motivation in political life was not the defence of Empire, it was certainly a primary objective in his war leadership. But in August 1941, as part of the price for United States support for the British war effort, Churchill committed Britain to upholding the principles of the Atlantic Charter, one of which pledged the signatories to 'respect the right of all peoples to choose the form of government under which they will live'. On his return from Newfoundland, where the Charter had been signed, Churchill insisted in the House of Commons that this principle was to be applied to those currently 'under the Nazi yoke',[217] and thus, implicitly, not to the peoples of the British Empire.[218] Churchill made his views on self-determination within the British Empire quite explicit on at least two subsequent wartime occasions. In 1942 he famously told the House of Commons that he had not 'become the King's First Minister in order to preside over the liquidation of the British Empire'.[219] During the Yalta Conference of 1945 he insisted that the self-determination clauses of the Yalta Accords 'did not apply to the British Empire'.[220]

---

214 Minutes of CP Political Bureau, 13 November 1936. CPA, Moscow Microfilm reel 16, @ PHM.
215 'Manifesto of the People's Convention', *Labour Monthly*, November 1940.
216 Morgan 1989, p. 188.
217 Roberts 2009, p. 130.
218 A few days later, Attlee told a gathering of West African students in London that the principles of the Charter 'applied to all races'. PREM 4 43A/3 @ NAK. Probably, Attlee was quite genuine in giving this assurance, but it was worthless.
219 Louis 1977, p. 200.
220 Kolko 1969, p. 249.

The Labour Party did not let its nominal commitment to colonial freedom hinder its wartime alliance with Churchill's ferociously pro-Empire Conservative party. But then Labour's principles were notoriously flexible. 'Jimmy' Thomas, the Colonial Secretary in the first Labour Government of 1924, had famously remarked on taking office that he was there 'to see that there was no mucking about with the British Empire'.[221] True to his word, the Labour Governments of 1924 and 1929–31 were responsible for brutal suppression of the nationalist movement in India.[222]

Colonial freedom did not feature in the various demands for postwar reform made by labour leaders in the first phase of the war. Admittedly, at the Labour Party's 1939 annual conference, the Reverend Reginald Sorenson, MP for Leyton West, sponsored an appropriately pious resolution on colonial policy. Sorenson, who was a harsh critic of Tory colonial policy, argued that in contrast 'the first and supreme purpose of [Labour's] colonial policy' should be 'the promotion of the moral and material welfare of the native peoples'. The delegates were quite happy to pass this resolution, as the conference report stressed, 'by a very large majority'.[223] Needless to say, it had no impact on the pro-imperialist policy of Labour's leaders.

Soon after the German invasion of the Soviet Union, the CP pledged its full support for the allied war effort. The People's Convention and the campaign for a People's Government were now anomalous. But a recalled Convention met on the 5th of July and issued a new call for a People's Government,[224] though the character of the People's Government deemed necessary was now revised: it would be one which, in 'close friendship with the Soviet Union, can appeal to the German people and all other oppressed peoples of Europe' and lead to peace.[225]

What role did anti-colonial struggles have in the now anti-fascist war? In September 1941, the Soviet Party's journal *Bolshevik* signalled, by calling for greater mobilisation of the resources of the British Empire, that colonial freedom must await the defeat of fascism.[226] This stance, after some confusion and

---

221 Ward 1998, p. 185.
222 Ahmed 1987, pp. 53–70.
223 Labour Party, *Labour Party Annual Conference Report 1939* (London, 1939), pp. 309–15.
224 Probably reflecting differences of opinion in the party's leadership over strategy in the new situation in the war, the Convention continued to lead a shadowy existence for some time. The campaign for a people's government was quietly dropped. See Redfern 2005, pp. 110–18, 136–7.
225 *Daily Worker*, 18 July 1941.
226 'The Role of the British Empire in the Current War', cited in Overstreet and Windmiller 1959, p. 194.

difficulty, was adopted by the Indian Party.[227] The British party's nominal commitment to supporting anti-colonial struggles was sloughed off, at least for the duration, as quickly as Japanese imperialism defeated British imperialism in the Far East in the wake of the Japanese attack on the US base at Pearl Harbor, Hawaii in December 1941. In early 1942, Hong Kong, Malaya and Singapore were 'lost' to Japan. The CP was particularly alarmed by the 'loss' of Malaya, 'a country fabulously rich in tin and rubber'. The 'people of Britain' were said to be 'amazed and angry'.[228] And, as the CP's old India hand, Ben Bradley, warned, 'now Burma is in peril, and India'.[229]

The British government did not need a warning from Bradley to be aware of the danger to India. In October 1941 India's Congress Party had started a campaign of civil disobedience which led to the imprisonment of tens of thousands. In early 1942, faced with a twin threat from Japan (which had by then conquered most of Burma and seemed poised to invade India) and the independence movement, Britain released imprisoned Congress leaders. In March 1942 the British cabinet minister Stafford Cripps (known to Nehru and other Congress leaders as Stifford Crapps) flew to India to try to find a way, short of granting independence, of gaining the support of Congress for the war effort. Cripps was a leading figure on the Labour left, a Tribunite who had long been in favour of Indian independence and who had built friendly relations with Congress leaders. During the negotiations, *Tribune* offered gratuitous advice to Congress: 'The overriding consideration which ... the Indians should keep in mind is the imminent danger of Japanese invasion. [Japanese] General Tojo is likely to be much less sympathetic to Indian aspirations than Sir Stafford Cripps'.[230]

The CP tried to raise public support for Congress demands for self-government. A handbill (100,000 were produced according to a marginal note on one of them in the hand of the party's chief ideologue and theoretician, Rajani Palme Dutt) used to promote a rally at Manchester's Belle Vue, insisted that 'democratic opinion in this country must insist upon the immediate establishment of a Provisional Government, so that the mighty resources of Britain and India alongside those of the Soviet Union, America and China can achieve victory over fascism this year'.[231] But the 'Cripps Mission' failed. Congress leaders were not seduced by promises of full independence after the war: while

---

227 Gupta 2006, pp. 208–12.
228 'Malaya "End of an Epoch"', *World News and Views*, 31 January 1942.
229 Bradley 1942.
230 *The Tribune*, 3 April 1942.
231 *India. Statement Issued by the Communist Party*, CPA, CP/IND/DUTT/29/12 @ PHM.

they were prepared to wait for full independence, they were adamant that the price for support for the war effort was immediate self-government within the Empire.

The 'Cripps Mission' was one of the few colonial events which gained the attention of labour movement activists in and around our three towns. It is perhaps overly cynical to wonder if a concern for the future of Lancashire's cotton trade (Japan was Britain's chief rival in the Far East for the supply of finished cotton goods[232]) stirred up this concern. Whatever the reason, it was during the Cripps Mission that Ashton Trades Council responded to an offer of a speaker from the India League by deciding that the offer should 'lie on the table' (i.e. that the offer should not be accepted). William Garside denounced the decision: 'it seemed that the [Trades Council] was indifferent to the problems of India'.[233] Hyde Trades Council wrote to Churchill and to local MPs urging a renewal of negotiations with Congress with the aim of giving the Indian people 'the right to self-determination'.[234]

While some on the British left criticised the 'Cripps Mission' for being insufficiently sympathetic to the Indian nationalist movement – at a meeting of the India League, William Gallacher, the CP's sole MP, argued that it seemed that the British 'were appointed by God to rule over other peoples'[235] – labour movement activists, including Gallacher, were not deflected from their support of the British war effort.

At Labour's annual conference in May, the NEC tabled a resolution which disingenuously asked the delegates to express their 'profound sympathy with the people of India in the danger now threatening them from the Japanese aggressors'. The movement's complicity in the repression in India was not addressed. Few criticised the motion. Exceptionally, Alex Sloan of the ILP, an ex-miner, now an MP, accurately nailed the reason for failure of the 'Cripps Mission': it was due to a failure 'to recognise the immediate demand of the Indian National Congress for a National Government now, not in the distant future, when the Indians had undergone a probationary period and had proved their fitness to govern'. But the resolution was carried unanimously.[236]

Shortly after Cripps left India, Congress leaders had again been gaoled. In August, the 'Quit India' movement was launched. It soon escalated beyond

---

232   By 1938, Japan had replaced Britain as the chief exporter of cotton goods. Porter 1979, p. 29.
233   *Ashton Reporter*, 10 April 1942.
234   *Ashton Reporter*, 5 June 1942.
235   Topic Collection Political Attitudes and Behaviour, the India League 1942–43. Box 9, File F. @ Mass Observation Archive at the University of Sussex.
236   Labour Party, *Report of the 41st Labour Party Annual Conference* (London, 1942), pp. 160–4.

the renewed civil disobedience movement envisaged by Congress leaders into mass insurrection and was met with savage repression.²³⁷ At that September's annual conference of the TUC a few, a very few, delegates attacked the government's India policy. Mr W. Whitaker of the Burnley weavers reminded the delegates that as 'Nehru said, how could he fight for freedom if freedom was denied'. Sloan attacked Churchill: his Common's speech on the failure of the 'Cripps Mission' had been his 'most provocative and disgraceful for some time'. He 'had said that the situation in India was reassuring, and yet at the present time British soldiers were shooting down the natives of India'. For the General Council, Citrine claimed that 'Everyone knew that if so-called self-government were handed to India tomorrow, there would be such internal strife in the country that the Japanese would be able to walk in'. This was a clinching argument for the vast majority of delegates. A proposed 'reference back' (a rejection) of the General Council's annual report was heavily defeated.²³⁸

Clearly, far more members of the labour movement were concerned by threats to the Empire than by denials of colonial freedom. Earlier in the year, in the spring, the 'fall' to Germany of Tobruk, the Libyan fortress earlier captured from the Italian imperialists, had been seen by many as the latest, and greatest, of a series of military catastrophes caused by government and military incompetence dating back to 1940. The CP warned that the 'disaster that Britain has suffered in Libya meant that Axis forces now threatened Egypt, the Suez Canal and India'.²³⁹ In Ashton, a Second Front meeting was advertised by the legend 'Avenge Tobruk with Second Front'. Ashton people were urged to assemble 'at the baths for a march to the market ground' to hear Freda Devine (the wife of Pat Devine, the Secretary of the Lancashire District of the CP) speak in support of 'The Anglo-Soviet Pact for Victory in 1943'.²⁴⁰ The Manchester and Salford District of the CP, in publicity for a Second Front meeting, renewed calls to settle matters with India: 'Over 400 million people in India want to fight and work with us. They want their own national government. **They must have it**'.²⁴¹

Tobruk served to encourage those who, believing that Tory dominance of the government was responsible for such disasters as that at Tobruk, desired reform, preferably immediately, but certainly postwar. By the spring of 1942

---

237   See Hutchins 1973 and Bakshi 1986 for accounts of the 'Quit India' movement. See also Fay 1994 for an account of the India National Army, which allied itself with the Japanese.
238   Trades Union Congress, *Trades Union Congress 74th Conference Report* (London, 1942) pp. 299–301.
239   Political Bureau circular, 'The Lessons of Libya', 25 June 1942. IND/DUTT/31/13 @ PHM.
240   *Ashton Reporter*, 26 June 1942.
241   'Victory in 1942', Emphasis in the original. CPA, CP/LOC/NW/1/4 @ PHM.

rank-and-file members of the Labour and Communist parties had begun to chafe at the limitations set on campaigning for social reform by their leaders' insistence on electoral unity. Strains in the Labour Party on the matter of electoral unity had surfaced at the May annual conference. Many delegates clearly considered that the truce was preventing the Party from campaigning for socialism. A vote on a 'reference back' of the NEC's policy of maintaining the electoral truce was defeated very narrowly.[242] Many CP members had strongly objected to having to campaign for the coalition Conservative candidate at the Grantham by-election in March, won by an independent socialist candidate, Denis Kendall. Even stronger objections were raised by their party's support for right wing Conservative candidates in April by-elections at Wallasey and Rugby. Their objections were rejected by the Party's leadership, which insisted that national unity and hence the electoral truce were vital if the war was to be won.[243]

9   A Social-Imperialist Surge for Reform

The frustration felt by Labour and CP members must have been greatly exacerbated by the growing evidence of popular support for postwar reform demonstrated by the defeats of Conservatives at Grantham, Wallasey and Rugby.[244] *The Tribune*, commenting on the imminent Maldon by-election, believed Tobruk had 'awakened the British people from the half-doze into which they had been lulled by ill-conceived propaganda and by an insular conceit born of centuries of successful war-making'.[245]

Tom Driberg's spectacular June 1942 victory at Maldon showed, even more than Kendall's at Grantham, that the so-called 'movement away from party' of 1942[246] was in essence not a movement away from party *per se*, but a reaction against Conservatism and conservatism in favour of reform. Steven Fielding, while arguing that there had been such a movement, provides convincing contrary evidence – notably that by-election swings against the Conservatives averaged 44.4 percent, but only 10.3 percent against Labour – that these by-election results were in fact a manifestation of anti-Tory, pro-reform senti-

---

242   Labour Party, *Report of the 41st Labour Party Annual Conference* (London, 1942), pp. 145–50.
243   PB circular 'National Unity Means Victory', 7 May 1942. CPA, CP/CC/IND/DUT/29/12 @ PHM.
244   Jefferys 1991, p. 224.
245   *The Tribune*, 26 June 1942.
246   This term was coined at the time to describe what was seen literally as a movement away from the established political parties of the time. Calder 1969, p. 336.

ment.[247] Driberg, standing as an independent socialist candidate, campaigned on an explicitly social-imperialist platform. 'Our sons and daughters fighting in far lands hang on desperately for munitions that don't turn up, while profiteers haggle with the government'. At home, Driberg argued, there must be reform. He insisted, for instance, that there must be nationalisation of 'inefficient' industries and increased pensions.[248] Driberg turned a Conservative majority of 8,000 into a majority of 6,000 for himself.[249]

Perhaps the most significant harbinger of reform had been the appointment – to the dismay of many Conservative MPs – in February 1942, of the Christian socialist William Temple as Archbishop of Canterbury. The author of *Christianity and the Social Order*, a Penguin Special which sold 139,000 copies, Temple 'thought it wrong for banks to make private profit from the supply of credit, wrong that shares could be inherited, and wrong that dividends, rather than wages, should be the first charge on industrial profits'.[250] In less elevated circles, Streat had argued that 'commerce and industry after the war must be put to work for the service of the people, for otherwise they will perish'.[251] The Cotton Control Board argued that 'all the signs and portents point to great and world-wide changes after the war, in which the Lancashire industry must be ready to play a powerful role'.[252]

Reform sentiments were growing swiftly too in our three towns in 1942. In Oldham, the Rotary Club held a series of meetings on postwar reform. The Borough Engineer and Surveyor argued that there would be a 'huge demand' for new houses and for 'older ones (no one could be satisfied with their standard) to be renovated'.[253] In the summer, a paper calling for the introduction of family allowances was presented. Children were said to be 'a national asset of the highest value'. They were the responsibility of the whole of society, not just of their parents.[254] The town's Labour Party's women's section held a meeting to discuss their Party's new pamphlet *The Old World and a New Society*,[255] which as we shall see in the next chapter, was an early prospectus for postwar reform. At a Trades Council meeting, objections were raised to funding hospitals by flag days. It was time the town council 'took strong objection to charity

---

247 Fielding 1995, p. 48.
248 'Three Reasons for Voting for Tom Driberg'. LPA, LPL/MAL/2/3 @ PHM.
249 Jefferys 1991, p. 224.
250 Cited in Addison 1977, pp. 187–8.
251 Streat Papers. Diaries 1939–45, 6 May 1942. GB133=133 ERS @ JRSC.
252 Cotton Board, *Cotton Board Trade Letter*, 22 May 1942.
253 *Oldham Weekly Chronicle*, 21 March 1942.
254 *Oldham Weekly Chronicle*, 23 July 1942.
255 *Oldham Weekly Chronicle*, 8 May 1942.

appeals'. Hospitals should be funded by the Government 'instead of having to belittle themselves' as 'professional cadgers'.[256] In the autumn, the town council began to consider how to improve housing after the war: 'in postwar housing schemes provision should be made for community centres and there should be adequate open spaces for out-door games'. The members of the Housing Committee noted 'that as overcrowding appears to be a contributory factor to delinquency, schemes for slum clearance should be proceeded with at the earliest possible moment'. The next month the Committee discussed a 'provisional programme of postwar housing'.[257]

In Ashton, the council was turning its attention to the shape of the town's postwar built environment and its facilities (in parliament, a bill on postwar town planning had just passed its second reading).[258] Acting on a suggestion by Jowitt, members of the town council were to visit an institute in Slough which 'under one roof, provides recreational and educational facilities for both young and old'. They were to visit Cambridge too, to inspect an institution which 'caters for three hundred children from ten villages'.[259] The councillors returned from their visits much impressed, they 'arrived back determined that it would not be through want of their own effort if Ashton did not keep in step when the new order of social life arrived'. They were particularly impressed by the Slough Communal Centre designed by Walter Gropius and described, as the *Reporter* was anxious to inform its readers, by Professor C.H. Reilly in the *Manchester Guardian* as 'a social phenomenon of immense importance'. At the Centre, 'thirty-six sections operate under one roof'. It had a bar, citizen's advice bureau, library, music room, gymnasium and theatre. In the fields surrounding the Centre there were sports pitches.[260] The trades council, inspired by this vision of a new Ashton, decided to send delegates to a conference on post war planning organised by the Lancashire and Cheshire Federation of Trades Councils.[261]

---

256 *Oldham Weekly Chronicle*, 3 July 1942.
257 Oldham Council, Minutes of the Housing Committee 1941–44, 9 September 1942 and 11 October 1942. CBO/15/2/1/3 @ OLSA.
258 Oldham's council too took up the matter of town planning, but not until the summer of 1943, when it agreed to send three delegates to attend an October national housing and town planning conference in London. It was also agreed that the chairman of the Housing Committee and the housing manager attend an 'exhibition of postwar housing at Birmingham'. Oldham Council, Minutes of the Housing Committee 1941–44, 4 August 1943. CBO/15/2/1/3 @ OLSA.
259 *Ashton Reporter*, 10 July 1942.
260 *Ashton Reporter*, 24 July 1942.
261 Minutes of Ashton Trades Council, 7 July 1942. DDTC/8 @ TLSAC.

Reform sentiments had begun to emerge even in Mossley, but were for a time stymied by an obdurate town council. Members of the Maternity and Child Welfare Committee wished to establish a wartime nursery to help mothers move into industry. They had visited and were impressed by a recently opened nursery in Ashton[262] (in Oldham, there were seven nurseries by the summer of 1942).[263] But at a meeting of the full council in May, the usual delaying tactics were deployed. The Town Clerk had advised that though many people had once expressed support for a nursery, many of these had been evacuees who had since left the town.[264] By the end of the war, as in the case of the British Restaurant, a nursery had not been provided.

Perhaps the point of the fable of King Canute had been misunderstood. But not even the reactionaries on Mossley's council could hold back indefinitely the tide of reform in the town. An anticipation of the surge in the tide which would follow the publication of the Beveridge Report had come in the spring of 1942 in a debate on 'individualism versus communism' at the Christian Sunday School. Mr Harry Brook claimed that 'England's greatness' was due to 'competition and Manchesterism'.[265] But the pastor, the Reverend C.E. Read, insisted that 'competition has produced the slum and poverty, a population on the border-line of starvation ... Their own town ... was a condemnation of Manchesterism'. In contrast, in the socialist Soviet Union (admiration for the Red Army meant that playing the Soviet card had become a trump), 'the school leaving age was 18, there was no unemployment and health-care was free'. The *Reporter* judged that Read had won the debate.[266]

Perhaps the most significant indicator that there was a growing desire for a new, better world was the response of the Home Guard in Oldham's neighbour Chadderton to a talk organised by the Ministry of Information by Madame Soermus, a Russian pianist. Soermus, who was adamant that she was 'not a communist', painted a seductive picture of life in the Soviet Union. For instance, people retired at 55 on a pension of 85 percent of their wage. There was 'applause' when Soermus spoke of officers and men 'fraternising off duty'. At the end of the talk, the Liberal *Chronicle*, a paper not likely to have exaggerated socialist sentiments, reported that the men of the Home Guard rose, and 'spontaneously sang the "Red Flag"'.[267]

---

262 *Mossley and Saddleworth Reporter*, 20 March 1942.
263 *Oldham Weekly Chronicle*, 1 August 1942.
264 *Mossley and Saddleworth Reporter*, 2 May 1942.
265 By 'Manchesterism', Brook presumably meant the *laissez-faire* liberalism and utilitarianism typical of nineteenth century Lancashire mill-owners, satirised by Dickens in *Hard Times*.
266 *Mossley and Saddleworth Reporter*, 27 March 1942.
267 *Oldham Weekly Chronicle*, 24 October 1942.

Soon afterwards, the tide of war turned. In 1940–42 Germany had had considerable success in challenging British power in and around the Mediterranean. Partly for this reason, Britain had in 1942 won the agreement of the United States for a 'Mediterranean first' strategy, in which Britain and the USA would first confront Germany and Italy in what Churchill deemed 'the soft underbelly' of Europe (the United States had agreed to this strategy because there was no short-term possibility of launching an invasion of France). Britain's imperialist interests and objectives in this strategy were clear. The Mediterranean and its surrounds was one of the most concentrated arenas of British imperial power. There, Britain had colonies (sometimes, as in the case of Palestine, in the guise of a League of Nations mandate), bases, as in Malta and Aden, dependencies such as Egypt, Iraq and Greece, control of vital raw materials, especially oil, and, crucially, Suez and the passage to the Far East.

That this was not an anti-fascist strategy would have been clear to anyone who had bothered to ponder the matter. It would certainly have been clear to the leaders of the Labour Party, whether in or out of the War Cabinet. It had been very clear indeed to Dutt, who regularly exposed the imperialist designs of the government in his 'Notes of the Month' column in *Labour Monthly*. But neither Labour nor the CP had been thus deterred from offering wholehearted support for the British war effort.

The CP had been about to launch its National Deputations Day, a mass lobby of parliament in favour of a Second Front in France, when in November news of the British offensive at El Alamein in Egypt broke. Pollitt was insistent that 'whatever form the offensive takes it will have the unstinted support of the people'.[268] Rather than cause disruption with a mass lobby of Parliament, local authorities would be lobbied. This, the Manchester and Salford District Committee of the CP argued, would 'avoid any loss of work and in that way be a practical demonstration to the men and women in the armed forces of the industrial workers' sincere desire to back up with increased production the tremendous fight they have'.[269] Workers at Bolton's De Havilland aircraft plant were said to be 'planning a production drive bigger than anything before to support our armies in Egypt. In three of the main shops a petition was circulating, demanding that the Production Committee and the management immediately made plans for the beginning of a tremendous production drive'.[270]

British success at El Alamein in Egypt was swiftly followed by equally successful Anglo-US landings in Algeria and Morocco. On the 15th of November,

---

268 *Daily Worker*, 5 November 1942.
269 *Lancashire News*, November 7 1942.
270 *Daily Worker*, 12 November 1942.

church bells rang out throughout Britain for the first time since the invasion scare of the summer of 1940. Since then Britain had been on the defensive, but now the threat to Britain and its Empire from its imperial rivals had been halted (the Japanese offensive in the Far East had been stalled at the US-Japanese naval Battle of Midway in the summer). It was, as Churchill memorably said, the 'end of the beginning'. In Mossley, the news from El Alamein gave a fillip to pro-reform sentiment. At a special service of thanksgiving (amidst the jubilation, probably few paused to consider how imperialist contention in North Africa could be considered to be compatible with a war claimed to be a war in defence of democracy and for self-determination) at St. George's Church, the incumbent spoke of the 'poverty and unemployment' which had followed the First World War. How were we to get 'a better life' after this war? A *Reporter* editorial spoke to the 'importance of making plans for the prevention of unemployment' and 'looked forward' to impending proposals on social security from Beveridge's Committee.[271]

With Germany's Afrika Korps in retreat, the Beveridge Report, promising rewards for wartime blood, toil, tears and sweat, was published on the 1st of December 1942, to great, though not universal, acclaim. The BBC broadcast lengthy extracts in 22 languages. It was not a coincidence that the Report was published soon after the offensive in North Africa and a successful Soviet offensive at Stalingrad. Churchill sanctioned its release.[272] Now that there could be confidence in eventual victory, it was appropriate to consider how society should be reconstructed. In the next phase of the war, while Churchill remained preoccupied with military matters and the Tories showed themselves to be at best lukewarm on the matter, the Labour Party was increasingly identified with the cause of social reform. Expectations of postwar reform rose as quickly as British imperialism vanquished its rivals.

---

271 *Mossley and Saddleworth Reporter*, 20 November 1942.
272 Addison 1977, pp. 216–17.

CHAPTER 5

Building the Social-Imperialist Settlement

El Alamein was a watershed in Britain's war effort. In alliance with the Soviet Union and the USA, Britain embarked on a more or less continuous offensive against its imperial rivals. The Italian imperialists surrendered after successive invasions of Sicily and the mainland in 1943. The German imperialists held out for nearly a year after 'D-Day', the invasion of France, in June 1944. In the Far East, Britain regained all its colonies after Japan unconditionally surrendered after the USA dropped atomic bombs on Nagasaki and Hiroshima in August 1945. El Alamein was a watershed too in the construction of the postwar settlement between labour and capital. The labour movement continued to give full, if occasionally critical, support to the war effort while – supplementing the Beveridge Report of 1942, in the Education Act of 1944, the 1944 White Papers on Health, on Employment and on Social Security, and the 1945 White Paper on Housing – capital promised handsome rewards for that support.

1   Beveridge Promises a New World

Working class people were understandably susceptible to such social-imperialist sirens as Churchill, Attlee, Bevin, Beveridge and Keynes. Though there had been significant improvements in social conditions in the interwar years,[1] and some improvement in living standards,[2] and cotton workers enjoyed considerable improvements in welfare and recreational facilities,[3] the extravagant

---

1   Between 1913 and 1938 the proportion of British gross national product spent on social services had risen from 5.5 percent to 13 percent. Kirk 1994, p. 295. The effect of this increased spending was evident in, for instance, the infant mortality rate, which had progressively declined from 105 per 1,000 live births in 1910, to 85 in 1920, 60 in 1930, and 56 in 1940. McPherson and Coleman 1988, p. 56. These were averages: as we might expect, the rate for working class people was higher. Even so, in Oldham it had declined from 70.76 in 1931 to 61.79 in 1939. Oldham Council, Annual report of the Medical Officer of Health for 1939, filed with the Minutes of the Housing Committee, 1941–44. CBO/15/2/1/3 @ OLSA.
2   One indicator of rising living standards was the steady increase in the number of cinemas, made possible by rising disposable incomes. In Oldham the number rose from 6 in 1919 to 17 in 1939, in Ashton from 3 to 8. Jones 1987, p. 37.
3   Jones 1988, p. 189.

promises of social reform made in the last year or so of the Great War had been only partially fulfilled. Social and working conditions for many working class people, especially in London and the industrial areas of northern England, Scotland and Wales, were still poor. What particularly concerned working people, or at least the labour movement activists of our three towns, were the poor housing and unemployment (even those currently in work were well aware that they soon might not be) which blighted the lives of so many.

In Lancashire, the principal cause of unemployment was the decline of its cotton industry, mainly the result of a failure to modernise and the loss of Indian markets.[4] For most of the 1920s and 1930s registered unemployment in Lancashire was very high. In the cotton trade, unemployment peaked at 38.5 percent in 1931, two years after the Wall St. Crash. There was something of a recovery in subsequent years, but on the eve of the Second World War, unemployment in the trade was still 26.3 percent.[5] The misery of unemployment was alleviated to some extent by successive increases in the number of people covered by unemployment insurance. By the end of the 1930s, over 14.5 million people were covered by the provisions of the 1934 Unemployment Act. Moreover, the ultimate sanction of being committed to the workhouse had been virtually abolished. On the other hand, payments under the act were meagre, while the great number of people who were not covered by the scheme,[6] far more of them women than men, or whose entitlement to benefit had ended, had to apply to a public assistance committee (PAC) for strictly means-tested assistance. The humiliations of the means test passed into popular memory. The present writer's parents remembered many: aged grandparents, for instance, forced to maintain a grandson orphaned by the Great War and then laid off from a mill in Stockport.

Poor housing afflicted many working class people. A small minority lived in well-built, spacious council houses with, the prospectus of 1919 fulfilled, bathrooms and indoor lavatories. Over a million such houses were built between the wars.[7] In Oldham 2,500 were built[8] and in Ashton, a proportionately much

---

[4] Much to the chagrin of the Lancashire millocracy, Britain accepted Japanese penetration of the Indian textile market, hoping to maintain the Anglo-Japanese strategic alliance in the Far East. Cain and Hopkins 1993, p. 180. Between 1913 and 1939 Lancashire's cotton exports to India fell from 3,000 million yards to 145 million yards (Chatterji 1992, p. 3).

[5] Jones 1987, p. 37.

[6] In Oldham in 1940 only 58 percent of the working population were covered by the scheme. Oldham Council, Annual Report of Medical Officer of Health for 1940, filed with the Minutes of the Housing Committee, 1941–44. CBO/11/8/46 @OLSA.

[7] Malpass 2005, p. 40.

[8] Oldham County Borough Council 1949, pp. 61–5.

greater 2,752, reflecting the town's greater need.⁹ But in 1938 only 10 percent of people in England and Wales lived in council houses; 58 percent lived in private rented accommodation and 32 percent were owner-occupiers.¹⁰ It can safely be assumed that the great majority of those living in private rented accommodation were working class. Very few of their houses would have had bathrooms or indoor lavatories. Private landlords were notoriously loth to improve. Damp, overcrowding and vermin infestation were rife. In *The Road to Wigan Pier* George Orwell provided a vivid account of the deplorable state of much housing in northern towns in the 1930s.¹¹ According to Oldham T&LC, there had been virtually no improvement in the town's privately rented housing stock since 1918.¹² The Council's claim is given considerable credence by a 1938 report of the National House and Town Planning Council which argued that the 'slum problem' had not improved since 1918 and that there were at least 1,000,000 unfit and 2,000,000 overcrowded houses.¹³ According to the CP, in Ashton in 1939, 228 families were living in overcrowded accommodation and 194 living in houses unfit for human habitation. There were 2,277 families on the waiting list for council accommodation.¹⁴

The social-imperialist pact struck between labour and capital in 1939–40 led to a fundamental reappraisal of how such socio-economic problems should be addressed. In place of a reliance on charity, private enterprise and the piecemeal solutions – the friendly societies, the hospital clubs, the public assistance committees, the ladies' welfare committees and so on – there emerged a much greater emphasis on collective provision and the boards and the commissions of that modern Leviathan, the 'welfare state'.

The Beveridge Report was, ostensibly, a plan for social security 'from the cradle to the grave', but it was much more than that; it was, as Beveridge himself claimed,

> only part of an attack upon five giant evils; upon the physical Want with which it is directly concerned, upon Disease which often causes that Want and brings many other troubles in its train, upon Ignorance which no

---

9   Rybaczek 1995, p. 32.
10 HMG, *Command Paper 6851, Housing Policy, Technical Volume* (HMSO, London, 1977), table 1.23.
11 Orwell 1937.
12 *Oldham Weekly Chronicle*, 21 April 1945.
13 Burnett 1991, p. 237.
14 *Lancashire and Cheshire News*, 27 October 1945.

democracy can afford among its citizens, upon Squalor ... and upon the Idleness which destroys wealth and corrupts men.[15]

Clearly, Beveridge had exceeded his brief. *The Tribune* saw quasi-socialist implications in the report:

> 'Nobody goes so far', said Oliver Cromwell, 'as he who does not know how far he is going'. It would be impolite for us to apply this text ... [to Beveridge] ... but the words are still appropriate ... Sir William states plainly that human claims must come first. The claims of property must come second.[16]

Beveridge had recommended only a comprehensive system of social insurance and a state health service, free at the point of use. Beveridge was not a socialist, as he made very clear 18 months later, in his *Full Employment in a Free Society*.[17] But to defeat the 'five giants' there would have to be, at the very least, a greatly increased level, compared with pre-war norms, of public spending and continued postwar state intervention into the economy and into industry. Which is why alone of the daily press, the *Daily Telegraph*, the house journal of the Tory right, failed to welcome the report, why the Chancellor of the Exchequer, Kingsley Wood, promptly opposed the report in Cabinet, why the Director of the Confederation of British Employers insisted 'we did not start this war with Germany in order to improve our social services' and why many Tory MPs robustly attacked in February 1943 Beveridge and his report during the parliamentary debate on the matter.[18]

At the start of the debate, the government insisted that while it accepted most of Beveridge's recommendations in principle, it would not initiate legislation. Moreover, to do so could properly only be the business of a new government elected after the war. A labour backbench amendment committing the government to 'immediately legislate' was lost by 338 votes to 121.[19] But

---

15   Cited in Timms 1995, p. 4.
16   *The Tribune*, 4 December 1942.
17   Beveridge 1944. The title of the work was an implicit challenge to the common assumption that only in such 'totalitarian' societies as Nazi Germany and the Soviet Union could there be full employment. Beveridge assumed that the economic demand-management theories of his fellow-prophet of postwar enlightenment, Keynes, would govern postwar economic policy and thus there would be relative (around 5 percent unemployment) full employment.
18   Addison 1977, ch. VIII.
19   Jefferys 1991, p. 135.

the genie was out of the bottle. People queued to buy the report outside His Majesty's Stationery Office. Combined, around 635,000 copies of the full report and of the official summary were sold. A Gallup Poll found that 95 percent of the population had heard of the report and that 90 percent thought that it should be adopted.[20] The *Ashton Reporter* gave the report a fulsome tribute; it 'sounds the bugle call of a scheme aimed at freedom from want, work and leisure for all'.[21] Though the regular Oldham Weekly Chronicle columnist 'Round the Town' counselled caution,[22] the Oldham MP Sir Hamilton Kerr, a Tory, gave the Report a guarded welcome: it had 'filled the headlines. Few can quarrel … Here at last is a plan where one simple insurance stamp will give a measure of security from the cradle to the grave'.[23]

In contrast to the qualms, doubts and even hostility among Conservatives, Beveridge's proposals, unsurprisingly, given that they were very similar to those which had been submitted in evidence by the TUC early in 1942,[24] gained virtually unqualified support from the labour movement. While everybody would benefit from a state health service funded from general taxation, free at the point of use, Beveridge's proposals for insurance-based social security to cover sickness, unemployment and old age were most suited to people in stable employment. Others, people in irregular, unstable employment, for instance, might well not have built up sufficient contributions to qualify for benefit and would therefore have to apply for whatever means-tested assistance might be available. Housewives were effectively regarded as dependents of their hus-

---

20   Calder 1969, p. 609.
21   *Ashton Reporter*, 4 December 1942.
22   *Oldham Weekly Chronicle*, 5 December 1942. It was 'clear that heavy additional burdens will have to be borne by the cotton trade'. What these 'burdens' were was not specified. But presumably increased general taxation and a proposed employer contribution to the social insurance scheme were in mind.
23   *Oldham Weekly Chronicle*, 2 January 1943. Kerr was a Tory social-imperialist. In 1944 he supported an equal pay amendment to the Education Bill (*Oldham Weekly Chronicle*, 18 April 1944) and extolled, while addressing the Rotary Club, the proposals of the White Paper on Employment. *Oldham Weekly Chronicle*, 18 November 1944. In a speech to Oxford University's Conservative Association, he insisted that 'the first concrete objective of British foreign policy is to maintain the cohesion of the Empire. We cannot by ourselves play a great role in the world, but in conjunction with our Empire we can'. *Oldham Weekly Chronicle*, 20 May 1944.
24   The TUC had advocated an 'inclusive scheme to cover unemployment, sickness, maternity, non-compensatable accidents, invalidity, old age, blindness, death and widowhood and orphanhood'. The scheme should cover 'all gainfully occupied persons irrespective of income'. Those 'not entitled to benefit should be provided for by a body like the present Assistance Board'. TUC, *74th Annual Conference Report* (London, 1942), p. 39.

bands[25] and would not, for instance, qualify for an independent old age pension. Amidst the acclaim for Beveridge, some of these deficiencies were recognised at the time.[26]

But most members of the labour movement, mainly men in stable employment, would probably have regarded these deficiencies, if they were aware of or concerned by them, as subordinate to the great reforms advocated by Beveridge. Roberts of the Cardroom Amalgamation noted that 'already the opponents [of Beveridge] are in the field in an attempt to preserve vested interests ... We must be just as active in our support of the plan; we must show the government that the full weight of every trade unionist is behind the demand that the attack shall not only be made, but shall succeed in destroying want'.[27] At the annual conference of the Spinners Amalgamation, the delegates demanded that the 'government announces its decision without delay to implement the principles embodied in the Beveridge Report, and that legislation be introduced immediately on the lines advocated in the Report with a view to the principles becoming law at the earliest possible moment'.[28] The CP optimistically asserted that the report would 'receive the universal assent of all sections of the people. It corresponds to the deep desires of the soldiers; the workers in industry; the housewives; of all who fear want and insecurity after the war'.[29] The leaders of the Weavers' amalgamation believed the Report to be 'a masterly and epoch-making document. It was ... bold in conception'.[30] At its annual conference of 1943, the Labour Party rather grudgingly assessed Beveridge as a 'valuable contribution', an 'important advance towards a democratic social policy, such as the Labour Party envisages as an essential part of its postwar plans'. But the party's call 'upon the Government for the

---

25   Beveridge asserted that the 'attitude of the housewife to gainful employment outside the home is not and should not be the same as that of the single woman. She has other duties ... In the next thirty years housewives as mothers have a vital role in ensuring the adequate continuance of the British Race and of British ideals in the world'. Cited in Wilson 1977, p. 14.
26   A pamphlet for the Women's Freedom League pointed out that the provisions of the Report would 'leave [women] as before, a dependent, and not a partner'. Cited in Timms 1995, p. 57.
27   Cardroom Amalgamation, Reports and Minutes January 1941–November 45. Quarterly Report and Balance Sheet for the Quarter ending 26 December 1942. Report to District Officials from Alfred Roberts, General Secretary. TU/TEX/CARD/18 @ WCML.
28   Spinners' Amalgamation to UTFWA, 18 January 1943. ACS/6/3/20 @JRSC.
29   *World News and Views*, 12 December.
30   Weavers' Amalgamation Annual Report for year ending 31 March 1943. DDX 1123/1/38 @ LROP.

speedy preparation of the necessary legislation'[31] suggests that Labour rated Beveridge's report rather more highly than as merely a 'valuable contribution'.

2 The 'Old Gang' Takes an Ideological and Political Beating

After El Alamein and the publication of the Beveridge Report, popular expectations of postwar reform accelerated and led to increasing support for the Labour Party. The Conservative Party, the 'old gang' associated with pre-war depression, dole and appeasement, was not able to capitalise on Churchill's increasing success as war leader. Earlier in the war, there had been a number of by-elections when ILP candidates did far better than would normally be expected, probably because they were seen as surrogate Labour candidates.[32] But it was the Commonwealth Party which was initially the principal beneficiary of the post-El Alamein upsurge in reform sentiment.

Commonwealth had been founded by Sir Richard Acland, a Liberal turned socialist, after the 'fall' of Tobruk in 1942. The party grew rapidly. At its zenith in 1943–44 it had around 15,000 members in 300 branches. It called for 'common ownership' (by which it meant nationalisation) of vital industries, independence for the colonies and an extremely vague concept called 'vital democracy'.[33] According to Geoffrey Field, 'those attracted to the movement were overwhelmingly suburban and professional: schoolteachers, managers, students, technicians, lower civil servants, many young people, and members of the armed forces'.[34]

Capitalising on the electoral truce, Commonwealth contested several by-elections and did rather well. In February 1943, Tom Wintringham, ex-CP member and International Brigader, who had been instrumental in the forming of the Local Defence Volunteers or 'Home Guard',[35] nearly defeated the Conservative candidate in the Midlothian by-election. At the Watford by-election the same month, the Conservative candidate gaffed by calling the Beveridge Report

---

31 Several contributors to the debate insisted that the Tories could not be trusted to implement the report. An amendment to the resolution to that effect was lost. The substantive resolution and a second resolution calling for establishment of a state medical service were both carried unanimously. Labour Party, *Report of 42nd Labour Party Annual Conference* (London, 1943), pp. 136–46.
32 McIlroy and Campbell 2011, pp. 893–4.
33 Calder 1967.
34 Field 2011, p. 331.
35 Purcell 2004, p. 109.

a 'poet's dream', but then called for it to be put into 'immediate operation'. Many of Watford's voters must have suspected his sincerity, for the Conservative vote fell sharply.[36]

It was perhaps in an attempt to stem growing popular discontent that Churchill spoke on postwar reconstruction in a wireless broadcast in March 1943. While being careful not to explicitly refer to the Beveridge Report, he effectively endorsed it by claiming that his own plans included 'national compulsory insurance for all classes for all purposes from the cradle to the grave'. They also included, he claimed, full employment, a National Health Service and equal opportunity in education. But the government could not commit itself to early legislation.[37] Churchill's intervention may have simply served to draw attention to the opposition of many Conservatives to the report and to their parsimony and meanness in government in the interwar years. In the spring, Commonwealth, campaigning for the implementation of Beveridge, took Eddisbury from the National Liberals.[38] As in 1942, this and later by-election disasters for the government were not essentially manifestations of a 'movement away from party', but a pro-reform movement away from the Conservatives, which, as Paul Addison convincingly argues, anticipated Labour's landslide victory in the General Election of 1945.[39]

Our three solidly working class towns were not the sort of places where Commonwealth could flourish (though Acland spoke at meetings in Oldham and in Royton early in 1944[40] and a branch was formed in Ashton in March that year),[41] but the same political tendencies which nurtured Commonwealth were present in them. Probably because the government had not yet seriously turned its attention to the matter, it was the desperate need for better housing for working class people which particularly dominated discussions of postwar reform in Mossley and, especially, Ashton in 1943. Oldham people, probably because of the comparatively good record on housing of their council (as we saw in the last chapter, Oldham council had already begun to consider the shape of the town's postwar housing), seem not to have been so concerned. In general, Oldham people seem to have given little consideration to postwar problems in the early months of 1943, though in April Oldham Labour Party organised a public meeting on 'current problems'. From the Chair, Miss Kenyon claimed that 'cur-

---

36   Calder 1969, p. 631.
37   Calder 1969, p. 617.
38   Jefferys 1991, pp. 151, 225.
39   Addison 1977, pp. 249–52.
40   There were 'fair attendances' at both meetings. *Oldham Weekly Chronicle*, 5 February 1944.
41   *Ashton Reporter*, 17 March 1944.

rents of uneasiness were spreading throughout the country'. She particularly drew attention to the government's 'India policy' and the 'treatment accorded to the Beveridge Report'. From the floor, a Mr Hyde criticised the government's 'refusal to set up a Ministry of Social Security'.[42] Perhaps, as in the First World War, Oldham militancy was expressed in industrial action, rather than agitation on postwar reform. We shall see that throughout this last phase of the war Oldham saw considerably more industrial militancy than our other two towns.

In February 1943, editorials in the *Ashton Reporter* and in the *Mossley and Saddleworth Reporter* asserted that 'of the many plans for postwar improvements, postwar housing is one of the most important'. Attention was drawn to a memorandum of the Royal College of Physicians which had recently stated that postwar new houses should be bigger, that 'sunshine, dryness, warmth, light and air must be taken into consideration' and that 'a living room in which neither cooking nor washing is carried out is essential'.[43] In the town's labour movement, the 'broken promises' trope was beginning to assert itself. Councillor Allen said that 'during the last war we had a lot of talk about "Homes for Heroes". We are still waiting for them'.[44] Mr F.S. Fitzpatrick, a member of the AEU's Executive Council, speaking at a meeting of the Ashton District Committee of the union, insisted that there must not be a return to the unemployment 'which ruined the morale of the people as it did from 1921 to 1939'. The unions were fighting for a 'new world. They did not get it last time, but we were going to get it this time'.[45]

In March, Attlee and Jowitt spoke in Ashton at a 'well attended' public meeting. Attlee had said that he 'wanted a world designed not for the speculators but for the real producers of wealth'. Contradicting Churchill, Attlee claimed that the government was actively preparing to implement Beveridge, 'not only the principles, but the greater part of all its actual proposals'. Jowitt, who, as Minister without Portfolio since 1940, had been involved in government discussions on postwar reconstruction, said that 'the first and most important duty after the war was to see that there were jobs for the people to do and that to his mind this was by far the most important form of social security'.[46]

But that same month, the *Reporter's* columnist 'Ashtonian' contradicted Jowitt by claiming that 'housing will be one of the greatest postwar problems in Ashton'. A 1935 survey had shown that Ashton's overcrowding figure (10.8

---

42   *Oldham Weekly Chronicle*, 3 April 1943.
43   *Ashton Reporter*, 5 February 1943: *Mossley and Saddleworth Reporter*, 5 February 1943.
44   *Ashton Reporter*, 12 February 1943.
45   *Ashton Reporter*, 28 May 1943.
46   *Ashton Reporter*, 5 March 1943.

percent) was the highest in Lancashire. Though a survey had shown that 1,500 houses were needed, the council had done very little and on the outbreak of war had plans for only 200.[47] Ashton Council did though now seem to be taking housing reform more seriously. In April the Housing Committee referred a letter from the Ministry of Health regarding postwar housing to a Standing Sub-committee 'for early consideration'.[48]

In Mossley, sentiment that there must be better working class housing was emerging. Councillor Martin, (who had taken the place, unopposed, of the recently deceased Farr) referred to such things as public baths and playgrounds 'which Mossley does not possess' but should. He claimed that Mossley 'lagged behind many other boroughs'. For instance, 75 percent of houses lacked 'modern methods of sanitation' (by which he meant that lavatories were not connected to the sewage system).[49] But even in Mossley, where only 220 council houses had been built between the wars, the council was beginning to take such matters seriously. In May, it was reported that the council was considering building 50 council houses immediately after the war.[50]

Resentment at the government's failure to act on Beveridge grew steadily in Mossley in 1943. 'Pennine' urged people to attend a public meeting at the Co-operative Hall which would discuss the matter. A resolution expressing the meeting's dissatisfaction with the government's attitude to the Report and urging it to 'appoint immediately a minister of Social Security and to proceed with all possible speed' to implement Beveridge was passed.[51] In May an 'enthusiastic meeting' of 40 representatives of 'religious, political and trade union organisations' agreed to hold a mass meeting on Beveridge.[52] The meeting was held at the Co-op Hall in June. The main speaker insisted that the time was 'bound to come when there would be an alignment of the forces determined that social insecurity should not continue against those who only paid lip service'. He regretted that housewives were 'not properly covered' by Beveridge's plan and 'looked forward to the time when the fear of want would be banished from all members of the community'.[53]

By the summer firm plans for housing reform were beginning to be formulated in Ashton. In August, the Housing Committee decided to send its Chair-

---

47   *Ashton Reporter*, 19 March 1943.
48   Ashton Council. Minutes of Housing Committee, meeting of 1 April 1943. CA/ASH 111/55 @ TLSAC.
49   *Mossley and Saddleworth Reporter*, 19 March 1943.
50   *Mossley and Saddleworth Reporter*, 7 May 1943.
51   *Mossley and Saddleworth Reporter*, 16 April 1943; 23 April 1943.
52   *Mossley and Saddleworth Reporter*, 14 May 1943.
53   *Mossley and Saddleworth Reporter*, 11 June 1943.

man and the Housing Manager to a conference of the National Housing and Town Planning Association, which was to discuss postwar housing. Despite shouts of 'hear, hear', which in November had greeted a complacent speech by the new Mayor, Lieutenant-Colonel W.L. Connery, who argued that 'Ashton has made substantial progress. We have cleared the old slum areas of Crickety and Charlestown and we have substituted a housing site comparable with any in the country',[54] pressure from central government and the local opposition ensured that the council continued to make plans. In December, in response to a demand from the Ministry of Health, the Committee agreed that 250 council houses should be built in the first postwar year.[55]

3 A Resurgence of Industrial Unrest

The incidence of strikes increased considerably after El Alamein. This strongly suggests that if most workers were prepared to eschew strikes during the national crisis of 1940, they were no longer quite so prepared to do so once victory seemed assured, as most probably thought it was after El Alamein. This, combined with the upsurge in pro-reform sentiment, prompted an acceleration of preparations for postwar reconstruction and reform in government and the civil service.

As we have previously noted, national unity did necessarily lead to class harmony. Though there were far fewer strikes in the Second World War than in the First,[56] more needs to be said. Industrial unrest accelerated as the war progressed. In 1940, when a German victory seemed a distinct possibility, the number of working days – 940,000 – lost to strikes was the lowest since the start of the century. But 1,808,000 days were lost in 1943 (the greatest since 1932) and 3,714,000 in 1944.[57] Miners (the miners' strikes of the spring of 1944, which we will consider later, were probably the most serious strikes of the entire war, threatening preparations for 'D-Day')[58] and dockers were just some of those who took part in unofficial strikes. Of course, it could be argued that wartime virtual full employment made strikes more likely. On the other hand, this was

---

54 *Ashton Reporter*, 12 November 1943.
55 Ashton Council, Minutes of the Housing Committee, meeting of 30 December 1943. CA/ASH 111/55 @ TLSAC.
56 In 1917–18, the height of unrest in 1914–18, 11,530,000 days were lost; in 1944–45, the height in 1939–45, 6,549,000 days. Pelling 1987, pp. 298–9.
57 Pelling 1987, pp. 289–90; Clegg 1994, p. 240.
58 See Gildart 2009, and McIlroy and Campbell 2011.

surely more than offset by ideological pressure against striking in wartime and the possibly severe consequences, including imprisonment.

The most serious strike in Lancashire, perhaps in the country, in 1943 was that of engineers engaged in vital war work at the vast Vickers-Armstrong shipyard and engineering plant in Barrow in the late summer and early autumn. As in most strikes of the time, the issue was a pay award. In this case, one which the management tried to implement in a way which would have left most of their workers worse off. The workers were supported by local officials and the District Committee of the AEU. When notice of the strike was given, the CP, unwilling to acknowledge the fundamental cause of the dispute, blamed it on outside Trotskyist agitators who 'stood for the defeat of the Soviet Union and its allies' and who to this end were determined to stir up trouble. The Party supported the decision of the AEU's national leadership to suspend its Barrow District Committee.[59] The majority of the CP's members in Barrow resigned.[60] After three weeks the strike was ended by a substantially increased pay offer.[61] The CP then considered it expedient to concede that the root cause of the strike was employer provocation, not Trotskyist agitation. More, it warned the government that it could not, 'without danger to the war effort, permit employers to adopt a provocative and negative attitude when the workers raise their just grievance'.[62]

None of our three towns saw a strike of comparable seriousness to that in Barrow. Oldham, where workers were perhaps fired up by memories and knowledge of the militancy of 1917–19, saw an upsurge in militancy early in 1943. In its annual report of January 1943, the Oldham Master Cotton Spinners Association reported that 'there is much absenteeism amongst the younger operatives which cannot be described as unavoidable … The great majority of our operatives are patriotic and loyal, but with a decline of discipline the minority … are out of hand'. A sudden increase in employee 'truculence' was reported:

> Reports continue to reach the office of firms being held up by men refusing to perform extra work … war production cannot be allowed to be interfered with at the caprice of men who try to use the occasion for extorting conditions and payments to which they are not entitled.[63]

---

59 *Daily Worker*, 5 September 1943.
60 Bornstein and Richardson undated, p. 110.
61 See Croucher 1982, pp. 218–28, for a full account of the strike.
62 *Daily Worker*, 10 October 1943.
63 Oldham Master Cotton Spinners Association, Reports 1943–46, Report of 30 January 1943. AAN/1/1/2/9 @ JRSC.

Strikes in February at the Woodstock Mill over the withdrawal of canteen facilities and at the Cape Mill over a man who refused to join the union[64] were but two of many strikes of short duration in Oldham's cotton mills early in 1943. In May, the town's bus and tram workers took part in a national strike over a pay award. In Manchester, 'hundreds' of bus and tram workers 'marched to Piccadilly, stopping trams and buses and urging the drivers to drive into the depots' which many, thinking that an official strike had been called, did. 'Some of the demonstrators pulled trolley-poles off wires, and several, including some women conductors, were taken to Newton Street police station'.[65] In August, Liverpool dockers briefly struck in protest over an arbitrary dismissal.[66] Pay was the issue in a September electrician's strike, including workers from Ashton and Oldham, in the greater Manchester area. At the same time 'several hundred' draughtsmen and fitters were on strike 'at a North-west aircraft factory' and a 'hundred women' from 'the machine shop of a North-west aircraft works' were on strike.[67] In Chadderton, 173 workers from the Greengate Works who had struck were each fined £5 under Order 1305.[68]

4   A Touch on the Reform Accelerator

Increasing suspicion that the government was not fully committed to the cause of postwar reform and the escalating industrial unrest may well have convinced Churchill to take seriously the persistent warnings of Labour members of the government of the dangers of neglecting reform. Probably because education reform was relatively uncontroversial (at least in government and Tory circles), the first fruit of a renewed commitment to reform was a White Paper on Education in the summer of 1943, followed by a bill in the autumn. Education reform in general was relatively uncontroversial, but the government's proposals for reform of denominational education stirred up a great deal of opposition, especially in Catholic circles. In November, clearly intended as reassurance of the government's sincerity on the matter of reform, the formation of a new Reconstruction Committee (the Reconstruction Committee which had been appointed in 1940 had never seriously got down to business) was announced. However,

---

64   *Oldham Weekly Chronicle*, 20 February 1943.
65   *Manchester Guardian*, 17 May 1943.
66   *Manchester Evening News*, 20 August 1943.
67   *Manchester Guardian*, 15 September 1943.
68   *Oldham Weekly Chronicle*, 25 September 1943.

the Committee seems to have acted as a sorting office for proposals from various ministries, rather than initiating proposals itself.[69]

Educational reform had been given an impetus by Beveridge and his insistence that 'ignorance' was one of the 'five giants' which had to be slain. Education was the responsibility of R.A. ('Rab') Butler, who was to be one of the main architects of postwar consensual Toryism, and his deputy, the Labour MP Chuter Ede. The Education Bill and the eventual Butler Act were, even for the time, conservative. Acceptance of the deficiencies of the 1944 Education Act by most labour movement activists particularly shows the degree to which they were still ideologically in thrall to the bourgeoisie. The act met the two main aspirations of the labour movement – free secondary education[70] and raising the school leaving age to 15[71] – but the act ensured that in other respects the existing elitist education system was preserved intact. The public schools, one of the main foundations of bourgeois power and privilege, were left untouched, a selective tripartite system in secondary education, which retained the grammar schools and assumed that most children would best benefit from a severely practical education, was introduced, denominational education was allowed and subsidised, and government threats ensured that an amendment to the act to provide for equal pay for women teachers was defeated.[72]

The ideological foundation of the proposed tripartite system was Eugenic doctrine, which held that the mass of people were quite dim intellectually.[73] The Butler Education Act acting upon the recommendations of the pre-war Spens Report, established a selective system based on an implicit assumption that all children were one of three Platonic types. The gold, the most able, would attend grammar schools and would typically enter the professions; the silver would attend technical schools and become technicians and artisans of various sorts;[74] the bronze, the least able, implicitly working class, children

---

69 Brooke 1992, pp. 177–83.
70 This had been an objective of the movement since the publication of its *Secondary Education for All* in 1922. Timms 1995, p. 74.
71 The Butler Act incorporated legislation passed in 1936 but never implemented. It was assumed that the school leaving age would soon be raised to 16, but this did not happen until 1972.
72 Timms 1995, p. 90.
73 Even the Marxist intellectual, J.B.S. Haldane, subscribed to Eugenics. He claimed that if working class people were to continue to reproduce at a higher rate than the rest of the population, then 'a slow decline of perhaps 1 or 2 percent per generation in the mean intelligence quotient of the country could be expected'. Haldane 1938, p. 117.
74 In April 1943, Butler had addressed a conference of cotton trade employers and workers at the Houldsworth Hall, Manchester, where he had indicated that such schools, clearly already taking shape in his mind, would teach, 'in addition to general subjects ... work-

would attend secondary moderns, where they would not be troubled by such subjects as French and Physics, but would learn appropriate manual skills. When preparing to establish these schools, planners in Oldham assumed that 10 percent of children would attend grammar schools, 12 percent technical schools and 78 percent secondary moderns.[75]

In 1943, critics of selective education were in a minority, but there were some in our three towns. Ashton's Labour Alderman Massey (the same Massey we encountered in Chapter 3) was presumably not one of them, for in the spring of that year he had presided over Ashton Grammar School's[76] first annual speech day since 1940.[77] But early in 1944, as the bill was making its way through Parliament, Mrs Smith of Oldham NUT called for 'multilateral' (comprehensive) education, but was chided for 'trying to mix oil and water' by 'Round the Town'.[78] At a Mossley public meeting held to discuss the education bill, Mr Davies of the NUT argued that 'the greatest evil had been that the boy or girl who left school at 14 believed he or she was inferior to the boy or girl who had a secondary education and that inferiority complex persisted throughout adult life'.[79] In 1945 at the annual meeting of Ashton and Dukinfield branch of the NUT, its incoming President, Miss E.H. Taylor, criticised those 'people, even in high places and our own profession, who believe that "hewers of wood" and "drawers of water"[80] need only a utility education'.[81]

---

shop processes, workshop drawing and various forms of craftwork'. Cotton Control Board, *Cotton Board Trade Letter*, 16 April 1943.

75   *Manchester Guardian*, 14 August 1945.
76   Probably due to the extremely narrow social base from which this school, like all grammar schools, recruited its teachers and pupils, it was a centre of reaction. In 1934, a master's description of a school trip to Germany undertaken the previous summer, revealed, even allowing for hindsight, truly shocking reactionary attitudes. At the entrance to Hamburg railway station, he had been 'delighted to see a small band of Nazis in their brown uniforms and with their swastika badges'. Later, in Lublin on the Baltic Coast, they had hoped to 'attach ourselves to one of the Labour Camps, organised by Herr Hitler, chiefly for boys leaving school. They are not military in character, though the discipline is fairly strict and a good deal of drilling and exercise is done'. They were not allowed to join the camp, but held 'political discussions' there, led by a 'Professor of Law'. The master was very impressed with Germany and 'left with the feeling that it was my second home'. *The Ashtonian* (the magazine of Ashton Grammar School), Easter 1934. ESR44/12/8 @ TLSAC.
77   *Ashton Reporter*, 21 May 1943. Massey presided again in 1944, when he remarked that no doubt the school 'would be carried on with same efficiency under the new act as under the old'. *Ashton Reporter*, 22 December 1944.
78   *Oldham Weekly Chronicle*, 5 February 1944.
79   *Mossley and Saddleworth Reporter*, 4 February 1944.
80   The fate (to be forever slaves) assigned by the God of the Christian Bible's Old Testament (Joshua 9.23) to the Gideonites, who had disobeyed him.
81   *Ashton Reporter*, 9 March 1945.

But Dr J.E. Richardson, the Principal of Oldham Technical College, subscribed to majority opinion on the matter. In January 1944 he addressed the Chamber of Commerce. 'In general', he claimed, there was 'profound admiration for the [education] bill'. He accepted the proposed tripartite system. He assumed that 84 percent of the town's children would not be capable of benefitting from a grammar or technical schooling.[82] And in Mossley, the Mossley Teachers Association held at the Co-op Hall a 'well attended' public meeting on the Education Bill. The main speaker, Lady Simon (Shena Simon),[83] supported the proposed tripartite system – children 'should have the sort of education that would best suit them'.[84]

For most labour movement activists, the introduction of free secondary education was the main consideration. As we saw in Chapter 2, the Fisher Act of 1918 had provided that fees, out of the reach of the vast majority of working class families, were payable for secondary education. A few working class children did go to secondary schools on scholarships. But in 1938, 88 percent of children, virtually all them working class, received only an elementary education.[85] The proposed abolition of fees for secondary education meant that critics of selective education found it hard to get a hearing. At the Labour Party's annual conference held late in 1944, after the Butler Act had been passed, the delegates supported an NEC resolution which gave a general welcome to the act. In an anodyne debate there was some criticism of the public schools, one delegate claiming that they provided '56% of the members of the House of Commons', but no delegate criticised the proposed tripartite system.[86]

If the government's commitment to selective education aroused little opposition in our three towns, its policy on denominational schools was quite another matter. Historically, the churches had been responsible for much of the country's educational provision. In 1943 the churches still ran half of British schools, many of them ill-equipped and poorly maintained.[87] To make such schools fit for secondary education would incur a great deal of expense. The government's solution to the problem of permitting denominational schools (there was not the slightest possibility that it would not permit religious in-

---

82 *Oldham Weekly Chronicle*, 22 January 1944.
83 Shena Simon had been a prominent Labour member of Manchester City Council. For a while she had been the Chair of the City's Education Committee. She had served on the Spens Committee on the reform of education. She became 'Lady' Simon by virtue of the knighthood conferred on her husband.
84 *Mossley and Saddleworth Reporter*, 4 February 1944.
85 Thom, 1986, p. 101.
86 Labour Party, *Report of 43rd Labour Party Annual Conference* (London, 1944), pp. 182–5.
87 Jefferys 1991, p. 126.

struction in schools) was to create two classes of such schools. The White Paper proposed that 'controlled' schools would be state maintained and that local authorities would control the appointment of teachers and ensure nondenominational religious instruction. Anglicans, the majority Christian denomination, had little to fear from 'controlled' schools in a society where the Anglican version of Protestantism was the established church. Moreover, the requirement in the act that each school day should start with an act of 'collective worship'[88] gave considerable scope for the propagation of Anglicanism. But those denominations which wished to appoint their own teachers and determine the content of religious instruction would have to opt for 'Aided' schools, for which the state would fund only half the cost.[89] The Catholic hierarchy, which considered it imperative that Catholic children were indoctrinated with their version of Christianity and no other, was outraged.

The TUC's 1942 memorandum on education had proposed ending state subsidies for church schools.[90] The memorandum undoubtedly reflected majority opinion in the labour movement, which held that they were reservoirs of superstition and fosterers of sectarianism. At a 1943 meeting of Ashton Trades Council, convened to discuss the education bill, E. Gartside claimed that it would be better for education to be taken out of the hands of religious bodies because the 'fables' they taught were often 'in contradiction to modern knowledge' and at the 1944 Mossley meeting Davies of the NUT claimed that because of their parents' religious beliefs, some children 'had been condemned to being taught in insanitary, out-of-date and musty buildings'.[91] But such views were not universally held in Lancashire, the heartland of British Catholicism. At the Ashton Trades Council meeting, several delegates argued that parents must have the right to have their child educated 'in the religion to which they belonged'. Miss Jones, a Catholic, said that 'without religion, people become monsters, not human beings'. Jones, who subscribed to the common misconception that the Nazis were atheists, insisted that their 'godlessness had caused the war'.[92]

Though Oldham T&LC resolved that they 'did not intend to invite speakers' when offered them by the Catholic Association of Hyde, Stalybridge and Dukinfield,[93] labour movement activists in Lancashire seem not to have opposed

---

88 Calder 1969, p. 629.
89 Jefferys 1991, p. 126.
90 Trades Union Congress, *Memorandum on Education after the War* (London, 1942), p. 8.
91 *Mossley and Saddleworth Reporter*, 4 February 1944.
92 *Ashton Reporter*, 4 December 1943.
93 *Oldham Weekly Chronicle*, 10 March 1944.

the Catholic hierarchy's reactionary campaign against the government's funding proposals, probably through fear of losing the mainly Labour Catholic vote. In October 1943, many of Ashton's Catholics joined a demonstration of around 30,000 people at the Belle Vue gardens in Manchester, where the Bishop of Salford said that many of the proposed reforms were 'admirable' but who would pay for it? Catholics would have to pay for the state sector through the rates and for their own schools through voluntary contributions. Later that month 1,000 of Ashton's Catholics travelled to Manchester city centre by chartered trolley-busses to attend a demonstration in Piccadilly Gardens. A speaker claimed that 'our schools shall be slowly but surely extinguished'.[94] 'Demanding justice for Catholic schools and repudiating the financial proposals of the White Paper on Education', 'thousands of Catholics from Oldham and district' marched in procession to a mass meeting, where a speaker claimed that Catholics must 'work for the full emancipation of Catholics as citizens of this country. They were now faced with the greatest menace that had ever confronted them'.[95] The campaign failed. The Butler Act ensured that those denominations which insisted on denominational education would have to substantially contribute towards it.

A markedly conservative feature of the existing educational system, one which the Education Act did nothing to change and which caused no controversy in our three towns, was its assumptions regarding the proper education of girls. At the first of the speech days of Ashton Grammar School presided over by Massey, it had been reported that girl pupils at the grammar school had 'adopted a day nursery school' and had gone to the district infirmary where they had spent 'their time mending, sewing and helping in the domestic arrangements'.[96] Such practices and the assumptions which underpinned them were widespread. The Headmistress of Fairfield High School for Girls, Miss Bradley, clearly opposed to prevailing attitudes, appealed to parents at the school speech day of 1945 'not to take girls away before their time'. But the main speech was given by John Coatman, the Northern Regional Director of the BBC. He hoped that while many girls would take up new opportunities, 'the greatest career for girls was the oldest career for girls, namely that of making a home. He did not mean, as the Nazis did, that girls should simply sit at home,

---

94 *Ashton Reporter*, 1 October 1943; 15 October 1943.
95 *Oldham Weekly Chronicle*, 30 October 1943. The speaker was no doubt referring to the fact that until Catholic Emancipation (the passing of the Roman Catholic Relief Act of 1829), Catholics were subject to various forms of discrimination. They could not, for instance, be Members of Parliament. But this speaker was demanding privilege, not emancipation.
96 *Ashton Reporter*, 21 May 1943.

scrub floors, cook meals and look after babies. In these days, home-making meant much more than that. The human family was the cornerstone of civilisation'.[97]

5 More Promises, More Unrest, More Discontent

While the Education Bill was making its way through Parliament, Britain, the Soviet Union and the USA were making plans for the final stages of the war. A meeting of foreign ministers in Moscow hammered out a unified military strategy for the last phase of the war and was followed by a first meeting of the 'Big Three'. Churchill, Roosevelt and Stalin conferred in Teheran between the 28th of November and the 1st of December 1943. Churchill's proposal for a thrust into Germany through the Balkans and Austria was rejected in favour of an invasion of northern France in May 1944. The *Teheran Declaration*, a document which, like the Atlantic Charter, served to conceal the imperialist nature of the war, was released at the end of the conference. The 'Big Three' insisted that when peace came with the final defeat of the Axis, it would be an enduring peace which would 'command the goodwill of the overwhelming masses of the peoples of the world and banish the scourge and terror of war for many generations'. The Allies would 'seek the cooperation and active participation of all nations, large and small, whose peoples in heart and mind are dedicated, as are our own peoples, to the elimination of tyranny and slavery, oppression and intolerance'.[98]

In the middle of the carnage and suffering of war the sophistries of the *Teheran Declaration* found a receptive audience. The *Times* and the *Manchester Guardian* gave greater coverage to the military aspects of the *Declaration*, its insistence on the Allies' united strategy, than its promises for the postwar world, but welcomed these.[99] Locally, the assurances of a peaceful postwar world attracted more attention. The *Ashton Reporter* welcomed the Allies' determination to build an 'enduring peace'.[100] The *Oldham Chronicle* welcomed their commitment to the 'elimination of tyranny and slavery, oppression and intolerance'.[101]

---

97   *Ashton Reporter*, 27 April 1945.
98   Edmonds 1981, p. 273.
99   *Times*, 7 December 1943. The *Manchester Guardian* printed the declaration in full. *Manchester Guardian*, 7 December 1943.
100 *Ashton Reporter*, 10 December 1943.
101 *Oldham Weekly Chronicle*, 15 December 1943.

Shortly after the Moscow meeting of foreign ministers, the Lancashire and Cheshire District Committee of the CP had declared that the meeting 'opens a new perspective ... the Moscow agreement brings the factory front near to the extended battle areas therefore, we have decided to call a District meeting of our comrades serving on JPCs, to discuss and develop a production policy based on the requirements arising from future extended military operations'.[102] After Teheran, an elated CP leadership retailed its membership with the promises of the *Declaration* and assured them that the second front was now assured and that in the postwar world there would be no return to 'poverty, strife and hunger'.[103]

But the CP had had, and continued to have, some difficulties in convincing workers of the merits of class collaboration. In the summer of 1943 a shop floor critic of the Manchester and Salford branch's *Factory News* had complained that on 'reading the Factory news I find that the main subject is production. This, I think is a managerial problem. Trade Unionism is ours'. But, the party had rejoined, 'Brother Morton seems to forget there is a war on. In occupied Europe today the Gestapo are shooting anyone found with a trade union card ... We should be even more concerned about production than the management, for we have more to lose if fascism wins'.[104] The Lancashire and Cheshire District of the Party later reported that 'some workers' were suspicious of JPCs and 'easy prey for Trotskyists, who [seek] to create suspicion by charging the J.P.C. representatives of being agents of the management'.[105]

Shortly before the Moscow and Teheran conferences, the *Daily Worker* had commented, disapprovingly, that many 'workers believe that as the war is going well the fight against the employers can be given preference'.[106] It is quite likely then that these conferences had the unintended consequence of intensifying such sentiments. It may well have been in anticipation of such a development that after Teheran the party's Lancashire and Cheshire District Committee argued that in the interest of boosting production it was necessary that there should be 'close relations ... between the Shop Stewards Committees and the JPCs [which] should be encouraged to issue Production Bulletins'.[107]

---

102   Report of Lancashire and Cheshire District Committee to Political Bureau, 2 December 1943. CPA, CP/CENT/ORG/6/4/ @ PHM.
103   'Teheran and the Next Steps in Britain', circular of 10 December 1943. CPA, CP/IND.DUTT/ 29/12 @ PHM.
104   *Factory News*, June 1943.
105   *Lancashire and Cheshire News*, 2 December 1943.
106   *Daily Worker*, 11 October 1943.
107   'Statement of District Party Policy on the Role of JPCs in Production', 20 January 1944. CPA, CP/LOC/NW/1/5 @ PHM.

But despite the CP's admonitions and exhortations, the number of days lost to strikes in 1944 was, as we have seen, nearly 50 percent greater than that of 1943. In early 1944 preparations for the invasion of France were well advanced, but were threatened by strikes. Particularly serious were a six-week strike of shipyard and munitions workers in Belfast in February and March and of miners in several coal fields from February to April.

The strike in Belfast involved 36,000 munitions workers and nearly led to a general strike when lay union officials were imprisoned.[108] The CP had little influence in Belfast. But it did among the miners. In a mainly coal-powered economy, the miners' strike over a pay award had the potential to halt preparations for 'D-Day'. Arthur Horner, a prominent miner's leader and CP member, warned the South Wales members against striking at a time 'when thousands upon thousands are due to die in the great onslaught on the continent of Europe'.[109] Signs of trouble in the Lancashire coalfield at the end of January were greeted with the claim that troublemakers were aiming to 'impede the successful prosecution of the war'.[110] The entreaties of the CP and of their union were ignored. Between February and April around 200,000 miners in the Lancashire, South Wales, Yorkshire, North-East and Scottish coalfields struck. Just as the miners were returning to work after an improved pay award,[111] engineering apprentices on the Clyde, the Tyne and in Yorkshire struck.[112]

More outbreaks of industrial unrest in Oldham's cotton mills came in the spring and autumn. In May, spinners at the Coldhurst mill in Oldham staged a brief sit-in strike over low staffing levels. They claimed not enough piecers were employed.[113] There were more strikes, of spinners at Gresham Mill, Oldham and piecers at Fir Mill, Royton, on this issue in the autumn.[114] Around the same time, 400 cardroom workers at the Victoria Mill, Rochdale struck over the refusal of eight women to join the union. After eight weeks on strike, the women agreed to join the union.[115] The Executive Committee of Oldham's spinners reported several other strikes that autumn.[116]

---

108 Field 2011, p. 109.
109 Broomfield 1979, p. 497.
110 *Daily Worker*, 1 February 1944.
111 Calder 1969, pp. 508–10. For the strike in South Wales, see Francis and Smith 1998, pp. 410–14.
112 Croucher 1982, pp. 232–41.
113 *Oldham Weekly Chronicle*, 13 May 1944.
114 *Manchester Guardian*, 16 September 1944.
115 *Oldham Weekly Chronicle*, 18 November 1944.
116 Spinners' Amalgamation, Oldham Committee Minutes, 1944. TU/1/1/60 @ OLSA.

Popular discontent had been manifest in by-elections as well as in industrial militancy. In January 1944 Commonwealth had won the Skipton by-election in a 12 percent swing against the Conservatives. Defying their leaders' support for the electoral truce, the local Labour Party supported the Commonwealth candidate.[117] A few weeks later, an independent labour candidate won at West Derbyshire, a Conservative seat which for decades had been in the pocket of the Dukes of Devonshire, whose seat at Chatsworth was in the constituency. In contrast, on the same day the Labour candidate at Kirkculdy contained the anti-government swing to 4.7 percent and retained the seat.[118] As the CP commented, in an implicit rejection of the notion of a movement away from party, 'the conclusion is obvious. Labour men can win seats, but there is a mass convulsion against the Tories'.[119]

Capitalising on the upset in Skipton, an article in the ILP journal, *Labour's Northern Voice* (which, judging by its content, was mainly the work of ILP members in the Manchester area), by Alva Barker, the Secretary of Skipton's weavers was given the headline 'To Save Cotton Industry Textile Operatives Recommend Socialisation' (a reference to a UTFWA report of 1943 which we will consider later). Despite the ILP's official opposition to the war effort, *Labour's Northern Voice* made no effort to stir up anti-war feeling, concentrating instead on insisting that plans for postwar reform were insufficiently radical. Barker criticised the failures of private ownership, noting, for instance, the fall in exports of finished 'piece goods' from 7.1million yards in 1913 to 1.4million yards in 1939. There was no mention of the imperialist relations on which these exports had relied.[120]

It is unlikely to be coincidental that a White Paper on Health had been published in February, at the height of the industrial unrest which was threatening the preparations for D-Day, or that a White Paper on Employment was published in May, just before D-Day. Both directly addressed major and longstanding concerns of the labour movement. The present writer has been unable to find any direct evidence of cause and effect, but it is surely significant that just after D-Day Bevin claimed in Parliament that when he and Churchill went to speak to British troops awaiting embarkation for Normandy, 'the one question they put to me when I went through their ranks was "Ernie, when we have done this job for you are we going back on the dole?" ... Both the Prime Minister and I answered: "No, you are not"'.[121]

---

117 Calder 1969, p. 637.
118 Jefferys 1991, p. 225.
119 *Daily Worker*, 19 February 1944.
120 *Labour's Northern Voice*, March 1944.
121 Cited in Addision 1977, p. 242.

The White Paper on Health was mainly the work of the Conservative Minister of Health, Henry Willink (though his predecessor the National Liberal Ernest Brown had done a great deal of preparatory work). While there had been some significant improvements in health services in the interwar period, notably a great increase in the number of hospital beds available,[122] it had been the policy of the Labour Party for some time that to overcome major deficiencies in healthcare,[123] which particularly affected working class people, there should be a comprehensive, free national health service run by local authorities.[124] The White Paper more than met labour movement aspirations: it proposed that everyone 'irrespective of means, age, sex or occupation shall have equal opportunity to benefit from the best and most-up-to-date medical and allied services available' and that such treatment should be 'free of charge'.[125]

Nothing happened in our three towns comparable to the upsets at Skipton and West Derbyshire, but it is clear that many people aspired to a postwar world radically better than that of the 1930s. In Ashton, the Council's commitment to postwar housing improvement was sustained. Early in 1944, the Housing Committee resolved that because of 'widespread distress and social discontent occasioned by the present acute housing shortage in this borough, and generally throughout the country', the government 'should allow local authorities to build the maximum possible number of houses now and not wait till the end of the war'.[126] At a full council meeting, Labour's Mrs Mamourian referred to the 'desperate' need for new houses. 'Perhaps the saddest cases were those of young married women who were expectant mothers. Some must reluctantly

---

122 Timms 1995, p. 106.
123 The healthcare available and the standard of care could be very variable (at Stepping Hill hospital in Stockport, for instance, pain relief was not always available on the obstetric ward) and was dependent on the money raised for each hospital (voluntary hospitals relied on charitable donations while local authority hospitals were funded via the rates). Hospital care was severely means-tested, with the result that many conditions went untreated, either because care could not be afforded, or through reluctance to submit to a means test. While most of the working population were members of the State Health Insurance scheme established by the pre-First World War Liberal government, housewives, children, pensioners, and so on were not covered. The state scheme did not cover hospital treatment, dentistry or ophthalmic needs.
124 Honigsbaum 1989, p. 81.
125 Timms 1995, p. 111.
126 Ashton Council, Minutes of the Housing Committee, 27 January 1944. CA/ASH/111/56 @ TLSAC. The committee was probably trying to take advantage of the severe housing shortage caused by bombing in some places, but not Ashton. So bomb-free was Ashton that a party of 285 evacuees was sent there from London during 'flying bomb' attacks towards the end of the war. Minutes of Education Committee, 17 July 1944. CA/ASH/111/56 @ TLSAC. 1,750 were evacuated to Oldham. *Oldham Weekly Chronicle*, 22 July 1944.

accept overcrowded conditions ... and some were in lodgings which they were liable to lose when the fact of pregnancy became known'.[127]

In May, Ashton Trades Council heard F.H. Duffy of the Painters' Society argue that a decisive stage of the war had been reached and the time had arrived when post war matters should be discussed. A delegate said that the Council would 'play a big part after the war in deciding what kind of life and peace they wanted'.[128] Later in May, a May Day demonstration on the Market Ground was chaired by G. Crompton of the CP, who stressed that this year workers were 'tensed for the greatest contribution towards international solidarity ever made – the liberation of Europe'. T. Shaw of the AEU District Committee 'called upon those in industry to be as ready as those in the fighting forces ... the invasion of Europe would make greater demands than were at present realised'.[129]

Delegates from Oldham's cardrooms attended UTFWA's annual conference in April 1944, where they heard fraternal greetings from the prominent Labour Party intellectual and NEC member Harold Laski, who was insistent that: 'When the war was over the people should not be cheated of the fruits of victory. He remembered only too vividly the ghastly unemployment that followed the last war ... If [the workers of Britain] had the courage to organise they had the courage and power to become the masters of their own fate'.[130]

In Mossley, in an extraordinary move, considering the council's traditional parsimony, the council agreed by 10 votes to 7 to increase the rates by a 1/- in the pound to fund increased public spending. Supporting the proposal, Councillor Buckley was adamant that the council must look to the future. In comparison with 'many a town, social amenities in Mossley were sadly lacking'. New sewers, a public baths and slum clearance were urgently needed. (Alderman Coe who had led the resistance against providing a British Restaurant was prominent among those opposing a rate increase).[131]

Work on postwar employment policy had started in 1943, shortly after the publication of the Beveridge Report. Beveridge's proposals on social security were posited on an assumption that idleness, one of the 'five giants', would be vanquished in the postwar world. The eventual White Paper on Employment,[132] published in May, was rather vague on how postwar full employment

---

127   *Ashton Reporter*, 11 February 1944.
128   *Ashton Reporter*, 5 May 1944.
129   *Ashton Reporter*, 19 May 1944.
130   Cardroom Amalgamation. Reports and Minutes January 1941–November 45. Quarterly Report and Balance Sheet for the Quarter ending 24 June 1944. Report to District Officials from Alfred Roberts, General Secretary. TU/TEX/CARD/18 @ WCML.
131   *Mossley and Saddleworth Reporter*, 21 April 1944.
132   The White Paper on Employment was supplemented by a White Paper on Social Security

might be attained. But whatever the means, the Government unequivocally accepted, in the opening words of the White Paper, 'as one of their primary aims and responsibilities the maintenance of a high and stable level of employment after the war'.[133] It is impossible to determine if, as Bevin had clearly hoped, the White Paper served to sustain morale prior to D-Day, though Home Intelligence reported that 'many people, especially workers, while approving the plan, are sceptical as to it ever becoming law in anything like its present shape'.[134]

Labour movement reaction to the White Pater was mixed. The unions were broadly supportive, but some on the labour left, believing that full employment in a capitalist society was impossible, were sceptical or even hostile. The trade unions gave the White Paper guarded support. An editorial in the AEU's journal supported it and noted that it was based on Keynes's 'maintenance of consumption rather than the pre-war "balanced budget" approach'.[135] Roberts of the cardroom workers was enthusiastic:

> The White Paper on Employment has rightly been hailed as a remarkable advance in the direction which organised labour has claimed for so long. The opening statement of the Paper [on government responsibility for full employment] is clear and unequivocal and decisively rejects the longstanding policy of 'laissez-faire'.

Roberts did argue that some parts of the paper were vague – what, for instance, he wondered was meant by 'high and stable'? But overall the report was to be warmly welcomed.[136] The spinners' Executive Council too welcomed it, noting that it was of 'special significance in view of the sad experience of textile workers' before the war.[137]

(in the long-term just as significant as the earlier White Paper) in September 1944, welcomed in a local editorial as a scheme which would banish 'the gaunt, grim spectre of a poverty-ridden old age'. *Mossley and Saddleworth Reporter*, 9 September 1944. In anticipation of legislation on both white papers, a Ministry of National Insurance was established in November 1944.

133 Timms 1995, pp. 132–3.
134 Addison 1977, p. 247.
135 Amalgamated Engineering Union, *Monthly Journal*, July 1944, pp. 193–4.
136 Cardroom Amalgamation, Reports and Minutes January 1941–November 1945. Quarterly Report and Balance Sheet for the Quarter ending 24 June 1944, Report to District Officials from Alfred Roberts, General Secretary. TU/TEX/CARD/18 @ WCML.
137 Quarterly Report of Executive Council of the Spinners' Amalgamation for quarter ended 31 July 1944. ACS/1/51 @ JRSC.

The nominally Marxist CP had fallen in love with Beveridge and Keynes. The Party claimed that 'A policy of high and steadily increasing real wages is not solely in the interests of [trade union members] but represents the national interest in a prosperous Britain contributing to the prosperity of the world'.[138] In a review of *Full Employment in a Free Society*, J.R. Campbell, one of the Party's most influential leaders, argued 'Spend on social reforms, Sir William argues, and you will stimulate demand for goods and so increase employment'.[139]

The Tribune on the other hand regarded the proposals of the White Paper as an attempt to save capitalism from its inevitable doom: the 'White Paper admits the justice of Socialist criticism – and draws the conclusion that Capitalism must be saved at all cost'.[140] ILP members had similar views. The proposals of the White Paper, they argued, 'aim not at the abolition of unemployment but at its regulation ... after the immediate postwar boom, which may last two years, the Labour remedies will have to be adopted if the problem is to be mastered'.[141] Many delegates to the Labour Party annual conference that December were critical. For them, only socialism (or rather the Labour Party's version of socialism – planning and state ownership) could ensure full employment. The NEC's resolution on full employment reaffirmed its 'contention that full employment and a high standard of living for those who work by hand or by brain can only be secured within a planned economy'. The aptly named delegate Jack Blitz contended, in what was to become the main dividing line between Labour and the Conservatives in the looming General Election, that in a document on full employment it should 'be shown quite clearly that the socialisation of the basic industries is a necessity to full employment because of the inherent contradictions of capitalism which produce unemployment'. The NEC resolution was carried.[142]

6 Social Imperialism Triumphant: the Last Phase of the War

It became abundantly clear after El Alamein that the sunny new world promised by the Allies would apply only to the people of the imperialist countries.

---

138 Communist Party, *Higher Wages and Full Employment. Memorandum of the Executive Committee* (London, 1944).
139 *Daily Worker*, 20 November 1944.
140 'A Nation of Fully Employed Tramps', *The Tribune*, 2 June 1944.
141 *Labour's Northern Voice*, August 1944.
142 Labour Party, *Report of 43rd Labour Party Annual Conference 1944* (London, 1944), pp. 160–8.

For the peoples subject to exploitation and oppression by these countries, little would change. But the Labour Party and the CP continued to insist, as they had on the matter of Indian independence, that everything must be subordinated to the perceived immediate necessity of defeating the Axis powers. As the imperialist nature of the war became increasingly apparent and as it become correspondingly increasingly difficult to justify support for the war on antifascist grounds, both the Labour left and the CP resorted to appealing to the imperialists not to behave like imperialists.

One of the few, the very few, expressions of concern from our three towns regarding the government's colonial policy came from the Secretary of Mossley's Labour Party. He wrote to the Party's headquarters to state that he had attended a lecture on India and had heard convincing criticisms of the Government's India policy, in particular its refusal to countenance immediate independence. In reply, William Gillies, Labour's International Secretary, stated that while Labour was committed to postwar independence, the Government could not ignore the 'Quit India' movement of civil disobedience and that to accept the Congress Party's demand of independence now 'would be foolhardy and would lead to civil war'.[143] Presumably, these arguments were found convincing, for no more expressions of concern from Mossley are to be found in the LP archive (there were very few at all). The matter of the Empire surfaced too in Oldham, where, in 1945, D.J. Williams, the one-time Assistant Bishop of British Honduras, addressed a public meeting on the 'awful poverty' he had witnessed in the West Indies. 'In one case, a whole family of four lived in a shack scarcely large enough to house a small car'. His audience was reminded that 'Lancashire people owed much of their prosperity to the products of the West Indies, and so they had an obligation to see that the natives were given better treatment'.[144]

But these were rare exceptions, certainly in the labour movement. Without any evident qualms or reservations, the CP continued to urge working class people to work harder to support Britain's assertion of imperial interests in and around the Mediterranean. Lancashire members cited a 'woman in Oldham, who says "the African offensive makes big demands and calls for sacrifices". In this spirit the majority of Lancashire women are going to the mills'.[145] A handbill publicising a CP rally at Belle Vue, Manchester, urged support for 'our' armed forces 'in the hard fighting in Tunisia' who were 'on their toes, ready for the all-out, final assault on Germany' (the CP was then expecting an immin-

---

143 J. Pennington to Labour Party Head Office, undated; William Gillies to J. Pennington, 18 September 1944. LP/ID/IND110–111 @ PHM.
144 *Oldham Weekly Chronicle*, 2 June 1945.
145 'Low Pay in Mills Hinders Output', *Lancashire News*, 5 December 1942.

ent invasion of France). Several months elapsed before Axis armies in North Africa were finally defeated. 'Glory to the men of the Eighth and First Armies and to Britain's working people who gave them the tools', declared a Lancashire District of the CP handbill.[146]

The CP asserted in that summer of 1943 that the

> peoples of Britain ... approach the fifth year of War with confidence of victory over fascism ... Now, thanks to the Red Army and the heroic Soviet people, and the achievements of the armed forces in North Africa, a position has been reached when decisive blows can be delivered, not only against Nazi Germany, but for the final defeat of the Axis powers.

But, the party warned, the British people 'must make it clear' that the self-determination clause of the Atlantic Charter 'shall be applied to all countries'.[147] How was this to be done? The government, not the people, held power. And the government and the labour movement were as one in being determined to work 'for the final defeat of the Axis powers'. The CP could only entreat the government not to behave like an imperialist government and make futile criticisms when it did. The Labour Party's resolutions on colonial freedom and the CP's denunciations of the government's colonial policy were sanctimonious, given their support for British assertion of imperial interests. Apart from the offer of postwar full independence to the Congress Party of India, dismissed by Gandhi as a 'post-dated cheque', there was no social-imperialist contract for the peoples of the Empire. The Atlantic Charter was a chimera.

After the victories in North Africa, Streat began to ponder the future of Lancashire's cotton industry and in particular how to take advantage of victory over Japan. In April 1943 he discussed this matter with Keynes at the House of Lords. Keynes had 'thought it probable that the result of the war would give us much relief as against Japan: his theory was that Peace Terms with Japan would be very savage'. In July he had a meeting with Wavell, the new Viceroy of India to urge him to 'bear in mind the interests of Lancashire cotton'. He also met Oliver Stanley, the new Colonial Secretary. Streat thought that 'economic exploitation of colonial territories was not a right or desirable policy'. But, on the other hand, he had hoped that Stanley 'would not be so lofty in his outlook as to lose the necessary touch with hard facts and practical issues'. He thought that 'time for adjustment might prove to be politically justifiable' and that the 'inhabitants of

---

146 Lancashire District and Manchester and Salford Branch of the CP ephemera. CPA, CP/LOC/NW/01/05 @ PHM.

147 Communist Party, *16th Congress Discussion Statement on Colonies* (London, 1943), p. 12.

the colonial territories might be the losers by a too pedantic adherence to the doctrine of the freedom to buy in the cheapest market'.[148]

Streat's views were but one manifestation of the popular assumption we noted in earlier chapters, fed by Empire Days and press coverage, that Britain's colonies were vital to its future prosperity. Lancashire's workers had for decades been fed tales of colonial benevolence and images of the colourful ways of the Empire's colonial subjects. In 1941, in Mossley, the Centenary of Livingstone's departure for Africa had been celebrated at Abney Congregational Church. Children had performed a play. A tableau of 'events in the explorer's life' had been on display, as had 'many exhibits from Africa'.[149] In 1943, Ashton's Girl Guides presented a 'Masque of Empire' at the Town Hall. At a service at St. John's on the eve of Empire Day, the vicar, the Reverend W. Brandwood, preached on the history of the Empire and claimed that 'historical evidence showed that this country was the servant nation of the world'.[150] There were frequent reports in the local press of the colonial outposts in which local members of the armed forces were carrying out their imperial duties. Sergeant K.H. Roberts wrote from the Gold Coast (Ghana since independence): 'Africans love colour. One of my most painful experiences here was to see an African wearing a complete suit ... of similar colours to the Ashton Grammar School Old Boys ... all the stripes running vertically!'[151] Sapper G. Brown wrote from Egypt on his work supervising 'gangs of natives', who, 'chanting their ancient songs', worked on the Nile and associated canals.[152] Early in 1944, a soldier's report from India caused the local Mossley paper to comment on 'the kindness and hospitality shown to our boys by people in all parts of the Empire'.[153]

Unsurprisingly then, the views of the cotton unions on their trade were, like Streat's, partly shaped by social-imperialist assumptions. In September 1943,

---

148   Streat Papers, Diaries 1939–45, 17 April 1943; 15 July 1943; 28 July 1943. GB133=133 ERS @ JRSC. In 1944, Oldham and Rochdale textile employers were arguing that as Japan 'is now an enemy', the Congo Basin Treaty (they were referring to the Treaty of Berlin of 1884 which, *inter alia*, gave its signatories access to markets and resources in the Congo Basin), 'which it is generally understood has operated unjustly against British exports and proved helpful to Japanese interests' should be abrogated. ORTEA Annual Reports 1943–46, report for 1944. AAN/1/1/2/9 @ OLSA. Prior to the war this had been the demand of the Burnley Labour MP Wilfred Burke. Gupta 1975, p. 233.
149   *Mossley and Saddleworth Reporter*, 28 March 1941.
150   *Ashton Reporter*, 28 May 1943.
151   *Ashton Reporter*, 8 October 1943.
152   *Oldham Weekly* Chronicle, 19 November 1943.
153   *Mossley and Saddleworth Reporter*, 14 January 1944.

UTFWA submitted to Streat a report containing proposals for the postwar structure and stability of the cotton industry (Streat had been asked by Hugh Dalton, the President of the Board of Trade, to draw up a plan for the postwar reconstruction of the cotton industry). The report's authors (this was the report referred to by Alva Barker of Skipton's weavers) assumed a common interest of 'labour and the nation', but not of labour and the millocracy, whose response to Japanese competition had been 'reduction in wages, increased working hours ... more looms'. Heavily influenced by social-imperialism, the main recommendation of the report was the 'socialisation' (actually state ownership – the report had nothing to say on ending the exploitation of the workforce, workers control, and so on) of the trade. This would be the best way to 'meet foreign competition [and] satisfy the aspirations of the workers for a better life'.[154] To deal with foreign competition, an International Control Board should allocate to each exporting country its quota of finished piece goods and fix the price of such goods. But Japan, the authors were keen to assert, should receive supplies sufficient only 'to satisfy her own requirements before she attempts to regain her foreign markets'.[155]

We should not be surprised that the authors of the report had nothing to say on the independence movement in India, where the mass insurrection of the Quit India movement was beginning to subside in the wake of savage repression. Perhaps this omission was due to concern that Indian independence would be disadvantageous to Lancashire's cotton trade. The response of the cotton unions, discussed in the previous chapter, to the Japanese 'threat' to India and the clear anxiety manifest in Streat's discussions with various notables that Japan be excluded from export markets, strongly suggests that this may have been the case. Even those nominally in favour of Indian independence, such as the CP, tended to argue for independence on the grounds that this would increase the demand for Lancashire's cotton exports: 'If the cotton consumption of India and China were to be doubled, world cotton consumption would be increased ... by 34%', insisted Lancashire's communists: therefore,

---

154 UTFWA *Report of the Legislative Council on Ways and Means of Improving the Economic Stability of the Cotton Textile Industry, September 1943* (Ashton-under-Lyne, 1943), pp. 84–5.
155 UTFWA *Report of the Legislative Council on Ways and Means of Improving the Economic Stability of the Cotton Textile Industry, September 1943* (Ashton-under-Lyne, 1943), pp. 94, 81–3. Union anxieties regarding postwar competition intensified. Shortly after the war in Europe ended, Andrew Naismith, the Secretary of the Weavers' Amalgamation, addressed Oldham Rotary Club. Prosperity, he argued, depended on 'recognising the common interests of workers and employers, especially in view of the prospective intensity of international postwar competition'. *Oldham Weekly Chronicle*, 9 June 1945.

'LANCASHIRE WORKERS HAVE A SPECIAL INTEREST IN ATTAINING INDIAN FREEDOM'.[156]

But while the CP called for (eventual) colonial freedom throughout the war, it also, objectively, campaigned for an intensification of the exploitation of the colonial peoples. Not long after 'D-Day', the CP would complain that:

> in the great world-wide struggle now being waged to destroy the forces of fascism and achieve peace, freedom and democracy for the peoples, the continent of Africa and the millions of Africa's people have already made quite a considerable contribution. Unfortunately, however, Africa's contribution still falls very short of what it actually could and should be were its resources in natural wealth and man-power really effectively mobilised.[157]

The war had stimulated attempts to extort a greater 'contribution' from the colonies to the war effort, especially in food for consumption in Britain, where supplies were threatened by submarine warfare.[158] A major reason why the 'contribution' of Africa had not been bigger had been the resistance of black Africans to such practices as forced labour.[159] In 1943, the CP had made a call for the better mobilisation of 'negroes' in the war effort. To this end, it had demanded 'the abrogation of forced labour enactments recently passed in Kenya, Northern Rhodesia and Nigeria'.[160] This demand was not made in the 1944 article.

Forced labour was not the only means of extorting from Africans a 'contribution' to the British war effort. The appalling labour conditions in, for instance, South Africa's gold mines and on cotton plantations in the Sudan, Tanganyika (one of the spoils of the First World War, now part of Tanzania), Nigeria, Southern Rhodesia (now Zambia), South Africa and the West Indies, were known to those who wished to know.[161] The CP certainly knew. Its *Colonial Information*

---

156 *Lancashire News*, 8 July (emphasis in original).
157 'Africa's Contribution to Victory', *World News and Views*, 24 June 1944.
158 In many places in Africa and in other parts of the Empire, there was hunger and even starvation, notably in the Bengal Famine of 1943–44, in which perhaps as many as three million people died from starvation and disease as a result of an implacable determination to maintain food supplies to Britain. Collingham 2011, ch. 7. For a full account of the Bengal Famine, see Greenhough 1983.
159 See Tembo 2013 for a discussion of wartime forced labour in Northern Rhodesia.
160 'The Negro Peoples and the War', *World News and Views*, 27 February 1943.
161 Knowledge of these conditions had begun to seep out in the early twentieth century. Porter 1985, pp. 309–10. Every January, the *Oldham Weekly Chronicle* carried reviews of the

Bulletin had regularly carried *exposés* on these plantations. The ILP too did. The May Day 1944 edition of *Labour's Northern Voice* reported on the dreadful conditions of 'native' labourers in South Africa.[162]

It is hard not to conclude that the CP's demands for a bigger 'contribution' from Africa involved self-deception on a grand scale. It was maintained throughout 1944 and 1945 as British imperial interests were forcibly asserted in such places as Greece, Burma and Malaya. As for the Labour Party, it was not thought necessary to discuss the colonial question at either its 1944 or its 1945 annual conferences, provoking, at the 1945 conference, delegate Trevor Pugh to protest that there was 'no reference here to great colonial questions. The black man is our brother. We have got to do something about the imposition of British imperialism'.[163]

But the 'imposition' of imperialism, British and other, had been proceeding swiftly since El Alamein and had accelerated since 'D-Day'. In the year or so afterwards, incipient revolt, especially in Italy, France and Greece, was suppressed. In this, the imperialist armies had the invaluable ideological, political and practical help of the international communist movement. In Italy, for instance, Togliatti, the leader of the Italian party, made it quite clear that this was the task of the Italian workers. After years of exile in the Soviet Union, Togliatti returned to Italy after the 'liberation' of Rome in June 1943. In his first speech after his return he was insistent that 'The problem for the Italian workers today is not to do what was done in Russia'. No, the task was to 'guarantee order and discipline in the rear of the allied armies'. The Italian communists carried out this task even as the allied imperialists disarmed partisans who had seized power in several northern Italian cities in April 1945.[164]

In the autumn of 1944, Britain intervened in an incipient Greek civil war. Greece was crucial to British supremacy in the eastern Mediterranean. The dominance of British finance capital in the Greek economy had ensured that Greek governments, including the pre-war quasi-fascist government, were friendly to Britain.[165] When, in the wake of Germany's withdrawal from Greece,

---

cotton trade. The review by the British Cotton Growing Association on African plantations never mentioned labour conditions. In 1945, for instance, the only reference to indigenous peoples was a passing mention that the 'natives' of Nyasaland were 'engaged in growing food and performing other duties'. *Oldham Weekly Chronicle*, 6 January 1945. Oldham's spinners never bothered to draw attention to the matter of labour conditions on these plantations.

162   *Labour's Northern Voice*, May 1944.
163   Labour Party, *Report of 44th Labour Party Annual Conference Report* (London, 1945), p. 96.
164   Claudin 1975, pp. 354, 360–1.
165   Sfikas 1994, ch. 1.

it seemed possible that communists might seize power, the British government despatched in October 60,000 troops to ensure that they did not. Over the next few months these troops were used to forcibly supress communists and other radicals and install a reliably pro-British government.[166]

The British intervention in Greece provoked far more opposition among the British left than any other nakedly imperialist action in this last phase of the war. Perhaps the denial of self-determination to Europeans stimulated support denied to others. The Greek business was another occasion (almost certainly not to the knowledge of the CP) where imperialism was rendered assistance by the international communist movement. Stalin had intimated that he accepted British dominance of Greece in a meeting with Churchill that October.[167] At the final conference of the 'Big Three', at Yalta early in 1945, Stalin told Churchill that he 'had no intention of criticising British actions [in Greece] or interfering' there.[168]

Bevan and Acland led a condemnation of the intervention in a parliamentary debate at the beginning of December, but only 23 Labour MPs were prepared to vote against the government.[169] Several Labour Party branches, including Salford Central and Liverpool, passed resolutions condemning the intervention (though, it is perhaps superfluous to mention, without withdrawing support for the war).[170] But at Labour's annual conference that December, the delegates were presented with an emollient resolution by the NEC which regretted the 'tragic situation' in Greece. Bevan denounced the intervention, claiming that only 'Fascist Spain, Fascist Portugal and the majority of Tories in the House of Commons' supported Britain's intervention. Typical of the Labour left though, while insisting that 'we cannot go much further along this road', he still did not 'want to break up the national government'.[171] After hearing Bevin argue that Britain could not 'abandon its position in the Mediterranean', the delegates supported the NEC resolution.[172]

After some initial equivocation, the CP opposed the intervention, but was careful not to threaten the war effort. At a lobby of Parliament, a worker from Napier's aircraft factory disingenuously claimed that 'we are not making planes to be used against our fellow anti-fascists in Greece'.[173] It was then announced

---

166 Sfikas 1994, ch. 2.
167 Kolko 1969, pp. 144–5.
168 Kolko 1969, p. 359.
169 Calder 1969, p. 651.
170 Thorpe 2006, pp. 180–3.
171 *Manchester Guardian*, 14 December 1944.
172 Labour Party, *Report of 43rd Labour Party Annual Conference* (London, 1944), p. 147.
173 *Daily Worker*, 18 December 1944.

that the North London District of the AEU was to 'down tools' in protest. But the strike did not take place. It was called off in view of the German offensive in the Ardennes (the so-called 'Battle of the Bulge').[174] Following the national lead, the Lancashire and Cheshire District Committee initially called for a strike – *Lancashire and Cheshire News* carried a page one headline 'Hands off Greece. All Out on December 17th' – but then reported only factory gate meetings, a public meeting attended by 1,600 people in Liverpool and a petition calling for a ceasefire.[175] Sam Wild spoke for the CP, along with speakers from Commonwealth, the India League and the Negro Association, at a rally of several thousand in Manchester's Piccadilly Gardens.[176] Attempting to justify his Party's timid response to the British intervention in Greece, this far-away country, Pollitt claimed that the intervention had to be seen 'against the background of the whole war against fascism, now nearing its final battles'.[177] In January 1945, at the height of the British suppression of the Greek left, the Lancashire and Cheshire District Committee provided another master class in wishful thinking by declaring that 'with inexorable might … the free people of the world … are advancing to victory'.[178]

Around the same time, the British reconquest of its far eastern possessions, made possible by a final US offensive against Japan (by June 1945, the US had conquered Okinawa, ready for an assault on the Japanese mainland, made unnecessary by the use of atomic bombs) began with an invasion of Burma. It soon became clear that Britain, as Churchill had always made very clear, had no intention of offering self-determination to the peoples of its far eastern colonies. Undeterred, those on the left who were troubled by such matters adopted their usual stance of treating British oppression of other nations and peoples as a matter of government policy rather than as an inherent aspect of imperialism.

Members of the ILP blamed 'Churchill, and … the little clique of imperialists around him who still dominate Britain's war councils' for the government's patently imperialist designs. It was clear that Attlee, Bevin and company were not to be regarded as members of the 'little clique'.[179] As for the CP, in March it welcomed 'the magnificent fighting march of the 14th army through the jungle hills of North Burma which has brought them out into the plains of Central Burma'.

---

174   *Daily Worker*, 20 December 1944.
175   *Lancashire and Cheshire News*, 16 December 1944; 23 December 1944.
176   *Manchester Guardian*, 18 December 1944.
177   *World News and Views*, 20 December 1944.
178   *Lancashire and Cheshire News*, 1 January 1945.
179   *Labour's Northern Voice*, December 1944.

But, the Party insisted, it was 'important that the British armies really come as liberators'.[180] Burmese communists wrote to the CP to condemn the activities of the British imperialists in the newly liberated Burma. They were forcibly dispersing meetings and confiscating newspapers.[181] The CP suppressed the letter in favour of publicising a rather different one from Burma expressing confidence that 'Britain, America and the Soviet Union' would 'help Burma in [its] national effort'.[182]

7   Labour to Power: the End of the War and the General Election

The future was much brighter for such British working class people as M.J. Crane of the Oldham District Committee of the AEU. He declared in the autumn of 1944 that his union had made 'great contributions' to the war effort and that his members now 'had a right to something better than 1939 ... They were not prepared to accept such conditions as existed after the last war'.[183] They would not have to. We have seen that since El Alamein, to meet the needs and aspirations of those such as Crane, educational reform had been enacted and that concrete proposals regarding social security, health, and employment had been made. In the new year, proposals for the final component of the postwar settlement, housing reform, would be made in the White Paper on Housing.

The war saw too the beginnings of an improvement in working conditions in the cotton mills. Before the war, most cotton mills were grim places indeed. One worker remembered that in interwar Ashton, the toilets were 'infested with cockroaches'. But even before the war conditions were beginning to improve. In some factories baths were being installed – 'you could put your name down and have a bath in your lunch time ... 'cos there weren't many people had baths'.[184] But the mill with baths was an exceptional mill. In 1945, the editor of the *Cotton Board Trade Letters* commented on the reluctance of young people to work in the mills, quoting a young woman who said she 'would rather go to prison than go to work in cotton'. However, after taking up an invitation from a 'progressive young manager' to inspect his mill, she changed her mind. The 'air condition was as near perfect as possible ... and the sanitary arrangements were very good. Slipper, foot and shower baths were provided ... The canteen was

---

180   *World News and Views*, 31 March 1945.
181   CPA, CP/CENT/INT/13/01 @ PHM.
182   *Inside the Empire*, October 1945.
183   *Oldham Weekly Chronicle*, 7 October 1944.
184   Abendstern et al. 2004, p. 48.

arranged with comfortable chairs ... To all mill girls like myself I say "your future will be happier"'.[185] Presumably, this was a fabricated story, aimed at improving recruitment. Even so, the improvements in conditions described were real enough, though perhaps not so comprehensive nor as widespread as the *Trade Letter* implied.

We have seen that holidays with pay had been introduced. In a further significant improvement, the government had encouraged, and, in some cases, compelled, employers to provide works canteens. The number increased from around 1,500 (though with virtually none in cotton mills) to 18,500 in 1944.[186] Food in canteens was 'off the ration' and thus provided one means for war workers to supplement meagre rations. They also, like British Restaurants, alleviated some of the domestic burden of women workers.

The first factory canteen in Oldham had been opened in late 1940, at the premises of Platt Brothers, manufacturers of textile machinery and one of the largest employers in the town. The factory already had a 'dining hall', where workers could go to eat food they had brought in, but now cooking facilities for the use of a 'large firm of London caterers' had been installed in a canteen where 'freshly cooked meals' could be obtained.[187] Another canteen was opened at the Marlborough Mill in neighbouring Failsworth in March 1942.[188] A week later, the first works canteen in Mossley was opened at Woodend Mill, with the Mayor and the Secretary of the South East Lancashire Cardroom Amalgamation in attendance. Testifying to their appreciation of this great improvement in working conditions, a concert was given by the employees.[189] At the end of the year, the CCB noted that 'the generation of workers to whom dinner at work meant a mug of strong tea and a meat pie by the loomside is passing ... More and more firms ... are telling the Cotton Board ... that operatives show increasing interest in general amenities, good working facilities, canteen facilities and other aspects of welfare'. There were now 81 canteens in Lancashire cotton mills, with another 101 in construction.[190]

The cotton unions considered that canteens should be merely one aspect of greatly improved postwar working conditions. In their 1943 proposals for postwar reconstruction, UTFWA had argued that in the postwar nationalised industry they advocated there should be, *inter alia*, 'installation of modern air

---

185   Cotton Control Board, *Cotton Board Trade Letter*, 7 August 1945.
186   Calder 1969, p. 446.
187   *Oldham Weekly Chronicle*, 11 November 1940.
188   *Oldham Weekly Chronicle*, 21 March 1942.
189   *Mossley and Saddleworth Reporter*, 27 March 1942.
190   Cotton Control Board, *Cotton Board, Trade Letter*, 15 December 1942.

conditioning plants ... lighting of sheds to be done by electricity ... an ample supply of sanitary conveniences and wash basins ... lockers, cloakrooms, suitable overalls, together with clinics, rest rooms and canteens should be provided ... in all mills'.[191]

In 1944, Streat, while drafting his proposals for postwar reconstruction of the cotton industry, visited David Whitehead and Company's mill in Rawtenstall, where the manager, George Whittaker, a 'passionate believer in some of the most radical theories of relationships with work people', had established a canteen and a works council. Streat believed that 'on balance ... there is a future for this sort of thing. It satisfies a good deal of the democratic instinct'.[192] 'This sort of thing' was being introduced at Lily Mills in Oldham, where 'a new building which is to comprise the mill's own surgery and shower baths is already nearing completion. Air conditioning is being installed so that operatives can work in as clean an atmosphere as possible'.[193]

In 1945, Mancunians and others could visit an exhibition designed to bolster recruitment to the cotton industry. A pamphlet (with a photograph on the back page showing a bright new modern mill with new WCs and women dressed in smart working clothes) noted that:

> We in the Recruitment and Training Department of the Cotton Board have been pleading for good conditions since our inception in 1943. Nothing fancy. Just ... a clean atmosphere, room to move about, adequate lighting and cheerful surroundings, modern lavatory and washing facilities, cloakroom ... and, especially where women and girls are employed, first aid and rest rooms.

The Recruitment and Training Department was quite clear that these improved conditions were in the interests of meeting competition from Britain's imperial rivals: the 'problems of the postwar world ... make it apparent that our whole national future prosperity, our standard of living and our share in world markets will depend, in large measure, on the constant development of our industrial techniques and skill'.[194]

Proposals for better conditions in the mills, while approved of, did not arouse a great deal of popular interest. Housing though, where there really had been

---

191 UTFWA, *Report of the Legislative Council on Ways and Means of Improving the Economic Stability of the Cotton Textile Industry* (Ashton-under-Lyne, 1943), pp. 84–5.
192 Streat Papers, Diaries 1939–45, 2 August 1944. GB133=133 ERS @ JRSC.
193 *Oldham Weekly Chronicle*, 9 September 1944.
194 Cotton Board, *The Modern Cotton Mill* (Manchester, 1945).

'broken promises' which still rankled in the labour movement, was another matter. Government attention to the housing question intensified in 1944. Just before D-Day, Churchill promised in a wireless broadcast that immediately after the war around half a million prefabricated houses ('prefabs') would be provided to meet immediate need and that 200,000–300,000 permanent houses would be built in the first two or so years after the war.[195] The success of the D-Day landings served to focus even more attention on housing. In the autumn, Lord Woolton, the Minister of Reconstruction, asserted that the housing problem was 'the most urgent and one of the most important from the point of view of future stability and public contentment'.[196]

Other than in the great cities of Liverpool and Manchester and a few centres of war materials production such as Barrow, the principal housing problem in Lancashire was not bomb damage but the historical legacy of jerry-built housing, slums and overcrowding. *Labour's Northern Voice* insisted that 'Practically all low-rented housing property in the north is unfit for habitation. It has stood through two long wars ... It has been unable to show a profit, no matter what the consequences'. The paper was opposed to the plan for prefabs ('Churchill homes'): 'we get this sudden spurt to provide 500,000 very inferior and frequently faulty low-roofed structures'.[197]

Utopians, visionaries and radicals were beginning to argue that housing reform was not just a question of building new houses: more fundamental changes were needed. The opening speaker at a conference on housing in Manchester convened by the Lancashire Federation of Trade Councils called for the nationalisation of land, arguing that 'the evils of land monopoly were easily appreciated in Lancashire, where at the beginning of the last century, when houses were needed for the rapidly swelling population, the excessive prices charged for land caused builders to pack as many houses as possible to the acre and thus provide for the formation of slums and overcrowding'.[198]

We have seen that in 1942 the members of Ashton's Housing Committee had been impressed by the communal facilities in Slough, but this would not be enough for some reformers. In October 1944, Ashton T&LC was addressed by E.L. Leeming, the Borough Engineer and Surveyor of Urmston Council, who spoke on postwar town planning. He insisted that 35 new towns must be built. They should be built in such a way that no-one would be more than ten minutes' walk from a community centre, where 'every kind of social amenity

---

195   Calder 1969, p. 619.
196   Malpass 2005, p. 57.
197   *Labour's Northern Voice*, July 1944.
198   *Labour's Northern Voice*, December 1944.

would be provided'. 'In 1950', he dreamt, 'no one will own anything individually, everything will belong to the community'.[199] In the summer of 1945, grand plans for the regeneration of several towns, including Ashton and Oldham, were revealed by the surveyor of the Oldham and District Regional Planning Committee. Under a plan for the next '25 to 50 years', these towns were to be broken up into separate neighbourhoods surrounded by 'wide green belts'. Each neighbourhood would have a 'large communal hall with facilities for leisure, pleasure, art, games, clubs, etc. [and] a compact shopping centre ... Houses will radiate around the centre in such a way that parallel rows will be spaced about seventy feet apart, each with a garden'.[200]

Perhaps unsurprisingly, these visions and plans remained mere visions and plans. But the *Ashton Reporter* made the far from utopian suggestion that 'women ought to be consulted more in regard to the type of house and the fittings they require, especially cupboards and kitchen arrangements, places to put garden tools and perambulators, cellars and coal storage, arrangements for the washing and ironing of clothes'. Stretford Council was praised for using a questionnaire to solicit opinions.[201] Labour Councillor Arthur Allen thought people other than those on the Housing Committee should be involved in the design of the houses. Existing council houses were 'nice to look at, but one had to live in them to realise their shortcomings'. But for Councillor Farnworth, the Conservative Chairman of the Committee, these ideas were far too radical. The Committee had sufficient designs in front of them 'without having to consult members of the public; that would lead to utter confusion'. Model homes in Manchester had been inspected.[202] Farnworth prevailed.

Churchill and Woolton assumed that most new postwar housing would be private housing, but our three councils were preparing to participate in the great postwar expansion of council housing. Even Mossley Council was making concrete plans for the provision of council houses. In September 1944 the council decided on the compulsory purchase of a site for the 'first postwar year's housing programme'. Later in the year, the council agreed to appoint an architect for the housing scheme and to send delegates to a conference of the National Housing and Town Planning Council in London in the New Year.[203] But reactionary die-hards continued to fight against reform. In the

---

199 *Ashton Reporter*, 6 October 1944.
200 *Manchester Guardian*, 14 August 1945.
201 *Ashton Reporter*, 13 October 1944.
202 *Ashton Reporter*, 25 October 1944.
203 Mossley Council, Minutes of the Housing and Baths Committee, Minutes of Meetings of 5 September 1944 and 5 December 1944. CA/MOSS1/22 @ TLSAC.

summer of 1945 the full council held a discussion on the outdated sanitary system in the town. A scheme for new sewers and conversion of the many 'pail closets' in the town to water closets was discussed. A member of the Health Committee opposed conversion: 'the use of disinfectants was good enough for anybody'.[204] Despite such opposition, in the autumn of 1945, architect's plans for 22 three-bed and 32 two-bed houses were submitted to the council.[205]

In Oldham, despite the council's comparatively good record on housing, the Chronicle declared in September 1944 that 'The need for houses is desperate'. Young married couples, for instance, 'did not want to stay for ever with their parents'.[206] The council, which was planning to build 'three hundred and fifty council houses in the first year of peace', was discussing using 'factory-made [prefabricated] houses'.[207] The Chairman of the Housing Committee had said that he hoped 'never to see' such houses in Oldham, but changed his mind after members of the Housing Committee had inspected 'prefabs' in several places, including Birmingham and London. Given that the town needed '12,000 houses in ten years', the council had decided to order 'four hundred prefabs' which would 'meet immediate and urgent need'.[208] But there were still sceptics. In nearby Failsworth, Councillor Evans claimed that 'prefabs' were 'not suitable for a damp climate'; he wanted 'decent houses, not shanties'.[209]

In Ashton, plans to build council houses on two sites had been drawn up by the summer of 1944. One hundred and fifty-two houses were to be built in the nearby township of Waterloo and 700 on a site near the town centre.[210] In December the council resolved to take possession of various sites to build 'temporary accommodation' ('prefabs'),[211] while the new Mayor cut the first sod on what would be the first estate of permanent three bedroom council houses, all with a bathroom and indoor toilet.[212]

Two years in gestation, the Housing White Paper was published in March 1945. Asserting a desperate need for new houses, the paper estimated that in

---

204 *Mossley and Saddleworth Reporter*, 22 June 1945.
205 Mossley Council, Minutes of Housing and Baths Committee, 4 September 1945. CA/MOSS 101/23 @TLSAC.
206 *Oldham Weekly Chronicle*, 9 September 1944.
207 Oldham Council, Housing Committee Minutes, meeting of 6 September 1944. CBO/15/2/1/3 @OLSA.
208 *Oldham Weekly Chronicle*, 21 October 1944.
209 *Oldham Weekly Chronicle*, 3 March 1945.
210 *Ashton Reporter*, 24 March 1944; 4 August 1944.
211 Ashton Council Minutes 1944, meeting of 13 December 1944. CA/ASH 100/40 @ TLSAC.
212 *Ashton Reporter*, 15 December 1944.

the first postwar decade three to four million new houses would be required. Willink (housing was then the responsibility of the Ministry of Health) presumed that most of these would be private houses.[213] Following the release of the White Paper, Oldham's reform-minded council resolved that it believed that housing was 'the supreme test by which the sincerity of the government can be judged towards fulfilling its repeated democratic ideals'.[214]

When the Housing White Paper was published, preparations to celebrate victory in Europe were underway. Employers and UTFWA agreed that cotton workers would get three celebratory days off with pay; further, 'If the announcement of the ending of hostilities is made when a mill is working, it will close at once'.[215] Victory in Europe Day (VE-Day) was the 8th of May 1945. From Hartshead Pike (a hill overlooking all three of our towns) a 'huge "V" flashed the victory sign every few seconds'. In Ashton, Labour Alderman Flowers addressed the crowd in the market place. He insisted that people must 'unite in one solemn pledge that we will work together for the benefit of the peace as we have worked together for victory in war' so that Ashton would enjoy 'freedom from want, freedom from fear, a happy, healthy band of people rejoicing in the beautiful manifestations of the creator'.[216] In Oldham, thousands attended services of thanksgivings, but, according to the *Chronicle*, a more triumphalist note was also present: 'Soon after dusk ... a crowd gathered ... near the war memorial singing *Land of Hope and Glory* and *There'll always be an England*'.[217]

The coalition broke up very quickly after the German surrender. Churchill resigned and was appointed Prime Minister of a caretaker administration, pending the election of a new government. Labour's annual conference coincided with the end of the coalition. The main business was a discussion of the NEC's draft election manifesto, *Let Us Face the Future*. It is extraordinary, given all the talk of a new world free from hunger, fear, want, etc., that there was no discussion of the colonial question. But perhaps it is not so extraordinary after all. Pugh's voice at Labour's annual conference had been a lone voice. True, *Let Us Face the Future* stated that Labour would seek 'the advancement of India to responsible self-government, and the planned progress of our Colonial Dependencies'. But, clearly, Labour considered that it should paternalistically decide when the colonial peoples were ready for independence. The social-

---

213 Malpass 2005, pp. 58–9.
214 Oldham Council, Council Minutes, Meeting of 11 April 1945. CBO/1/1/43 @ OLSA.
215 *Oldham Weekly Chronicle*, 14 April 1945.
216 *Ashton Reporter*, 11 May 1945.
217 *Oldham Weekly Chronicle*, 12 May 1945.

chauvinist tenor of Labour's attitude to international relations was perhaps best expressed by delegate Rene Saran, who demanded that Japan and Germany 'be disarmed' and not allowed 'to make war in future. On that I think we can all agree'.[218]

Endorsed by the conference, *Let Us Face the Future* opened with a robust statement of social-imperialist intent:

> Victory is assured for us, and our allies, in the European war. The war in the East goes the same way ... The people will have won both struggles. The gallant men and women in the Fighting Services, in the Merchant Navy, Home Guard and Civil Defence, in the factories and in the bombed areas – they deserve and must be assured a happier future than faced so many of them after the last war. Labour regards their welfare as a sacred trust.[219]

Labour declared that it was 'a socialist party, and proud of it'. But in what sense was it socialist? As we have seen, it was certainly not socialist in a Marxist sense. Labour aimed at serving the nation. Lest anybody not grasp this, *Let Us Face the Future* had the subtitle '*a declaration of Labour Policy for the Consideration of the Nation*' and was superimposed on a prominent 'V for victory' on its title page. For Labour the point of its commitment to nationalisation and planning – its principal difference with the Conservatives – was to ensure that Britain had an 'industry organised to enable it to yield the best that human knowledge and skill can provide. Only so can our people reap the full benefits of this age of discovery and Britain keep her place as a Great Power'.[220]

The CP, though still nominally a Marxist party committed to class struggle, argued that the national unity it had fought for since 1935 should be maintained into the peace. National unity would be essential for successful postwar reconstruction, which would in turn lay the foundations for a peaceful transition to socialism. In early 1945 it had been seduced by the sophistries of the Yalta Communique, in which the 'Big Three', while carving up the world in the spirit of the Congress of Berlin, had promised continuing postwar co-operation to build a 'world order under law, dedicated to peace, security, freedom and the gen-

---

218 Labour Party, *Report of 44th Labour Party Annual Conference Report, 1945* (London, 1945), p. 96.
219 Labour Party, *Let us Face the Future: A declaration of Labour Policy for the Consideration of the Nation* (London, 1945), p. 1.
220 Labour Party, *Let us Face the Future: A declaration of Labour Policy for the Consideration of the Nation* (London, 1945), p. 12.

eral well-being of all mankind'.[221] According to the CP, even 'progressive' Tories could participate in a national government committed to such perspectives.[222]

In April, Lancashire communists had attracted 5,000 people to a rally at Manchester's Belle Vue and 2,500 to a rally at Liverpool's Philharmonic Hall. 'A feature of both rallies' was said to have been 'the enthusiastic welcome' given to the Communist Party's 'plea for the return of a majority of Labour, Communist and Progressive MPs to form a National Government'.[223] But soon afterwards, in a tweak to international communist policy directed by the Soviet party,[224] the party abandoned its call for a National Government. Thereafter, it continued to argue for national unity, but campaigned for a Labour Government. The CP fielded 22 candidates in the General Election, including Pat Devine at Preston. Devine's campaign was claimed to be 'characterised by ... a concentration on the Tories [and] a friendliness to Labour and a refusal to be provoked' (presumably by Labour attacks).[225] Two Communist MPs – Phil Piratin at London's Mile End and Willie Gallacher at Fife West – were returned. In the municipal elections of November, the party won 42 of the 356 contests it fought, none of them in Lancashire. In London, it gained 27 percent of the vote in the wards it contested.[226]

The Conservatives ran a disastrous election campaign, over-reliant on Churchill's prestige as a war leader and on misjudged attacks on Labour, notably the claim that a British 'Gestapo' would be required to implement Labour's programme should it win.[227] During his visit to Oldham, Churchill visited the Ferranti factory, where the workers 'gave him a great cheer'. But this probably manifested mostly an appreciation of his leadership of the war effort. Those who 'booed him and ... held aloft a red flag with the hammer and sickle'[228] (famously, Churchill was also booed at Walthamstow dog track[229]) offered a

---

221 Edmonds 1991, p. 494.
222 See Redfern 2002, pp. 38–43.
223 *Lancashire and Cheshire News*, 21 April 1945.
224 An article, published in a French Communist Party journal, but written by members of the Soviet party and approved by Stalin prior to publication, criticised 'Browderism', the specific form of wartime class collaboration promoted by the US party. Not only had it dissolved itself, it had 'transformed' the Teheran Declaration, a diplomatic agreement, 'into a political platform of class peace'. Probably, the point of this episode was to make clear to the western allies of the Soviet Union that its co-operation in the postwar world should not be taken for granted. See Redfern 2005, pp. 190–4, for a fuller discussion.
225 *Lancashire and Cheshire News*, 28 July 1945.
226 *World News and Views*, 3 November 1945.
227 See Field 2011, pp. 358–72, for a concise description of the national campaign.
228 *Oldham Weekly Chronicle*, 30 June 1945.
229 *Manchester Guardian*, 4 July 1945.

better indicator of the opinion of many working class electors of his suitability for leading the task of postwar reform and reconstruction.

Of course, not all electors were working class. There were many middle class voters in the sprawling two-member Oldham constituency which contained a great deal of suburban and semi-rural territory. Even so, Kerr was probably unwise to devote most of his adoption speech to international relations, endorsing the 'general principles enunciated at San Francisco' (where the United Nations Organisation was being established) and only briefly mentioning his party's plans for postwar social reform.[230] In contrast, Labour's Frank Fairburn, a cotton worker himself, while being careful to speak on postwar reform, addressed the problems of the cotton industry. Fairburn argued that 'had the war not intervened, they would have witnessed, probably by now, the slow death, in face of Japanese competition, of what was formerly a great export trade'. He argued for the swift postwar implementation of the Platt report into the future of the cotton trade.[231] The two Labour candidates won a combined 47.5 percent of the vote to the 38.5 percent of the two retiring MPs.[232] The Labour vote in Oldham proper was considerably higher in November's municipal elections. The Party gained ten wards from the Conservatives and won overall control of the council.[233]

In the much more compact, mostly working class constituency of Ashton, the Tory candidate, Captain Goodheart, addressed more than Kerr the issue of postwar reform, but did so in a distinctively Tory way, ill-judged for the Ashton of 1945. In his adoption speech, Goodheart spoke mainly on how Britain must 'achieve greatness again'. He spoke also on housing, but argued that private enterprise should be relied upon. This would almost certainly not have gone down well in a town where private enterprise had spectacularly failed to solve the housing problem, nor would his claim that taxes should be lowered as there

---

230   *Oldham Weekly Chronicle*, 23 June 1945. The Conservative manifesto promised to maintain a 'high and stable level of employment', that the 'provision of homes will be the greatest domestic task', to introduce a 'nation-wide and compulsory scheme of National Insurance' and a 'comprehensive health service' which would not deny treatment to those could not afford it. Conservative Party, Winston Churchill's Declaration of Policy to the Electors (London, 1945).

231   *Oldham Weekly Chronicle*, 30 June 1945. Sir Frank Platt, wartime Cotton Controller, had visited the USA in 1944. In his report he had unfavourably compared British with US cotton spinning. He had been especially critical of the low productivity of the British trade and had advocated a move towards ring spinning. Fowler 1987a, p. 199.

232   *Oldham Weekly Chronicle*, 28 July 1945. One of the retiring MPs was a National Liberal, effectively a Conservative.

233   *Oldham Weekly Chronicle*, 3 November 1945.

were 'not many rich people left in the country'.[234] Jowitt's adoption speech was adroit, at a time when many working class people seemed to appreciate what Churchill had done as a war leader, but were doubtful of his credentials as a peace-time leader. He criticised the Tory slogan 'Let him [Churchill] finish the job': 'What is this job? It's not just a matter of the Japanese war. I'm quite happy to let him finish that. But what of social insurance ... housing? We have to do away with overcrowding, with bad housing, and all the diseases which spring from overcrowding and bad housing'.[235] In a straight fight with Goodheart, Jowitt won the 'notoriously fickle Ashton-under-Lyne'[236] easily, by 56.4 percent to 43.6 percent.[237] In the November municipal elections, Labour made 11 gains, ten from the Tories, one from the Liberals, to take control of the council for the first time.[238]

Mossley had much in common with Oldham, being a sprawling, much more socially mixed constituency than Ashton. The Labour candidate there, the Reverend G.S. Woods had been campaigning for months. In February he had argued at a public meeting that it was 'absurd' to think that there could be a return to pre-war conditions. 'It would only mean, for most, the old life of insecurity, subject to boom and slump with mass unemployment, with anxious preparation for another and even more horrible war'.[239]

The over-confident incumbent, Austin Hopkinson, had been, except for 1929–31, the town's MP in various political guises for the entire interwar period. He specialised in gratuitously insulting the labour movement. In 1919, in response to criticism from Hyde Trades Council of his opposition to an increase in old age pensions, he had replied that 'I told them the unpleasant truth instead of lying to them and licking their boots'.[240] In 1941 he had claimed that it was 'preposterous' to put Bevin, 'a man whom the craftsmen say "is only a labourer"', in charge 'of the whole labour affairs of the country'.[241] In 1945, he insulted the miners by claiming that the biggest problem in the mines was 'to induce the miner to work hard when he didn't particularly want to. The best way to deal with the problem was to set up a dogtrack near every big colliery. Then a man would have his money taken away from him as quickly as he earned it'.[242] But

---

234   *Ashton Reporter*, 15 June 1945.
235   *Ashton Reporter*, 22 June 1945.
236   *Manchester Guardian*, 27 July 1945.
237   *Ashton Reporter*, 29 July 1945.
238   *Ashton Reporter*, 2 November 1945.
239   *Mossley and Saddleworth Reporter*, 23 February 1945.
240   *Manchester Guardian*, 23 August 1919.
241   *Mossley and Saddleworth Reporter*, 11 July 1941.
242   *Mossley and Saddleworth Reporter*, 20 March 1945.

in 1945 the worms turned. In an election in which Woods topped the poll with 47.5 percent of the vote, Hopkinson, standing as an Independent, came last of four candidates and lost his deposit.[243] But in Mossley proper's municipal elections, its persistent deference reasserted itself. Of the eight councillors elected, only one was a Labour councillor.[244]

In the General Election overall (held on the 5th of July, but the count had been delayed until the 20th of July to allow time for soldiers' postal votes to arrive from overseas) Labour won 393 seats (47.7 percent of the vote) to the Conservative's 197 seats (36.2 percent of the vote). Labour's landslide victory greatly surprised most contemporary observers but should not have done. In the interwar period there had been a steady increase in working class support for Labour. The initial breakthrough of 1918–19 had been followed by a slow if inconsistent consolidation. Labour won many cotton towns in the general election of 1929, including our three, but lost them in the Labour *debacle* of 1931. The party recovered somewhat in the election of 1935, winning Ashton again and substantially increasing its support in Oldham (where Mathew Farr was one of the two losing Labour candidates). Between 1919 and 1938 the number of Labour councillors in Ashton increased from 5 to 14 and in Oldham from 2 to 16. But in obstinately deferential Mossley, while the Labour vote crept up, the number of councillors had increased only from 1 to 2.

Much more important than Labour's existing electoral base was the great boost to Labour support provided by wartime sentiment that postwar Britain must be a new Britain. Steven Fielding has argued that in 1945 the British people were mostly little interested in such issues as social security and housing, that Labour's victory was not the result of a tide of popular enthusiasm for its programme, but rather of vague pro-reform and anti-Conservative sentiments.[245] But is it likely that lukewarm support for Labour would have led to a 10 percent surge (from 38 percent to 48 percent on a high turnout) in support since the previous general election of 1935? This surge in support was much more marked in the working class: from 30 percent to 61 percent in skilled workers and from 41 percent to 65 percent among 'the poor'.[246]

It was striking too that for the first time Labour won more support among working class women than the Conservatives (42 percent to 29 percent),[247] illustrating the transition the party had made from a party of narrow trade uni-

---

243 *Mossley and Saddleworth Reporter*, 29 July 1945.
244 *Mossley and Saddleworth Reporter*, 2 November 1945.
245 Fielding 1992. Fielding et al. 1995 made similar claims.
246 Bonham 1954, p. 166.
247 Hinton 1998, p. 63.

onism to one that appealed to working class (and some middle class) people generally. Even in our Lancashire, the heartland of working class Toryism, Labour won 29 seats to the Conservative's 14. Data at ward level are not available for general elections, but ward data from the municipal elections of November show similar surges. In Ashton, for instance, in the three central overwhelmingly working class wards, the average Labour vote increased from 46.37 percent in 1938 (the last municipal elections before the war) to 55.22 percent in 1945.[248]

Surely, the best explanation for Labour's thumping victory is that a majority of working people did desire postwar reform, distrusted the Conservatives and had decided that Labour was the best party to enact reform. Probably few of them had read Labour's election manifesto, but the party's proposals were well aired in newspapers and on the wireless. And might Labour's surge in support also have something to do with an interaction between labour movement activists – whose hopes and expectations have been documented here – and the mass of working class people? There would have been innumerable unrecorded political conversations between such activists and other working class people in homes, workplaces, shops, pubs, clubs and so on. These are essentially the arguments too of James Hinton in his critique of Fielding and his school.[249] For months prior to the election the sentiments expressed by Arthur Deakin (in 1940 Deakin had replaced Bevin as the leader of the TGWU) at a Conference of Lancashire and Cheshire trade councils – that they 'were the common people, and for their contribution [to the war effort] they are entitled to play their part in rebuilding our civilisation on such a basis that fear, insecurity and want are banished'[250] – had been common currency in the labour movement.

Labour might not have quite won a majority of the popular vote in 1945, but it had won a decisive majority of working class votes. For the first time it had a parliamentary majority – a substantial majority at that – and, arguably, a mandate for a radical reconstruction of society. Henceforth, the representatives of the working class and the people generally would ensure that society would be run in the interests of the majority of the people. Or would it? In our conclusion and postscript we will consider the significance of Labour's triumph and the consequences of that triumph.

---

248   *Ashton Reporter*, 8 November 1938 and 2 November 1945.
249   Hinton 1997.
250   *Labour's Northern Voice*, February 1945.

Conclusion and Postscript

The author was writing this conclusion when the result of the British referendum of June 2016 – fought between two equally reactionary factions of monopoly capital – on whether to remain a member of the European Union (EU) or to leave was declared. The Remain Campaign narrowly lost. A key factor in the victory of the Leave Campaign was stirring up xenophobia and racism, diverting from capital to migrant workers the anger of many poor, marginalised, disaffected, fearful, desperate or alienated indigenous working class people at unemployment, poor pay, zero-hours contracts, housing shortages, pressures on schools, health and social services and so on.[1] The EU referendum had posed for working class people, for all those exploited or oppressed by capital, the same question posed in the two world wars: who are our friends, who are our enemies?

The support for the British war effort by virtually all working class people in 1914–18 showed that the bourgeoisie had achieved ideological hegemony over the working class, due not least to the changes in British imperialist society over the previous 50 years or so. That internationalist sentiments were rare was demonstrated, for instance, by the chauvinist or at best indifferent response of most of the left to the Easter Rising in Ireland and of the cotton unions to the imposition of duties on exports of cotton finished goods to India.

The suffering and turmoil of war caused considerable unrest and class antagonism but this was not, in most cases, translated into a questioning of the justness of Britain's war. The Russian Revolutions of 1917 suggested to a few, especially on the Clyde and in South Wales (but to hardly any in Lancashire), that British workers should overthrow capitalism by revolution. Already committed to reform to improve the fitness and readiness of the working class to defend the national interest and anxious to maintain a secure home front, the government promised postwar reform. Significant reforms, notably in the franchise, in education and in social insurance, were delivered towards the end of and just after the war. But these reforms did nothing to end the subordination of labour to capital: rather they reinforced it. In the General Election of 1918,

---

1 In many working class areas, voter turnout was much higher than usual. The Leavers achieved the greatest margins of victory in the most deprived areas of Britain – in Sunderland, for instance, by 61 percent to 39 percent – and in those areas that had seen great waves of migrant labour from the poorer countries of the EU – in Thurrock, for instance – by 72 percent to 28 percent. *Daily Telegraph*, 25 June 2016.

newly enfranchised working class voters voted overwhelmingly for the Conservative Party, the party of crown, country and empire.

What did this election signify? If it signified that the vast majority of the working class were still patriotic, it did not signify a return to the deferential politics characteristic of pre-war days. The war had created the conditions for a breakthrough for the deeply reformist and constitutional Labour Party, which had become the party of the organised working class. If few working class people desired revolution, many of them had become insistent that the postwar world must be one much more in tune with their perceived needs and aspirations. In the municipal elections of 1919 the Labour Party began a steady ascent to national and municipal power.

Immediately after the General Election, festering class resentments and antagonisms, which had been contained by the ideological and political pressures of war, burst out in a year of social unrest. But only here and there and from time to time was 1919 a 'Red Year' in Britain. The strikes of 1919, at least in Lancashire, were mostly economic in character, were not aimed at challenging the power of capital. Certainly, the militancy of that year and its potential for transcending the merely economic should be celebrated and popularised, but those who, like Chanie Rosenburg of the Socialist Workers' Party, insist that Britain was 'on the brink of revolution' in 1919[2] do their revolutionary cause a disservice by grossly underestimating the depth of penetration of bourgeois ideology into the working class. Protected to a considerable degree by postwar reforms, the hardships of the interwar depression did little to dent the patriotism of the mass of working men and women while the labour movement's social-chauvinism and reformism was, if anything, reinforced.

The October Revolution in Russia had presented a revolutionary alternative to social-chauvinism and reformism. The Comintern was formed to spread the lessons of October around the world. The main lesson it sought to teach was that the principal enemy of the working class of the imperialist countries is 'at home', is its 'own' bourgeoisie. What this meant concretely was the subject of lively debates in the Comintern. For the working class of the imperialist countries, the most important conclusion of these debates was that there was little prospect of overthrowing capital in those countries unless vigorous support was given to revolutionary struggles in the colonies and semi-colonies. For, as Lenin argued, in the 'final analysis' the outcome of the communist movement's struggle for world revolution would be 'determined by the fact that Russia, China, India, etc., account for the overwhelming majority of the population

---

2 Rosenburg 1999.

of the globe. And during the past few years it is this majority which has been drawn into the struggle for emancipation with extraordinary rapidity'.[3]

But the Comintern succumbed to social-chauvinism and reformism just as the Second International had. After its Seventh Congress of 1935, the Comintern began to rapidly downgrade the importance it attached to revolutionary movements in the colonies and semi-colonies. In Britain, both the Labour Party and the CP had no hesitation in supporting the British war effort in the second imperialist world war. The ILP and the Trotskyists resisted the chauvinist tide, but had little influence. For those who had doubts, the imperialist nature of the war was obscured by specious anti-fascist rhetoric. Even when the war of the imperialist protagonists spilled over into such places as Libya, Egypt, Burma and Malaya, few withdrew their support for war. In the labour movement, the social-chauvinist trope of 'broken promises' was used to help ensure that labour would be amply rewarded by capital for its support in another imperialist war. The wartime experience and the record of the Tories in the interwar year helped Labour to a landslide win in the General Election of 1945.

What was the significance of Labour's victory? It was part of a general move in imperialist countries towards the so-called 'golden age' of mixed state and corporate capital, high-wage, full employment, reform-orientated economies, generated not only by the demands of powerful labour movements but also by the palpable failure of pre-war economic policy and the bourgeoisie's acceptance of the critique of that policy by such influential intellectuals as Keynes, and by the ideological and political challenge of the Soviet Union.

But to those on the left, 1945 was the end of a long teleological process towards the new Jerusalem, the end of what Francis Williams called a 'fifty years march'.[4] In Ashton, the new Labour councillors said that they would be 'partners with the Government in the great enterprise of laying the foundations for real progress in the place of the morass left by the old social order'.[5] Communist Party shop stewards at Ferguson Pailin's electrical engineering factory in Openshaw, midway between Ashton and Manchester, rebuked a worker there who was disgusted with CP attempts to continue a JPC. He was a 'rip van winkle', who should wake up: 'We are no longer busy manufacturing millionaires. We have today a Government without a single company director'.[6] The leaders of the Weavers' Amalgamation lyrically argued that all 'the hopes of a nobler Britain were expressed [in Labour's victory]. The remembrance of long years of

---

3 Lenin 1971, p. 787.
4 Williams 1949.
5 *Ashton Reporter*, 9 November 1945.
6 *Trade Union News and Tatler*, October 1945.

poverty, insecurity, low wages, unemployment, bad housing had at last found corporate expression ... Our hopes for the future – not only for our own country, but the whole world – are high'.[7]

What did Labour do in power? Internationally, Labour endeavoured to preserve Britain's great power status in a new international world order dominated by US imperialism. Britain played a crucial role – in, for instance, Vietnam, Indonesia and Korea – in creating the new world order by combatting communist-led national liberation movements. Britain participated – through such wartime creations as the World Bank, the United Nations and the International Monetary Fund – in the creation of the new world order.[8] An independent India became one of the first neo-colonies.

Unknown, presumably, to most of its beneficiaries, Britain's Empire played a crucial role in financing postwar reconstruction at home. The Labour Government, however, knew well the importance of the Empire. Ernest Bevin, Foreign Secretary in the 1945–51 Labour Government, proclaimed his social-imperialist sentiments in the House of Commons in 1946: 'I am not prepared to sacrifice the British Empire ... I know that if the British Empire fell ... it would mean that the standard of life of our constituents would fall considerably'.[9] Labour fought energetically to defend the Empire in such places as Kenya. Cash crops, for instance, grown in the empire were a crucial source of dollars[10] without which the 'welfare state' could not have been financed.

Domestically, these Labour Governments laid the foundations for the postwar social-imperialist settlement between labour and capital. The expansion of secondary education promised in the 1944 Education Act was begun. The principal recommendations of the Beveridge Report – a comprehensive system of social insurance (though Beveridge's assumptions regarding the proper role of married women were reflected in the legislation) and a national health service, free at the point of use – were implemented, although its steady erosion began in 1951 with the introduction of charges for false teeth and spectacles. A great programme of slum clearance and expansion of council house provision began. Between 1945 and 1951 a million council houses, all with a bathroom and an indoor toilet, were built.[11] In Oldham, for instance, several hundred were built

---

7   Weavers' Amalgamation, EC Annual Report for year ending 31 March 1946. DDX 1123/1/41 @ LROP.
8   For Britain's role in creating the new postwar international order see, for instance, Bayley and Harper 2007. Carr 1993 and Kolko 1969.
9   Cited in Ramdin 1987, p. 63.
10 For the postwar financing of social reform, see, for instance, Cain and Hopkins 1993, ch. 11, Callaghan 1983 and Gupta 1983.
11 Timms 1995, p. 147.

in the first three postwar years.[12] Even under the Conservatives, it was not until 1959 that more private than council houses were built.[13]

Nationalisation of key industries such as the mines, railways and steel, satisfied constituency Labour Party activists, who regarded nationalisation as a crucial aspect of building socialism, and trade unionists in those industries, for whom pay and conditions improved (miners, for instance, much appreciated the much greater provision of pithead baths). As in Western Europe generally, the nationalised industries were fully integrated with and served the interests of capital, becoming a state capitalist sector of the economy.

Although there were improvements in working conditions in the cotton trade (in 1946, for instance, it was agreed that working hours would be reduced from 48 to 45 and (a cause for great rejoicing) that there would be no Saturday morning working, allowing two lie-ins a week),[14] the unions' demand for nationalisation was not met. The probably inevitable decline of Lancashire's cotton trade continued. Eventually, Lancashire was exporting less cloth than it imported. Membership of the Spinners' Amalgamation declined from 22,866 in 1951 to 1,758 in 1970.[15] But postwar prosperity and the honouring of the commitment to full employment in the White Paper on Employment[16] meant that there were ample opportunities for employment in other industries.

But the postwar settlement began to crumble in the late 1960s. National decline – decline, that is, relative to other imperialist countries – began to be attributed by the bourgeoisie to allegedly over-powerful trade unions. Rapidly rising inflation (peaking at 25 percent per annum in 1975, after which control of inflation replaced the maintenance of full employment as a key goal of economic policy) was blamed on trade union power. Initial attacks on the unions in 1969–74 by both Conservative and Labour governments were defeated. But the Industrial Relations Acts of the 1979–87 Tory governments, aided by sharply increasing unemployment, severely weakened the unions. The defeated miners' strike of 1984–85 completed a collapse in the power and morale of the trade unions.

Britain's economic malaise was merely part of a growing international crisis of imperialism. The so-called 'golden age' of postwar growth and prosperity (for

---

12 Oldham Council 1949, pp. 61–5. This publication contained photographs of solidly-built new houses with fitted kitchens, bathrooms, and indoor toilets sited in estates with lawns, shops, community centres, health centres, and so on.
13 Malpass 2005, pp. 68, 84.
14 Spinners' Amalgamation EC circular, 18 November 1946. ACS/6/5/18 @ JRSC.
15 Fowler 1987a, p. 197.
16 The unemployment rate averaged 2 percent between 1945 and 1975. Calculation based on statistics in Her Majesty's Government Statistical Service 1996, pp. 244–5.

most) in the imperialist countries ended abruptly with the crisis of 1973–75, when industrial production declined by 10 percent and international trade by 13 percent.[17] Conveniently and chauvinistically blamed on oil prices imposed by the Organisation of Petroleum Exporting Countries (OPEC), it was actually a classic crisis of profitability, the outcome of a falling rate of profit.[18] Imperialism now began to move away from Keynesianism[19] and to embrace neoliberalism in an attempt to extract more surplus value from the working class by privatisation, minimising regulation of capital and, through 'globalisation', facilitating capital's ability to seek out the cheapest sources of labour power while forcing many workers to compete ever more desperately for available work under ever-worsening conditions. But, just as Keynesianism could not, so neoliberalism cannot resolve the fundamental contradictions of capitalism. Since the crisis of 1973–75, despite the temporary fillip given to western imperialism by the collapse of the Soviet bloc and consequent investment opportunities in that bloc, imperialism has lurched from crisis to crisis. At the time of writing, imperialism is in the eighth year of stagnation ushered in by the banking crisis of 2008.

Given their need to ensure continuing relative social peace at home, imperialists can only go so far in their attempts to maximise the amount of surplus value from the domestic working class. Moreover, as Amin, Lotta and Nabudere have argued, while domestic production might well provide the mass of surplus value in the imperialist countries, surplus value from exploitation abroad is the key to expanding domestic production. Since the end of the Second World War, Britain, probably the most parasitic of imperialist states, has been a junior partner of US imperialism's semi-permanent war against the peoples and nations of Asia, Africa and Latin America, including in the recent and current wars in the Middle East and Afghanistan.

There was little opposition in Britain to these wars. Moreover, Britain's own war against Argentina in 1982 over the Malvinas engendered little opposition and saw a surge in chauvinistic sentiment comparable to that which apparently accompanied the 'relief' of Mafeking in 1900. Phenomena such as this, and a surge in racist attacks which followed the victory of the Leave Campaign in the

---

17 Armstrong et al. 1991, p. 225.
18 For a discussion of the falling rate of profit in Britain, see Freeman 1991.
19 In Britain, this shift was marked by a speech by the Labour Prime Minister James Callaghan in 1976. Callaghan told the Labour Party conference that 'We used to think you could spend your way out of a recession and increase employment by boosting government spending, but I tell you in all candour that that option no longer exists'. Labour Party, *Report of 75th Labour Party Annual Conference* (London, 1976), p. 188.

EU referendum, are the result of the ideological hegemony which the British bourgeoisie has over the British proletariat and the British people generally. We cannot know how the working class in Britain will eventually emancipate itself from the rule of capital. But we can say that as long as it continues to support British imperialism in its wars with other imperialist states and its exploitation and oppression of other peoples and nations, and as long as it allows itself to be duped by racist demagogues, it will be unable to do so. This has been the case since Marx studied the question of Ireland nearly a 150 years ago. Let Marx have the final word on the subject of this work, social-imperialism in Britain:

> After studying the Irish question for many years I have come to the conclusion that the decisive blow against the English ruling classes (and it will be decisive for the workers' movement all over the world) cannot be delivered *in England* but *only in Ireland* ... And most important of all! Every industrial and commercial centre in England now possesses a working class divided into two *hostile* camps, English proletarians and Irish proletarians. The ordinary English worker hates the Irish worker as a competitor who lowers his standard of life. In relation to the Irish worker he regards himself as a member of the *ruling* nation and consequently he becomes a tool of the English aristocrats and capitalists against Ireland, thus strengthening their domination *over himself*. He cherishes religious, social, and national prejudices against the Irish worker. His attitude towards him is much the same as that of the 'poor whites' to the Negroes in the former slave states of the USA. The Irishman pays him back with interest in his own money. He sees in the English worker both the accomplice and the stupid tool of the *English rulers in Ireland*.[20]

---

20 Marx to Meyer and Vogt in New York, 9 April 1870, in Marx and Engels 1971, pp. 220–4 (emphasis in the original).

Bibliography

Primary Sources

Principal Archives Visited
The Labour Archive and Study Centre at the People's History Museum, Manchester, holds records of the main parties and organisations of the labour movement, including the archives of the Labour and Communist parties, and the War Emergency Workers' National Committee.

The Lancashire Record Office at Preston has the records of the Amalgamated Weavers' Association and of Lancashire County Council.

Manchester, Oldham and Tameside central libraries have extensive holdings of local newspapers and records and ephemera of many different bodies and organisation. At Oldham, the records of the trades council and Oldham and Rochdale Textile Employers Association and at Tameside of Ashton and Mossley town councils proved particularly informative.

The John Rylands University Library, Deansgate, Manchester has many relevant special collections, including the records of the Amalgamated Association of Operative Cotton Spinners and Twiners and the Ashton and District Textile Employers Association.

A visit to the National Archives at Kew found a few items of interest.

The Working Class Movement Library in Salford is a treasure trove of working class records, pamphlets, journals and pamphlets. It has, for instance, the records of Manchester and Salford Trades Councils, the Manchester District of the Amalgamated Engineering Union and the Amalgamated Association of Card and Blowing Room Operatives.

Principal Newspapers, Journals and Periodicals Consulted
Particularly informative papers were:

Ashton Herald; Ashton Reporter; Cotton Factory Times; Daily Herald; Daily Worker; Labour Leader; Labour Monthly; Labour's Northern Voice; Manchester Evening News; Manchester Guardian; Mossley and Saddleworth Reporter; Oldham Chronicle; Oldham Evening Chronicle; Oldham Weekly Chronicle; Times; World News and Views.

It is not very fashionable in these postmodern times to find local newspapers a valuable source of information. But they are. Until comparatively recently, editors thought it their duty to inform citizens of the doings of trades councils, the meetings of councils and so on.

Other Primary Sources

Lenin, V.I. 1971 [1922], 'Better Fewer, But Better', *Selected Works, Vol. 3*, Moscow: Progress Publishers.

Lenin, V.I. 1974 [1915], 'The Collapse of the Second International', *Collected Works, Vol. 23*, Moscow: Progress Publishers.

Lenin, V.I. 1974 [1916], 'Imperialism and the Split in Socialism', *Collected Works, Vol. 23*, Moscow: Progress Publishers.

Marx, K. 1974 [1844], 'Introduction to the Critique of Hegel's Philosophy of Right', *Collected Works, Vol. 3*, Moscow: Progress Publishers.

Marx, K. and F. Engels 1971, *Selected Correspondence*, Moscow: Progress Publishers.

Document Collections

Adler, A. (ed.) 1980, *Theses, Resolutions and Manifestos of the First Four Congresses of the Communist International*, London: Inklinks.

Dale, I. (ed.) 1962, *British Political Party Manifestos, 1900–1997, Vol. 2, Labour Party General Election Manifestos 1900–1997*, London: Routledge.

Degas, J. (ed.) 1965, *The Communist International 1919–1943: Documents, Vol. 2*, London: Frank Cass.

Degas, J. (ed.) 1971, *The Communist International 1919–1943: Documents, Vol. 3*, London: Frank Cass.

Riddell, J. (ed.) 1986, *The Communist International in Lenin's Time. The German Revolution and the Debate on Soviet Power. Documents: 1918–1919 Preparing the Founding Congress*, New York: Pathfinder.

Riddell, J. (ed.) 1987, *The Communist International in Lenin's Time. Founding the Communist International. Proceedings and Documents of the First Congress: March 1919*, New York: Pathfinder.

[Editor uncited] 1977, *The Second Congress of the Communist International Minutes of the Proceedings, Vols 1 & 2*, New York: New Park.

Secondary Sources

Theses

Bowker, D. 1983, 'Ashton Weavers in the Age of Labour Unrest (1910–1920)', BA thesis, Manchester Polytechnic.

Broomfield, S. 1979, 'South Wales during the Second World War: The Coal Industry and its Community', PhD thesis, University of Wales.

Bruton, P. 1990, 'Women in Cotton Trade Unions. A Case Study: Ashton Weavers 1919–1939', BA thesis, Manchester Polytechnic.

Calder, A. 1967, 'The Commonwealth Party, 1942–45', PhD thesis, University of Sussex.

Eckersley, T.P. 1991, 'The Growth of the Cotton Industry in Mossley with Special Reference to the Mayalls', MA thesis, Manchester Polytechnic.

Hall, A.A. 1975, 'Social Control and the Working Class Challenge in Ashton-under-Lyne 1886–1914', MA thesis, University of Lancaster.

McNama, M. 1983, 'A Study of Local Responses to the Means Test and Unemployment in Ashton-under-Lyne, 1931–34', BA thesis, Salford.

Poole, E. 2014, 'Troublesome Priests: Christianity and Marxism in the Church of England, 1906–1969', MPhil thesis, University of Manchester.

Upham, M. 1980, 'The History of British Trotskyism to 1949', PhD thesis, University of Hull.

Other Secondary Sources

Abendstern, M. et al. 2004, 'The Struggle for Sanitary Reform in the Lancashire Cotton Mills 1920–1970', *Journal of Advanced Nursing*, 48, 3: 257–65.

Adams, T. 2000, 'Labour Vanguard, Tory Bastion or the Triumph of New Liberalism? Manchester Politics 1900 to 1914 in Comparative Perspective', *Manchester Region History Review*, 14: 25–38.

Addison, P. 1977, *The Road to 1945*, London: Quartet.

Ahmed, M. 1987, *The British Labour Party and the Indian Independence Movement 1917–1939*, New York: Envoy.

Amin, S. 1977, *Imperialism and Unequal Development*, New York: Monthly Review.

Angus, I. and S. Orwell (eds) 1968, *The Collected Essays, Journalism and Letters of George Orwell, Vol. II*, London: Secker and Warburg.

Armstrong, P., A. Glynn and J. Harrison 1991, *Capitalism since 1945*, Oxford: Basil Blackwell.

Attlee, C.R. 1940, *War Comes to Britain*, London.

Bakshi, S.R. 1986, *Congress and the Quit India Movement*, New Delhi: Criterion.

Barrow, H. 2010, 'Weaving Tales of Empire: Gandhi's Visit to Lancashire, 1931', in C. Horner and N. Mansfield (eds.), *The British Labour Movement and Imperialism*, Newcastle: Cambridge Scholars.

Bateson, H. 1949, *Centenary History of Oldham*, Oldham: Oldham County Borough.

Bayley, C. and T. Harper 2007, *Forgotten Wars: The End of Britain's Asian Empire*, London: Penguin.

Beckett, I.F.W. and K. Simpson 1985, *A Nation in Arms*, Manchester: Tom Donovan.

Beddoe, D. 1989, *Back to Home and Duty: Women between the Wars 1919–1939*, London: Pandora.

Benson, J. 1989, *The Working Class in Britain 1850–1939*, London: Longman.

Beveridge, W. 1944, *Full Employment in a Free Society: A Report*, London: G. Allen.

Billings, J. and D. Copland 1992, *The Ashton Munitions Explosion of 1917*, Ashton-under-Lyne: Tameside Leisure Services.

Blackburn, S. 1991, 'Ideology and Social Policy: the Origins of the Trade Boards Act', *Historical Journal*, 34: 43–64.

Bonham, J. 1954, *The Middle Class Vote*, London: Faber.

Bonner, M. 2011, *The Manchester Regiment, the 63rd and 96th Regiments of Foot*, Ashton-under-Lyne: Tameside Leisure Services.

Boothby, R. 1962, *My Yesterday, Your Tomorrow*, London: Hutchinson.

Bornstein, S. and A. Richardson n.d. *Two Steps Back: Communists and the Wider Labour Movement*, Ilford: Socialist Platform.

Bowden, S. and D.M. Higgins 1999, '"Productivity on the Cheap"? The "More Looms" Experiment and the Lancashire Weaving Industry during the Inter-War Years', *Business History*, 41, 3: 21–41.

Bowker, D. 1990, 'Parks and Baths: Sport, Recreation and Municipal Government in Ashton-under-Lyne Between the Wars', in R. Holt (ed.), *Sport and the Working Class in Modern Britain*, Manchester: Manchester University Press.

Bowker, D. 1997, 'The Cotton Industry and the Ashton Weavers' Association', in A. Lock (ed.), *Looking Back at Ashton*, Ashton-under-Lyne: Tameside Leisure Services.

Bradley, B. 1942, *India: What We Must Do*.

Branson, N. 1997, *History of the Communist Party of Great Britain 1941–1951*, London: Lawrence and Wishart.

Braybon, G. 1981, *Women Workers in the First World War*, London: Routledge.

Braybon, G. and P. Summerfield 1987, *Out of the Cage: Women's Experiences in Two World Wars*, London: Pandora.

Bridgen, P. 2009, *The Labour Party and the Politics of War and Peace, 1900–1924*, London: Boydell.

Brooke, S. 1992, *Labour's War the Labour Party during the Second World War*, Oxford: Clarendon Press.

Bullen, A. and A. Fowler 1986, *The Cardroom Workers Union: A Centenary History of the Amalgamated Association of Card and Blowing Room Operatives*, Manchester: Amalgamated Textile Workers Union.

Bullen, A. 1984, *The Lancashire Weavers Union a Commemorative History*, Manchester: Amalgamated Textile Workers Union.

Burnett, D. 1978, *A Social History of Housing 1815–1970*, Newton Abbot: Routledge.

Burnham, P. 2014, 'The Radical Ex-Servicemen of 1918', in C. Horner and N. Mansfield (eds), *The British Labour Movement and Imperialism*, Newcastle: Cambridge Scholars.

Cain, P.J. and A.G. Hopkins 1993, *British Imperialism: Crisis and Deconstruction 1914–1990*, Harlow: Longman.

Calder, A. 1982 [1969], *The People's War*, London: Granada.

Callaghan, J. 1984, *British Trotskyism Theory and Practice*, Oxford: Basil Blackwell.

Callaghan, J. 1993, 'In Search of El Dorado Labour's Colonial Economic Policy', in J. Fyrth (ed.), *Labour's High Noon: The Government and the Economy 1945–51*, London: Lawrence and Wishart.

Cannadine, D. 2001, *Ornamentalism: How the British Saw their Empire*, London: Allen Lane.

Carr, F. 1993, 'Cold War: The Economy and Foreign Policy', in J. Fyrth (ed.), *Labour's High Noon: The Government and the Economy 1945–51*, London: Lawrence and Wishart.

Cass, E., A. Fowler and T. Wyke 1998, 'The Remarkable Rise and Long Decline of the Cotton Factory Times', *Media History*, 4, 2: 141–59.

Challinor, R. 1995, *The Struggle for Hearts and Minds Essays on the Second World War*, Whitley Bay: Bewick.

Challinor, R. 1997, *The Origins of British Bolshevism*, London: Croom Helm.

Chatterji, B. 1992, *Trade, Tariffs and Empire Lancashire and British Policy in India 1919–1939*, Delhi: Oxford University Press.

Chisholm, A. and M. Davis 1992, *Beaverbrook: A Life*, London: Pimlico.

Clarke, P.F. 1977, *Lancashire and the New Liberalism*, Cambridge: Cambridge University Press.

Claudin, F. 1975, *The Communist Movement from Comintern to Cominform, Part Two: The Zenith of Stalinism*, New York: Monthly Review.

Clegg, H. 1985, *A History of British Trade Unions Since 1889, Vol. II 1911–1933*, Oxford: Clarendon Press.

Clegg, H. 1994, *A History of British Trade Unions Since 1889, Vol. III 1934–1951*, Oxford: Clarendon Press.

Cohen, G. 2001, 'The Independent Labour Party, Disaffiliation, Revolution and Standing Orders', *History*, 86, 2: 180–99.

Collette, C. 1989, *For Labour and for Women: The Women's Labour League 1906–1918*, Manchester: Manchester University Press.

Colley, L. 1996, *Britons: Forging the Nation 1701–1837*, New Haven: Yale University Press.

Collingham, L. 2011, *The Taste of War World War Two and the Battle for Food*, London: Allen Lane.

Conacher, J.B. 1971, *The Emergence of British Parliamentary Democracy in the Nineteenth Century The Passing of the Reform Acts of 1832, 1867, and 1884–85*, New York: Chichester.

Cowden, M.H. 1984, *Russian Bolshevism and British Labor 1917–1921*, New York: Boulder.

Cronin, J.E. 1983, 'Labor Insurgency and Class Formation: Comparative Perspectives on the Crisis of 1917–1920', in J.E. Cronin and C. Sirianni (eds), *Work, Community and Power the Experience of Labour in Europe and America 1900–1925*, Philadelphia: Temple University Press.

Cronin, J.E. 1989, 'The Crisis of State and Society in Britain 1917–1922', in L. Haimson and C. Tilly (eds), *Strikes, Wars and Revolution in International Perspective*, Cambridge: Cambridge University Press.

Croucher, R. 1982, *Engineers at War 1939–1945*, London: Merlin.

Croucher, R. 1987, *We Refuse to Starve in Silence*, London; Lawrence and Wishart.

Crowley, M. 1998, 'Communist Engineers and the Second World War in Manchester', *North West Labour History*, 22: 82–91.

Davies, A. and S. Fielding 1992, *Workers' Worlds Cultures and Communities in Manchester and Salford 1880–1939*, Manchester: Manchester University Press.

Davies, S. and B. Morley 2000, 'The Politics of Place: a Comparative Analysis of Electoral Politics in Four Lancashire Cotton Textile Towns, 1919–1939', *Manchester Region History Review*, 14: 63–78.

Davis, L.E. and R.A. Huttenback 1986, *Mammon and the Pursuit of Empire: The Political Economy of British Imperialism, 1860–1912*, Cambridge: Cambridge University Press.

Drake, B. 1920, *Women in Trade Unions*, London: Allen and Unwin.

Edmonds, R. 1991, *The Big Three Churchill, Roosevelt and Stalin in Peace and War*, Harmondsworth: Penguin.

English, J. 2006, 'Empire Day in Britain 1904–1958', *Historical Journal*, 49, 1: 247–76.

Farnie, D. 1982, 'The Emergence of Victorian Oldham as the Centre of the Cotton Spinning Industry', *Saddleworth Historical Society Bulletin*, 12: 41–53.

Farnie, D. 1998, 'Introduction', to D. Gurr and J. Hunt, *The Cotton Mills of Oldham*, Oldham: Oldham Leisure Services.

Fay, P.W. 1994, *The Forgotten Army: India's Armed Struggle for Independence*, Michigan: University of Michigan Press.

Field, G. 1992, 'Social Patriotism and the British Working Class: Appearance and Disappearance of a Tradition', *International Labor and Working Class History*, 42: 20–39.

Field, G. 2011, *Blood Sweat and Toil: Remaking the British Working Class 1939–45*, Oxford: Oxford University Press.

Fieldhouse, D.K. 1984, *Economics and Empire*, London: MacMillan.

Fielding, S. 1992, 'What did the People Want? The Meaning of the 1945 General Election', *Historical Journal*, 35, 3: 623–39.

Fielding, S. 1993, *Class and Ethnicity Irish Catholics in England 1880–1939*, Oxford: Oxford University Press.

Fielding, S. 1995, 'The Second World War and Popular Radicalism: The Significance of the "Movement Away from Party"', *History*, 80, 258: 38–58.

Fielding, S. et al. 1995, *England Arise: The Labour Party and Popular Politics in 1940s Britain*, Manchester: Manchester University Press.

Fishman, N. 1995, *The British Communist Party and the Trade Unions, 1933–45*, Aldershot: Scolar Press.
Flynn, A. 2000, 'Irish Catholics in South-East Lancashire: A Conflict of Interest?', *Manchester Region History* Review, 14: 79–90.
Foley, A. 1973, *A Bolton Childhood*, Manchester: Manchester University Extra-Mural Department.
Foster, J. 1993, 'The Clyde 1917–20', in C. Wrigley (ed.), *Challenges of Labour Central and Western Europe 1917–1920*, London: Routledge.
Fowkes, B. 1984, *Communism in Germany under the Weimar Republic*, London: MacMillan.
Fowler, A. 1987a, 'Decline of the Amalgamation', in A. Fowler and T. Wyke (eds), *The Barefoot Aristocrats: A History of the Amalgamated Association of Operative Cotton Spinners*, Littleborough: George Kelsall.
Fowler, A. 1987b, 'Spinners in the Inter-War Years', in A. Fowler and T. Wyke (eds), *The Barefoot Aristocrats: A History of the Amalgamated Association of Operative Cotton Spinners*, Littleborough: George Kelsall.
Fowler, A. 1987c, 'War and Labour Unrest', in A. Fowler and T. Wyke (eds), *The Barefoot Aristocrats: A History of the Amalgamated Association of Operative Cotton Spinners*, Littleborough: George Kelsall.
Fowler, A. 1995, *Lancashire Cotton Operatives and Work, 1900–1950*, Aldershot: Ashgate.
Fowler, A. and T. Wyke 2003, *Mirth in the Mill: The Gradely World of Sam Fitton*, Oldham: Oldham Leisure Services.
Francis, H. and D. Smith 1998, *The Fed: A History of the South Wales Miners in the Twentieth Century*, London: Lawrence and Wishart.
Frank, W. et al. (eds) 2010, *The British Labour Movement and Imperialism*, Newcastle: Cambridge Scholars.
Fraser, D. 1984, *The Evolution of the British Welfare State: A History of Social Policy since the Industrial Revolution*, Basingstoke: MacMillan.
Freeman, A. 1991, 'National Accounts in Value Terms: The Social Wage and the Profit Rate in Britain, 1950–1986', in P. Dunne (ed.), *Quantitative Marxism*, Oxford: Polity.
Gallacher, W. 1978 [1936], *Revolt on the Clyde*, London: Lawrence and Wishart.
Gardiner, J. 2004, *Wartime Britain 1939–45*, London: Headline.
Garside, W.A. 2002, *British Unemployment: A Study in Public Policy 1919–1939*, Cambridge: Cambridge University Press.
Gazeley, I. and A. Newell 2013, 'The First World War and Working Class Food Consumption in Britain', *European Review of Economic History*, 17: 71–94.
Geary, D. 1981, *European Labour Protest 1948–1939*, New York: St. Martin's Press.
Gibson, I. 2013, 'The British Parliamentary Labour Party and the Government of Ireland Act 1920', *Parliamentary History*, 37, 3: 506–21.
Gilbert, B. 1970, *British Social Policy 1914–1939*, London: Batsford.

Gildart, K. 2009, 'Coal Strikes on the Home Front: Miners, Militancy and Socialist Politics in the Second World War', *Twentieth Century British History*, 20, 2: 121–51.

Glynn, A. 2005, 'Labour's Family: Local Labour Parties, Trades Unions and Trades Councils in Cotton Lancashire, 1931–39', in M. Worley (ed.), *Labour's Grass Roots: Essays on the Activities of Local Labour Parties and Members, 1918–45*, Aldershot: Ashgate.

Greenough, P.R. 1983, *Poverty and Misery in Modern Bengal: The Famine of 1943–1944*, Oxford: Oxford University Press.

Gregory, A. 2008, *The Last Great War British Society and the First World War*, Cambridge: Cambridge University Press.

Grieves, K. 1988, *The Politics of Manpower, 1914–1918*, Manchester: Manchester University Press.

Griffiths, T. 2001, *The Lancashire Working Classes, c. 1880–1930*, Oxford: Oxford University Press.

Gupta, P.S. 1983, 'Imperialism and the Labour Government of 1945–51', in J.M. Winter (ed.), *The Working Class in Modern British History: Essays in Honour of Henry Pelling*, Cambridge: Cambridge University Press.

Gupta, P.S. 2002 [1975], *Imperialism and the British Labour Movement 1914–1964*, New Delhi: Thousand Oaks.

Gupta, S.D. 2006, *Comintern and the Destiny of Communism in India 1919–1943: Dialectics of Real and a Possible History*, Kolkata: Thousand Oaks.

Haffner, S. 1973, *Failure of a Revolution: Germany 1918–1919*, London: Deutsch.

Haldane, J.B.S. 1938, *Heredity and Politics*, London: George Allen and Unwin.

Hannington, W. 1977 [1936], *Unemployed Struggles 1918–1936: My Life and Struggles amongst the Unemployed*, London: Lawrence and Wishart.

Harrison, R. 1971, 'The War Emergency National Workers' Committee', in A. Briggs and J. Saville (eds), *Essays in Labour History 1886–1923*, London: MacMillan.

Hatton, T. 1997, 'Trade Boards and Minimum Wages, 1909–39', *Economic Affairs*, 17, 2: 22–8.

Heim, C. 1986, 'Interwar Responses to Regional Decline', in B. Elbaum and W. Lazonick (eds), *The Decline of the British Economy*, Oxford: Clarendon Press.

Her Majesty's Government Statistical Service 1996, *Unemployment Statistics from 1881 to the Present Day*, London: Her Majesty's Stationery Office.

Herbert, M. 2001, *The Wearing of the Green a Political History of the Irish in Manchester*, London: Irish in Britain Representation Group.

Hill, J. 1992, 'The ILP in Lancashire and the North West', in D. James et al., *The Centennial History of the ILP*, Halifax: Ryburn Press.

Himmelfarb, G. 1991, *Poverty and Compassion the Moral Imagination of the Late Victorians*, New York: Knopf,

Hinton, J. 1973, *The First Shop Stewards Movement*, London: Allen Unwin.

Hinton, J. 1983, *Labour and Socialism: A History of the British Labour Movement 1867–1914*, Brighton: Wheatsheaf.

Hinton, J. 1992, 'Essays in Labour Statistics: Women and the Labour Vote', *Labour History Review*, 57, 3: 59–66.

Hinton, J. 1994, *Shop Floor Citizens: Engineering Democracy in 1940s Britain*, Aldershot: Edward Elgar.

Hinton, J. 1997, '1945 and the Apathy School', *History Workshop Journal*, 43: 266–73.

Hobsbawm, E. 1984 [1972], 'The Formation of British Working Class Culture', in *Worlds of Labour: Further Studies in the History of Labour*, London: Wiedenfeld and Nicolson.

Honigsbaum, F. 1989, *Health, Happiness and Security: The Creation of the National Health Service*, London: Routledge,

Horne, A. 1991, *Labour at War France and Britain 1914–1918*, Oxford: Clarendon Press.

Howe, S. 1994, *Anti-colonialism in British Politics: The Left and the End of Empire 1918–1964*, Oxford: Oxford University Press.

Howell, D. 1976, *British Social Democracy: A Study in Development and Decay*, London: Croom Helm.

Howell, D. 1983, *British Workers and the Independent Labour Party 1888–1906*, Manchester: Manchester University Press.

Hunt, C. 2014, *The National Federation of Women Workers*, Basingstoke: Palgrave MacMillan.

Hunt, K. 2005, 'Making Politics in Local Communities: Labour Women in Interwar Manchester', in M. Worley (ed.), *Labour's Grass Roots: Essays on the Activities of Local Labour Parties and Members, 1918–45*, Aldershot: Ashgate.

Hutchins, F.G. 1973, *India's Revolution: Gandhi and the Quit India Movement*, Cambridge, MA: Harvard University Press.

James, D. 2010 [1995], *Class and Politics in a Northern Industrial Town, Keighley 1880–1914*, Edinburgh: Edinburgh University Press.

Jefferys, K. 1991, *The Churchill Coalition and Wartime Politics 1940–45*, Manchester: Manchester University Press.

Jenkinson, J. 2009, *Black 1919: Riots, Racism and Resistance in Imperial Britain*, Liverpool: Liverpool University Press.

Johnstone, M. 1997, 'The CPGB, the Comintern and the War 1939–1941: Filling in the Blank Spots', *Science and Society*, 61, 1: 27–45.

Jones, H. 1994, *Health and Society in Twentieth-Century Britain*, Harlow: Longman.

Jones, S.G. 1985, 'The Lancashire Cotton Industry and the Development of Paid Holidays in the Nineteen Thirties', *Transactions of the Historic Society of Lancashire and Cheshire*, 135: 99–115.

Jones, S.G. 1987, 'Work, Leisure and the Political Economy of the Cotton Districts Between the Wars', *Textile History*, 18: 33–57.

Jones, S.G. 1988, 'Cotton Employers and Industrial Welfare between the Wars', in J.A. Jowitt and A. McIvor (eds), *Employers and Labour in the English Textile Industries, 1850–1939*, London: Routledge.

Joyce, P. 1980, *Work, Society and Politics: The Culture of the Factory in Late Victorian England*, Cambridge: Cambridge University Press.

Kelly, K. and M. Richardson 1996, 'The Shaping of the Bristol Labour Movement 1885–1985', in M. Dresser and P. Ollerenshaw (eds), *The Making of Modern Bristol*, Tiverton: Tiverton Press.

Kendall, W. 1969, *The Revolutionary Movement in Britain 1900–1921*, London: Wiedenfeld and Nicolson.

Kirk, N. 1980, 'Ethnicity, Class and Popular Toryism 1850–1870', in K. Lunn (ed.), *Hosts: Immigrants and Minorities. Historical Responses to Newcomers in British Society 1870–1914*, Folkestone: Dawson.

Kirk, N. 1985, *The Growth of Working Class Reformism in Mid-Victorian England*, London: Croom Helm.

Kirk, N. 1994, *Labour and Society in Britain and the USA, Vol. 2: Challenge and Accommodation 1850–1939*, Aldershot: Scolar Press.

Kirk, N. 2011, *Labour and the Politics of Empire Britain and Australia 1900 to the Present*, Manchester: Manchester University Press.

Klugman, J. 1969, *History of the Communist Party of Great Britain, Vol. 1: Formation and Early Years 1919–1924*, London: Lawrence and Wishart.

Kolko, G. 1969, *The Politics of War: Allied Diplomacy and the World Crisis of 1943–45*, London: Wiedenfeld and Nicolson.

Laybourn, K. 1995, *The Evolution of British Social Policy and the Welfare State*, Keele: Ryburn.

Lazonick, W. 1986, 'The Cotton Industry', in B. Elbaum and W. Lazonick (eds), *The Decline of the British Economy*, Oxford: Clarendon Press.

Liddington, J. 2006, *Rebel Girls: Their Fight for the Vote*, London: Virago.

Liddington, J. and J. Norris 1978, *One Hand Tied Behind Us: The Rise of the Women's Suffrage Movement*, London: Virago.

Locke, A. 1997, 'Robert W. Cummings, the "Communist" Vicar of Hurst', in A. Locke (ed.), *Looking Back at Ashton*, Ashton-under-Lyne: Tameside Leisure Services.

Lotta, R. 1984, *America in Decline*, Chicago: Banner Press.

Louis, W.R. 1977, *Imperialism at Bay 1941–45: The United States and the Decolonization of the British Empire*, Oxford: Clarendon Press.

Lowe, R. 1978, 'The Failure of Consensus in Britain: The National Industrial Conference, 1919–1921', *The Historical Journal*, 21, 3: 649–75.

Lummis, T. 1994, *The Labour Aristocracy 1851–1914*, Aldershot: Scolar Press.

MacFarlane, L.J. 1966, *The British Communist Party: Its Origins and Development until 1929*, London: McGibbon and Kee.

Macintyre, S. 1980, *A Proletarian Science: Marxism in Britain, 1917–1933*, London: Lawrence and Wishart.
MacKenzie, J.M. 1985, *Propaganda and Empire: The Manipulation of British Public Opinion 1880–1960*, Manchester: Manchester University Press.
Malpass, P. 2005, *Housing and the Welfare State: The Development of Housing Policy in Britain*, Basingstoke: Palgrave MacMillan.
Martin, D.E. 1974, 'James Seddon', in J.M. Bellamy and J. Saville (eds), *Dictionary of Labour Biography, Vol. II*, London: MacMillan,
Marwick, A. 1968, *Britain in the Century of Total War, Peace and Social Change 1900–1967*, London: Bodley Head.
Marwick, A. 1991 [1965], *The Deluge*, London: MacMillan,
Mason, T. 1996 [1975], 'Internal Crisis and War of Aggression', in *Nazism, Fascism and the Working Class*, Cambridge: Cambridge University Press.
Mayhall, L.E.N. 2000, 'Reclaiming the Political: Women and the Social History of Suffrage in Great Britain, France and the United States', *Journal of Women's History*, 12, 1: 172–81.
McHugh, J. and B. Ripley 1987, 'The Spinners and the Rise of Labour', in A. Fowler and T. Wyke (eds), *The Barefoot Aristocrats: A History of the Amalgamated Association of Operative Cotton Spinners*, Littleborough: George Kelsall.
McIlroy, J. and A. Campbell 2011, 'The Last Chance Saloon? The Independent Labour Party and Miners' Militancy in the Second World War Revisited', *Journal of Contemporary History*, 46, 4: 871–96.
McKibbin, R. 1974, *The Evolution of the Labour Party 1910–1924*, Oxford: Clarendon Press.
McKibbin, R. 1994 [1984], 'The Franchise Factor in the Rise of Labour', in *The Ideologies of Class Social Relations in Britain 1880–1950*, Oxford: Clarendon Press.
McLean, I. 1983, *The Legend of Red Clydeside*, Edinburgh: Donald.
McPherson, K. and D. Coleman 1988, 'Health', in A. Halsey (ed.), *British Social Trends since 1900: A Guide to the Changing Social Structure of Britain*, Basingstoke: Palgrave MacMillan.
Millman, B. 2000, *Managing Domestic Dissent in First World War Britain 1914–1918*, London: Frank Cass.
Minkin, L. 1991, *The Contentious Alliance: Trade Unions and the Labour Party*, Edinburgh: Edinburgh University Press.
Monger, D. 2012, *Patriotism and Propaganda in First World War Britain: The National War Aims Committee and Civilian Morale*, Liverpool: Liverpool University Press.
Morgan, K. 1989, *Against Fascism and War: Ruptures and Continuities in British Communist Politics 1935–1941*, Manchester: Manchester University Press.
Nabudere, D.W. 1977, *The Political Economy of Imperialism*, London: Zed Press.
Neal, F. 1992, 'English-Irish Conflict in the North-West of England: Economics, Racism,

Anti-Catholicism or Simple Xenophobia?', *Bulletin of the North West Labour History Group*, 16: 20–5.

Nevell, M. 1993, *Tameside 1700–1930*, Tameside: Tameside Metropolitan Borough Council.

Nevell, M. and P. Walker 2004, *The Archaeology of Twentieth Century Tameside*, Tameside: Tameside Metropolitan Borough Council.

Newton, D. 1985, *British Labour, European Socialism and the Struggle for Peace, 1889–1914*, Oxford: Clarendon Press.

O'Brien, P.K. 1988, 'The Costs and Benefits of British Imperialism 1846–1914', *Past and Present*, 120: 163–200.

Oldham County Borough Council 1949, *Oldham Centenary: A History of Local Government*, Oldham: Oldham County Borough Council.

Olechowicz, A. 2000, 'Union First, Politics After: Oldham, Cotton Unions and the Labour Party before 1914', *Manchester Region History Review*, 14: 3–12.

Orbach, L. 1977, *Homes for Heroes: A Study of British Public Housing 1915–1921*, London: Seeley.

Orwell, G. 1962 [1937], *The Road to Wigan Pier*, Harmondsworth: Penguin.

Overstreet, G.D. and M. Windmiller 1959, *Communism in India*, Berkeley: University of California Press.

Owen, N. 2007, *The British Left and India Metropolitan Anti-Imperialism 1885–1947*, Oxford: Oxford University Press.

Peden, G. 2000, *The Treasury and British Public Policy 1906–1959*, Oxford: Oxford University Press.

Pelling, H. 1987 [1963], *A History of British Trade Unionism*, Harmondsworth: Penguin.

Pennell, C. 2012, *A Kingdom United: Popular Responses to the Outbreak of War in Britain and Ireland*, Cambridge: Cambridge University Press.

Pollitt, H. 1940, *Serving My Time: An Apprenticeship to Politics*, London: Lawrence and Wishart.

Porter, B. 1984 [1975], *The Lion's Share: A Short History of British Imperialism 1850–1983*, London: Longman.

Porter, J.H. 1979, 'Cotton and Wool Textiles', in N.K. Buxton and D.H. Aldcroft (eds), *British Industry Between the Wars*, London: Scolar Press.

Price, K. 1988, 'Changes on the "Kitchen Front": The Case of British Restaurants in World War II', *North East Labour History*, 22: 20–32.

Pugh, M. 1974, 'Politicians and the Women's Vote 1914–18', *History*, 59, 197: 358–74.

Pugh, M. 1978, *Electoral Reform in War and Peace 1906–1918*, London: Routledge and Kegan Paul.

Pugh, M. 1985, *The Tories and the People 1880–1935*, Oxford: Blackwell.

Pugh, M. 1993, *The Making of Modern British Politics 1867–1939*, Oxford: Blackwell.

Pugh, M. 2002, 'The Rise of Labour and Political Culture of Conservatism, 1890–1945', *History*, 87, 288: 514–37.
Purcell, H. 2004, *The Last English Revolutionary*, Stroud: Sutton Publishing.
Ramdin, R. 1987, *The Making of the Black British Working Class in Britain*, London; Gower.
Redfern, N. 2002, 'Winning the Peace: British Communists, the Soviet Union and the General Election of 1945', *Contemporary British History*, 16, 1: 29–50.
Redfern, N. 2005, *Class or Nation: Communists, Imperialism and Two World Wars*, London: I.B. Tauris.
Redfern, N. 2013, 'Labour Failure and Liberal Survival: The Impact of the Great War on the Labour Movement in Mossley', *Manchester Region History Review*, 24: 15–30.
Reid, A.J. 1988, 'The Impact of the First World War on British Workers', in A. Wall and J. Winter (eds), *The Upheaval of War: Family, Work and Welfare in Europe 1914–1918* Cambridge: Cambridge University Press.
Reid, A.J. 2000, 'Labour and the Trade Unions', in D. Tanner et al. (eds), *Labour's First Century*, Cambridge: Cambridge University Press.
Roberts, A. 2009, *The Storm of War: A New History of the Second World War*, London: Allen Lane.
Ronan, A. 2013, 'The Women's War Interest Committee in Manchester and Salford: A Snapshot of Feminist Activism in the First World War', *Manchester Region History Review*, 24: 31–44.
Rosenburg, C. 1999, 'From World War to Class War', *Socialist Review*, 226: 18–24.
Rowlinson, F. 1949, *Contribution to Victory: An Account of Some of the Special Work of the Metropolitan-Vickers Electrical Company Limited in the Second World War*, Manchester: Metropolitan Vickers Company.
Rybaczek, A. 1995, *Homes Fit for Heroes in Inter-war Ashton: Did they stop a Revolution?*, Ashton-under-Lyne: Tameside Leisure Services.
Savage, M. 1987, *The Dynamics of Working Class Politics: The Labour Movement in Preston 1880–1940*, Cambridge: Cambridge University Press.
Schumpeter, J.A. 1951, *Imperialism and Social Classes*, New York: Kelley.
Seddon, J.A. 1917, *Why British Labour Supports the War*, London.
Semmel, B. 1960, Imperialism *and Social Reform: English Social-Imperialist Thought 1895–1914*, London: Allen and Unwin.
Sfikas, T.D. 1994, *The British Labour Government and the Greek Civil War 1939–45: The Imperialism of Non-Intervention*, Keele: Ryburn.
Sherington, G. 1981, *English Education, Social Change and War 1911–1920*, Manchester: Manchester University Press.
Silbey, D. 2005, *The British Working Class and Enthusiasm for War 1914–1916*, London: Frank Cass.

Silver, A. 1966, *Manchester Men and Indian Cotton 1846–1872*, Manchester: Manchester University Press.

Smith, H.L. 1981, 'The Problem of "Equal Pay for Equal Work" in Great Britain in World War II', *Journal of Modern History*, 53: 652–72.

Summerfield, P. 1989, *Women Workers in the Second World War: Production and Patriarchy in Conflict*, London: Routledge.

Swartz, M. 1971, *The Union of Democratic Control in British Politics during the First World War*, Oxford: Clarendon Press.

Swift, D. 2014, 'Labour Patriotism in Lancashire and London, 1914–1918', in C. Horner and N. Mansfield (eds), *The Great War: Localities and Regional Identities*, Newcastle: Cambridge Scolars.

Swift, D. 2016, 'Labour and the War Emergency: The Workers' National Committee during the First World War', *History Workshop Journal*, 81: 84–105.

Tanner, D. 1990, *Political Change and the Labour Party 1900–1918*, Cambridge: Cambridge University Press.

Taplin, E. 1993, 'James Sexton', in J.M. Bellamy and J. Saville (eds), *Dictionary of Labour Biography, Vol. IX*, Basingstoke: MacMillan.

Taylor, A.J.P. 1965, *English History 1914–45*, Oxford: Clarendon Press.

Taylor, M. 1992, 'Patriotism, History and the Left in Twentieth Century Britain', *The Historical Journal*, 33, 4: 971–87.

Tembo, A. 2013, 'Rubber Production in Northern Rhodesia during the Second World War 1942–46', *African Economic History*, 41: 223–59.

Terkel, S. 1985, *'The Good War': An Oral History of World War Two*, London: Hamilton.

Thane, P. 1996, *Foundations of the Welfare State*, Harlow: Longman.

Thom, D. 1986, 'The 1944 Education Act: The "art of the possible"?', in H.L. Smith (ed.), *War and Social Change: British Society in the Second World War*, Manchester: Manchester University Press.

Thom, D. 1988, 'Women and Work in Wartime Britain', in A. Wall and J. Winter (eds.), *The Upheaval of War: Family, Work and Welfare in Europe 1914–1918*, Cambridge; Cambridge University Press.

Thom, D. 1998, *Nice Girls and Rude Girls: Women Workers in World War I*, London: I.B. Tauris.

Thompson, A. 2000, *Imperial Britain: The Empire in British Politics c. 1880–1932*, Harlow: Longman.

Thompson, A. 2005, *The Empire Strikes Back? The Impact of Imperialism on Britain from the Mid-Nineteenth Century*, Harlow: Longman.

Thompson, F.M.L. 1990, *The Cambridge Social History of Britain 1750–1950*, Cambridge: Cambridge University Press.

Thorpe, A. 1997, *A History of the British Labour Party*, Basingstoke: MacMillan.

Thorpe, A. 2000, *The British Communist Party and Moscow 1920–43*, Manchester: Manchester University Press.

Thorpe, A. 2006, '"In a Rather Emotional State"? The Labour Party and British Intervention in Greece, 1944–45', *English Historical Review*, 121: 1075–105.

Timms, N. 1995, *The Five Giants: A Biography of the Welfare State*, London: Harper Collins.

Turner, J. 1992, *British Politics and the Great War Coalition and Conflict 1915–1918*, New Haven: Yale University Press.

Waites, B. 1987, *A Class Society at War England 1914–18*, Leamington Spa: Berg.

Ward, P. 1998, *Red Flag and Union Jack England: Patriotism and the British Left, 1881–1924*, Woodbridge: Boydell Press.

Weiler, P. 1993, *Ernest Bevin*, Manchester: Manchester University Press.

White, J.L. 1978, *The Limits of Trade Union Militancy: The Lancashire Textile Workers 1910–1914*, Westport: Greenwood Press.

White, S. 1974, 'Soviets in Britain: The Leeds Convention of 1917', *International Review of Social History*, 19, 2: 165–93.

Whitehead, J. 1987, 'No Place for a Lady: How the Unions tried to Keep Women out of Office – A Case Study of Alice Foley', *North West Labour History*, 12: 12–18.

Wild, P. 1979, 'Recreation in Rochdale, 1900–1940', in J. Clarke et al., *Working Class Culture: Studies in History and Theory*, London: Hutchinson.

Williams, F. 1949, *Fifty Years March: The Rise of the Labour Party*, London: Odhams.

Williams, M.A. 2002, *A Forgotten Army: Female Munitions Workers of South Wales, 1939–1945*, Cardiff: University of Wales Press.

Wilson, E. 1977, *Women and the Welfare State*, London: Tavistock.

Wilson, T. 1968, *The Downfall of the Liberal Party 1914–1935*, London: Collins.

Winstanley, M. 1996, 'The Factory Workforce', in M. Rose (ed.), *The Lancashire Cotton Industry: A History Since 1770*, Preston: Lancashire County Books.

Winter, J.M. 1993 [1974], *Socialism and the Challenge of War: Ideas and Politics in Britain 1912–1918*, Aldershot: Gregg Revivals.

Winter, J.M. 2003, *The Great War and the British People*, Basingstoke: Palgrave MacMillan.

Wooton, G. 1956, *The Official History of the British Legion*, London: MacDonald and Evans.

Worley, M. 2005, *Labour Inside the Gate: A History of the British Labour Party Between the Wars*, London: I.B. Tauris.

Wrigley, C. 1993, 'The State and the Challenge of Labour in Britain 1917–1920', in C. Wrigley (ed.), *Challenges of Labour: Central and Western Europe 1917–1920*, London: Routledge.

Index

Acland, Sir Richard   195–6, 221
'Addison Act'   124, 128n180, 129
Addison, Christopher   71, 71n122
Addison, Paul   6, 152, 196
Aden   187
Africa   11, 55, 104, 137–8, 150, 157, 178n218, 188, 215–7, 219, 219n157, 219n158, 220, 241
Aitken, Max   4
Allaun, Frank   170
Amalgamated Association of Card and Blowing Room Operatives see Cardroom Amalgamation
Amalgamated Association of Operative Cotton Spinners and Twiners see Spinners' Amalgamation
Amalgamated Society of Engineers (ASE), Amalgamated Engineering Union (AEU) (see also strikes, trade unions)   144, 144n12, 145, 152, 167, 169, 170, 176, 197, 200, 213, 222–3
Amalgamated Weavers' Association see Weavers' Amalgamation
Amin, Samir   8
Ardwick   160
Ashton (Ashton-under-Lyne)   2–4, 8n44, 9n48, 18, 19–22, 24, 26–8, 30, 41–4, 45–7, 49–51, 52, 57, 58, 61, 63, 65, 67–8, 76, 78–9, 82–90, 96–8, 99, 101, 134, 136, 146–8, 153, 156, 158–9, 160–2, 165, 175, 206
    general and municipal elections of 1945   232–5
    general election of 1918   108–17
    housing   72–7, 124–5, 185–6, 190–2, 197–9, 211, 211n126, 226–9
    municipal elections of 1919 & 1922   127–8, 130–4
    strikes   32–7, 90–3, 118–23, 166–7, 176, 201, 203
Ashton and Stalybridge Women's Suffrage Society   100
Ashton Co-operative Society   109
Ashton, Dukinfield and District Trades Council (Ashton Trades Council)   17, 24, 47, 50–4, 65, 70, 75, 99, 104–6, 110, 114, 142, 153, 181, 205, 212
Ashton Grammar School   203n76, 206, 217
Ashton, Margaret   105, 105n46
Ashton Munitions Explosion   76
Ashton Power-loom Weavers   104
Ashton Property Owners' Association   77
Ashton Reporter   62, 67, 76, 82, 85, 116, 158, 160, 175, 185, 197, 226
Ashton Textile Employers' Association (ATEA)   41, 44, 49
Ashton Unionist Association   132
Askwith, George   34, 60, 63, 66, 83
Asquith, Herbert Henry   28, 63, 117n110
Astor, Lady   56n36, 177
Atlantic Charter   178, 178n218, 207, 216
Attlee, Clement   149, 152, 154, 156, 178n218, 188, 197
Audenshaw   68, 115, 162
Australia   7, 55, 150

Baldwin, Stanley   128
Barnes, George   37, 64, 70, 117
Barrow   200, 226
Bengal Famine   219n158
Benn 'Tony'   7
Bevan, Aneurin   150, 178, 221
Beveridge Report   156, 186, 188, 189, 191, 194, 195–7, 198, 202, 212, 239
    and women   193–4, 194n25, 194n26, 198
Beveridge, William   151, 157, 188, 192, 192n17, 193, 214
Bevin, Ernest   149, 154, 155, 156, 157, 167, 210, 233, 239
Birkenhead   68
Birmingham   62, 185n258, 228
Blackburn   2n9, 124
'Black Friday'   129
'Blitz', 'Christmas Blitz', bomb damage, bombing   144, 160, 165, 211n126, 222, 230
Board of Education   78, 78n152, 156
Board of Guardians   26, 128, 132, 132n203
Board of Trade   38, 62, 82–3, 115, 116, 137, 174, 218
Boer War   3, 4, 20, 104
Bolshevik   179

INDEX

Bolshevism, Bolsheviks, influence of   12, 49, 66–7, 69, 70, 85, 86, 89, 93, 94, 96, 119, 128, 131, 132, 132n206, 141
Bolton   40n159, 44, 106, 187
Bombs, Bombing see Blitz
Bondfield, Margaret   15, 15n13, 42, 99, 100, 104, 161, 161n112
Boothby, Robert   150
Bradford   59, 177
Bradley, Ben   180
Brailsford, Henry   66
Bramley, Ted   177
Branson, Noreen   177
Brasiers and Sheetmetal Workers   61
Britain, and its allies and rivals
 Austria-Hungary   11, 12, 94, 95
 Belgium   11, 14–5, 18, 87, 116, 150
 France   4, 11, 12, 66, 69, 87, 116, 141–3, 147, 149–51, 154, 158, 187, 189, 207, 209, 216, 220
 Germany   4, 10, 11, 13, 34, 66, 71, 81, 87, 95, 96, 113, 116, 136, 141, 142, 143, 149, 150, 151, 182, 187–8, 207, 220
 Italy   4, 141, 150, 182, 187
 Japan   1, 141, 142, 180, 181, 188, 189, 216, 217–8, 222, 233
 Russia/Soviet Union   11, 141, 142, 148, 151, 180, 189, 207
 Turkey   4, 11, 12, 95, 136n232
 United States of America (USA)   96, 150, 180, 223, 241
British Legion   116
British Restaurants   160–2, 177, 186, 212, 224
British Socialist Party (BSP)   13n4, 18, 19, 19n36, 31, 32, 32n108, 38, 52–3, 53n20, 53n21, 54, 55, 55n30, 69, 96n5, 108, 109, 114, 117, 129, 130, 131, 132
British Workers' League (BWL)   71, 71n119
Brooke, Stephen   149, 152
Brocklehurst, Fred   22
Brown, Gordon   11
Burma   4, 7, 180, 220, 222, 223, 238
By-elections see Parliamentary by-elections
Butler, 'Rab'   151, 202, 202n74

Calder, Angus   6
Call, The   55, 55n30
Cambridge   185
Canada   150

Cannadine, David   6
Canteens see Cotton Mill working conditions
Cardiff   135
Cardroom Amalgamation (see also strikes, trade unions)   16, 19, 23, 41n160, 45, 48, 57, 73, 79, 81, 92, 94, 119, 137–140, 153, 155, 171, 171n177, 174–5, 176, 194, 212, 213, 224
Carr, E.H.   81, 156
Catering Wages Bill   156
Chadderton   3, 186, 201
Chamberlain, Austen   57
Chamberlain, Neville   62, 143, 149
China   15, 56, 56n38, 180, 218, 237
Christianity and the Social Order   184
Churchill, Winston   4, 149, 150, 151, 178, 179, 181, 182, 187, 188, 189, 195, 196, 197, 201, 207, 210, 221, 222, 226, 227, 229, 231, 233
Citrine, Sir Walter   143, 147, 153, 182
Clyde, Clyde Workers' Committee (CWC)   28, 66–7, 69–70, 85, 96, 117, 118, 167, 236
Clynes, J.R.   15–6, 18, 44–5, 65, 68, 85, 103, 106, 111
Clynes, Mary   103
Cocker, Harry   53, 130, 130n192, 131, 132, 133, 133n212
Colley, Linda   6
Colne   124
Colonial Information Bulletin   219–20
Colonies, colonialism   1, 3, 1n5, 3, 5, 6, 7, 11, 12, 14, 16, 20, 23, 26, 52, 54–6, 58, 66, 87, 110, 113, 129, 133–4, 136–40, 151, 157, 177–8, 178–83, 186, 187, 188, 214–20, 229, 241–2
Comintern (Communist International)   130, 132, 134, 138, 142, 142n4, 178, 220, 221, 237–8
Committee of Enquiry into Industrial Unrest   60, 68, 71
Committee on National Expenditure   129
Commonwealth Party   193, 195–6, 210, 222
Communist, Communist Party of Great Britain (CP)   13n4, 53, 61, 70, 71n120, 94, 96n4, 98n12, 129, 130, 130n192, 132, 154–5, 158, 159, 164, 164n130, 164n131, 164n132, 171, 177, 180, 194, 230, 238
 colonies   134, 138, 139, 178, 180, 181, 182, 187, 214–20, 223
 general election of 1945   230–1

Greece   221–2
Joint Production Committees (JPCs)   168–70, 171, 172, 208
People's Convention   162–3, 165, 179
social reform   208, 213–4
stance on war   142–3, 147, 151
strikes   200, 209
Communist Party of Germany   98n12
Communist Party of India (CPI)   180
Communist Party of the Soviet Union (CPSU)   179, 231, 231, 231n224
Congress Party of India   180, 181, 182, 215, 216
Confederation of British Employers   192
Conscientious Objectors ('conchies')   51–2, 97, 148
Conscription   23–4, 27, 48, 49–51, 66–8, 86, 88–9, 148, 155, 172
Conservatives, Conservatism, Conservative Party   4, 5, 6, 18, 21, 27, 29, 30, 31n101, 62, 72, 76, 77, 82, 95n2, 98, 99, 108, 114–7, 123, 125–7, 135, 146, 151, 156, 179, 183–4, 188, 191, 193n23, 195, 195n31, 196, 202, 210–11, 214, 221, 227, 231–2, 232n230, 232n232, 233–5, 237–8, 240
Cotton Board   171, 171n179, 223–5
Cotton Board Trade Letters   223–4
Cotton Control Board (CCB)   66, 82–4, 90–3, 172, 184, 224
Cotton Factory Times   5, 42, 43, 44, 56, 80, 104, 123
Cotton Industry Act (1938)   172
Cotton mill working conditions   171n179, 223–5
Cotton Trade League   151
Cotton Trade Reconstruction Committee   121
Crinion, James   48, 83, 116
'Cripps Mission'   180–2
Cripps, Sir Stafford   180
Croucher, Richard   128n181, 152
Cummings, Reverend   77, 97, 130

Daily Herald   12, 14, 18, 23, 52, 54, 66, 67, 105, 118–9, 141–2
Daily News and Leader   72, 72n125
Daily Telegraph   192
Daily Worker   159, 163n121, 164n132, 165, 208

Dalton, Hugh   152, 154
Deakin, Arthur   235
Defence of the Realm Act (DORA)   27, 68, 92, 93
de Freece, Sir Walter   127–8, 132
Denmark   149
Denton   120
Devine, Freda   182
Devine, Pat   182, 231
Derby, Lord, 'Derby Scheme'   25–6
'Dilution'   30, 33, 39, 41–7, 67, 68, 145, 147, 173, 175
Domestic service   3, 104n28, 128n180
Dresden   144
Driberg, Tom   183–4
Droylsden   122
Dublin lock-out   103, 103n35
Dunkirk   150, 156, 158, 165, 166, 170
Dutt, Rajani Palme   180, 187

Ede, Chuter   202
Education   71, 78–81, 107, 140, 151
   1918 Education Act (Fisher Act)   78, 204
   1944 Education Act   201–7, 240
   denominational Education   204–6
   education of girls   206–7
   'half-timers'   79–80
   school leaving age   202, 203–4
   secondary education   202, 204
   selective education   202, 203n80, 204, 204n83, 205
   Spens Report   202
Egypt   3, 11, 134, 136, 136n233, 137, 182, 187, 217, 238
El Alamein   157, 166, 187–8, 189, 195, 199, 214, 220, 223
Electoral Reform, Electorate see Franchise
Emergency Powers Act   155
Empire see colonies
Empire Cotton Growing Association   136
Empire Day   58, 58n49, 139, 217
Engels, Frederick   153
Engineering and Allied Employers National Federation   145
Engineers (see also strikes, trade unions)   3, 8, 35, 39, 40, 49, 52, 60, 64–5, 67, 84, 86, 88–9, 105, 115, 142, 144–5, 147, 154–5, 164, 167, 170, 171n178, 172–6, 200, 209, 238

INDEX 261

Enlisting, Enlistment see recruitment
'Equality of Sacrifice' 32, 35, 48, 50, 52, 61–2, 92
Equal Pay 39, 105–6, 112, 145, 175–7, 193n23, 202
Essential Work Orders (EWOs) 167, 172

Fabians, Fabian Society 5, 102, 111–2
Failsworth 3, 20, 161, 224, 228
Farnworth 159, 227
Farr, Mathew 19–20, 50, 73–5, 82, 105, 109, 110, 120, 126, 136, 146, 159, 198
Fascism 141–3, 144, 159n96, 162, 165, 168, 178–9, 180, 192n17, 203n76, 205, 206, 208, 216, 219, 222
Federation of Master Cotton Spinners' Associations 41
Field, Geoffrey 6
Fieldhouse, D.K. 6
Fielding, Steven 183, 234, 235
Finland 147–8
Fisher Act see Education Act 1918
Fishman, Nina 154, 168
Fitton, Sam 5
Foley, Alice 106
Food 28–31, 33, 35–6, 44, 52, 59, 60–5, 68, 82–6, 90–4, 145, 161–2, 166
Food Policy Committee 156
Food Vigilance Committees 65
Forced Labour 219n161, 220
Fowler, Alan 91n232, 121, 123
France see Britain's allies and rivals
Franchise 9, 15n14, 29, 71, 95, 98–101, 110, 124, 124n155
Full Employment see White Paper on Employment
Full Employment in a Free Society 192

Gallipoli (Dardanelles) 11, 24
Gallacher, 'Willy' 71n120, 96n4, 151, 181, 231
Gandhi, Mahatma 4, 216
Geddes, Sir Aukland 86, 89
Geddes, Sir Eric, 'Geddes Axe' 129
Germany see Britain's allies and rivals
Glasgow 18, 32, 37–8, 72, 96, 100, 118, 134n219, 135, 167, 175, 177
Goggins, S.T. 50
Greece 136n231, 187, 220–2
Greenfield 97, 116

Gregory, Adrian 6, 20, 34, 50
Griffiths, Trevor 6
Guide Bridge 44, 175
Gupta, P.S. 7–8

Haldane, J.B.S. 202n73
Hannington, 'Wal' 140
Hardie, Kier 13
Health 5, 22, 73, 74–6, 76n143, 77, 102, 103, 115, 140, 151, 157, 176, 177, 184–5, 186, 189, 189n1, 190n6, 192–3, 196, 198, 199, 210–11, 211n123, 223, 228, 229, 232n230, 236, 239, 240n12
Hector, Emily 176
Henderson, Arthur 13, 14, 28, 28n88, 34, 52, 64, 70, 114n88, 118
Hinton, James 30, 39, 67, 88–9, 96n4, 235
Hitler, Adolf 172, 203n76, 142, 147
Hitlerism see fascism
Hiroshima 189
Hodges, John 64
Holidays with Pay 145, 145n20, 224
Holland 150
Hong Kong 56n38, 180
Hopkinson, Austen 115, 233–4
Horner, Arthur 209
Hospitals see Health
Housing 5, 8, 15n14, 29, 38n148, 71, 72–5, 76–78, 107, 113, 117, 124, 125–7, 140, 184, 186, 192, 240, 241
  council houses 73, 125–6, 190–1, 197–9, 225–9, 239–40
  'prefabs' 226, 228
Howe, Stephen 6
Hull 65, 124
Hurst 77, 96
Hutt, Allan 169
Hyde 19, 50, 82, 120, 122, 205
Hyde Trades Council 181, 233
Hyndman, Henry Mayers 18

Independent Labour Party (ILP) 3, 18–20, 48, 53–5, 69, 99, 108, 109, 110, 117, 143, 143n8, 146, 181, 210, 220, 221
India 1, 3, 3n17, 4, 55, 56, 56n40, 57, 57n47, 112, 133, 134, 137, 139, 179, 180, 181, 182, 190, 215, 216, 218, 219n158, 236–7
India League 181, 222

Indonesia 7, 239
Industrial disputes see strikes
Inflation 32, 34–7, 45, 47, 59, 60–3, 65, 84, 166
International communist movement see Comintern
International Federation of Textile Workers 54, 143–4
Iraq 7, 134
Ireland, Irish, Irish Republican Army 54–5, 87, 87n204, 111n74, 112, 133, 134, 135, 135n223, 136, 138, 236, 242
Italy see Britain's allies and rivals

Japan see Britain's allies and rivals
Jay, Douglas 154, 154n74
Jefferys, Kevin 152
Johnstone, Monty 151
Joint Advisory Council 145
Joint Consultative Council (JCC) 155, 169
Joint Emergency Committee 145
Joint Production Committees (JPCs) 167, 168–72, 176, 187, 238
Jones, Stephen 60
Jowitt, Lady 162
Jowitt, Sir William 146, 185, 197, 233
Joyce, Patrick 5
Judson, Edward 41, 44, 49, 50, 61, 76–7, 83, 92, 106, 109, 119, 121, 131

Kirk, Neville 7
Kitchener, Lord Herbert 21, 23
Kendall, Dennis 183
Kenney, Annie 93
Kenya 219, 239
Kerr, Sir Hamilton 193, 193n23, 232
Keynesian 158, 241
Keynes, John Maynard 151, 189, 192n17, 213, 214, 216, 238

Labour and the New Social Order 102, 107, 133
Labour's Northern Voice 210, 220, 226
Labour Party (for elections see Ashton, Mossley and Oldham) 5, 18, 27–8, 28n88, 29–31, 48, 59, 62, 70, 98, 99, 99n18, 149–51, 155, 237
  colonies 1, 86–7, 133–5, 135n222, 139, 159, 179, 181–2, 187, 215–6, 220, 239

governments of 1945–51 239–40
outbreak of war 12, 13, 13n4, 14, 15, 141, 145
social-reform 71, 71n122, 72, 77–8, 81, 101–2, 107–8, 152–4, 159, 183–4, 188, 194–5, 195n31, 196, 204, 210–12, 214, 239
Labour Problems after the War 105
Labour Representation Committee (LRC) 29–30, 108
Laissez-faire see Liberalism
Lancashire 1, 2, 2n7, 3, 4, 8, 15, 20–21, 30, 34, 35, 39, 40, 41n161, 44, 50, 52, 53n21, 56–7, 60, 64, 65, 67, 69, 78n152, 81, 93, 96, 97, 101, 102, 103, 103n33, 105, 116, 117–8, 120–1, 129, 130n192, 134, 135, 136, 137, 139, 143n8, 146, 147, 148, 151, 152, 157, 158, 164, 166–7, 169, 171, 171n179, 177, 181, 182, 184, 190, 190n4, 198, 200, 205, 209, 215–6, 217, 218, 224, 226, 231, 235, 236, 240
Lancashire Federation of Trades Councils 60, 185, 226
Lansbury, George 12, 42, 45, 66, 100
Laski, Harold 212
Law, Andrew Bonar 95n4, 113
League of Nations 143, 147
Leeds 69, 124
Leeds Soviet Convention 69, 70
Lehman, Beatrice 177
Lenin, V.I, Leninist 1, 7–8, 128, 130, 237
Let us Face the Future 229–30
Liberalism, Liberals, Liberal Party, neo-liberalism 5, 6, 12, 15, 20, 21, 23–4, 25, 27–8, 29, 30–1, 31n101, 47, 71n122, 74, 76, 82, 85, 98–9, 101, 107, 108, 109n61, 111, 111n74, 114–5, 116–7, 117n11, 125, 126, 127–8, 136, 146, 151, 186, 186n265, 195, 196, 211, 211n123, 233, 241
Libya 182
Lister, Thomas 114–6
Liverpool 8, 68, 72, 82, 116n108, 134n219, 201, 221, 222, 226, 231
Lloyd George, David 28, 34, 62, 63, 70, 71n132, 86–7, 93, 95n2, 96, 101, 113, 117n110, 119, 127
Lloyd George, Megan 177
Local Government Board 25, 73, 74, 76, 76n143, 77, 105, 124, 126, 127

INDEX

London 15n14, 22, 42, 42n169, 45, 65, 72, 92, 94, 124, 140, 148, 149, 165, 169, 172, 177, 178, 185n258, 190, 211n126, 222, 224, 227, 228, 231
Long, Walter 96
Lotta, Raymond 8
Luxemburg 150

MacArthur, Mary 14
MacDonald, Margaret 40
MacDonald, Ramsay 14, 28n88, 48, 117
MacKensie, John 4
MacLean, John 18, 69, 117
Maclean, Neil 117
MacManamen, T.J. 23
MacManus, Arthur 70, 71, 71n120
MacMillan, Harold 151
Malta 187
Malaya 7, 180, 220, 238
Mamourian, Councillor Mrs 161, 211, 213
Manchester 2n9, 3, 4, 8, 15, 16, 21, 22, 32, 44, 54, 56, 67–8, 70–3, 75, 76n143, 88–93, 96, 98–101, 106, 112, 120, 123, 124, 125, 130n192, 144, 147, 151, 155, 158, 160, 164, 165, 168, 170, 171, 175, 177, 180, 182, 187, 201, 202n74, 204n83, 206, 208, 210, 215, 222, 226–7, 231, 238
Manchester and District Federation of Women's Suffrage Societies 100
Manchester and Salford Trades Council 76n143, 163–4
Manchester Evening News 70
'Manchesterism' 186, 186n265
Manchester Guardian 57, 121, 157, 185, 207
Manchester Regiment 1, 3–4, 24, 98, 136
Manchester Women's War Interests Committee 105
Mann, Tom 94, 153
Manpower Bill 67
Manpower Conference(s) 86, 88
Manpower Requirements Committee 173
Marsland, William 32, 50, 52, 75n135, 80
Marwick, Arthur 6, 120
Marx, Karl 242
Mason, Tim 2n6
Massey, James 75, 82, 127, 131, 203, 203n212, 205
Mawdsley, James 4

McLean, Ian 39, 96n4
Means Test 190, 193, 211n123
Mediterranean 11, 187, 215–6, 220–1
Meeks, Edward 127, 130, 131, 132, 133, 133n212, 153, 153n72
Memorandum on War Aims 86–7
Mesopotamia 4
Middleton, James 14, 100
Military Service Bill 48, 49, 89
Miners (see also strikes, trades unions) 14, 36, 62, 62n74, 63, 68, 96, 118, 119, 119n121, 120, 129, 199, 209, 233, 240
Ministry of Food 64–5, 85, 162
Ministry of Health 72, 102, 140, 157, 198, 199
Ministry of Information 164, 186
Ministry of Labour 64, 120, 167, 175
Ministry of Munitions 28, 68
Ministry of Reconstruction 49, 71, 201
Morocco 11, 187
Morrison, Herbert 149
Mosley, Wright 19, 82, 126
Mossley 1–2, 2n8, 17, 17n25, 19–23, 26, 50, 53, 57–8, 70, 82–3, 91–2, 99n15, 105, 106, 106n52, 109, 135, 146–7, 159–60, 162, 176, 186, 188, 198, 203–5, 212, 215, 217, 224
  general and municipal elections of 1945 233–4
  general election of 1918 109–15
  housing 72–4, 125–6, 196–7, 211, 211n126, 227–8
  municipal elections of 1919 126–7
  strikes 36–7, 43, 45, 60–1, 64, 87–8, 90–3, 118–22
Mossley and Saddleworth Reporter 160, 186, 197, 198, 207
Mossley Trades Council 24, 31, 36, 50, 65, 110n70
'Movement away from Party' 183–4, 196, 210
Mullins, William 16, 57, 79, 92, 137
Municipal Employees Association 16
Munitions 27–8, 33–4, 38, 40, 49, 60, 61–3, 67–8, 76, 86, 88–90, 100–1, 104n38, 105, 119, 173, 175, 184, 209
Munitions of War Act 28, 38, 61, 62n74, 83

Nabudere, Dan 8
Nagasaki 189
Naismith, Andrew 218n155

National Council for Adult Suffrage 100
National Federation of Discharged and Demobilised Sailors and Soldiers (NFDDSS) 59–60, 97, 114–6, 127
National Federation of Women Workers 14
National Industrial Conference 118
National Insurance Act 1911 128
Nationalisation 29, 71, 107, 111, 112, 115, 118, 184, 195, 226, 239–40
National Health Service see Health
National Housing and Town Planning Council 74, 191, 199, 227
National Service Act 173
National Union of Railwaymen (NUR) (see also strikes, trade unions) 17, 109, 120, 127
National Union of Teachers (NUT) 158
National Union of Unemployed Workers (NUWM) 131, 132, 140
National Union of Women's Suffrage Societies (NUWSS) 40, 42n168, 99, 99n18
Nazis see fascism
Negro Association 222
Nehru, Jawaharlal 180, 182
Newcastle-on-Tyne 177
New Zealand 54, 150
Nigeria 219
No-Conscription Fellowship see Conscientious Objectors
Norway 149

Oldham 2, 4, 15–6, 19–20, 22–6, 31, 33, 39, 46–7, 49, 58, 65, 68–9, 70, 72, 78–81, 82, 85–6, 94, 96, 96n5, 97, 97n9, 99, 99n15, 100–4, 106, 106n52, 129, 130, 135, 145, 146n30, 148, 152, 155, 158, 159, 160–1, 172, 173–5, 176, 184, 185n258, 186, 190n6, 196, 203–4, 206, 211n126, 212, 215, 219n161, 221, 224–5
   general and municipal elections of 1945 231–4
   general election of 1918 108–15
   housing 73, 124–5, 190–1, 196, 211, 211n126, 227–9, 239
   municipal elections of 1919 125
   strikes 35–8, 41–5, 60–1, 66–8, 83–4, 88, 90–3, 119–24, 166–7, 170, 197, 200–1, 209

Oldham and Rochdale Textile Employers Association (ORTEA) 83–4, 91, 166–7, 217n148
Oldham Chamber of Commerce 119, 176, 204
Oldham Chronicle 62, 78, 115, 119, 125, 161, 186, 193, 193n22, 207, 228
Oldham Master Cotton Spinners Association 113, 200, 204
Oldham Trades and Labour Council (Oldham T&LC) 17, 23, 31–2, 36, 38, 47–8, 51, 55, 57, 59, 64–5, 70, 83, 100, 105, 112, 205
Old World and a New Society, The 184
Openshaw 19, 238
Order 1305 155, 166–7, 169, 201
Orwell, George 150, 191

Palestine 4, 86, 136, 187
'Pals' Battalions 22–3
Pankhurst, Christabel 42n168
Pankhurst, Emmeline 42n168, 93
Pankhurst, Sylvia 42, 42n168, 54, 100
Parliamentary by-elections 163, 148–49, 195, 195, 183, 195–6, 210
Passchendaele 86
Paul, William 96n5
Pennell, Catriona 20
Pensions 5, 27, 59, 60, 64, 116, 118, 151, 184, 186, 233
People's Convention 162–3, 164–5, 177, 178, 179, 179n224
Phillips, Marion 15, 15n15, 42, 104
Piratin, Phil 23
Platt Report 232, 232n231
Poland 134, 141, 147n35
Pollitt, Harry 19, 19n36, 134, 148, 151, 154, 168, 178, 187
Poor Laws 72, 102, 111, 128
Position of Women in the Readjustment of Labour after the War, The 105
Post-war reform see Social-Reform
Primrose League 4, 103
Preston 2, 68, 231
'Profiteers', 'Profiteering' 9, 14n12, 35–8, 52, 52, 61–2, 64–5, 68, 76, 85–6, 102, 111–12, 119, 138, 156, 165, 184
Public Assistance Committees (PACs) 34, 190–1

INDEX

'Quit India' Campaign   181–2, 182n237, 215

'Rack-Renting'   38–9, 65, 75
Radek, Karl   134
Railway workers (see also unions, strikes)   17, 24, 96, 104, 109, 116, 118, 120, 128n180, 129
Rathbone, Eleanor   177
Rationing   82, 84, 85, 90, 166
Reconstruction (see also Ministry of Reconstruction)   49, 58, 71, 71n122, 72, 72n123, 88, 102, 107, 116, 121, 156–7, 194, 197, 199, 201, 218, 224–5, 226, 230, 232, 235, 239
Recruitment   9n2, 21–2, 23, 26, 48, 49–51
'Red Year' of 1919   94, 95–8, 237
Rent and Mortgage Interest (War Restrictions) Act (Rent Restrictions Act)   38
Representation of the People Acts   95, 101
Rhodesia   219
Rhondda, Lord   82
Richardson, Dr. J.E   204
Riding, Edith   104
Roberts, Alfred   171, 171n177, 174, 194, 213
Robinson, W.C.   25, 37, 48, 94, 100, 113, 114–5, 128
Rochdale   8n44, 19, 31n101, 32, 37, 61, 67, 88, 135, 209, 217n148
Ronan. Alison   105
Roosevelt, F.D.   207
Royton   3, 136, 146, 166, 196
Royton and Shaw Trades Council   136
Runciman, Walter   34, 62
Russia see Britain's rivals and allies
Russian revolutions   54, 59, 65, 66, 69, 134, 236–7
Rust, Tamara   177

Salford   82, 135, 195, 206, 221
Salter, Ada   15n14, 40
Sankey Commission   118–9
Savage, Mike   6
Scanlon, Hugh   169
Schumpeter, Joseph   6
Second International   17, 30, 53, 69, 238
Seddon, James   15
Semmel, Bernard   5–6
Sexton, James   16, 16n20
Shackleton, David   30, 41, 92

Shaw   136, 146
Sheffield   89
'Shells and Fuses' Agreement   34, 40
Shop Stewards   39, 65–70, 73, 83–4, 86–94, 96, 121–3, 142, 154, 168, 169–71, 172, 175, 208, 238
Silbey, David   20
Simon, Lady (Shena Simon)   204, 204n83
Singapore   4, 180
Sloan, Alex   181–2
Smales, Fred   74, 79
Smillie, Robert   14
Smith, Alice   42, 104, 123
Smith, Sir Alan   118
Snowden, Phillip   117
Social-Democratic Federation (SDF)   30
Socialist Labour Party (SLP)   18, 38, 70
Social-Imperialism, Social-Imperialist   1–2, 2n6, 2n9, 4, 5, 7, 9, 10, 79, 95, 104, 113, 149, 151, 183, 184, 189, 191, 193n23, 216, 217–8, 230, 239, 242
Social Reform   5, 49, 62, 66, 71, 72–81, 81–2, 94, 95, 98, 113–6, 117, 118, 128, 149, 151, 152–3, 157–8, 158–62, 182–3, 183–8, 189n1, 190, 220, 237–8
South Africa   104, 150, 219, 220
South Wales   177, 236
Soviet Union see Britain's allies and rivals
Spinners' Amalgamation (see also, strikes, trade unions)   21, 32, 35, 41–2, 44, 50, 52, 57, 75n135, 75n137, 80, 83, 88, 93, 121, 139, 144, 144n16, 145n20, 146, 147, 155, 172, 174, 194, 209, 213, 240
Stalin, Joseph   142, 221, 231n224
Stalingrad   168, 188
Stalybridge   23, 37, 43, 81, 110n70, 122, 135, 205
Stalybridge, Mossley and Millbrook Trades Council see Mossley Trades Council
Stanley, Oliver   216
Stanley, Sir Albert   115–116, 127
Stockholm International Conference of Socialists   69–70
Stockport   70, 71n120, 88, 135, 190, 211n123
Streat, Sir Raymond   157, 172, 184, 216–7, 218, 225
Stretford   227

Strikes (and industrial disputes and industrial unrest)   28, 34, 36, 52, 59, 59n54, 63, 65, 71, 118–9, 154, 166, 168, 237
  bakers   119
  cotton workers   35, 37–8, 43–4, 60, 66, 83–4, 90–3, 118–23, 129, 166, 201, 209
  council employees   37
  days lost   90, 118, 199–200, 209
  dockers   199–200
  engineers, munitions workers   28, 34, 49, 57, 60, 67, 88, 90, 167–8, 175–6, 200, 209
  hatters   119
  miners   36, 118–9, 129, 209
  police   119
  railway workers   96, 118, 120, 129
  tram conductors   45
Sudan   219
Suez Canal   11, 182, 187
Suffrage see Franchise
Suffragettes see Women's Social and Political Union
Suffragists see National Union of Women's Suffrage Societies
Swanson, Walter   168
Sykes-Picot Agreement   12, 86

Tanganyika   219
Taylor, A.J.P.   63
Teheran Conference, *Teheran Declaration*   207–8, 231n224
Temple, William   184
Tenants Defence Leagues (TDLs)   38, 38n224, 65, 75
Terkel, Studs   6
Third International see Comintern
Thomas, 'Jimmy'   127, 179
Thomasson, William   139–40
Thompson, Andrew   3
Tillett, Ben   42, 42n109
Times   207
Tobruk   182–3, 195
Togliatti, Palmiro   220
Tories see Conservatives
Trade Card Scheme   67, 68
Trades Disputes Act (1927)   148
Trade Unionists, Trade Unions, Trade Union Congress (TUC) (see also 'dilution', shop stewards and strikes)   1, 4, 5, 21, 29, 31–2, 34, 36, 38, 49, 52, 70, 78–80, 92–3, 100–5, 109, 111–15, 117–18, 131, 136, 139, 152, 154, 155–6, 175, 182, 193, 197, 198, 205, 213, 240
  and colonies   54–7, 217–8, 218n155
  and Joint Production Committees   168, 170–1, 171n178
  outbreak of war   12–7, 143–8
  overtime   32–5, 41, 144, 144n16, 145, 154, 166
Trafalgar Day   58, 58n53
Tribune, The, 'Tribunites'   149, 150, 151, 159, 159n96, 169, 180, 183, 192, 214
Trotsky, Trotskyists   128, 143n7, 200, 208, 238
Tunisia   215
Turkey see Britain's allies and rivals

Unemployment   27–9, 53, 72n125, 75, 92, 128n180, 129, 131, 151, 161n112, 166, 186, 188, 190, 192n17, 193n24, 197, 212, 214, 233, 236, 239, 240, 240n16
Unemployment Act 1934   190
Unemployment Insurance Act 1920   128
Union of Democratic Control (UDC)   47, 47n196, 48, 51
Unions see trade unions
United States of America (USA) see Britain's allies and rivals
United Textile Factory Workers' Association (UTFWA)   25, 30, 31, 48, 79–80, 91, 100, 102, 109n64, 113, 118, 120–3, 128, 210, 212, 218, 224, 229

Volunteering see recruitment

Waites, Bernard   9, 34, 59, 59n54
Wallasey   183
War Aims, War Aims Committee(s)   15, 57–8, 86–7, 151, 163
Ward, Paul   1
War Emergency Workers' National Committee (WEWNC)   14, 28, 28n90, 29, 31, 32, 38–9, 48, 63, 72, 99, 112
Wavell, Earl Archibald   216
Weavers' Amalgamation (see also strikes, trade unions)   14, 21, 23, 31, 33, 36, 42, 48, 52, 56, 59, 61, 65, 72, 80, 99, 112, 121, 137, 143–5, 148, 172, 194, 218n155, 238–9
Webb, Sydney   5, 14, 71, 72, 112, 154
Welfare State   9, 152, 156, 191, 239

INDEX   267

West Indies   215, 219
White Paper on Education   201, 205–6
White Paper on Employment   189, 193, 210–11, 212, 212n132, 213, 213n132, 214, 240
White Paper on Health   189, 210–11
White Paper on Housing   189, 223, 228–29
White Paper on Social Security   189, 212n132
Wild, Sam   159, 164, 222
Wilkinson, Ellen   42, 104, 138
Williams, Francis   238
Willink, Henry   151, 211
Wimpenny, Booth   61, 130, 131, 133n212
Wintringham, Tom   195
Women (see also 'dilution' and franchise)   2n9, 3, 39–47, 55, 64, 67, 79, 85, 90, 97, 97n10, 98–101, 112, 120, 124–5, 145, 147, 155, 159, 161, 172–3, 173–8, 184, 186, 215, 224, 239
  influence on labour movement   40, 40n156, 44, 100, 102–7, 109, 173, 174, 176

Women's Appeal to Women   43
Women's Citizens Associations   106, 159
Women's Freedom League   194n26
Women's International League for Peace and Freedom   100
Women's Labour League (WLL)   15, 15n14, 40, 103, 103n33, 105, 109n61
Women's Parliaments   171, 177–8
Women's Social and Political Union (WSPU), Women's Emergency Corps   42, 42n168, 43, 99, 103n32, 177
Wood, Kingsley   192
Woodhouses   85
Woolton, Lord   226, 227
Workers and the War, The   29n95, 72
Workers' Educational Association (WEA)   104
Workers' Socialist Federation (WSF)   54
Worley, Mathew   153

Yalta Conference   178, 221, 230–1

www.ingramcontent.com/pod-product-compliance
Lightning Source LLC
Chambersburg PA
CBHW071152070526
44584CB00019B/2758